GRACE
&
STEEL

GRACE
&
STEEL

Dorothy, Barbara, Laura, and the
Women of the Bush Dynasty

J. Randy Taraborrelli

ST. MARTIN'S PRESS
NEW YORK

First published in the United States by St. Martin's Press,

an imprint of St. Martin's Publishing Group

APR 2 9 2021

GRACE AND STEEL. Copyright © 2021 by Rose Books, Inc. All rights reserved.

Printed in the United States of America. For information, address

St. Martin's Publishing Group, 120 Broadway, New York, NY 10271.

www.stmartins.com

Library of Congress Cataloging-in-Publication Data

Names: Taraborrelli, J. Randy, author.

Title: Grace & steel : Dorothy, Barbara, Laura, and the women of the Bush
   dynasty / J. Randy Taraborrelli.

Other titles: Dorothy, Barbara, Laura, and the women of the Bush dynasty

Description: First edition. | New York : St. Martin's Press, 2021. |
   Includes bibliographical references and index.

Identifiers: LCCN 2020040968 | ISBN 9781250248718 (hardcover) |
   ISBN 9781250248701 (ebook)

Subjects: LCSH: Bush family. | Bush, Barbara, 1925-2018. | Bush, George,
   1924-2018—Family. | Bush, Laura Welch, 1946- | Bush, George W. (George
   Walker), 1946—Family. | Presidents' spouses—United States—Biography. |
   Politicians' spouses—United States—Biography. | Presidents—United
   States—Family—Biography. | Children of presidents—United States—
   Biography. | United States—Politics and government—1945-1989. |
   United States—Politics and government—1989-

Classification: LCC E883.B87 T37 2021 | DDC 973.931092/2 [B]—dc23

LC record available at https://lccn.loc.gov/2020040968

Our books may be purchased in bulk for promotional, educational, or business use.
Please contact your local bookseller or the Macmillan Corporate and Premium
Sales Department at 1-800-221-7945, extension 5442, or by email at
MacmillanSpecialMarkets@macmillan.com.

First Edition: 2021

10 9 8 7 6 5 4 3 2 1

To mothers, sisters, and daughters everywhere,
for the love you give and all you hold,
for the resiliency out of which you persist
despite adversity, setback, and struggle,
and the courage to nonetheless carry on,
and endure, on all things.

God waits until you've experienced all of life's ups and downs, every one of them, before he presents you with your toughest competitor: old age.

—DOROTHY WALKER BUSH (MOTHER OF GEORGE H. W. BUSH), 1901–1992

Our family, *your* family, *their* family . . . the one thing we all have in common is . . . family.

—JENNA HAWKINS WELCH (MOTHER OF LAURA BUSH), 1919–2019

Think about it. All that really matters are the three f's: faith, family and freedom.

—PAULINE ROBINSON PIERCE (MOTHER OF BARBARA BUSH), 1896–1949

Our success as a society depends *not* on what happens in the White House, but on what happens inside your house.

—BARBARA BUSH (WIFE OF PRESIDENT GEORGE H. W. BUSH), 1925–2018

The White house is just for now. The marriage is forever.

—LAURA BUSH (WIFE OF PRESIDENT GEORGE W. BUSH), 1946–

Never in my wildest dreams, after twenty-two years of marriage, would I have ever believed that I had to fight for my dignity and financial stability.

—SHARON BUSH (FORMER WIFE OF NEIL BUSH), 1952–

No one prepares you for a life in politics. But what was helpful to me was having a very strong faith that I got from my mother. When you're strong in faith, you don't lose hope.

—COLUMBA BUSH (WIFE OF GOVERNOR JEB BUSH), 1953–

Contents

Prologue

It was the end of February 2000. Laura Bush sat in the backseat of a black SUV and watched through tinted glass as people jostled one another while coming and going from the *Dallas Morning News* office building. On Young Street, traffic was jammed, as was usually the case in these parts. Laura's vehicle was double-parked, a typical demonstration of entitlement by the Secret Service not at all appreciated by impatient drivers trying to get by while leaning on their horns. Behind her car were two more vehicles, also Secret Service agents, all part of a convoy. Laura glanced out the window and shook her head in dismay.

According to photographs taken on the day, Laura was dressed conservatively, as was her way, in a navy blue wool day suit with a long skirt. She also wore a matching tailored jacket cut to her waist, which appeared to be made of merino wool, over a white silk blouse with a high neck. Her hair was a glossy chestnut color. At fifty-three, she was stunning, with her flawless complexion and eyes so deeply blue they were almost violet. Thin creases around her eyes and some at her mouth, too, just made her look more real, more authentic. Her beauty was austere and somehow even autocratic. She was also a powerful woman, as she'd demonstrated many times over the years. Sometimes it felt like the best was yet to come for Laura Bush . . . but was it? In her lap was a tabloid newspaper with the startling headline

"Revealed! Bush's Wife Killed Boyfriend." As the agent watched in the rear-view mirror, she nervously rolled the paper into the shape of a tube and then flattened it out again.

It had to happen eventually, and she knew it. How long could any scandal of this magnitude be kept out of the public view? After all, it had been thirty-seven years. It was amazing that this particular story hadn't come to light yet considering the high-profile nature of her life. Her father-in-law, George H.W., had been Vice President for eight years and then President for four. Her husband, George W., had been governor of Texas for the last six years and was now campaigning for the Republican presidential nomination. How was it possible that no reporter had uncovered this scoop before now? She'd been dreading it for so long, maybe she should've been grateful that, finally, some writer she didn't even know had relieved her of this burden. But why did it have to be a tabloid reporter, and why did he have to work for something called *Star*?

Sighing deeply, she folded the newspaper in quarters and quickly stuffed it into her purse, as if making the decision to stop obsessing over it. To hear her recall this time many years later, her primary concern was how the story might affect George's campaign. He'd worked so hard and, as far as she was concerned, was by far the best candidate. The idea that she could ruin things for him now was crushing. Her next thought was obvious: How would it affect her family? Most people, even close relatives, didn't know about this misadventure. It had taken her years to come to terms with this *private* heartache. Finally, she had come to understand that in no way did this terrible event—which had happened when she was just seventeen—define her. Still, it was mortifying to now have the whole world read about it, and, making it worse, many of the details weren't even accurate.

What might people think of her in light of this story? As she sat in the backseat of her car, surrounded on all sides by the maddening cacophony of bustling Dallas, she must have felt completely and utterly trapped. She tried to lower the tinted window to get some air. It was locked. "Can we put this down just a bit?" she asked the agent. He pushed a button and the window lowered about an inch. "A bit more?" she asked. He gave her another half inch. "Any more's not safe, ma'am," he told her. "I know," she said with a sigh. "I know." She asked him to turn on the air. When he did, she tilted her head back and fanned herself with her hand.

The campaign had been a real roller coaster, down one moment, up the next. George was now on top with fresh primary wins in the states of Washington, Virginia, and South Carolina. Yet neither he nor his opponent for the nomination, Senator John McCain, had the momentum for a landslide victory, especially after McCain took New Hampshire. For months, these two men had been viciously attacking each other, and it had gotten very personal. For instance, McCain authorized advertisements that branded George as being anti-Catholic. George was furious, but no more so than his wife. Laura knew that George's unwavering Christian faith was the rock upon which his whole life was built and that he would never have a pejorative word for anyone else's religion. It was a low blow, and the senator had to know better, or at least Laura thought so. "You have to fight back, Bushie," she told George, using her pet name for him. "You can't let him walk all over you. Show strength for goodness sake!" Even as the words came from her lips, she had to have been astonished by them. When did she become such a brawler, this woman who had once so eschewed politics that she'd made George promise upon marrying him that he would never make her give a speech? Now, a little more than twenty years on, politics was pretty much in her bones, and, she had to admit, that was a pretty scary thought.

Over the last year, Laura had been making stops with her mother-in-law, Barbara Bush, usually flying on the official campaign plane with George but sometimes off on their own. Right now, she was waiting for Barbara to emerge from the *Dallas Morning News* building, where she'd been giving an interview. The Bush women would then be taken to the Dallas airport. Barbara was headed home. Laura was scheduled to board a flight to yet another tour stop, where she'd meet up with her husband.

Laura was so lost in thought, it had to have jarred her when the door was flung open and Barbara quickly slid into the car. One of the Secret Service agents closed the door behind her. "Fiddlesticks," Barbara exclaimed as she organized herself next to Laura. "What a waste of time." When Laura asked what happened, Barbara said she hadn't even done the interview.

As the car slowly lurched from the curb, soon to be followed by the others, Barbara explained that the designated reporter had called in sick and that his replacement was late showing up. She didn't feel like waiting. With a malicious gleam in her eyes, she recalled telling them, "Here's an idea: *Next time, plan better.*" Then she turned on her heels and walked out. She said a gaggle of anxious people trailed her all the way down the hall. The way she described the scene, it called to mind mallard ducklings following their mother, all the while making quacking noises that sounded like *Mrs. Bush! Mrs. Bush! Mrs. Bush!* But she just kept on walking, she said, straight for the elevator, down to the lobby, and then right out the door. "And that's the way the cookie crumbles," she concluded with an airy wave of her hand. Laura gasped, her eyes wide. She would never have handled it that way. No, she would have waited until the last possible moment, and then she would have waited a little while longer. But she and Barbara were very different in how they dealt with impatience, and Laura had always admired that about her mother-in-law.

Upon hearing Barbara's story, the Secret Service agents seated in the front of the vehicle turned to each other and smiled. "Very Barbara Bush," one said to the other. He nodded. "*Very* Barbara Bush."

And she *looked* "very Barbara Bush," too, with that snowy-white hair of hers, those large, expressive gray eyes, and the signature creamy pearls, three strands and fake, of course. She was seventy-four and didn't mind that she looked every bit her age. She felt she'd earned each wrinkle and was proud of the life she'd thus far lived. As a former First Lady and Second Lady, too, she was always self-assured, in public anyway, exuding an aura of undeniable power. There was also an undeniable grandmotherly quality about her. People would actually come up to her and, instead of paying obeisance to her as they might other First Ladies, ask if she enjoyed baking apple pies for her family. She would chuckle and say, "Oh, sure." In fact, she couldn't remember the last time she'd baked a pie. Her skills in the kitchen were practically nonexistent. "But disabusing people of harmless notions is such a bore," she would say. "Why can't we just let people be happy, for heaven's sake?"

Barbara was nothing if not a real patriot; some might even call her an American icon. She loved her country, and no one doubted it. She had been deep in the trenches of many a contentious campaign, including the presidential race in 1992 between the current incumbent, Bill Clinton, and her husband, George H. W. Bush. It, too, had gotten vicious. It wasn't always easy for Barbara to parse out her feelings about what should be taken personally and what should just be chalked up to political combat. While one side fended off attacks and the other launched more, all she could do was try not to be hardened by the warfare. "As the wife, it's easy to become jaded if you're not careful," she once said. "But it's the husband running for office who has the greater burden. After all, no one really understands what it takes to govern."

Unfortunately, George H. W. Bush lost that particular race in 1992, making him a one-term president. But what were the chances that not only would he have had the great honor of serving in high office but that now his son might, as well? That had only happened once before in American history, back in the late eighteenth and early nineteenth centuries when John Quincy Adams became the sixth president after his father, John Adams, had been the second. And to think that Barbara's daughter-in-law Laura might also find herself in the White House? It seemed impossible to imagine, but, as she'd long ago learned, there was no limit to what could be expected from anyone with the last name of Bush.

On the way to the airport, Barbara and Laura didn't say much, both seeming lost in contemplation. Generally, they got along well these days, though they'd traveled a long and sometimes difficult road on the way to their present détente.

Had Barbara known Laura's secret? Laura figured she must have known, yet not once in the twenty-three years Laura had been married to George did Barbara ever mention it. So, Laura never knew for sure and, truth be told, she didn't want to know. Communication between the two could sometimes be challenging under the best of circumstances. What would *that* conversation be like? Now, she felt Barbara had to know everything. *Everyone* knew. The phone at George's campaign headquarters had been ringing off the hook with requests for comments. Her spokesman was working on a statement to give to *The Dallas Morning News*. She'd also just learned that the Associated Press had been trying to obtain the police report. It was just a matter of time. There was no telling how any of this would turn out for her, for George, or for their family, which included twin daughters, Barbara and Jenna.

"We're calling ahead to say we might be late," the agent who was driving said as he glanced in the rearview mirror at the Bush women. "There's some kind of tie-up ahead, I'm afraid. No telling what's going on."

Laura knew Barbara well enough to know she'd never put her on the spot and mention the tabloid report, not while two Secret Service agents in the front seat listened in on every word. Instead, Barbara just sat silently while biting her lip and looking out the window to her left. As traffic moved slowly along, Laura stared straight ahead, her eyes seemingly laser focused on the back of the driver's head. The silence was deafening.

After about ten more minutes of awkwardness, the agent who wasn't driving noticed something in the rearview mirror. Barbara, as if reacting to a flash of intuition, suddenly reached out and gently touched Laura's cheek. Laura took Barbara's hand, held it in her own, and squeezed it. It was an unexpected moment of tenderness. But then Barbara pulled her hand away, completely breaking the spell. It seemed harsh—unkind, even. From her expression, Laura was surprised and maybe even a little hurt. Barbara then slipped off her heavy wool glove. She opened her large knit handbag, placed the glove inside, and refastened the kissing-lock closure. Then, she reached over again and, this time with her bare hand, took Laura's into her own. It was as if she'd wanted only warmth between them, nothing else. For just a second, Barbara's eyes rested on Laura before she turned and, once again, stared straight ahead. Laura bit her lip, striving for composure. She blinked a few times.

They continued to hold hands, Barbara and Laura, with no words spoken between them. But, then again, they didn't need words. Not these two. Not after all these years.

PART ONE

Dorothy Walker and Prescott Bush

George H. W. Bush's Parents

Fit for a Queen

Some see leadership as high drama, and the sound of trumpets calling, and sometimes it is that. But I see history as a book with many pages, and each day we fill a page with acts of hopefulness and meaning. The new breeze blows, a page turns, the story unfolds. And so today a chapter begins, a small and stately story of unity, diversity, and generosity—shared, and written, together.

It was Saturday morning, January 21, 1989, and as Dorothy Walker Bush lay in bed reading those words, quick tears came to her eyes. It was such an eloquent declaration of American idealism and just one of the many powerful statements made by her son President George H. W. Bush yesterday during his inaugural address to the nation. How proud she had been as she watched him being sworn in as the forty-first President of the United States of America. Now, as she read and reread the transcript of his speech, which she'd asked to be delivered to her room last night while everyone was at the inaugural balls, her heart was still full.

Dorothy hadn't slept a wink, which was not unusual for her. A chronic insomniac, she would sometimes quip, "I slept once in the 1950s and was sorry to lose the hours." She was only half joking. In her younger years, she had always been busy with a life so full, the idea of falling into a black hole of unconsciousness seemed like an enormous waste of time. However, she was eighty-seven now, and her world had shrunk so much that she had few, if any, responsibilities. Every day was a challenge as she coped with arthritis, a heart condition, high blood pressure, and other physical maladies. She hated no longer being the live wire she'd been in her youth.

Leaving the house was such an ordeal these days, especially now that she was in a wheelchair. However, she wouldn't miss her son's inauguration. There had been no shortage of drama, though, in getting her from her winter home in Florida to Washington, D.C. Her daughter-in-law Barbara Bush arranged for a private medical airplane transport, meaning a jet fully equipped with every lifesaving tool imaginable, to transport her. Her own doctor and a nurse flew at her side, as well as the air ambulance service's experienced medical team. While she didn't believe these precautions were necessary, others disagreed. After all, how much of a damper would it have put on things if the President-elect's mother suddenly passed away in the air on her way to his inauguration?

As she looked around, Dorothy had to have been awed by her surroundings. After all, she was in the Queens' Bedroom in the White House. Again, it was Barbara who'd decided that she, as the family's matriarch, should sleep here.

The stately Queens' Bedroom on the second floor of the White House was named in honor of the many royal guests who'd slept in it over the years—queens of Norway, the Netherlands, Great Britain, and Greece, among others. In years to come, whenever Assistant Chief White House Usher Chris Emery would give a tour of the White House to guests of the Bushes during parties they'd host, he would always allow Barbara to take over when they got to this special room. She knew the history of all the queens who'd stayed here and would always enjoy regaling her guests with those stories.

The room was elegantly decorated in the Federal style with rose-colored walls and had two north-facing floor-to-ceiling windows, each framed by heavy Scalamandré drapes. But it was the nearly eight-foot-by-six-foot Sheraton four-poster bed with its rosewood headboard and floral pink-and-green canopy that most distinguished it. Donated around 1902, this bed was first used in the Lincoln Bedroom, which was right across the hall; it had supposedly once belonged to Andrew Jackson. "Fit for a queen," Barbara had said of the accommodations, "and very appropriate that Ganny [the family's loving appellation for Dorothy] should sleep there."

Dorothy might have had a restful night in such an august room had it not been for two nuisances: the doctor and nurse sitting on two straight-back chairs to the right of her, *all night long.*

"Ganny, look. Look!" an excited Barbara Bush said as she burst into the room. She was with Dorothy's great-granddaughter, seven-year-old Jenna, one of the twins belonging to George W. and Laura. "Outside," Barbara exclaimed. "You won't believe your eyes.*"*

The physician jumped to his feet and helped Dorothy to hers, after which the nurse draped her in a long robe. The two then slowly walked her to one of the windows. It seemed to take forever. Below, thirty thousand people had gathered outside the North Portico to pay their respects to the new President and First Lady. Dorothy stood transfixed as the throng—now delighted to catch a glimpse of the President's mother—waved at her while applauding and shouting out good wishes. It was breathtaking, a virtual mob of smiling faces as far as the eye could see. "My God, Bar. I've never seen anything like this," Dorothy exclaimed.

As Dorothy waved back at the multitude, Barbara rested her hands on her mother-in-law's slight shoulders. Suddenly, much to their surprise, the crowd started singing Irving Berlin's "God Bless America." Dorothy and Barbara, along with the doctor and nurse, all stood at full attention, swept away by such a stunning display of patriotism. Dorothy fumbled for her handkerchief to blot the corners of her eyes. Even little Jenna seemed enchanted.

"I guess this is our life now," Dorothy said as the crowd finished its song. She then turned to face her daughter-in-law. "For sure, we'll be remembered now, won't we, Bar?" she asked, her eyes damp.

Barbara smiled at her. "Yes, Ganny," she said. "For sure, we'll be remembered now."

A Woman of Substance

As Dorothy Bush sat down at her classic Queen Anne desk, circa 1770—a birthday gift from her husband, Senator Prescott Bush—she told her long-time Irish maid, Lucy Larkin, that she didn't want to be disturbed for at least an hour. Before her was a green Underwood Leader typewriter, another present from the man who she once noted, tongue-in-cheek, "showers me with so many gifts you have to wonder about his conscience." All around her were books about American history, biographies of Presidents, and photographic volumes illustrating many of the states of the union. She'd never been much of a student of history, that is until she started dating Prescott in 1919, two years before they wed. He had spoken so intelligently about the Constitution during one of their early dinners, she knew she'd have her work cut out for her if she wanted to be able to converse with him at his level. A competitive woman, she started reading history books just so that he wouldn't always be the more knowledgeable of the two.

Dorothy's study was large with a high ceilings, as were most of the rooms in the sprawling, two-story Victorian home at 15 Grove Lane in Greenwich, Connecticut, the house in which she had raised her five children: Prescott Jr., now thirty-one; George, twenty-nine; Nancy, twenty-seven; Jonathan, twenty-two; and William, known as "Bucky," fifteen and presently at boarding school. It was a large gray-wood, brown-shingled 1902 Victorian with a wraparound porch surrounded by two and a half acres of verdant lawn resembling rolls of stretched-out emerald velvet. When Dorothy first laid eyes on this house, she noticed the way it shimmered in the brilliant morning light, and she knew she had to have it. Back in 1931, though, there was no way Prescott could afford it. So she appealed to her father, Bert, not the most generous man. Much to her surprise, he decided to purchase the estate and put it in her name. She came to realize, though, that the only reason he accommodated her was to get under Prescott's skin by lording control over him and his family. Soon she would forget the reasons Bert had purchased the estate—though Prescott never did.

In the study were two desks, her dainty Queen Anne on one side completely dwarfed by Prescott's enormous Chippendale on the other side. When they'd moved into this house, Prescott figured this room would be his private study, his inner sanctum. However, Dorothy, who was about thirty at the time, rejected the notion that he should have his own place to work, one that would ostensibly be off-limits to her. The idea of it reminded her of her father's den, entrée to which was forbidden to all. She would never forget the sight of her mother creeping about the door, wondering if her husband was in there or not and afraid to knock for fear of possibly disturbing him. Dorothy couldn't fathom how a wife could be so fearful of her husband. That was never going to be the case in her marriage, she decided.

When the Bushes moved into this grand house, Prescott set up his office in the brightest, airiest room, whose windows looked out onto the back of the lush property lined with flowering bushes and tall trees. A week later, while he was away, Dorothy and the maid, Lucy—known to the family as "Lizzie"—somehow managed to carry the Queen Anne desk from the master bedroom to the study, which meant dragging it down a treacherous flight of stairs. "She almost broke her neck on those stairs," Dorothy would recall of Lizzie many years later. Most women were, as she put it, "a little weak." But not Dorothy, who was as strong as an ox—even though she was pregnant with her fourth child, Jonathan, when she moved that desk.

What's perhaps more fascinating than the fact that Dorothy hadn't cleared with Prescott the decision to relocate the furniture is the fact that when he got home and saw what she'd done, he didn't question it. He knew his wife well and recognized the statement she was making with the placement of her desk in that room, and it was fine with him.

When the children were young and obstreperous, Dorothy and Prescott would secrete themselves in this study—*their* study—for peace and quiet while Lizzie looked after their brood; they also had two other maids, a nurse, a laundress, and a cook living out in the carriage house. They needed refuge not just from the children but also from all the help, and this study was their sanctuary. The couple would spend hours in here nestled on the couch together, their feet intertwined, talking about their lives or their children's futures. They would sometimes play soft music in the background. It was romantic and intimate, but it was also serious. Prescott's political ambitions were always the subject of great discussion, the bills he was trying to pass, the important work in Congress he so valued. Dorothy was his greatest ally, the one person he knew he could count on. It's not that they agreed on everything, either. They often disagreed on important matters, but they respected each other's views. Within these walls, they could share any secret without judgment. "She knows me better than I know myself," Prescott would say, and in many ways that was true. They also prayed in here, which the religious Dorothy insisted was the most important thing they could do together; she was even known to read devotions to her family at the breakfast table.

According to photos of this well-appointed room, between the two desks was a comfortable sofa covered in a fabric the color of which family members recall as a deep blue floral chintz. On either side were comfortable cream-colored velvet chairs. The heavy tied-back drapes at the tall windows matched the colors of the chairs. Covering the dark wood floor was a large, classic Aubusson rug. It's difficult to know the shades of the rug given that surviving photographs are all in black-and-white, but a family member recalls it as a blue, green, and red floral design. The walls were said to be painted a pale golden color. The lighting in here at night was always purposely soft; most of the silk shades on the lamps were beige. On one wall were hung several landscapes by French masters. There were also graceful floral displays on several tables. A fireplace was on another wall, above which hung two large oil paintings—one of her mother and one of his. Two more walls were dominated by wooden built-in shelves made of curled maple, upon which the Bushes' prized books were arranged in alphabetical order by author. Dorothy was just a little fanatical about keeping them that way, too. Anytime someone—usually one of the children when they were younger—would take a book and return it to the wrong spot, she would know it as soon as she walked into the room. She could sense it. Prescott said it was "a gift," the fact that his "Dotty" could take two steps into their study and instantly be able to intuit that just one of the many hundreds of volumes was out of order. She would make a beeline for that book, say something about how thoughtless it was that "some people" had no respect for the alphabet, and return it to its rightful spot. She was nothing if not exacting.

Dorothy Wear Walker Bush—known to loved ones and friends as "Dotty," to her children as "Mum," and later to her grandchildren as "Ganny"—was remarkable in many ways. She was born in Kennebunkport, Maine, on July 1, 1901, to George Herbert Walker—known as "Bert"—and Lucretia Wear—known as "Luli" (sometimes spelled "Loulie"). She was the second child of six; her siblings were Nancy, George Herbert Jr. ("Herbie"), Jimmy, Louis, and Johnny.

Dorothy was a petite, wiry woman; once, someone referred to her as "dainty," and she responded by walloping him on the shoulder. In 1953, she was fifty-two and stood at maybe five feet three inches, if that tall, and had a closely cropped, wavy salt-and-pepper hairstyle and cobalt blue eyes. Her face was mostly unlined; her skin glowed. She had a square-jawed countenance and a determined air about her: a serious, no-nonsense type. Hasty impressions of her were deceptive, though. She could also be funny, charming, and endearing. She enjoyed competitive sports and had always been an excellent athlete.

Dorothy was a lot tougher and more formidable than she would be described by family members in years to come. Perhaps she is the most misunderstood of all the Bush women. In interview after interview over the passing of decade after decade, one Bush progeny after another sings her praises the benign way her grandson, George W. Bush, did in 1987: "She is the sweetest, kindest, most gentle soul who ever lived. She was miraculous." While that was true of Dorothy, it certainly wasn't her totality. She was anything but bland. She had more backbone, more spunk, more *daring* than most of her descendants acknowledge. It's not pejorative on their parts, either, not an effort to diminish her. Dorothy actually had a way of embodying all the characteristics they so admired about her—the sweetness, the kindness, the gentleness—while at the same time being a very ballsy, outspoken kind of woman who could never be intimidated. Maybe the fact that she was able to project so many sides of herself and be for her loved ones exactly who they needed her to be was the truly "miraculous" thing about her. "George's mother is a woman of substance," her daughter-in-law Barbara Bush once said of her in a description more in line with the truth, "and I don't think I have ever used that term to describe a person before, but there's no better way to describe her."

Like most Bush women and those associated with the Bush family, Dorothy also had a hunger for politics and thought of herself as a patriot. Nothing made her prouder than knowing that Prescott was a United States senator. He was being of service to his country and so was she in her own way. Every week, she was charged with writing a column for a syndicate that distributed it in newspapers across the state. It was called "Washington Life as Seen by a Senator's Wife by Mrs. Prescott Bush," and, though she'd only been at it for about a month, it had already become a staple of the editorial pages of the newspapers that carried it.

On this morning, Dorothy had a deadline. She had handwritten some text on a tablet and now sat down to type it up, pecking out the words slowly and deliberately. Her notes read:

My husband, Prescott, or Senator Bush as he is known, has a great many dreams for this country which, of course, pleases me as it should all who care deeply about America. However, on a more personal scale, when I think of his insistence of a code by which our children live, my heart fills with pride. "To do unto others as you would have done unto you is a good way to live," he told our son, George, the other morning over breakfast. "But doing unto others better than you'd expect to be done unto you is even greater. To give more, that's what's truly American." The Senator's words made me think. Indeed, what is more patriotic than to give more than you'd expect to be given? How fortunate are we to live in a country with such unlimited riches and abundant blessings, where all of us have so much opportunity. I think what the Senator was hoping to impart to our son was this: we must resist the all-too-human urge of self-involvement. We have so much let's not take it for granted. Be generous, if not of wallet because perhaps you can't afford it, but of heart because that, most certainly, is never in short supply.

"Enough for now," she would always tell Lizzie as she rose from her desk after any writing session, adding that she was lucky she'd gotten that far. After all, she didn't even really know how to type properly. She did the best she could, pecking about on the keys, making mistakes and then losing her train of thought as she corrected them, always pushing forward, as was her way, determined to finish the task at hand. "Perhaps it's not important, this little column of mine," she said in an interview for a women's magazine at the end of 1953, "but it's the thing I'm doing right now, and so it's the thing in which I take pride. Whatever it is we do, we must give it our all. I don't believe in half an effort, no matter what. I taught my children to give everything they have to everything they do. That's always been my way. It was my way long before I became the wife of a senator."

Buccaneer and Playboy

George Herbert Walker's family, the Walkers, had emigrated from England to America in the early seventeenth century, settling in Maine. By the nineteenth century, they had migrated to St. Louis. His father, David Davis (D.D.) Walker, born in 1840, was a true American success story in that he came from nothing, the son of a farmer who'd gone bankrupt, and through hard work and dedication, eventually made a fortune as cofounder of Ely, Walker and Company, a large supplier of dry goods that distributed to stores such as J. C. Penney. A staunch Democrat, he would become one of about seven thousand millionaires in America during his time.

George, who was known as Bert, was born in St. Louis in 1875. Jacob Weisberg, in his book *The Bush Tragedy,* described him as a "buccaneer and raucous playboy" who "was raised like a Midwestern prince." Apparently he took his valet with him when he attended the Jesuit boarding school Stonyhurst in England.

A former collegiate heavyweight boxing champion (while attending Washington University, where he studied law after studying medicine at Edinburgh), Bert could be contentious and defiant for no good reason other than just being the way he was wired. Like his father, he could also be short-tempered, erratic, and given to bizarre fulminations. For instance, once when he was stung by a wasp he got out his shotgun and started shooting at it, leaving large, gaping holes in the dining room ceiling. Luli was horrified. "Don't blame me," he told her, "blame the damn bee."

Bert ruled his family with an iron fist and was, according to most accounts, a fearsome character. "He was a tough old bastard," Elsie Walker, one of his grandchildren, said. "There really wasn't a lot of love on the part of the boys for their father." If his sons had a disagreement about anything, Bert would lace them up with boxing gloves and have them duke it out in a ring he had set up in the house—no rules, no restrictions, and whoever came out the least bloodied was the winner. "The old man figured that the one left standing was right," said Bert's son Louis, "and whoever was laying on his ass was wrong."

One family story has it that Louis once showed up drunk for a doubles tennis match with Dorothy and another couple; apparently, he'd stumbled upon a wedding reception in the clubhouse during a break in the action and enjoyed six glasses of champagne in rapid succession. Bert felt his son had thoroughly disrespected the game. As punishment, he pulled Louis out of Yale and sent him to work in a steel mill in Pennsylvania for two years. "That's something you just don't get over," observed Louis Walker many years later.

Those who knew him well found it hard to believe that Bert had once almost become a priest; he sure didn't seem like the religious type. His Catholic parents had sent him to a Catholic seminary with the priesthood in mind; he rebelled by dropping out and marrying Luli, a Protestant. D.D. warned him that if he married her, he would go straight to hell. "I'll tell you one thing," Bert shot back, "I'll go straight to hell if I don't." It was a line he later repeated to a priest who had given him pretty much the same admonition. In the end, he would wed his beloved outside of the Catholic Church. D.D. staged his own revolt by refusing to attend the wedding.

A few years before his death in 1918, D.D. seemed to be losing his mind, or at least that's what his sons thought as he started giving away his fortune, equal to more than $3 million in today's money, in just a few years' time. He had also become outspoken about the most reprehensible of personal views, which he proudly espoused in editorials, such as one on the front page of *The St. Louis Republic* in 1914: "I am in favor of segregating the Negroes in all

communities. I consider them more of a menace than the social evil [prosti-
tution], and all other evils combined. I am completely in favor of the unwrit-
ten law—lynching for assaults on women, no matter whether the criminal
be black or white. For humanity's sake, I am in favor of putting to death all
children who come into the world hopeless invalids or badly deformed."

Bert and his brother, David Davis Jr., were sure their father was going
senile. They sued to prevent him from squandering their inheritance and
charged him with being mentally unfit. He countersued. None of it was
resolved before D.D. died, but it left Bert, in particular, angry and resentful.
Some felt his resentment of his father was the driving force that propelled
him to not only reject Democratic politics as well as Catholicism, but to
be bigger and better in business and have more fun doing it than the old
man ever had, and he did just that. Bert went on to become a successful
banker with his own firm, the G. H. Walker & Co. (one of the first investment banking firms in the Midwest), and later became the president of the
U.S. Golfing Association and established the Walker Cup championship, a
competition that pitted American golfers against their British counterparts.
He raced horses, had his own stables, and served as a New York state racing
commissioner. He also was a partner in the Racquet Club in St. Louis and
the Deepdale Golf Club in Great Neck, Long Island. A smart investor, he
made many more millions than D.D. ever had; he would always be proud to
say he had topped his father in pretty much every way.

At the age of twenty-six, Bert built 12 Hortense Place in St. Louis,
which resembled an Italian Renaissance manse with its marble bathrooms,
a portico, and carriage house. In 1920, he would set up a second home in
Manhattan after taking a position heading up W. A. Harriman & Co., an
investment banking organization specializing in foreign stocks and bonds.
There, the Walkers would live even more affluently than they did in St.
Louis, in an opulent manse at 453 Madison Avenue. Later, they would have
a luxurious penthouse at 1 Sutton Place. They also had a weekend home in
Long Island and a sumptuous estate in Santa Barbara, he and Luli each with
their own chauffeur-driven Rolls-Royce. "My grandfather was the worldliest
man that ever lived, the very worldliest," says Nancy Bush Ellis. "Two Rolls-

Royces, the place on Long Island, and two butlers, First Man and Second Man. One did the silver and one was his valet."

Bert was so shrewd with money, even the stock market crash didn't affect his wealth. It could easily be argued that thanks to Bert the next couple of generations of Walkers and Bushes wouldn't have to fret about finances—that is unless a parent made the specific decision to withhold money in order to teach some sort of life lesson about persistence or tenacity.

Into this cushy life of privilege was born Dorothy Walker. Over the course of her youth, she would enjoy the many opulent Walker estates, her favorite being their ten-thousand-acre estate called Duncannon Plantation in South Carolina. When she was a young girl, Bert would load his private train car with all their family members and friends and servants and take them all down to the plantation for Thanksgiving and Christmas. They'd all stay together in an enormous mansion, built back in 1820. While vacationing there, Dorothy learned to hunt; she became an excellent quail shooter. She also excelled as a horsewoman and polo player, making her father proud. Few in the family, if any, were as athletic as Dorothy, who, in 1918, became a runner-up in the first National Girls' Tennis Championship at the Merion Cricket Club near Philadelphia. She was accustomed to butlers and maids and other functionaries catering to her every whim at the family's stately manor at 12 Hortense Place, as well as at all their other estates; it's just the way she and her siblings were raised, and they knew no other life.

The Walker Sisters

As they passed through adolescence, Dorothy Walker and her older sister by two years, Nancy, couldn't have been more different from each other. Though Dorothy was quite pretty, with a flawless skin tone and shoulder-length blond hair (even if in some photos from the era it seems rather dark), she wasn't very focused on her appearance. She wore little makeup for a fresh, clean appearance, whereas Nancy—or "Nan," as she was known—was a brunette and was much more beauty conscious. She sometimes seemed nearly preoccupied with cosmetics. Both girls had a wholesome look, though, with clear complexions, great smiles, and conservative hairstyles apropos of the times.

Whereas Dorothy was pragmatic, Nancy was whimsical. She loved high society, studied couture in fashion magazines, and daydreamed about traveling the world. She enjoyed dressing in the best styles of the day. At least three times a year, her father would arrange for her and Dorothy to receive the latest Parisian fashions, packed carefully in boxes and sent to them directly from France. It was one of Bert's indulgences of his daughters, and one that appealed much more to Nancy than to Dorothy. She loved wearing the wardrobe, underneath which would always be a corset, and, for Nancy, the tighter the better. Dorothy hated wearing corsets, but Luli insisted on them for her daughters, and, like most wealthy people at the time, even had a "fainting room" in their home. This was a small cubicle off one of the bedrooms where women who were, perhaps, party guests or happened to be at the manor for one reason or another could retreat after becoming woozy because their corsets were too tight.

Another of Bert and Luli's indulgences of their daughters was that they saw to it that they had a French governess, Lena Gremillot, taking care of their every need throughout their childhood and into their teen years. It would be years, though, before Dorothy would appreciate this particular perk. "I remember so well as a child my ingratitude and almost resentment at having a French governess and having to walk in the afternoon with *mademoiselle* instead of playing baseball with my brothers," she recalled in May of 1961. "Now, occasions present themselves in Washington when I bless mother over and over again for persevering in spite of my protests."

Though equally pampered, there was a friendly competition going on with the two sisters. Which daughter was the most favored by their father was always a big concern. Bert didn't help matters by saying Nancy was his favorite and then going off to spend the day skeet shooting with Dorothy. It bothered Nancy more than it did Dorothy, though. "Dotty was always the more self-confident sister," said one relative, "and, in that respect, didn't feel much of a need to compete."

Nancy was a bit of a paradox. Even though she loved high fashion and was more given to what some might have viewed as the superficial, she was also a serious young woman with a definite streak of activism about her. She was a member of the Junior League, for instance, and dedicated herself to clothing drives for the poor. She assisted in organizing fund-raisers at Children's Hospital—at one she sold cigarettes and tulips to wealthy young men who could contribute to the hospital's coffers; at another she participated in a "dollar dance" to raise thirty thousand dollars to reopen the hospital's convalescent home. "She cared about people," Dorothy would write many years later. "She was maybe the more socially conscious of the two of us, just one of the many differences between we sisters. I was more interested in higher education, though."

After Dorothy graduated from Mary Institute, the elite girls' school in St. Louis, she approached her father about college. All her brothers would attend Yale, and Dorothy wanted to go to Vassar. Luli certainly hadn't gone to college. Whether she'd even graduated from high school was an open question in the family, which had been fine with Bert. "[Bert] thought that college just made women tough and argumentative," said Dorothy's daughter, Nancy Bush Ellis, many years later. "So, no, he was not for it. Not at all."

"You're not going to Vassar, and that's the end of it," Bert told Dorothy, in a voice that forbade argument. His reasons weren't that complex: A woman's place was in the home, maybe not a surprising opinion considering the times, the early twentieth century. She should marry well, be at her husband's beck and call, raise a good family, and be satisfied with that kind of life. However, Dorothy told him it was her dream to go to Vassar and asked, "Aren't I allowed to dream?" According to the family's history, Bert shouted at her, "Who do you think you are? You have no right to ambition," and when Bert raised his voice, it could shake the rafters. Distraught, and maybe a little frightened, too, Dorothy ran off in tears.

Bert did have a plan for Dorothy, though. He sent her to Miss Porter's School in Farmington, Connecticut, but only because it was a finishing school for young girls and it would help her snag a good husband. Nancy had just graduated from a two-year program there; she was fine with the education she received at Miss Porter's and felt she needed nothing more.

In 1919, Bert allowed the sisters to spend about six months in France with their eccentric and fun-loving aunt Min, and he did so for the same reason he had them educated at Miss Porter's—to polish them up enough for them to land good husbands. Even wealthy young women of this era from the Midwest were seldom able to travel overseas, so this really was a big deal. It was actually the second time the girls had been to Europe; they had both been presented as debutantes at the Court of St. James's in London, just a year earlier.

Sixty-one-year-old Minnie Holliday Nave was a maternal aunt of Luli Walker. She had an apartment on Paris's Place Monceau, which she had bought after her husband died in 1901. She was just forty-three when he passed, determined to continue to live her life and not spend the rest of it being what she called "a sad, old widow." She also had a house in Biarritz on the Bay of Biscay. She was living a good life and eager to expose her nieces to it.

Dorothy and Nancy would never forget their time with Aunt Min, who gave them free rein to enjoy every new experience that came their way. Their time in the City of Lights and on the Bay of Biscay was filled with romantic horse-and-buggy evenings with exciting men; both were pampered and, as Dorothy would later recall it, "treated just a little bit like royalty." The sisters also took in every museum they could find, completely immersing themselves in the culture, so much so that by the time their vacation was over, they'd become fluent in French. Much to Bert's later dismay, Aunt Min also taught the girls how to play poker; she was proficient at the game, always winning large sums of money.

After this vacation, the sisters would have enough stories about Aunt Min to last a lifetime, such as the time she invited a minister to tea, a man with a struggling church who seemed to need all the help he could get. She told him, "Reverend, I want you to know that first of all I love my God, then my children, then my country, and finally . . . gambling." She explained that the previous night she'd had a winning streak and wanted to now use her profits to buy him a new suit. She hoped he would accept it, but she wanted to be honest about how she bought it in case he'd be offended. He said he'd be honored to accept the present. She then bought him a purple shirt with a white collar and a gray suit that, in her eyes, seemed suitable for a minister. "This is the nicest thing anyone has ever done for me," he told her with tears in his eyes when she presented it to him. That particular story resonated with both sisters as a demonstration that, as Dorothy put it many years later—almost thirty years later, which suggests just how much of an impact it made on her—"it's worth it to be generous and not so self-involved."

Dorothy's Gamble

In 1919, after the Walker sisters returned from Paris, Nancy was selected to participate in the Veiled Prophet Ball. This event, a St. Louis tradition, was comprised of a parade and pageant sponsored each year by the Veiled Prophet Organization, founded by prominent St. Louisians back in the late nineteenth century. Every year, a male member of this order was selected to preside over the Veiled Prophet Ball. Then six young women were chosen for the "Veiled Prophet's Court of Honor." Before one of them was crowned, a runner-up called "Queen of Love and Beauty" (also known as "First Maid") was selected. It was like a Miss America pageant—but a lot more complicated.

Because of the war, the ball had been canceled for the last two years. Therefore, this one, in 1919, marked a grand return to the tradition and, thus, was highly anticipated. Not only would there be the ball, but also scheduled was a grand parade earlier that same day, which was known to attract huge crowds. (The Veiled Prophet Ball and Parade are still held in St. Louis today.)

In 1919, the Veiled Prophet Ball was to be held on October 7. Among the women in the Court of Honor along with Nancy was a young brunette named Marian Franciscus. As fate would have it, Marian's father, James Franciscus, happened to be one of Bert's avowed enemies. The two men had had failed business dealings years earlier involving the Third National Bank, of which Franciscus was vice president.

When Bert found out that James Franciscus's daughter could possibly end up queen, he put his foot down and said he wouldn't allow Nancy to risk being one of her "lowly" maids. He then refused to allow her to go to the ball. This caused no shortage of tears and outrage from Nancy, who believed the honor of participating was more important than any animosity her father may have had for the father of one of her competitors.

Though Dorothy thought the ball was frivolous and a waste of time and money, she knew it was important to her sister. So when Nancy asked her to try to reason with their father, Dorothy said she would give it a shot. Dorothy then asked Bert for a few moments in his study, a daring move on her part. The Walker children all knew they were never allowed access to Bert's inner sanctum. When they were younger, they would gather at the door and press their ears against it to hear what was going on in there, because whatever their father was doing in that secret room was a true mystery. Very often, they would hear Bert bellowing into the telephone and they'd look at each other with wide-eyed fear. Sometimes a visitor would be in there with him, and they'd hear Bert repeatedly pounding his fist on the desk as he shouted. Their mother would shoo them away out of fear that Bert would suddenly open the door and find them crouched behind it.

Now, at eighteen, Dorothy sat in this forbidden room on one side of an enormous mahogany desk, facing her father. As she looked around, she would have noticed the walls lined with shelves that were filled with books and periodicals. There were no windows, just artificial light from lamps that Bert kept dimmed. Sometimes he put auburn bulbs in the fixtures to keep them from burning too brightly because he said it hurt his eyes. Though a large space, it was dark and claustrophobic, not at all welcoming. It also reeked of Bert's favorite stogies, which Dorothy, her sister, and her mother found to be a nauseating smell. As if it could get any worse in there, every surface in the room was coated with a thick patina of dust because Bert wouldn't allow the help to tidy up for fear they'd rearrange his prized possessions.

Dorothy started by trying to appeal to Bert's affection for Nancy. She told him she would be devastated if she wasn't allowed to participate in the ball. This wasn't the best strategy given Bert's personality. "Dotty, I don't allow empathy to distort my judgment," he told her. His problem was with James Franciscus, he reminded her, not with Nancy. There was no way he would ever allow his daughter to be a handmaiden to any daughter of Franciscus's if she was selected to be queen.

Dorothy then changed tactics to one she knew would better resonate with him, which was pointing out the shame that would result if he didn't allow Nancy to go to the ball. Dorothy reminded Bert that people would be talking about it for years to come, and the family would thus be scandalized. *That* made an impression on Bert. Furthermore, Dorothy said, she doubted that Marian Franciscus would win, and her money was on Nancy. She was prettier, Dorothy said, and her gown was more beautiful; she and her mother had helped Nancy select the elegant cream-colored sheath she'd wear to the ball. Bert told Dorothy he would think about it. "Now, go," he told her, pointing at the door. She got up and left and, according to what she wrote decades later, couldn't wait to get out of there. As soon as she was in the hallway, she found Nancy waiting for her. She had been on the other side of the door the entire time, trying to listen in. "What happened, Dotty?" she asked urgently. "Did he say yes?"

"Well, you know Father," Dorothy said with uncertainty. She explained that she had appealed to his brain, not his heart, because she figured his brain was probably the bigger target.

In the end, Dorothy was successful in her mission; Bert changed his mind and decided to allow Nancy to participate. Many years later, he would say he was proud of Dorothy for having the courage to confront him and assert herself. She really showed him what she was made of, and he never forgot it. Or, as he put it, "Dotty showed me something I didn't know she had." On one hand, he didn't want his daughters to have backbone because he didn't think it was ladylike. On the other, he respected strong-minded people just on principle, even if they did happen to be women.

In support of her sister, Dorothy participated in the festivities every way she could by attending all the ancillary dances, dinners, and then the ball it-self, as well as the parade. In the end, much to the Walkers' disappointment,

Marian Franciscus did end up being crowned queen. The only silver lining to her triumph was that the Walker sisters were able to see the look on their father's face when the crown was placed on the head of the daughter of an enemy. Somehow, that made the whole thing seem worthwhile. Nancy was named First Maid, just as Bert had feared. He blamed Dorothy and didn't speak to her for almost a month. She said it was worth it, though, if that's what it took for her sister to have such a memorable experience. She also quipped that she had a whole lifetime to talk to her father, and she was certain he wouldn't hesitate to catch her up on anything she'd missed.

About a month later, in November, both Dorothy and Nancy had their "coming out" as debutantes with a lavish reception hosted by their parents at their home or, as one report had it, "The Misses Walker made their formal bow to society."

There were any number of debutante festivities that year, not just for the Walker sisters but for their friends as well, such as a dinner at the St. Louis Club hosted by Mr. and Mrs. Neil A. McMillan, the wealthy parents of one of the girls' friends. This one was a costume party with Egyptian culture as its theme. Dorothy wore jade green and silver, Nancy an elaborate headdress of purple, rose, and white plumes. At the party, Nancy met a young man named Prescott Bush. According to one press account, he came "dressed as an Egyptian gentleman." He was good-looking and interesting at twenty-four, and Nancy was taken with him. About a week later, she saw him again for lunch. As it happened, she had a couple of tickets to the St. Louis Symphony Orchestra at the Odeon, which she couldn't use because of a prior commitment. She offered them to Prescott, maybe to curry favor with him. He suggested he return the good turn, perhaps with dinner and maybe dancing, too. They then put a date on the books; she was excited by the prospect.

On the afternoon Prescott Bush came to the Walker home to pick up the tickets, Luli was hosting a dressy, midday cocktail party for the society women of one of her many charity interests. Embarrassed about the intrusion, especially since he wasn't dressed appropriately, Prescott offered to wait in one of the parlors. Luli told him not to be silly; he looked just fine. She took his hand and escorted him into the drawing room, which was dominated by an enormous oil painting of herself (by Hungarian master Philip Alexius de László), in which she was wearing a diaphanous pink gown with her hands divinely extended as if to a deity. As soon as he walked into the room many of the young women present made an immediate beeline for Prescott, wanting to get to know him. Meanwhile, Nancy was up in her bedroom, primping for her own grand entrance. Maybe she waited a little too long, though, because, as fate would have it, there was a rustle in the entryway as someone came bursting through the front door. "Oh my God, I'm late. *I'm late,*" came the voice, according to the family's history. "Mother is going to *kill* me." Eighteen-year-old Dorothy Walker then came sweeping into the parlor, wearing her cute ankle-length tennis outfit. Luli shook her head. "Really, Dotty?" she asked, exasperated. "I mean . . . *really?*" According to what Dorothy's daughter, Nancy, would recall many decades later, Dorothy was "blond and breathless after a tennis game, and in that moment, Prescott Bush spotted a kindred spirit."

Prescott

B y the time Dorothy Walker met him, Prescott Sheldon Bush was already a unique man. In years to come he would be the architect of the Bush dynasty as a senator, the father of a President, and the grandfather of two governors and *another* President. The Bushes would always, as a family, reject the notion of a dynasty, though. Tim McBride, a personal aide and assistant to President George H. W. Bush, observed, "Their family commitment was one of service. And if that suggests dynasty, then so be it, but that was not the driving force. The driving force behind the family's engagement in public life was service to others, in all things, at early ages and throughout their careers. And this is true of all the Bushes, not just the two Presidents."

Prescott would always be the Bush family's biggest inspiration, the man from whom they would draw their greatest example of not only how to survive in the cutthroat world of politics, but also how to raise a close-knit family. At a looming six foot four and 250 pounds, he would dominate any room he walked into, and not just because of his physicality but also his force of personality. He had a deep, booming voice, which, when provoked to anger, could shake the walls. Though he always exuded charisma as a businessman and politician, something about him kept people at arm's length. He seemed unknowable.

It's not easy to put into words the way Prescott affected people with the passing of time, even his own family. His children loved him but also feared him, and his grandchildren especially viewed him as a frightening presence in their lives. The walking stick he carried everywhere didn't help matters; to a youngster's eyes it probably looked like a weapon. Years later, George W. would wonder just what his grandfather was thinking as the old man sat in his easy chair puffing on his cigar and watching the news with a scowl on his face, his hand resting on that walking stick. When he was caught pulling a dog's tail by Prescott, the old man lit into George so hard that his mother, Barbara, slowly backed into a closet and, according to her memory, and said to herself, "Okay, well, that kid's on his own now."

All that would come much later, though.

In 1919, Prescott Bush was just twenty-four and fully on the upward trajectory of his life. Prescott Sheldon Bush was born on May 15, 1894, the oldest of four surviving siblings, along with Mary, Margaret, and James; a brother, Robert, died of scarlet fever at the age of three and a half. All published accounts have Prescott's birth as 1895. However, fresh research conducted by the Ohio Genealogical Society, utilizing the Franklin County, Ohio, birth register 1893–1897, volume 6, page 126–127, now proves 1894 as his actual birth year. (The year is even wrong on Prescott's grave marker.)

His father, Samuel Bush, born in 1863, was a railroad manager and later a successful steel manufacturer who, during World War I, worked for the government as a coordinator of weapons contractors. "He was a stern man, that's what my father always said," Teensie Bush Cole, daughter of James Bush, recalled of Samuel. "It was that era of seen and not heard. He kept that attitude throughout his life."

Prescott's mother, Flora Sheldon Bush, whose name appears in society columns as a guest at various affairs as early as 1893, married Samuel on June 20, 1894, at the age of twenty-two. An elegant young woman who adored her husband, she later became known in the family for her flowery letters full of care and concern for him as he traveled on business.

Though close to his mother, Prescott constantly butted heads with his father. Later in life, he wouldn't even talk about him to family members, and when Samuel died in 1948, Prescott would eschew his inheritance, giving it all to his sisters. He wanted nothing from Samuel, he said, because Samuel had nothing worthwhile to give him.

After attending Douglas Elementary School in Columbus, Ohio, and then the all-boys preparatory St. George's School in Middletown, Rhode Island, where he was an excellent student and even an actor, Prescott then went on to a successful college education at Yale, from which he graduated in 1917. During his time at Yale, he was a member of the elitist and secretive Skull and Bones society, as were later his son George H. W. Bush and his grandson George W. (Though there have always been rumors that Prescott was one of the Bonesmen who'd excavated the skull of Geronimo from his grave in Oklahoma, most scholars have debunked the story.) He was also known for his bass singing voice and was a member of the Glee Club, the Yale Men's Choir, and the Whiffenpoofs.

Pretty much right from Yale, Prescott went into the service and was soon commissioned a captain in field artillery in France and Germany during World War I. He returned home after two years. Though he thought he might go to law school, he ended up taking a good job with the Simmons Hardware Company after moving to St. Louis in 1919, which is where he met Dorothy Walker.

As soon as she laid eyes on Prescott, Dorothy was impressed. The next thing everyone knew, she was telling Nancy that *she* was going out on a date with him. Nancy tried not to be upset about it, but this was difficult for her. It seemed so unfair. She would make statements she'd later in life admit were trite, along the lines of *but I saw him first.* At the time, though, it did seem wrong to Nancy that Dorothy hadn't thought to ask her for permission to go out with someone she had, in a sense, brought home.

Nancy had always had her share of good-looking men, though; she was popular and social. However, Dorothy was always more practical when it came to the opposite sex. The two would sit on the uncomfortable, straight-back Queen Anne sofa in the drawing room at Hortense Place and make lists of the men they knew and then discuss the pros and cons of each. Nancy always leaned toward the most handsome of the bunch, but not Dorothy. She wanted more in a mate than just good looks. He would have to be ambitious and enterprising, like her father. He would also have to be a quality person at his core, someone she could admire—unlike her father. He couldn't be selfish; she hated self-involvement in a man. If he was also attractive, more the better, but it wasn't necessarily a requirement. It was for Nancy, though. She would say she could never get to the part where he was a good person if a good face couldn't be her starting point.

Prescott almost came between the Walker sisters. However, Luli would have none of any sisterly dispute over someone they'd just met and who, she speculated, might not even be in their lives in two weeks. She told Nancy to just let it play out and not worry about it. It was hard for Nancy to stay mad, anyway. After all, Dorothy had always been her biggest champion. Even if they did have their competitive moments, she always knew her sister would support her, as she'd done with their father over the matter of the Veiled Prophet Ball. She so adored Dotty, it was impossible for her to imagine any kind of protracted conflict with her.

As it would turn out, after their first couple of dates, Dorothy was more taken with Prescott than anyone might have expected. He was good-looking with short, dark hair parted in the middle and deep-set brown eyes, a prominent forehead, full lips, and a smooth and rounded jawline. But there was a kind of depth about him to which Dorothy really responded. He was smart and well-spoken, and he appreciated art and history, especially American history. He was also religious—Episcopalian—and could quote scripture with ease. While he didn't talk about his faith openly, if asked he was eager to discuss it. Because Dorothy was raised with such strict religious values, she appreciated his zeal; it made her feel comfortable and at home with him.

There was a bit of a bump in the road for Dorothy, though. During her third date with Prescott, at a social gathering hosted by the Midland Valley Country Club, she dropped her napkin onto the floor. Prescott came forward to pick it up for her. While he was bent down, he spent a few extra seconds staring at her legs. It was so obvious, it made her uncomfortable. When she told her sister about it, Nancy didn't think it was so bad. She said she thought it was flattering. Dorothy didn't agree, saying there were better ways to flatter a woman. "Fine. If you don't want him, Dotty, hand him over," Nancy said with a wink. Already, the sting of losing Prescott to her sister had lifted and his presence was viewed in a more lighthearted way. No, Dorothy decided with a smile, not just yet.

In getting to know Prescott, Dorothy quickly came to the conclusion that he was a real romantic, or at least that was her first-blush impression. She would say that she never felt as taken care of as she did on those early dates. He lavished her with thoughtful presents—a diamond bracelet, a silver picture frame, and a leather-bound diary. He also praised her constantly. It was difficult to resist falling for him.

For his part, Prescott felt Dorothy, who was six years his junior, was quite the catch. She was gorgeous, a major part of her appeal. She came from money, which mattered to him as it did to his family. More important, though, she had a crucial quality he sensed right away: loyalty. In talking to her about the way she treated her friends and family members, her undying devotion to them was always evident.

Once, early in the courtship, Prescott made the mistake of criticizing Nancy by venturing an opinion, during an otherwise romantic dinner at the Hotel Statler, that she wasn't as smart as Dorothy. Who knows why he would have had such a pejorative view of her, because Nancy was actually quite intelligent. More provocative, though, was the question of why he would think it appropriate to offer such a dim view of her to her beloved sister? Dorothy was put off by it. She demanded to know what right he had to be critical of Nancy, or of any member of her family for that matter. He thought she had a lot of nerve standing up to him like that—and he hated that kind of nerve in a woman.

The couple didn't speak for a week. Prescott refused to apologize. He dug his heels in and wasn't very diplomatic about it, either. "You'll never be in a position to tell me what to say or how to act," he told Dorothy, "so you may as well accept that if we're to continue." In the minds of many young women, his attitude might have inspired a cautionary voice, perhaps one that might signal potential trouble down the road. For Dorothy, though, it reminded her of familiar terrain. It would seem she'd fallen for someone just like her father. She actually wasn't put off by Prescott's attitude as much as she was drawn to it. It presented a challenge, anyway, and if there was one thing Dorothy Walker liked, it was a good, old-fashioned challenge. Still, after she held her ground and told him she'd never allow herself to be cowed by him, the two found themselves at an impasse.

By this time, Prescott had already started golfing with Bert at the prestigious and incredibly discriminating St. Louis Country Club—no blacks, no Jews, no Catholics, and no brewers (of beer). The two men got along famously, mostly because Bert admired Prescott's focus and ambition, especially on the golf course. When Dorothy told her father that she and Prescott were having problems, he said she'd better do something to solve them. He had worked "too damn hard," he told her, to get her to the place where she could be thought of as interesting to an accomplished man like Prescott Bush. In other words, he didn't want her to blow it.

Finally, after about two more weeks of silence from Prescott and a lot of badgering about it by Bert, Dorothy decided to just give in and apologize. It had to remind her of the way she'd seen Luli act contrite to Bert about fights for which she was most certainly not to blame. "I gave in but I didn't like it," Dorothy recounted a good fifty years later to her caretaker, Virginia Mason. "I didn't like it one bit."

Nancy's Broken Heart

Autumn of 1920 proved to be a heady time for Dorothy Walker and Prescott Bush, who had rapidly fallen in love with each other. But, then, on September 4, tragedy struck. His parents, Samuel and Flora, had been vacationing in Rhode Island with his younger brother, James, when Flora was struck by a car and killed instantly. She was just forty-eight. Samuel was devastated; his marriage had been a happy one and there are many letters from Flora to him that prove it. "You and I are so much to each other we don't need others," she had recently written. "I want you, need you more every year, and we must take good care of each other."

Dorothy wanted to be at Prescott's side at the funeral in St. Louis. However, Luli wouldn't allow it, saying it wasn't appropriate for a young, single woman to traipse off to St. Louis with a beau, even if it was for the services of his mother. Dorothy agonized over it the whole time Prescott was gone and, says her daughter, Nancy, "she was more convinced than ever that she wanted to marry my father after that happened, more convinced than ever."

When he returned, Prescott proposed to Dorothy after asking Bert for her hand in marriage. "Miss Dorothy Walker to Wed P.S. Bush," ran the headline in the *St. Louis Post-Dispatch* on November 23, 1920, once the engagement was official. The couple was married eight months later on August 6, 1921, at the Church of Saint Ann-by-the-Sea in Kennebunkport in what the *Post-Dispatch* had predicted would be "one of the notable weddings of the summer." The reception, attended by dozens of Bushes and Walkers, was held at Surf Ledge, the Walkers' Victorian home on a cliff's edge at Kennebunkport. Of Dorothy's dress, the same paper described it as "white tulle, embroidered in seed pearls. Her veil of rose point lace fell from a coronet of orange blossoms over a satin court train." Dorothy had seven bridesmaids, including Nancy as her maid of honor, who, according to the *Post-Dispatch,* "wore a frock of cream lace over lavender charmeuse and a lace hat to match." The wedding was perfectly planned by Luli, again according to the same newspaper account, "as brilliant and as perfect as the good taste of Mrs. G. Herbert Walker could make it."

Though happy for her sister, Dorothy's wedding was difficult for Nancy, especially given that Bert had so immediately approved of Prescott and had so adamantly disapproved of someone she'd begun to see just after Prescott came into their lives. He was a minister, the Reverend James Baker, whom Nancy had met at a benefit. After just a month, she fell in love and urged him to ask Bert for permission for them to marry. When he did, Bert didn't give an immediate answer, saying he needed time to consider it. For weeks, the proposal was put on hold as Bert supposedly mulled things over. Frantic, Nancy asked Dorothy to intervene since she did seem to have sway over their father. Dorothy did her best with Bert, trying everything she could think of to get him to make the right decision. This time, though, she was unsuccessful. However, at least Dorothy was able to figure out the reasons for Bert's lack of enthusiasm. He wanted Nancy to marry well, he explained, and felt she wouldn't have a good life on a minister's salary. Maybe he was well-intentioned, but why did it take him a month to come to that conclusion? It felt to Nancy as if he'd never intended to give his permission and was just trying to torture her. Finally, he called the reverend into his office and told him, "No, absolutely not. I won't allow it."

At that point, Nancy wanted to run off and elope, but James wouldn't agree to it. As a man of the cloth, he said it just somehow felt wrong. Instead, he ended it with her, truly breaking her heart. From that point on, it would seem that Nancy was afraid to date for fear of once again falling for someone her father wouldn't approve of and then having to endure that kind of hurt all over again. Or at least that's what she said with the passing of the years. It doesn't answer the question, though, as to why she didn't date long after Bert was dead and gone. "I actually don't remember her ever talking about having dated when she was much older and would reflect on her life," said one of her relatives. "I think she just closed that part off in her. She was such a warm and giving person, it was a shame that she wasn't willing to take another chance on love. She was so deserving of it."

Marital Problems

After he and Dorothy married, Prescott Bush became a sales manager for a company his father worked for, Hupp Products, which produced floor coverings. It was a tough decision for Prescott since there was no love lost for Samuel, but he needed the job. He was tired of getting handouts from Dorothy's father, Bert, who was living the high life now on Madison Avenue in New York with Luli. However, Hupp went out of business in a year. It was Prescott who then discovered that a former owner had somehow found a way to skim profits from the company; he made certain that person was prosecuted to the fullest extent of the law, hoping it would ingratiate him to his father. It didn't. He then went to work for the new owners, Stedman Products, and that's when he and Dorothy relocated to a large Victorian house just outside Boston.

Soon after they were married, Dorothy found that Prescott was like her father in more ways than just his stubborn nature. "Prescott wanted Dotty to stay in her place, not have opinions, just be at home, a wife who would soon have his kids," said one family member. "That's not who Dotty was, though. She wanted to travel the world, she wanted to meet new challenges . . . she wanted to work. She wanted to grow, to live and have an exciting life. But she was in a marriage now to someone who didn't want any of that for her, and she would just have to figure it out."

Dorothy knew one thing for sure: Prescott may have been like her father, but in her marriage to him she would be nothing like her mother. Poor Luli always seemed intimidated by Bert, and with good reason. He constantly berated her, criticized her, and talked about her behind her back. Once, she was putting on her lipstick while looking into her compact as Bert stood behind her. When she finished, she whirled around and asked, "How's this?" He shrugged and said, "Could be better." Dorothy hated the way he treated her, but what she hated more was the fact that Luli put up with it. "If it were me," she used to say, "I'd tell him to go jump in a lake." Luli did her best to pray away her problems; she would retreat to her spirituality whenever troubled by Bert. That was fine for her mother, Dorothy decided, but never would she be so subservient to any man.

Another issue that constantly came up between Dorothy and Prescott was a more surprising one. Every time they had a little argument, Prescott escalated it by accusing her of marrying him just to get away from Bert. In his mind, Dorothy probably would have done anything to escape from her father, even marrying someone with whom she truly wasn't in love. None of this was true. It had never even occurred to Dorothy to marry someone just to get away from her father, and the fact that Prescott had come to believe it hurt her. It suggested that he didn't think her feelings were genuine. How had he come to such a conclusion? It was Nancy who cleared it up. She heard from one of Prescott's friends that it had been Bert who planted seeds of doubt in his mind. "I gave that girl everything," he told Prescott one day while golfing, at least according to what Nancy heard. "But she just couldn't wait to get out of the house, and then you came along in the nick of time. So I'll bet Dotty thanks her lucky stars for you." Once told this story, Dorothy had to wonder: If Nancy had heard it, how many other people had as well, and how many of them believed it? Now she was mortified. There wasn't much she could do about it, though, other than just continue to deny it whenever it came up, which was pretty often in the first year of her marriage.

After two years in Boston, Prescott got another job, this one with the U.S. Rubber Company, based in New York. It was time to pick up and move again, and Dorothy was happy to now be closer to her mother and sister. By this time, she and Prescott had two children—Prescott Sheldon Bush Jr., born August 10, 1922, and George Herbert Walker Bush, born on June 12, 1924. (Since Dorothy sometimes called her father, Bert, "Pop," his namesake was immediately called "Little Pop" or "Poppy.")

A Leg Up

By 1926, Dorothy was again pregnant; her only daughter, who she'd name after her beloved sister, Nancy, would be born later in the year. Ever since she and Prescott married, he had been going from one job to the next. Now he was with the U.S. Rubber Company in New York. Though the family was living large in Greenwich, their house at 11 Stanwich Road had been bought and paid for by Dorothy's father, Bert. To make it even more humiliating for Prescott, Bert put the estate in Dorothy's name only. That was quite a blow to Prescott's ego. However, because trying to keep up appearances had become increasingly difficult, he agreed to the purchase provided no one knew the truth about it. Meanwhile, Bert also paid for the couple's cook, governess, and even a nurse. Bert was fine with it; he enjoyed the idea that, on some level, he was controlling his daughter and her husband, but that was just Bert's way.

It just so happened that at this same time Bert had a substantial interest in the investment banking firm W. A. Harriman & Co. The firm was owned by railroad baron E. H. Harriman, who put his son, Averell, in a supervisory role.

Dorothy had been working on an idea in her head for about a month, and when she thought the time was right she decided to try to see it through. One day, she took her father to lunch at one of the best restaurants in New

York and leveled with him. Prescott had been going from job to job, and she wanted to help him find something more permanent. Their family was growing, and it was time for this instability to come to an end. Would he consider hiring Prescott at W. A. Harriman?

Unfortunately, the specific details of Dorothy's appeal to Bert are lost to memory all these many years later, but suffice it to say she was successful with it. "Before the luncheon was over, Bert had agreed to talk to Harriman about hiring Prescott," recalled William Bush (no relation to the Bush family), whose grandfather, also named William, was an executive at the company. "My grandfather—who was one of Bert's best friends and maybe wasn't objective—speculated that Bert had softened, was being magnanimous and just wanted to help out. However, I know that many others in the company felt he did it so that he'd be able to hold over Prescott's head the fact that he and his daughter had given him a leg up in life—and that does sound more like Bert, at least from the stories I've heard about him. I think his daughter didn't know which was the case and didn't care; she was probably just glad her father had said yes."

Maybe it was predictable considering his personality, but when Dorothy told Prescott the good news over dinner that night, he was less than grateful. He said he didn't need her going out and begging her father to take care of him. She felt he was being foolish and that he should just take the job. She was firm about it, which perhaps wasn't the best way to appeal to Prescott, but this really was a crucial moment, and she knew it. This job could change everything for them. "The two ended up in a fight that lasted a week," said one of Dorothy's relatives. "She couldn't believe Prescott would let his pride get in the way of this opportunity. It just seemed ridiculous to her. But look at it this way: Bert bought their house, was paying their staff . . . he was pulling all the strings, and now he was giving him a job. Looking back on it, you can sort of see why Prescott would hesitate."

"My grandfather told me that the word back was that Prescott wasn't going to accept the job, which, if memory serves, was a vice presidency position," recalled William Bush. "There was some surprise about that news given that it was a plum position just being handed to him."

Prescott eventually did agree to the job. "I think he realized that he was being foolish," said William Bush. "This was such a great opportunity, and it made no sense to turn it down just because his father-in-law and wife had cooked it all up. He had a lot of pride, though, and my grandfather said it made sense that there was some vacillation about this."

It was fortuitous that he took the job, because from that time onward, Prescott's and Dorothy's life and that of their children would never be the same. Taking the new position with W. A. Harriman & Co. would be the catalyst for an upward trajectory that would see Prescott gain not only power and influence, but untold millions. He never gave Dorothy credit for it, though, and no one else did, either. Historically, she would always be completely edited out of the official account. "I do remember that I left U.S. Rubber on May 1, 1926, to become associated with W. A. Harriman and Co., which was an investment banking organization, principally owned by Averell Harriman and his brother, Roland," Prescott said in his massive 454-page oral history, found at Columbia University. Roland was a friend of Prescott's from Yale. "Mrs. Bush's father, G. H. Walker, was the president of it, but Averell was the chairman, and my father-in-law had a substantial interest in it," Prescott said. "We [Averell and Roland Harriman and G. H. Walker] talked it over and they seemed to think that I would have some possibilities in that field that they were looking for. At any rate, they offered me a job."

Prescott's apparent lack of gratitude and acknowledgment didn't seem to bother Dorothy. She really didn't need his appreciation. She was just satisfied knowing she'd done what she'd set out to do in helping him get the job. Later she would say she wasn't responsible for anything more than just opening the door for him; he was the one who had to walk through it and convince the Harrimans and even his father-in-law that he was the man for the job. That was just Dorothy being humble, as was always her way.

"She was the kind of woman who didn't worry about small things as long as big things were accomplished," said her daughter, Nancy, many years later. "Mother was tough, not really sentimental," added her son George. "She was someone who was all about the end result." Also, Dorothy said she knew that "deep down," Prescott appreciated what she'd done for him and their family, and that this was enough for her.

In 1931, after W. A. Harriman & Co. merged with the Brown Bros. & Co. merchant bank, Prescott became a full-fledged partner in Brown Brothers Harriman & Co., now a huge private investment firm for the very wealthy on Wall Street. In a short time, it would become the nation's largest private bank, this despite the uncertainty of the stock market and no small number of nearly cataclysmic troubles as a result of the Depression. This merger is largely responsible for the initial wealth attained by Prescott just by virtue of his stock holdings and then his salary as well as his significant involvement with several major accounts, such as the Columbia Broadcasting System; he helped William Paley buy a half interest in the company, which lined the pockets of everyone, Prescott included. During various times in the coming years, he was on the board of directors of CBS Television and also, as an avid golfer, the head of the United States Golf Association. He was on his way, and he never looked back.

By this time, Prescott and Dorothy had four children: George, Prescott Jr., and Nancy were joined by Jonathan, who was born in 1931, and, later, in 1938, William, known as "Bucky," came along.

In 1931, the Bushes moved into a new, larger Victorian house on two acres in Greenwich at 15 Grove Lane, with a separate carriage house for their functionaries, who included two cooks, three maids, a governess, and a chauffeur. "It was such a good life," Dorothy would tell her caretaker, Virginia Mason, almost fifty years later. "But you can't count on luck to have a good life. Prayer is essential. So is taking action."

As it would happen, the new estate was also bought by Bert Walker, again in Dorothy's name. By this time, Prescott had enough wealth to purchase the property on his own, but he decided to stick with the tried-and-true and just let Bert purchase the estate in Dorothy's name as he had previous properties. *Why not?* Prescott figured. He didn't want to spend money on the new property and decided that if his father-in-law wanted to buy it for his wife, he was fine with it. He no longer felt controlled by Bert, since he had his own money. That said, one thing that became very predictable about Prescott as he started accumulating wealth was that he would always feel "cash poor," no matter how much he had in the bank. "Father was known for worrying about money," said his daughter, Nancy. "It was always on his mind, whether we had enough, whether we didn't, even when we clearly did." Basically, it would seem Prescott decided to use Bert's penchant for wanting to control things against him. If he wanted to buy a big estate for his daughter, that was fine with Prescott. It was also the cheaper way to go.

Raising Bush

When Dorothy Walker married Prescott Bush in 1921, she had just turned twenty. By way of a wedding present, her father, Bert, built a lovely one-story bungalow for the newlyweds at Walker's Point in Kennebunkport, the family's summer retreat. It would be here in these bucolic and ocean-swept surroundings that Dorothy would spend each and every summer for the rest of her life. At the time of her marriage, her parents also summered in the Big House, the home in which everyone congregated and which would, at one point, end up being occupied by George H.W. and Barbara Bush. Dorothy's sister, Nancy, had her own little house on the point, too.

The quaint village of Kennebunkport, Maine, is situated at the mouth of the Kennebunk River, just at the juncture where it widens into a harbor and then flows into the Atlantic. Bert had come upon the village at the turn of the century in 1902, which was when he and his father, D. D. Walker, purchased this rocky, eleven-acre peninsula. It was here they would build the family's original summer home, called the Big House. This rambling tract—Walker's Point—is also where Bushes would build other cottages that would, for decades, be the place where they'd commune during the summer months. George H. W. Bush would one day tell Tom Fiedler of the *Miami Herald*, "Walker's Point has always been the anchor to windward. It was always here. Always stable. Long on memories. Long on values. Happiness. It just repeats."

As she raised her children, Dorothy became a formidable and memorable presence in all their lives. "Every mother has her own style. My mother's was a little like an Army drill sergeant's," George H.W. wrote in a 1985 Mother's Day tribute in *Greenwich Time*. "Dad was the commanding general, make no mistake about that, but Mother was the one out there day in and day out shaping up the troops. She expected total honesty, and she expected us all to have concern for others. There was never any question about the absolute importance of those values. She had five of us to raise—Pres, myself, Nancy, John, and Bucky—and she just felt that there was too much for us to learn and to do to waste any time on chaos. So we had very little chaos in our house."

It could be argued that George maybe had a romanticized view of life with Mother considering that, from most other accounts (even some of his own), there seemed to be no shortage of household "chaos." But since Dorothy did once write, "You can do with memories whatever you like," she might have approved.

For instance, there's the story of when Dorothy was nine months pregnant with Prescott Jr. and decided to play softball. She supposedly hit a home run, ran all the bases, and then just continued to run straight to the car, where she was driven to the hospital to deliver her child.

There's also the story that, while at Kennebunkport a few years later, Dorothy took little Pressie sailing out on their small sailboat, the *Shooting Star*, in the middle of a raging thunderstorm. When the boat almost sank, Prescott Sr. had to take a motorboat out to rescue them. Naturally, he was upset about it, but Dorothy suggested he just calm down. It had been a great adventure, she said, one their boy wouldn't soon forget—which, she added, had been the whole point. She was used to swimming a mile in the frigid Atlantic Ocean, anyway, she reminded her husband. "But what about Pressie?" Prescott asked. Her response: "Do you really think he can't float?"

There are many other stories handed down over the years having to do with the sense of audacity mixed with athleticism fostered by "Mum." For instance, she insisted little George learn how to play tennis using both hands.

"Why not be skilled with *both* sides?" she asked. In the end, it did make him a star player, just like her. In playing baseball, she had her left-handed son bat from the right side, this even though he caught with his left hand. Once, when someone suggested he might become confused by these ambidextrous lessons and that they might even hinder his writing and math skills, she scoffed. "What does *that* have to do with the price of the tea in China?" she asked. "If you have a limitation, you must find a way around it."

When he was about eight, George told her he'd lost a tennis match because "I was off my game." She found the statement boastful. "You don't even *have* a game," she sharply reminded him. She always lived by the proverb "Let another man praise thee and not thee, thyself." Years later, when George was on a football team, after he won a game she asked him, "How did it go?" He said that he played pretty well, even scored a touchdown. "That's not what I mean," she said. "How did the *team* do?"

During the family's summers at Kennebunkport when the children were barely teenagers, Dorothy customarily set up competitions among them in tennis, basketball, softball, and swimming. She timed them as they played, encouraging them to win against one another. While it mattered to her how well they played and that they not be boastful about victories, it also mattered to her that they won. "She felt strongly that a winning attitude in sports would influence the same attitude in life, and she wanted her kids to be winners," George once said. "I think it worked to the extent that as a youngster I hated losing, and I still hate losing and not just in sports. Close only counts with horseshoes and hand grenades." (His son George W. would often make the exact same statement.)

While Dorothy was teaching her children determination and persistence, Prescott was teaching them how to toe the line; he was the disciplinarian in the family. "Dad was really scary," George H. W. Bush once told the television interviewer David Frost. "Remember Teddy Roosevelt's 'Speak softly and carry a big stick'? My dad spoke loudly and carried the same big stick. He got our attention pretty quick. It never occurred to me to differ with him. I mean, he was up here, and I was this little guy down here."

A firm believer in corporal punishment, Prescott didn't hesitate to use a razor strap, a belt, or whatever other weapon he could lay his hands on in a heated moment. If a young Bush incurred his wrath, he took off his belt and snapped it, instilling fear in the heart of the poorly behaved youth, who then ran as fast as his feet could take him. If he was unlucky enough to get caught, he ended up on Prescott's knee and got, as Prescott Jr. once put it, "whooped . . . he had a strong arm and, boy, did we feel it. He was a tough Joe bastard." (It should be noted that these punishments seem to have been relegated to just the boys; Nancy has no memories of ever being hit as a child.)

"When it came to being supportive, though, I don't know that anyone could beat my father," George said. "And when it came to loyalty, forget it; you couldn't top my mother. I can't fault them for anything and we had fun, too, especially with Mother."

In his 1985 Mother's Day essay, George H. W. Bush wrote:

One morning at church, the Reverend Alfred Wilson was giving his sermon, and he took as his biblical text, "Comfort me with apples." For some reason, Pressie and I thought that was terribly funny, and we began to snicker out loud. Mother looked at us severely and that quieted us—until suddenly the whole pew began to wiggle and shake, and there was Mother, attacked by "the giggles." Of course, looking at her broke us all up, and the whole Bush family had to beat a hasty and ignominious retreat, vanishing outside into gales of laughter.

Another memorable, humorous family moment had to do with Dorothy's singing—and the fact that she couldn't. Though she loved music, she could never carry a tune. However, Prescott was very good and, throughout his life, was always a part of a barbershop quartet; he'd been a loyal member of the Whiffenpoofs at Yale. A favorite song of his was "Jeepers Creepers," whose lyrics were written back in 1938 by Johnny Mercer. He would begin the song in his booming and melodic voice: *"Jeepers Creepers, where'd you get those peepers/Jeepers Creepers . . ."* and then Dorothy would sing the next line terribly off-key, and not at all intentionally: *"Where'd you get those eyes."* It never failed to make everyone laugh. Soon, after being able to predict the reaction she'd get, Dorothy would purposely sing more off-key and even add a funny face to elicit more gales of laughter. Every time they brought down the house, she and Prescott would smile at each other and nod as if to say, *Job well done.*

PART TWO

Pauline Robinson and Marvin Pierce

Barbara Bush's Parents

An Imperfect Fit

"Pauline Robinson wears her hair back and looks like a Madonna" is how the Miami University yearbook referred to Barbara Bush's mother in 1915. With her porcelain complexion and her face so lean and angular, it could be said that she looked a lot more like a fashion model than anyone's idea of the Virgin Mary. Appearances aside, she was also a complex, confounding woman. Talking about her in years to come, Barbara noted that she "had it made with a loving family, a devoted husband and many good friends." It always perplexed Barbara, she said, that her mother never seemed able to find satisfaction in anything. Instead, "she constantly talked about what her life might one day be like when my ship comes in. I just never understood it."

Maybe Barbara didn't know a lot about her grandmother, Pauline's mother, Lulu, because if she had, her mother's wanderlust might have made more sense to her. Lulu Dell Flickinger Robinson, born on March 24, 1875, in Union County, Ohio, one of fourteen siblings, was an unusual woman in many respects. "They didn't come more unconventional than Lulu," said one of her descendants. "She was a strange one, put it that way."

Lulu married the attorney James Edgar Robinson of Marysville, Ohio, on May 31, 1893, when she was eighteen and he was twenty-five. The sixth cousin once removed of Winston Churchill, his mother, Sarah Coe, had descended from the noted early English settler Robert Coe. The couple went on to have four children, including Pauline—born on April 28, 1896—Sarah, Eloise, and James. They lived at 324 West Fifth Street in Marysville. In 1899, when Pauline was three, James was elected prosecuting attorney for Union County.

The problem with Lulu was that she was pretty much devoid of any sense of maternal responsibility. She just wasn't cut out to be a mother and probably never should have had children. Not satisfied with staying at home, she hired a governess to take care of her kids while she traveled all over the East Coast with friends. She couldn't drive, but she knew people who could—most of whom were young and single—and would eagerly take off with them to destinations unknown to her husband. "But where are you going?" James used to ask her. "I'll know when I get there" would be her answer as she walked out the door with her bags.

As long as Lulu wasn't stuck at home, she was happy. One of her great-nephews, Garret Bishop, said of her, "She used to say she had 'itchy feet.' James raised those kids on his own; he may as well have been divorced or a widower. They just got used to Lulu not being around. She'd leave, come back, spend a few weeks at home, and then leave for another month. It was normal in their household, all the children knew growing up was that their father was there for them and their mother was a visitor."

With the passing of the years, James became known for his work in family law, defending spouses accused of cheating and sometimes even battery. A Republican, he then went on to become an Ohio Supreme Court judge in 1918 and served two full terms. *The Union County History of 1915* noted of James Edgar Robinson, "He has been one of the leaders in county affairs for many years. He is a man of sterling qualities and because of his high professional standing he is eminently deserving of the position he holds in the esteem and confidence of his fellow citizens."

It wasn't easy for James to raise four children on his own given his full docket of work responsibilities. However, he'd seen too many families break up over "irreconcilable differences," with the children often separated and divvied out to warring parents. Therefore, even though he was unhappy with Lulu's chronic absences and, apparently, powerless to do anything about it, he devoted himself to trying to give his children as stable a home as possible. His daughters, Sarah, Eloise, and Pauline, would love him unconditionally for it, each always insisting they hoped to one day marry someone just like him.

Pauline graduated from Marysville High in 1914, after which she attended Miami University. As she got older, she started to understand what the role of a mother in a family was actually supposed to be, and that's when she started to resent Lulu for being so completely negligent. By the time she was eighteen, she wanted no relationship with her at all. She went to Miami University to become a teacher and graduated in 1916. She then started teaching second grade at the West School Building in Marysville, Ohio.

By the spring of 1918, Pauline was about to turn twenty-two, living at home and anxious to marry, if only to get away from Lulu, who still breezed in and out whenever she felt like it. In May, a college friend said she knew someone who might be perfect for Pauline. A star football player, he was a good-looking guy, twenty-six, and would "look just right" on the arm of a woman as striking as Pauline. It just so happened that he was home on leave from the army for a few days; if Pauline was interested, her friend told her, they needed to act quickly because he would be gone very soon. Two days later, Pauline was on a date with Marvin Pierce, and he did not disappoint. They got along so well that within days she was sure he was the man she wanted to marry.

Marvin Pierce was born on June 17, 1893, in Sharpsville, Mercer County, Pennsylvania, shortly after the Panic of 1893 caused a depression that would last for four years. Marvin had missed the good life by just a generation. His grandfather, Jonah, had made a fortune in the iron business but lost it due to the failing economy and bad business decisions. He ended up completely bankrupt. Marvin's father, Scott, one of Jonah's five children, would have to struggle most of his life to make ends meet. He dropped out of college after two years and went to work for a pig-iron dealership and then an insurance agency. His life was tough; there simply was never any money, and the stories of how his father had squandered the family's wealth didn't make things any easier. "Daddy's father, Scott Pierce, was not a success in life," Barbara Bush once frankly stated.

Scott met the woman who would go on to become his wife, Mabel Marvin, at Buchtel College in Akron, Ohio. In 1898, the couple and their two children, Mabel and Marvin, settled in Dayton, Ohio. Barbara would recall visiting them as a child. "They had a tiny little house and it was very, very hot in Dayton, and he would sleep in the basement," she said. "My auntie, the hunchback, stayed upstairs. My grandmother Mabel did, too, and my great-grandmother."

Good-looking, solidly built, and more than six feet tall, Marvin excelled in sports, specifically football. Known as "Monk Pierce," he quickly became one of the most renowned football players Steele High had ever seen. In his senior year, he was recruited by Miami University in Oxford, where he became a star running back and captain of the team. He also played basketball, baseball, and tennis. (He would be inducted into Miami's Athletic Hall of Fame in 1972.) He had all the girls he could ever have wanted and all the fun he could squeeze into between study periods. He put off going to college for a couple of years, instead working to support his family as a teaching assistant in botany. Finally enrolled in Miami University in 1912, he proved himself dedicated to his studies; he eventually earned a master's degree, graduating summa cum laude and Phi Beta Kappa. He then went on to MIT and Harvard College, where he obtained his degrees in civil and architectural engineering. In 1918, he was drafted into the Army Corps of Engineers Reserves, and it was while he was on leave that Second Lieutenant Pierce met Pauline Robinson.

Pauline loved Marvin's sense of humor. He could make her laugh, which wasn't always easy. However, she thought he was a little "rough around the edges," or so Barbara told a reporter for *Good Housekeeping* many years later in talking about her parents' early years. She also said her mother once told her "my dad needed some work, but that, still, she saw the good in him." In turn, Marvin had to wonder about Pauline's judgmental nature, or so Barbara also noted in that same interview. In some ways, it sounded like an imperfect fit. However, Barbara concluded, "They were still madly in love despite their differences, and I think they both knew it pretty quickly."

Marvin and Pauline married within four months in a Presbyterian ceremony in Marysville, Ohio, on August 6, 1918.

Marvin married into Pauline's family at an exciting time; her father,
James, was running for a seat on the Ohio Supreme Court. Marvin wouldn't
be around to celebrate his father-in-law's win, though. Just weeks after the
ceremony, he was deployed to Europe. The war was over after a few months,
however, and by the spring of 1919 Marvin was home again. Within a year,
he and Pauline welcomed their firstborn, Martha, in 1920.

Marvin wanted to work as an engineer; it's what he had majored in at college. Much to his frustration, though, he wasn't able to find employment in
that field after graduate school. It just so happened that a fraternity brother
was a comptroller at a local department store who ended up on the board
of directors at McCall, a publisher of women's magazines such as *McCall's*
and *Redbook*. He helped Marvin land a job there as a clerk in 1921. Within
just a year, he was assistant to the president, and five years after his hiring he
was a vice president. By 1945, he would be president of the company and,
later, publisher of *McCall's*.

In 1922, the Pierces welcomed a son, James. Then, on June 8, 1925,
Pauline gave birth to another daughter at Booth Memorial Hospital in Manhattan. Marvin wanted to name the baby Helen because he had three good
friends by that name. Because Pauline wasn't very enthused about naming
their daughter after one of Marvin's female friends, she pushed hard for
Catherine. After days of disagreeing about it, an exasperated Pauline finally
said, "Fine. We'll just call her Barbara." It was a name that had just come
off the top of her head in the moment, with no consideration at all. Marvin
said he wanted to keep the conversation about it going, but Pauline was
done with it. "Her name is Barbara," she told Marvin. He didn't have much
choice but to agree.

In 1930, Barbara Pierce was joined by a brother, Scott.

The Critical Mother

Spring 1937. "Eat up, Martha," Pauline Pierce would say as the waitstaff served large portions of chicken and rice onto the teenager's dish. Then, with a warning look, she would turn to her other daughter and snap, *"But not you, Barbara."* The inference was clear. Whereas Martha, seventeen, was slim with a perfectly proportioned figure, Barbara, twelve, was overweight and always appeared a little frumpy in clothing purposely sized large to disguise her figure. Pauline never let her forget it, either. Pauline liked to joke that carrying Barbara during pregnancy was a lot tougher on her than it had been with Martha. Why? "Because *Barbara* weighed a hundred pounds at birth." For the record, Barbara's weight as a newborn is not recorded on her birth certificate. She was 148 pounds by the time she was twelve.

Some of the adults in her life speculated that young Barbara Pierce was still just carrying "baby fat," unlike Martha, who seemed to pass through the awkward puberty stage with no trouble. Maybe Barbara really did have a weight problem. At her tender age, who could know for sure? Unfortunately, as she got older, she began to consider her weight to be the consequence of what she would later call "my issues with food." As had been ingrained in her thinking by her mother's criticisms, this would be the case for the rest of her life. "Eat it today, and wear it tomorrow," Pauline used to warn her, and, true to the way these things often seem to work out, Barbara would one day end up telling her own daughter the exact same thing. Making things all the more difficult for her, Barbara was also tall for her age at five foot eight. To compensate, she would slink down in her chair at the dinner table in hopes of making herself appear smaller.

One story passed down in the family has it that when a cousin was to marry, Barbara and Martha were selected as bridesmaids. They were given frilly yellow dresses to wear. Martha came out of the bedroom in hers and modeled it for Pauline, who immediately nodded her assent and praised her. Then Barbara came out in hers and stood awkwardly before her mother, whose gaze was cold and assessing. "My God, Barbara," she said, disheartened. "You look like a school bus in that thing."

Why was Pauline so cruel? Like Lulu, Pauline seemed to never be satisfied with the status quo, always feeling there was something better for her right around the corner. But like her father, she had a sense of obligation to her family. She wouldn't leave, as her mother had done, but she wouldn't be happy about staying, either. She was miserable, and she took it out on everyone else.

Pauline's father died of a heart attack at the age of sixty-three on January 27, 1932, a little more than a year into his third term as a Supreme Court judge. Now that he was gone, Lulu decided it was time to learn to drive. Once she got her license, she was even freer to travel, and not just on the East Coast but now all over the country. Teaming up with three other widows, she was determined to visit every city she could and not allow any grass to grow under her feet. After they were finished with the United States, the gray-haired coterie took on Canada and then Mexico. They even made the news with their unusual ventures, such as with a story in *The Indianapolis Star* headlined "Mexico Lures Four Widowed Grandmothers." The article quoted Lulu as saying, "We think life begins at sixty."

The fact that her mother was still having these kinds of adventures while Pauline was at home raising her family tapped into her nagging sense that life was just passing her by. As a result, she'd suffer moments of great sadness, times when she couldn't even get out of bed. The way her relatives describe it today, it sounds as if Pauline was suffering from clinical depression, which, because of the times, was left untreated. "She would sometimes burst into tears for no reason," said Lucille Bowman, whose mother was one of Pauline's cousins. "She was also very moody, high on life one day and just so sad the next." William "Bucky" Bush, George H. W. Bush's youngest brother, said, "Mrs. Pierce, she was tough to get along with. She was kind of a gloomy person."

"My mother told me that Lulu had no patience for any of it," added Patricia Bowman. "During those rare times she would visit her daughter, when she happened to be passing through, she would take her to task. 'You're responsible for your own happiness,' she would tell Pauline. 'Take a look around. You've got it made! Be happy about it.' When Barbara was a little older, she heard her grandma say those exact words to her mother again, and from the way it was explained to me, Lulu then turned to her granddaughter, pointed right at her and said, *'And you too, Barbara.'* That had to have made an impression on her. How could she ever forget a thing like that?"

That was probably the wisest advice Lulu ever gave her daughter and granddaughter. Lulu had done it by abdicating all parental responsibilities and taking off for adventures to parts unknown. Surely, there was a better way.

Desperately discontent, it's no surprise that Pauline became hypercritical of her children. Given Lulu's example, she didn't know how to be a supportive mother and, unfortunately, became just the opposite. The slightest bit of misbehavior could set her off. "Go stand by the door and pose," she would tell the disobedient child, which basically meant a "time-out" for about a half hour.

Pauline's constant chipping away at Barbara's self-esteem was all the more unfortunate in that Barbara really did have a lot going for her. Though maybe not beautiful in the traditonally accepted sense of the word, she was very pretty. Reddish-brown hair fell to her shoulders. She had a deeply set brow, a full mouth, and a smile that could light up the room. Her eyes were her most spectacular feature, though. Large and intelligent, they were gray . . . or were they green? It depended on how the light hit them; people sometimes had to look twice to figure it out.

Just prior to Barbara's birth, the Pierces moved to the small but posh Westchester County town of Rye, New York—Indian Village, specifically—

with its population at the time of no more than eight thousand people. Rye was quaint, upscale small-town living. Everyone seemed to know one another in what Barbara would later call "a bedroom community to New York City."

The Pierces lived at 31 Onondaga Street in a large three-story, five-bedroom brick Georgian Revival, which sat on a well-manicured, quarter-acre lot surrounded by gardens and an artificial pond. Marvin paid $14,500 for it, the equivalent of about $215,000 in today's money. The house was filled with fine art, crystal, and antiques. "Every time you turned around, you knocked a piece of Chinese export off the table," Barbara once recalled. "It was because of my mother's spending. She always had to have the best clothes, the best furnishings, the best, the best, *the best.*"

Maybe because Pauline was so unhappy with her own life, she felt the need to straighten out everyone else's. "Somewhere along the way, she decided it was her responsibility to improve the quality of life of everyone around her," said Linda McDonald, who knew Barbara's family in Rye. "Nothing had ever been good enough for Lulu, and now nothing was good enough for Pauline, except Pauline didn't leave like Lulu. Instead, she stuck around and tried to change things.

"She had two favorite words, *remarkable* and *unremarkable.* She would say, 'Oh my, that's *remarkable,*' which meant it—whatever it was—met with her approval, or 'No. That's *un*remarkable.' She wanted everything and everyone around her to be better, or 'remarkable.' The best clothes. The best furnishings. The best foods. The best of the best—that was Pauline Pierce. She thought of herself as a model of good taste, and she wanted her daughters to be the same way. Some people thought she was a snob, and that was okay with her. She was unashamed of it. 'I know who I am,' she liked to say. 'Everyone knows who I am and what I'm like. Nothing about me is much of a surprise. So, don't act surprised.'"

In *Barbara Bush: A Memoir*, she described a childhood that sounded typically middle-class in humble, suburban America. But incongruous with her description of it is this surprising disclosure: "The best food in the world came out of our kitchen. I don't remember what Mother cooked, but she knew good food and trained the helpers very well. Thursday and Sunday afternoons were their days off."

Helpers? Apparently, the Pierces could well afford them. By 1937, Marvin was making about $23,000 a year, which is more than $400,000 in today's money. When one considers that the average income at that time was barely $2,000 a year—the equivalent of about $35,000 today—it becomes clear that the Pierces were living well. However, Barbara would always downplay it in interviews about her youth, saying her family "pinched pennies." They actually had another family of Filipinos living with them—two parents and their teenaged son. The mother worked as the cook and maid, the father as a gardener as well as handyman, while the boy assisted both. The Pierces had virtually nothing to do with these people on a personal level, even though they lived in the same house in a guest wing. They didn't know where—or even if—the boy went to school, and they never asked. The children didn't even know their first names, and in years to come, Barbara wouldn't be able to recall their last. (It was Mercado, incidentally. Their first names have been lost to the ages.)

Dinnertime was always an important occasion at the Pierce home. As the meal was served by the cook and her son, the Pierces sat rigid in their dining room in straight-back chairs. There was never any skimping when it came to culinary delights, always the best cuts of meat and the freshest of vegetables with everything swimming in heavy cream or butter. Prior to every meal, the family was to say a prayer of thanks; Marvin made the decision as to which family member would have the honor. One night, he was so hungry, he started reciting the prayer himself as he was walking to the table and then finished it just as he was sitting down. The children loved it, and so did Pauline. Marvin could always make her laugh. From the very beginning, he could put a smile on her face.

Sometimes, though, Pauline was so perplexing that even Marvin didn't know what to make of her. For instance, one summer she became obsessed with the proliferation of starling birds in the family's backyard, which she found to be a nuisance. So she bought BB guns for her sons and offered to pay them a quarter for each bird they managed to shoot. (James, going for one of the birds, accidentally shot Barbara in the leg one day and threatened to "kill" her if she told their parents. Barbara would say she was "scared to death," of James; "for a week, I wore long, high woolen socks and feared death," she quipped years later. She was much closer to her other brother, Scott.)

At this same time, during World War II, meat was being rationed, as was sugar, bacon, butter, cheese, eggs, and many other food products. This rationing was because imports were severely restricted and farming was limited due to the large number of men who'd gone off to war. Many families were looking for alternatives to meat, and in that spirit Pauline sought out a recipe for starling pie—basically a puff pastry filled with chunks of starling bird meat. While this dish may sound completely unappetizing, actually, "game pie," as it's called, dates back to the Roman Empire, where the wealthiest ate such pies made of pheasants and pigeons. It later became popular in Victorian England, using thrushes, blackbirds, crows, and starlings. Pauline was intrigued by the idea and, even though she rarely did anything in the kitchen, slaved away one afternoon on her starling pie. That evening, her family assembled for dinner and she proudly brought the pie out and placed it in the middle of the table. When Marvin asked what it was, she explained that she'd taken the birds the boys had shot with their BB guns and . . . well . . . *voilà*. Marvin blanched and was almost sick right there at the table. He dashed from the room; his children burst out laughing. "Well, I'm not eating *that*," James said, and his siblings agreed. As Marvin was leaving, he bumped into Mrs. Mercado, the cook, who must have suspected Pauline's delicacy wouldn't go over well. She quickly placed a meatless vegetable stew on the table. Pauline was annoyed. After all, she'd worked hard on that meal and was used to a little more appreciation.

Linda McDonald recalled having a sleepover with Barbara at her home and slipping out of the room early to use the bathroom in the hallway. She stood at the bedroom door for a moment as the three Mercado servants walked very solemnly down the hallway, one behind the other in single file, each holding a silver tray—one with cereal, milk, and eggs, another with fresh fruit, and the other with a coffee serving. Approaching Pauline's bedroom, Mrs. Mercado knocked as softly as she could on the door. Then, with what looked to young Linda's eyes like extreme caution, she and her husband and son tiptoed into the room in order to serve the mistress of the house her daily breakfast in bed.

Though she was very often depressed, Pauline did have other aspects to her personality that bear noting. She was civic-minded, for instance, and convinced the city council to ban parking on the main shopping street of Rye so that it could be turned into a pedestrian thoroughfare. She just thought it would be nicer, and it was difficult to argue the results. They were . . . remarkable.

Pauline was also patriotic. She enjoyed reading about American history and had a large collection of books displayed on shelves in the study. (She would discard the books' dust covers because she thought the display looked better with just the unadorned spines.) A staunch Republican, she had helped coordinate voting processes in her county for the last several years. She had little time for people who weren't interested in politics, and she could suss out such a person quickly at a cocktail party with just a couple of questions. It was something else she had in common with Marvin. He was also raised a Republican, and enjoyed a lively debate about politics, especially when it came to President Roosevelt, whose policies he didn't approve of. "They both felt people should know what was going on in their government," said Garret Bishop. "She used to say, 'Don't complain if you don't vote.' I'm sure she passed on this civic duty mind-set to her children as well."

Private Heartbreak

The spark Pauline and Marvin felt for each other in their youth continued to glow with the passing of the years, despite Pauline's thorny personality. When Pauline first met him, Marvin carried himself with sure-footed athleticism. However, as he got older he began to put on weight and lose his hair. His gait became slower due to arthritis in his knees, a consequence of his old football days. Pauline wanted him to continue to work on himself, not let himself go. She still loved him madly, though. It was as if when she saw him she saw the young athlete she'd met long ago, and he was still that man for her. She also knew that in his eyes she could do no wrong. All Marvin wanted was for her to be happy, and it frustrated him that this never seemed to be the case. But he continued to try, often bringing her flowers, taking her to dinner, spending time with her. He remained the one bright spot in Pauline's life, and she in his. She'd extend herself for him in ways that she never would for others. For instance, he loved to golf. She hated it as she did pretty much anything that required physical exertion. Still, after he got home from work, Pauline would go with Marvin to the golf course and walk at his side as he golfed, just to spend time with him while he did something he enjoyed.

Pauline couldn't resist her nature to be critical when it came to Marvin. She tried to get him to watch his weight and would harp about one habit of his or another. He felt that this was just her way, though, and it didn't really bother him. His weight problem actually gave him more empathy for his daughter Barbara. He always tried to spend more time with her and boost her self-confidence in the face of her mother's constant barrage of criticism. As a result, he would always have a stronger bond with her than she did with her mother; she later described Marvin as "the fairest man I knew, until I met George Bush."

Because he would never challenge her, Pauline could also be very controlling of Marvin, and one telltale sign of this dynamic was detected when they occasionally smoked in public. Pauline would light the cigarette, take a puff, and then put it to Marvin's mouth so he could inhale from it. Then she would slip it between her own lips before returning it to his. Some viewed this exchange as an intimate gesture. When the two were at a table in a restaurant, for instance, onlookers thought it was sweet. But those who actually knew the couple saw it as another aspect of Pauline's controlling nature. There were those in his life who wished Marvin had a little more backbone, and certainly Barbara would later suggest as much in her own telling of her childhood. However, Marvin accepted that Pauline was the stronger, more dominant force in their marriage, and he liked it that way.

Very occasionally, Marvin would question Pauline about her harsh treatment of Barbara. She would tell him that she felt she had no choice but to be hard on their daughter because she feared that the odds would be stacked against her as an adult. She wasn't that pretty, Pauline said, and so she was going to have to be tough or she'd end up getting hurt somewhere along the way. It seemed so unkind to Marvin, this pejorative appraisal of their daughter, and it bothered him. Barbara would, years later, observe that as far as her father was concerned, a parent had three primary responsibilities to his children: "a fine education, a good example and all the love in the world." However, Marvin also couldn't escape the feeling that maybe, just maybe, Pauline knew what she was talking about and maybe, just maybe, she was right about Barbara. Therefore, he didn't challenge her.

In a household of so many complications having to do with personality and character, there was another problem completely out of their control, one that caused years of private grief for both Pauline and Marvin: their son Scott's chronic illness.

When he was about two, Scott toppled off a bike and fractured his collarbone. While X-raying him, doctors discovered a cyst on his right arm. Between the ages of three and nine—1933 to 1939—he would have to undergo five operations to dig out this cyst, which kept reappearing, and replace the missing bone with transplants from his shins and hip. It was awful and painful for the little guy; he'd have to spend months in the hospital. Heartsick about it, Pauline would sleep at his bedside, holding Scott's hand throughout the night.

Once, when he was nine, Scott became desperately ill and his father had to race him to a doctor. When the police pulled him over for speeding, Marvin fell to pieces and, sobbing, told the officer he needed to get his son to a hospital because he feared he was about to lose his arm. This was a real shock to Scott, who didn't know losing a limb was even a possibility. He, too, started to bawl. The policeman was so moved by all this emotion—and probably a little unnerved by it, too—that he decided to provide an escort to the hospital.

Pauline would spend hours on the road driving to New York to be with Scott in the hospital and then returning home in time to have dinner with her other children. Maybe she wasn't the best mother, but no one could fault her for trying her best with Scott. When he was home, it was vitally important that he not get sick. Therefore, if any of his brothers or sisters came down with a cold, that sibling would have to stay with friends. As a result of wanting to keep him quarantined, he completely missed the second grade; Pauline homeschooled him. "With Scott's illness, Pauline proved she had the capacity to be a good mother," said Garret Bishop. "Not only did she pray constantly for his recovery, she was proactive in every way in caring for him."

"Over the years, I often wished people knew about this side of Pauline, because if they did maybe they'd be less inclined to be so judgmental of her," added Linda McDonald. "You can't separate this pain from the rest of her life and expect to really understand who she was. Also, she and Marvin would never have gotten through it if not for each other. They pulled each other through. Whereas the illness of a child can sometimes cause friction between parents, that wasn't the case with the Pierces. If anything, it made them closer."

Despite Marvin's income during the years of his son's illness, the family's finances were strained. Marvin had no family health insurance through his employer and was forced to take out a $100,000 loan to pay for medical expenses—the equivalent of almost $2 million in today's money. It would take decades to pay it back, and some family members reported that the debt was never completely satisfied.

Rather than risk Marvin trying to cut back on the family's lifestyle in status-conscious Rye, Pauline decided that she would be the one to pay the bills. However, she was also avoidant when it came to these responsibilities. Therefore, she'd just stuff the bills in the top drawer of her nightstand as if she hoped they would somehow take care of themselves. Then, only when things got dire—such as when the utilities were about to be disconnected—would she start writing out checks. She'd then pay as little as possible just to keep the household going. As well as having household expenses in arrears, she also owed every department store in town. "Don't go to Best to buy that new coat," she would tell her daughters, "because I owe Best. Go over to Lord & Taylor's, instead." It was difficult for Marvin to take her to task about it, though. They had so much on their minds with their son's illness, this bad habit of Pauline's was the last thing he felt he needed to worry about.

Pauline Finds Satisfaction

By 1940, young Scott Pierce's medical issues were finally behind him, much to his parents' great relief. In June of that year, Pauline was asked to lead a four-week workshop for the Ladies' Aid Society of the Congregational Christian (Presbyterian) Church, the theme of which was to be "The Christian Citizen and Patriot." She was recommended by a friend in the society who knew she'd studied education in college and had been a teacher. Pauline was also somewhat religious; after college, she'd led the Christian Endeavor Society at the First Presbyterian Church. She was patriotic as well. She seemed like a good fit for the workshop, especially now that her son's illness was no longer a chief concern.

Pauline wasn't sure she could do what would be required of her for the seminar. She wanted to badly, she just wasn't confident about it. It was Marvin who convinced her that not only could she do it but she would be great at it. As always, he wanted her to find some happiness, and he must have sensed that this was something that might help her in that regard.

Pauline spent almost four months preparing for the workshop, going to the library to do research every day. It was important to her that the gathering be meaningful and that participants take away something of value from it. She personally typed up all the material to be utilized and took it to a print shop in Rye where a manual duplicator was used to make copies.

This project monopolized a great many of her hours, during which time she actually did seem a lot more content.

One Sunday afternoon after services, Pauline stood in the parking lot of the church, surrounded by people as she explained what her workshop would entail and why she felt it so important. She was so lovely and well-spoken, it was difficult to resist her. "Think about it: All that really matters are the three f's: faith, family, and freedom" was the headline on the flyer she distributed.

The following Friday night, Pauline dressed in a conservative silk dress with matching sweater along with a string of pearls. She came downstairs as her children, James, seventeen; Barbara, fifteen; and Scott, ten (Martha was at college), gathered around her to compliment her and offer encouragement. She was nervous, she said, but felt prepared. Everyone was excited for her and cheered her on. It must have felt good to Pauline to have this kind of support as Marvin opened the front door for her, walked her to the car, and then drove her to the church.

Donna Zimmerman, whose mother, Shirley, worked with Pauline on the workshop, recalled, "My mom told me Pauline was smart and well-spoken, very charismatic. She was also very prepared, had spent a lot of time researching her topic and how to relate to people. 'I studied to be a teacher,' she would say, 'so I know what I'm doing.' It was formal, not exactly relaxing, my mother said, but informative. She said, 'Pauline had planned out every second of spontaneity.'"

The idea behind Pauline's seminar was to stress the importance of patriotism, prayer, and family. She wanted people to become interested not only in civics but also in religion and explore the link between both with family values. To that end, she distributed copies of a book called *Life Together: The Classic Exploration of Christian Community*, by Dietrich Bonhoeffer, and had everyone read it and then submit a book report.

The monthlong workshop was a great success. From that time onward, Pauline would give at least four seminars a year and, when she wasn't leading her own, would assist with others. Not only did she find satisfaction in doing something she believed mattered, but she also must have felt she was fulfilling her personal mandate of bettering the lives of others. "It was a win-win for her," noted Donna Zimmerman with a chuckle. "She also became more interested in gardening and horticulture at this same time and joined the Garden Club of America. Soon, she became known for her golden thumb when it came to pollinating lilies. She grew barley in her basement and had worms to aerate the soil in the flats."

It would seem that things changed a little for Pauline Pierce after she started teaching her seminars and felt she had some purpose in her life other than just staying home and raising her children. Like Lulu, she hungered to do *something,* but unlike her mother, she stayed home while doing it. While she still had her moods and difficult habits, she seemed more settled and was usually in a better place, which made her family, especially her husband, Marvin, happy.

Leader of the Pack

Barbara Pierce attended the public Milton School from first to sixth grade. One can't resist drawing a parallel between the way she was treated at home by her mother and the disconcerting way she interacted with her friends at school. For instance, as part of a small clique of popular girls during the fourth and fifth grades, Barbara would make random decisions as to who in the group would be frozen out on any given day. June Biedler, who went to grade school with Barbara, recalled, "She would call all the girls the night before and say, 'Okay, tomorrow nobody's going to talk to June. Got it? *No one talks to June.*' So the next morning, I'd be sitting on the bus with my friends and no one would speak to me. What a dreadful feeling that was, being ostracized like that for no reason."

Posy Morgan Clarke, another of the students, recalled of Barbara, "She'd call ahead and say, 'Okay, now, tomorrow we're not going to speak to Posy. No one speaks to Posy. Got it? No one speaks to Posy.' It was horrible. I'd be on the bus wondering, what did I do, what did I say? Why is this happening to me? To have everyone turn on you like that? For a girl of twelve, that was hard to take. But, yes, you could say Barbara controlled the girls."

Looking back, it's possible that Barbara was acting preemptively to keep others from bullying her the way she felt tormented at home by her mother. Or maybe she was just reflecting the same behavior. Going a little deeper into her psychology, Posy Morgan Clarke feels Barbara's tactics may also have had to do with control. "I think she felt out of control in her home with a mother so critical and also with issues having to do with food," she theorized, "and the one way to exert control was to exercise it with us, her schoolmates. We were kids, you know? She was pretty powerful. We just did what she told us to do."

Barbara could also demonstrate a harassing nature in other ways. For instance, because June Biedler stammered when she spoke, Barbara made fun of her. "She'd mimic my stutter, point at me in a mocking way and make the other girls laugh at me," June recalled.

Sarah McDonald tells this story: "Barbara came home from school one day with a note from the teacher saying she had been mean to some of the other little girl students. *That* was embarrassing to Pauline. My grandmother told me that Pauline chased Barbara all over the house with a wire hanger. She tripped and fell, and once she was on the ground, Pauline lunged at her and let her have it a couple times on the rear end with the hanger. She told her to stop picking on the other girls. Barbara said she would stop, but I'm not sure she did."

Barbara attended the private Rye Country Day School through ninth grade, and then followed her sister into Ashley Hall, an exclusive boarding school in Charleston, South Carolina, from tenth to twelfth grade. Ashley Hall was very strict, with a code of conduct that had the girls wearing hats, gloves, and no lipstick while on campus. "Plus, the school stressed good behavior," Barbara later said, "and it was really a sort of finishing school. My mother sent me and my sister there to be . . . finished." Barbara also once remembered the student body as being "a lot of fat, squatty girls who were there to be transformed."

At Ashley, Barbara started coming into her own. She slimmed down, the result of strict dieting and, likely, also her new smoking habit. Later she would admit that she wouldn't dare stop smoking at the time for fear of putting weight back on, though eventually—in about twenty-five years—she broke the habit. She also blamed her many decades of smoking for the congestive heart failure and lung disease from which she would suffer much later in life.

Now at Ashley, Barbara still had the reddish-brown hair and bright hazel eyes of her youth, but was much prettier. For many years after college, she would remain slender and quite beautiful, though she would never think of herself that way. "When she would come home from Ashley, we would dance at Manursing, which was a country club in Bedford Hills, and she was delightful," recalled Stephen Miller, who had dated her sister, Martha. He's in his mid-nineties now, but his memories of the Pierces have never faded. "She had her own sort of allure," he said of Barbara. "But she would always think of herself as fat even when it wasn't true of her. She would also always be critical of other women and of their weight, expressing very often that someone could really only be beautiful if she was slim."

By the time Martha was out of Ashley, she, too, was lovely, though that had always been the case with her. At one point she was even chosen for the college issue of *Vogue*. Martha had been on the student council, the French club, the drama club. She won a prize in poetry and was an editor of the school yearbook. Barbara's time at Ashley paled in comparison; she got through it with Bs and Cs. The way Pauline continued to fuss over Martha only served to make Barbara feel more competitive with her. "It was tense between the sisters," said Stephen Miller. "I didn't see a lot of warmth between them."

They did have some pleasant times together, memories Barbara would cling to, such as when Pauline would take her and Martha to tea at the historic Charleston Place Hotel in Charleston. "I met them at Charleston Place one afternoon," recalled Stephen Miller, "and the thing I most remember about Mrs. Pierce—and this was a million years ago, but it still stands out—is that she took an eyedropper from her purse, stuck it into the creamer, and sucked out a few drops. Then she put those few drops into her tea, stirred it, and put the eyedropper back in her purse. She did all of this very nonchalantly, as if it were the most natural thing in the world.

"I also recall her saying something to the girls like, 'Thank goodness *you* two have a mother who's there for you all the time. I didn't have that and, boy, did I suffer. You have no idea how much I suffered.' Barbara and Martha didn't comment. They just sort of sat in silence. Then Mrs. Pierce reached into her purse and took out that blasted eyedropper again and added a few more drops of cream to her tea."

PART THREE

Barbara and George H.W.

Young Love

In 1941, when she was sixteen, Barbara Pierce attended a dance at the Greenwich Country Club in Greenwich, Connecticut, during her Christmas break from school, and it was there she met George Herbert Walker Bush. At seventeen and a senior at Phillips Academy Andover, George was so handsome and charming, she couldn't help but be drawn to him. For his part, George would, in years to come, say he knew immediately upon meeting her that Barbara was the girl he would one day marry. "It was one of those love at first sight situations," he would say, "the kind you don't know for sure really happens in life, until it happens to you."

That evening when she got home, Barbara excitedly told her mother about George—whose nickname, "Poppy," had been handed down to him by his father and his before him. By the next morning, Pauline had already done her research by calling a friend of hers and learning that Bush came from a good and upwardly mobile family who belonged to many of the same private clubs as the Pierces. Barbara was annoyed with her mother for having so immediately investigated George's background. In her mind, it had just been another way for her to try to control things. "It really burned me up," she would later say. Pauline would explain, "She was sixteen. Of course, I was watching out for her. *Of course.*"

The next night, Barbara saw George again at another dance, this one at the Apawamis Club in Rye, and a few days later at a basketball game where he then met her family. "The thing about him was that he was so funny," she recalled many years later. "No one made me laugh like he did. I think I needed that at the time, I needed laughter. He was funny, and I loved that." Afterward, the teenagers went back to their respective schools. For the next few months, they exchanged correspondence but were able to see each other only once more, during the upcoming spring break. Then, the week Barbara turned seventeen, George invited her to his prom, after which they shared their first kiss.

George Herbert Walker Bush was born in Milton, Massachusetts, on June 12, 1924, to Prescott and Dorothy Bush. He was educated at Greenwich Country Day School and then, beginning in 1938, Phillips Academy in Andover, Massachusetts. A gregarious and outgoing young man, he was a popular student—president of the senior class and captain of the varsity baseball and soccer teams. However, his life took a dramatic turn in December 1941 when the Japanese bombed Pearl Harbor. This attack served as a clarion call to all American students to mobilize and prepare to serve. A pervasive sense of patriotism among students made for a school fleet eager to enlist. George decided he wanted to be a pilot, though it was unclear even to him why he had this dream; he'd never flown a plane before yet had an intuition that it was the best way for him to serve.

About six months after his graduation from Phillips and on the occasion of his eighteenth birthday on June 12, 1942, George enlisted in the navy as a seaman second class. When Prescott saw his son off at Penn Station for a train that would take him to Chapel Hill, North Carolina, for basic training, he found himself uncharacteristically overcome by emotion. "It was the first time I had ever seen him cry," recalled George.

As he trained in Chapel Hill, George and Barbara stayed in touch, and she visited him there as well. Within a year, just before he turned nineteen, he received his wings and commission as an ensign; he was now one of the youngest pilots and flying Avenger bombers. Meanwhile, Barbara graduated from high school that same month and enrolled at Smith College, a private, independent women's liberal arts college in Northampton, Massachusetts, which her sister, Martha, had attended a few years earlier.

Barbara was delighted when, in August of 1943, George—on leave from the military—invited her to spend time with the Bush family at their summer home in Kennebunkport. "I'm George's mother," Dorothy Bush said as she walked toward young Barbara with her hand extended. "You can call me Dotty." When Barbara took Dorothy's hand for the first time, she may have been surprised at the strength of the grip. Dorothy also pulled her in by her wrist in a manner that may have felt a little aggressive. Her smile took any edge off the moment, though. Barbara took the gesture as an eagerness to know her better. She was impressed, not put off. Their eyes connected and, with their hands still joined, it was as if a current of energy passed between them. There was an immediate connection and, to hear them speak of it years later, an instant bond was forged.

"How about you and me play a little paddle tennis?" Dorothy suggested. "Sure, why not?" was Barbara's response. Barbara was pretty good at the game, so much so she was afraid to beat her new boyfriend's mother and maybe upset her. She needn't have worried; Dorothy was victorious—first by playing with her left hand, and then with her right. Then they played tennis, with Dorothy playing left-handed to make it easier on Barbara. Dorothy won again.

During her time at the family's compound, it became clear to Barbara that George's extended family was very important to him and that if she was to have a future with him she'd have to fit in with them. Everyone was extremely close; they all competed with one another and also ribbed each other mercilessly. It would turn out that Barbara wasn't exempt from such badinage even if new to this territory. It was at this time that she got the nickname "Bar," which would stick with her for the rest of her life. Many people over the years would naturally assume this appellation to be a shortened version of Barbara. However, it was actually the name of the Bush family's beloved horse, Barsil. This inglorious nickname was given to Barbara by George's brother, Prescott Jr., simply because in his mind "Barsil" sounded like "Barbara." While it may seem unkind given her personal history, remember that the Bushes knew nothing about her mother's criticisms of Barbara; there was no pejorative intent behind the gesture. Barbara didn't take offense, anyway. She viewed the fact that she now had a nickname as a sort of initiation into the family.

It was during this visit that Barbara, eighteen by this time, and George, nineteen, became "secretly" engaged, though, according to George's later memory, it was a secret "only to the extent that the German and Japanese high commands weren't aware of it." In other words, he told his family about it, and she told hers. Everyone was delighted. In George's eyes, Barbara was not only the prettiest girl he'd ever known, but she was also athletic and anything but shy or retiring, traits that reminded him of his mother. There was no equivocating for Dorothy when it came to her own opinion of Barbara. She and Prescott both thought she was a beautiful, smart young woman and, as they got to know her better, would become mystified as to why she was often so self-deprecating.

Dorothy wrote to Barbara on the day she learned of the engagement to tell her how delighted she was and that if George had "searched the world he couldn't have found anyone who would have pleased us as well. With so much to live for, he just has to come back safely, and I am sure he will." Meanwhile, Marvin wrote to his daughter, too, saying that he didn't know how Pauline felt about the big news—"she told me nothing about her intentions"—but he was happy about it. "I don't know what Mother said," he reiterated, "but, as for me, I accept your decision without any conditions."

Not surprisingly, the reaction to the engagement from Barbara's mother was more complex. When she first met George, according to one family member, Pauline's clipped response had been, "Well, he's *plausible,* anyway." It was difficult to know what she meant by that comment—it wasn't much of an endorsement—but at least she didn't seem adamantly opposed to him. "She was lukewarm about the whole thing," Barbara would say many years later.

Pauline's response wasn't very different from her reaction to Martha's announcement of her own engagement to a young man named Walter Rafferty, a junior at Yale. Martha was a senior at Smith at the time. Rafferty was from a wealthy Greenwich family and, like George, also an alumnus of Phillips Academy Andover. Pauline had also been ambivalent about Martha's plans. The fact that she wasn't going to be completely supportive of either daughters' engagement wasn't much of a surprise to them. They knew their mother well. In the end, Pauline decided Barbara was lucky to "get sorted out" so early in life, and decided not to oppose the marriage.

Now with plans to marry, Barbara began her freshman year at Smith College while George went back to the service. The couple finally announced their engagement in *The New York Times* on December 12, 1943: "Mr. and Mrs. Marvin Pierce have announced the engagement of their daughter, Barbara, to Ensign George Herbert Walker Bush, Naval Air Arm, son of Mr. and Mrs. Prescott S. Bush of Greenwich, Conn." In the accompanying photo, Barbara looked lovely in profile, her dark hair flowing to her shoulders, a thin strip of pearls at her neck. Her features were delicately drawn, her complexion flawless. It's difficult to imagine, judging from this picture anyway, how anyone could ever have had a critical opinion of her appearance. George wrote her a note the day the announcement was published to tell her how overjoyed he was to "open the paper and see our engagement" and "how lucky our children will be to have a mother like you." He finished by saying, "Goodnight, my beautiful. Every time I say beautiful you about kill me but you'll have to accept it."

George wanted to find just the right engagement ring for Barbara, and wrote to his mother to see if she had any ideas. Dorothy thought long and hard about it. She finally decided that a star sapphire ring that belonged to her sister, Nancy, would be ideal. Nancy prized that ring, though, and Dorothy didn't think she would ever give it up. She wondered how she could convince her. "Why don't you just ask her?" Prescott suggested. He reminded his wife that Nancy adored her and would do anything for her. He was right. Nancy absolutely wanted her nephew to have the ring for his fiancée, and handed it over immediately. When Dorothy then wrote to George and told him about it, he was elated.

In December 1943, Dorothy had the ring in her pocket when she and Barbara went to Philadelphia together for the ceremonial commission of the *San Jacinto*, the new carrier to which George was being assigned. "What kind of engagement ring do you think you want?" Dorothy asked Barbara while on the trip with her. "It doesn't matter to me," Barbara said. "Really, dear, what would make you happy? You're not the type to want *diamonds*, now, are you, dear?" It then occurred to Barbara that her future mother-in-law had an agenda. She went along with it and said diamonds didn't interest her in the least. Whatever George had in mind would be fine with her. "Just as I expected," Dorothy said, patting Barbara's arm and smiling approvingly. Later, in the shipyard, George presented Barbara with the sapphire ring—which she would wear until the day she died.

In March 1944, George shipped out for the South Pacific with his squadron. Meanwhile, Barbara decided she was no longer interested in higher education and dropped out of Smith soon after the start of the fall semester. While she would sometimes regret not continuing, "the truth is," she'd later admit, "all I could think about was George," or, as she put it, "Barbara Bush majored in George Bush at Smith College."

In September 1944, the families received the worst news imaginable: George's plane was shot down off the island of Chichi Jima in the Bonin Islands during an attack on Japanese installations there. Even though his plane was on fire and going down fast, George still managed to drop his five-hundred-pound bombs on an enemy radio station before bailing out into the ocean. "The flak was very heavy," he later told the U.S. Naval Institute in an interview. "You could just see it and hear it almost around you. It was when I saw the flames along the wing there that I said, 'I better get out of here.' I told the crewmen to get out. I dove out onto the wing. I hit my head on the tail, a glancing blow, and bleeding like a stuck pig. I dropped into the ocean, and I swam over and got into this life raft. I was sick to my stomach. I was scared. If somebody didn't pick me up, I would have been captured and killed. They were very brutal on Chichi Jima."

George's two-man crew was killed. For three very upsetting days, his fate would remain unknown as the Bushes and Pierces waited for news. Prescott refused to believe the worst, and any time Dorothy drifted toward dark thoughts, he did what he could to lift her spirits. "We can't have anything but the most prayerful of thoughts," he reminded her. Dorothy wholeheartedly agreed and tried to comfort herself with prayer and Bible study. It was almost more than she could bear, though. George had been constantly in touch with her while in the service; there are dozens of letters that still exist today as a testament to their closeness. She was exceedingly proud of him, loved him with all her heart, and couldn't imagine what her life would be like should he perish. Still, she knew she had to be strong, not just for her other children but also for Barbara, whom she would telephone several times a day. Their shared concern brought them even closer; Barbara's admiration for Dorothy grew.

Eventually, everyone learned George was safe, having spent four hours on the inflated raft, sick and vomiting, while protected by fighter aircraft above until being rescued by the submarine USS *Finback*. Now a bona fide war hero, he would later receive the Distinguished Flying Cross after having logged 1,228 hours in the air and fifty-eight combat missions. "People talk about, 'Wow, you're a hero,'" he said many years later. "Well there's nothing heroic about getting shot down. And I wondered why was I spared when two friends in the plane with me were killed. I don't know the answer."

George's close call made the couple all the more anxious to marry, or, as Barbara later explained, "In wartime, the rules change. You don't wait until tomorrow to do anything." She was nineteen and George twenty when they were finally wed on January 6, 1945, at the First Presbyterian Church in Rye. George's sister, Nancy, was maid of honor; Barbara's sister, Martha, matron of honor. The groom's brother Prescott was his best man. A reception for three hundred was held at the Apawamis Club in Rye. The newlyweds then honeymooned at the Cloister in Sea Island, Georgia. A photograph of Barbara as a bride in an ivory satin gown lined with pearls—looking brooding and forlorn, though that expression was fairly common in such photographs at that time—ran in the local papers with an accompanying announcement.

While Pauline seemed happy, it wasn't easy to discern her true feelings on her daughter's wedding day. It was Dorothy, though, who made the biggest impression on Barbara that day. As the bride put on a veil of heirloom princess and rose point lace—a "something borrowed" from Dorothy, who had worn it at her own wedding to Prescott—Barbara was heard saying, "You know, I just want to feel beautiful. Is that too much to ask?" Her tone was plaintive, almost as if she believed it could never happen. According to the family history, the two were standing in front of a full-length mirror, and Dorothy, positioned behind Barbara and a good foot shorter, gazed at their reflection and said, "You *are* beautiful, my dear. You must never forget it."

A Wife's Duty

For nearly the next year, Barbara and George would move from one army base boardinghouse to the next—Michigan, Maine, and then Virginia—before the war finally ended in the summer of 1945. After having flown fifty-eight combat missions, George was discharged with the Distinguished Flying Cross honor, three Air Medals, and the Presidential Unit Citation. Now he was on his way to Yale University, the alma mater of his father, brother, and uncles. Once enrolled there, he and Barbara moved to New Haven, Connecticut, where first they lived in a couple of small apartments before a boardinghouse for Yale students with as many as nine other families. These were lean years. Though the Bush parents had money, as did, to a lesser extent, the Pierces, they didn't extend themselves to the newlyweds. Rather, very much like people of their generation who'd been through the Depression, they felt their children should learn the value of money and make their own without expecting handouts. Because both Barbara and George were used to such a privileged lifestyle with maids and butlers, their new, more modest way of living took some adjustment. They were generally happy with their lives, though, and tried to sock away as much money as they could from jobs, which were later described by Barbara as "mundane."

On July 6, 1946, the couple welcomed their first child, George Walker. Barbara had gained sixty pounds while pregnant with him and later said,

"I then spent the rest of my life trying to lose that sixty pounds." She was elated. Watching the way Pauline held the new baby in her arms made her feel she'd finally done something to make her mother proud. It was interesting, though, that Pauline would say she didn't enjoy being alone with little George because if she didn't give him her undivided attention, he'd look at her with such a pitiful expression it made her feel guilty. Barbara had to laugh. "Finally, we have someone in the family capable of doing something no one else has ever been able to do," she said.

When she learned she was pregnant, Barbara began to seek a better understanding of her problematic relationship with Pauline. She now wanted to show a little more leniency where her mother was concerned and perhaps not become instantly offended by each and every criticism that rolled off her lips. "I know you think I made certain mistakes with you," Pauline told her during one luncheon. "Looking back," she said, "maybe I could have done better." It was about as close to an apology as Barbara was ever going to get from her, and she appreciated it. But then Pauline completely ruined the moment. She told Barbara that she was starting to look old because of threads of gray coming into her hair. She was only twenty-one. "You should dye it before it gets out of hand," Pauline suggested. Barbara did what her mother suggested; she started coloring her hair even though her gut told her not to do so.

Though she could still be so easily swayed by Pauline, Barbara tried to remember she was now an adult, the mother of a newborn, the wife of a man determined to see his family chart its own course. There was no use in dwelling on her dark past with Pauline, not with the future appearing to be so bright. She now wanted to focus on George and on his life objectives. "It was very important to George that he like his work," she once recalled. "He told me he had thought about it a great deal while standing night watch on the submarine deck after being rescued. He had decided he didn't want to work with intangibles; he wanted a product he could see and feel."

"What you need to do is head out to Texas and those oil fields," suggested George's mentor, Neil Mallon, who had been a classmate and close friend of his father's. "That's the place for ambitious, young people these days."

"The oil business sounded like a good idea to me," George later recounted. "I had heard you could make a pretty good penny in Texas. After toying with the idea of farming or even a place on my father's investment firm, I decided to take a job as a laborer on an assembly line for Pacific Pumps, a Dresser Industries oil business subsidiary, making something like $375 a month." It wasn't much of a stretch, actually. The company's CEO was Neil Mallon, and Prescott had been on the board since about 1929.

Taking this job represented a seminal moment for George. As he stated, he could have chosen to work with his father, but he wanted to chart his own way. Prescott had told him from the time he was a youngster that he should make his life worthwhile. "Give your life purpose," he would tell him. "Think about this: What is it you want to leave behind?" He drilled it into his head so often, George said he could hear those words reverberating in his head while trying to sleep.

Even though Prescott had been politically active in social issues, it really wasn't the focus of his life at this time. Though George H.W. and his siblings may have felt parental pressure to meet certain standards, it wasn't necessarily to be in politics. If Prescott had expected him to truly follow in his footsteps in the investment business, he probably would have discouraged George from getting into the oil business, even if he was on the board of Dresser Industries.

Somehow George H.W. didn't seem weighted down by expectations, unlike what would one day be the case with his own son, George W. It seemed H.W. accepted that his father just wanted him to excel at something, and he just wanted to make him proud. He rarely, if ever, complained about it. Years later, though, Dorothy would tell Barbara that she felt George and his siblings *did* feel the weight of expectation, but that they kept it to themselves. That made sense. Dorothy would never have tolerated complaints from them, and certainly neither would Prescott. "You knew exactly what you had to do," George H.W.'s brother, Prescott Jr., said in a 1977 interview. "You knew you were expected to contribute and you knew you should live a good life, but it was a different time. It's not like today where kids sit around caterwauling about what their parents expect from them. Back in my day, you just kept your head down and did the work without any bull." Maybe George H.W. summed it up best, though, when he said, "We knew what we had to do. My father could just look at you, and we knew."

In 1948, with the new job in hand, Barbara and George now had to move to Odessa, Texas. George didn't sit down with Barbara to discuss his taking the job or even their having to relocate; he just told her to start packing. It didn't occur to him to strategize with her, and it didn't occur to her to be unhappy about being left out of the decision. It speaks to the times in which they lived that Barbara just felt it was her duty to follow her husband's lead. She helped George load up the red 1947 two-door Studebaker Prescott had given him as a graduation present and sent him on his way to, truly, parts unknown. They had an understanding that he would find a place for them to live and then send for her and little Georgie.

Soon after arriving in Texas, George called and told Barbara to get on the plane, for he'd found what he would later call "a sorry little home." She packed up her suitcases, and she and her son were on their way. She didn't know what to expect in Texas; she'd never even met a Texan. It didn't matter, though. Once she got to Odessa, she was just so happy to be reunited with the husband she adored, nothing else mattered.

Barbara's first impression of Odessa? "Hot and flat," she said. Her second impression? "Very hot and very flat. A million miles away from anything I'd ever known in Rye." George had found a small two-room apartment in a building in which the Bushes would have to share a bathroom with three women who were, apparently, prostitutes. It was fine, though; the Bushes were just happy to have a bathroom when so many others had to use outhouses. Barbara was determined to make it work, but she didn't have to bear it for long. The little family soon moved to a new apartment where, thankfully, they even had their own facilities. It was small, though, just a living room, kitchen, bedroom, and that one bathroom.

In the spring of 1949, after almost a year in Odessa, George got a new job in an apprentice role at Dresser, which took the family to California. While there, he also worked as a salesman for Security Engineers Company, a manufacturer of drilling bits. The Bushes settled in modest accommodations, first in Whittier, then Ventura, Bakersfield, and finally Compton. It was as if they were constantly on the move. By the time George began working at yet another job, the Pacific Pumps factory, again related to the oil industry, Barbara was pregnant again.

No Goodbyes

On a fateful Friday, September 23, 1949, Marvin Pierce called his son-in-law George Bush with terrible news. He explained that he and Pauline had been driving through Harrison, Westchester County, to the Rye train station—from which Marvin traveled daily to the New York headquarters of *McCall's*—when they were involved in what could only be called a freak accident. Apparently, Pauline had placed an English bone china cup of hot coffee on the front seat between the two of them. In order to keep it from spilling, Marvin reached out to steady the cup. In doing so, he swerved and lost control of the vehicle. It then careened one hundred feet down a steep embankment, colliding with a tree and crashing into a stone wall. Marvin suffered a number of injuries, such as broken ribs, though none life-threatening. However, Pauline hit her head hard against the windshield. She died instantly of a fractured skull. She was fifty-three.

This was such a shock. Barbara had just seen Pauline at her brother Jimmy's wedding a couple of months earlier. They were, as usual, on uneasy terms.

Marvin told Barbara not to fly back for the funeral because she was six months pregnant. Barbara didn't put up much of a fight about it. As a result, she would never have closure where Pauline was concerned, or, as her brother Scott put it, "there was no resolution."

"Are you telling me Bar is not going to her own mother's funeral?" a surprised Dorothy asked Prescott when she heard about it. She couldn't believe it. She said she'd never heard of a daughter not attending her own mother's memorial services. She believed Barbara would always regret the decision and would never get over not having said goodbye. "I don't want her to go through that," Dorothy said. She wanted to talk to her and try to change her mind. However, Prescott encouraged her to just stay out of it. This delicate matter was between their son and his wife, he said, and they really didn't know Barbara or her family well enough to interfere. After some thought, Dorothy agreed. She then called Barbara and extended her sympathies, reminding her she would always be there for her.

In the weeks after Pauline's funeral, Barbara was besieged not only by grief but also with the sense that maybe she should've tried harder with her. She was also angry at Pauline for abandoning her before they'd had a chance to resolve things. She didn't want to talk about it, though, not to George or to anyone else. Occasionally, she would offer a sad observation, such as "My mother had many interests but, unfortunately, I wasn't one of them," but for the most part she bottled up her feelings. One friend recalled visiting Barbara during this time and noting that she seemed "almost bedridden. She just lay in that bed very, very depressed," she recalled, "and seemed to not want to be in the world. George told me he had said to her, 'Bar, one day you'll be happy again, I promise,' and she said, 'I don't want to be happy, Poppy. I like things just as they are.' So, yes, she was not herself."

"What a lonely, miserable time that was," Barbara would, years later, confirm.

Stephen Miller, now related to the Pierces by marriage, recalled a conversation he had with Barbara about two months after Pauline's death. The two were in Barbara's kitchen. "I remember that Bar was drinking Cold Duck and it was the middle of the day," he said. 'It's not liquor,' she told me, 'it's like a soda.' I said, 'Well, actually, Bar, it's wine mixed with champagne.' She chuckled and said, 'Oh, really? Well, I guess that explains a lot.'"

"I have this memory of my mother that I can't seem to shake," Barbara told Stephen. "It was 1931 and I was just starting first grade at Milton and so very nervous." Barbara recalled asking Pauline to walk her to the school.

She did so, but she wasn't happy about it; who knows what else Pauline had on her mind that day, but Barbara's anxiety wasn't on top of the list. Mother and daughter then went to the new classroom and met the teacher. While Barbara was talking to the instructor, she turned around to ask her mother a question. Pauline was gone.

"She didn't even say goodbye?" Miller asked.

"No," Barbara said sadly. "She never said goodbye."

On December 20, 1949, three months after Pauline's death, Barbara, now twenty-four, gave birth to her second child, a girl she and George named Pauline Robinson Bush in honor of Barbara's mother. It's interesting, though, that they would not call the baby "Pauline," as might have been expected. Maybe there was something painful for Barbara in the baby's first name, because she and George began calling the girl "Robin," an unlikely, shortened version of her middle name.

For Barbara, there was something special about giving birth to a daughter. As much as she loved little Georgie, who was now three, having a girl felt like a full-circle moment to her. She knew she'd do her best with her daughter and that she'd make certain it was more than enough. Whatever mistakes Pauline had made with her, Barbara was determined not to make with Robin. She wanted to get back to living again after the death of her mother, and hoped that maybe Robin would help give her a sense of purpose.

The next year, the family was on the move again, this time back to Texas, but now to the small town of Midland, about twenty miles away from their former home of Odessa. George was now working for the IDECO oil company as a salesman during a time when the oil industry was really booming.

At first blush, Midland was still "hot and flat," but somehow seemed a step up from Odessa. The people of Midland were close-knit and gracious, and Barbara felt completely welcomed by them. She couldn't help but note that even perfect strangers were hospitable in a manner she soon began to understand was just the Texan way. It was also a community of faith: People weren't just religious on Sundays; they took their faith with them the rest of the week, too.

After renting a couple of apartments, Barbara and George finally bought their first home, just 847 square feet and, as Barbara put it, "smack dab in the middle of a neighborhood where every house looked like the one before it, except a different color. Ours was blue. I looked around Midland, and I thought, yes . . . I can be truly, truly happy here. This is a town of survivors. Some people were struggling, and you could see that, but you could also sense their strength and, I don't know how to put it except to say, their *joy*. I felt that if you couldn't figure out a way to be happy in Midland well, then Midland wasn't really the problem. Maybe you were the problem. Plus, George had such a funny sense of humor and whenever I felt a little blue or confused he would make a face or crack a joke and all was right in my world."

"In a sense many of us had been uprooted and seemed to come from somewhere else," Barbara recalled of their neighbors. "We all had young children; and we were all having a lot of fun. The women joined the Midland Service League, and the men played touch football in the Martini Bowl. We all worked in the Little Theater and the YMCA and volunteered at the hospital. Most of us were active in church; George was an elder, and we both taught Sunday school at the First Presbyterian Church. We took turns having cookouts on our tiny patios or in our backyards, watching each other's children."

Martin Allday, who'd go on to become George's first campaign manager, said, "Midland doesn't have any mountains, it doesn't have any oceanfronts, it doesn't have any fishing holes or other similar niceties; what it did have were caring transplanted citizens, like the Bushes, who pitched in on every effort, from the Boy and Girl Scouts to the United Way and most everything in between. You can do a lot in a small town if you are willing, and the Bushes were—in spades."

Later that year, 1950, George continued to prove his entrepreneurial spirit by leaving his job and starting his own business. He and a friend named John Overbey, a gas and oil lease broker, formed Bush-Overbey Oil Development Company, Inc. Three years later, the firm would merge with the Liedtke brothers, Hugh and Bill, to form a new company, Zapata Petroleum Corp. (named after the Mexican revolutionary played by Marlon

Brando in the film *Viva Zapata!).* Its mandate was to explore opportunities in the oil business, more specifically locating mineral rights in areas being drilled for oil. George threw out a wide net for investors in this new business. His uncle Herbert Walker was good for $350,000. Family friend Eugene Meyer, who owned *The Washington Post* and was the father of Katharine Graham, chipped in $100,000. Prescott came in with just $50,000, which was a disappointment, but in the end, George was just grateful for whatever he could get from a father who really wasn't exactly generous when it came to money.

Meanwhile, Barbara's widowed father, Marvin, married Willa Gray Martin, an arts writer for the Associated Press in New York. She was eighteen years his junior and a widow from South Carolina. It had been almost four years since Pauline's passing. At first, Barbara didn't have much of a relationship with Willa. However, she felt her father deserved to be happy. She and her siblings look very pleased in the wedding photo; little Georgie standing in front of his uncle Scott and mother, Barbara, with her shoulder-length coif and in a fetching strapless gown. With the passing of the years, Barbara would become close to Willa, calling her a "wonderful woman" in her memoir.

Still, Willa would, in years to come, seem intimidated by Barbara, such as when she was contacted by reporter Marjorie Williams in 1992 for a profile in *Vanity Fair* called "Barbara's Backlash." In her diary, Barbara indicated that she was very displeased about it. "I could get in so much trouble if I said something she didn't agree with," Willa remarked. "Because you know how she is: she knows how she wants to appear to the world."

Marvin and Willa would have seventeen good years together before his death in 1969.

On February 11, 1953, Barbara and George welcomed another son into the fold, a boy they named John Ellis, nicknamed "Jeb" (the first initials of John Ellis Bush) or "Jebbie."

PART FOUR

Political Ambition

Dorothy Embraces Politics

While George H. W. Bush focused on his business concerns and his wife, Barbara, on family matters, his father, Prescott, entered a new and challenging phase of his own life. He had always felt the calling to be a public servant, going all the way back to 1920, when he was moderator of Greenwich town meetings, a position he enjoyed for about seventeen years. He got along with people and liked problem-solving, was civic-minded and, above all, patriotic, having been active in the Republican Party for many years. By the end of the 1940s, he'd made his fortune on Wall Street and was looking for exciting, new frontiers. So, in 1949, after serving as the Connecticut Republican finance chairman for the previous two years, he decided to throw his hat into the political arena by running for the Senate.

Dorothy wasn't just whiling away the hours at home wondering what she might do to assist her husband. In recent years, she'd been very active in Greenwich, working with the American Red Cross and establishing a children's shelter dedicated to placing displaced youth into foster homes. She was a member of the Garden Club and was an active member of the Greenwich Field Club tennis team. She was also raising a family. Content with her life, she feared politics might upend everything. She didn't want to be a public person, anyway, so she was skeptical of Prescott's running for office. "Politics wasn't for Mother from the very beginning," George H. W.

Bush would recall. The bigger problem, at least as Dorothy saw it, wasn't just that she had reservations about Prescott's idea, it was that he didn't care about her opinion. He'd made up his mind, and that was pretty much the end of it for him.

In one family story, Prescott decided to host a party at the family home for possible campaign donors and others who might be helpful to him. Dorothy was angry at him at this time for not wanting to engage with her about the Senate run, and she couldn't seem to get past it. Despite that quarrel, she said she'd still do her duty and host the party, even if she wouldn't enjoy it.

For the event, the Bushes hired a six-piece string and brass band to play in their drawing room and had cleared out most of the furniture to make way for a dance floor. After the event, one newspaper society columnist put it this way: "It was an evening of fine food, fine music, fine dancing all under the auspices of one of the city's finest couples in their stately and grand home. The waiters wore white gloves, which should tell you all you need to know. . . ." The food served was described as "a delightful, pecan-crusted lamb with red curried sweet potatoes, grilled artichokes and roasted eggplant soup." The paper also added that during the evening Dorothy sauntered about the room, talking to the guests, making each one feel special, doing her part, wearing what the reporter called "a smart pants outfit."

Apparently, Prescott didn't think women should wear slacks, and especially not at an important social gathering with political overtones. He was annoyed and found it difficult to hide his feelings. He and Dorothy were cool to each other the entire night.

Once she had engaged with everyone, Dorothy left the party early without saying a word to her husband about it. Prescott saw this as such a breach of etiquette, he was dumbfounded by it. Still, he played it off, ignoring the whispers of surprised guests and giving a rousing speech while also toasting the donors. Hours later, he and a few of the stragglers converged in the dining room, where he cleared the table and set up a game of tiddlywinks, a favorite pastime of his. Finally, once everyone had departed, Prescott retired to a guest room, where he slept alone.

The next morning, Prescott couldn't wait to confront Dorothy. According to the family history, he came down to the kitchen and found her having a leisurely breakfast. "Dotty, about last night," he began in an angry tone. She looked up from her meal and, in a voice just as stern, said, "No, Pres. I speak. *Then* you speak." He glared at her and sat down. She then let him have it, the gist of her argument being that if she was so important to him that he needed her to cohost essential parties, he should learn to ask for and then seriously consider her opinion. Otherwise, she said, in the future she'd just do what was required of her and disappear, just as she'd done the previous night. "Marriage is about respect, Prescott," she said, repeating a favorite phrase of hers and one in which she firmly believed. She said she wasn't going to just sit back and "let you run the show around here." She had "thoughts and feelings and ideas," she said and he would have to learn to respect them. He took it in and mulled it over. He couldn't very well argue with her, especially when she was right.

After a couple of weeks of discussions about it, Dorothy finally agreed to support Prescott in his political ambitions, but with one caveat: She wanted to be brought into every decision, especially if it impacted the family. He agreed. He wouldn't always keep his end of that bargain, but at least he would try his best, and when he didn't he would hear about it from her.

At this same time, a scandal unfolded that had the potential to jeopardize things for Prescott. Earlier, he'd been a founding member of the Union Banking Corporation, which was in business with Friedrich "Fritz" Thyssen, one of Germany's leading industrialists and an early proponent of the Third Reich; he became known as "Hitler's Angel." A tangled web of business entities and investment strategies through the 1930s would cause Prescott to be vulnerable for the rest of his life to criticism of being a Nazi sympathizer.

By 1941, Fritz Thyssen had broken with Hitler, but it was too late to thwart what would become a big story when the *New York Herald Tribune*, on July 31, 1941, did an investigative report into UBC's association with the notorious German leader. The article named Prescott as a director of UBC and implicated him as much as anyone else at the company for its dealings with former Nazi champion Thyssen. At the time, it was more of a public relations dilemma than anything else; the article pointed out that much of the business with Thyssen had occurred when "the present world tangle could hardly have been foreseen and when such courtesies were part of the normal routine of international banking relations."

Prescott never took a public stand one way or the other when it came to his company's relationship with Thyssen—he could have at least made a moral argument against it, but he didn't. Because of these whisperings, though, there was some concern that Bush's Senate run could be negatively impacted. All these many years later, there are people who still believe Prescott Bush seeded his family's fortune with the help of Nazis. Often, when his life and times are written about by historians, this rumor resurfaces and seems to raise a question about his patriotism. At the time, though, Dorothy really had no opinion about any of it other than that it was ridiculous to think her husband was in league with Nazis. "You have to know him," she would later write of her husband, "and if you spent just five minutes with him, you would know the truth about him. I think it's easy to believe the worst of people when they're not real in your mind."

Now that Dorothy was in alignment with Prescott's political goals, she and their children truly pulled together to campaign hard for him as he went up against the Democratic nominee, William Benton, for the Senate seat in 1950. While he traveled around the state giving speeches and shaking hands, Dorothy and her daughter, Nancy, hosted teas for Republican women's groups while Prescott Jr., John, and even young Bucky kept themselves busy at the campaign office raising money from donors, or out on the road with their father. Much to her surprise, Dorothy found herself in her element. After all, she loved competition, and this was certainly just that at a very high level. She was swept away by it all and found herself really wanting Prescott to have that Senate seat. She was also gratified to see the family pull together in an effort to achieve a common goal. There was just one Bush missing in all this action, and that was their son George.

By this time, George and Barbara had moved to Midland and George was working in the oil business. The word in the family was that Prescott had given George "a pass" because of everything going on in his life, Pauline's death, and Robin's birth. "We have enough Bushes here working in my favor," he said. While Prescott may have said as much publicly, privately he felt very differently. When George claimed he was too busy to campaign,

Prescott was irritated by it. He called George and told him they, as a family, had an opportunity to make history and that he needed him to be a part of it. "Use your head, George," he said angrily. George held his ground; he really was becoming a lot like Prescott, especially when it came to his stubborn nature. Or, as Dorothy so aptly put it, "Sons are their fathers." In the end, George decided he wouldn't leave his family and his business to campaign all around the state with his siblings. It was surprising, actually; he knew full well what was expected of him and decided not to do it.

Dorothy felt Prescott had handled it all wrong and called Barbara to ask her to talk to George. Dorothy admitted to Barbara that she'd had her reservations about Prescott's interest in politics. Now that they were in the game, though, she felt they had to win it and do so as a family. Barbara said no, she wouldn't talk to her husband because she knew it wouldn't do any good; he never listened to her, anyway. Dorothy hung up and, as was her custom, gave a lot of thought as to how to proceed because, truly, she was bothered by Barbara's point of view. A couple of days later, she called back. "May I be blunt?" she asked Barbara. Barbara must have known what she was in for, because her response was curt: "If you have something to say, Ganny, just say it."

Dorothy took the invitation as an opportunity to talk to her daughter-in-law about her lack of agency in her marriage. She told her that she didn't have to do everything George told her to do without question. "You get to have opinions, too, Bar," she said. "You must be firm and stand up for yourself." Barbara didn't see it that way. George made all the important decisions in their marriage, she explained, and she was happy with the status quo. "Yes, but are you *really*?" Dorothy asked her. Though Barbara insisted she was, Dorothy seriously doubted it. However, she also realized Barbara would have exactly the kind of marriage she wanted, and that there was nothing she could do about it. Therefore, she let it go. What choice did she have?

According to the family history, George eventually did call his father to apologize. However, in yet another interesting twist, Prescott seemed more agitated about the apology than he was about his son's decision not to participate in the political process. "Don't apologize," he told him angrily. "Never apologize. That's weak. Don't be weak."

Once it was finally sorted out that his eldest son would not be along for the ride, Prescott continued onward, running with a strong Republican platform of lower taxes and limiting the power of trade unions. Unfortunately, he wouldn't be successful. As it happened, two of the most popular columnists of the time, Walter Winchell and Drew Pearson, laid waste to Prescott's chances. They reported that flyers were being slipped into the pews of Catholic churches all over the state alerting the faithful to the fact that Prescott was president of the Birth Control League. Because Connecticut was so heavily Catholic and birth control was illegal, Winchell, in particular, theorized that Preston's affiliation with the league would ruin him in the state. They urged people to tune in to their radio broadcasts that night and learn more.

"The state at that time was probably 55 percent Catholic population with all the Italian and Polish, and the Catholic Church is very dominant here, and the archbishop was death on this birth control thing," Prescott said later in his oral history. "They fought repeal every time it came up in the legislature and we never did get rid of that prohibition until 1965."

The Bush family did what it could to refute the report. Dorothy denied it adamantly to every reporter who called her at home, and there were many. "I don't understand how anyone could say that," she told one journalist. "It's such a lie, it's just outrageous."

The problem was that the story was at least partly true: The Birth Control League had merged with other organizations of its nature in 1942 to become Planned Parenthood—and Prescott was its treasurer. His name was even on its letterhead. So, while it was technically true that Prescott wasn't a part of the Birth Control League, he most certainly *was* affiliated with Planned Parenthood. Besides that, he had long been a proponent of the birth control movement and family planning, and he felt strong in that position. Therefore, it was perhaps unfortunate that he and Dorothy decided to equivocate. However, with Prescott's campaign on the line, they felt they had no choice but to at least try to save the election for him any way they could. Dorothy didn't care if it was true or not. "Is it a surprise that there's a difference between public pronouncements and reality?" she later asked.

Based on that statement alone, it would seem that politics was beginning to change her; she was becoming more cynical, anyway.

As a result of this scandal, Prescott ended up losing the election to William Benton by the slimmest of margins: about a thousand votes. This loss was tough for the Bushes. Prescott was disappointed but didn't take it as personally as Dorothy did. She was angry about it, and it would be a while before she'd get over it. "How many times must I say it?" she asked. "Losing is not an option in this family. We don't lose. Period."

The Bushes would always be of the opinion that Prescott had been cheated out of a win. "The cards were handed out at noon in [Catholic] churches saying 'Listen to the broadcast tonight at six,'" Dorothy later recalled. "It was Sunday night. I do believe that if it had happened the week before so you could do something about it, we may have been able to—but it was just that very day, six o'clock, and there was nothing we could do. We didn't have enough time. It was completely unfair and made me question the process, I must say."

Later, when a reporter came to the house to do an interview with Prescott, he got into a debate with Dorothy over why her husband had lost the election. She wasn't having it. "Does this conversation need to continue?" she asked him. Before he could answer the question she said, "No. It does not," and escorted him from the room. Though Prescott was a little troubled by how emotional Dorothy was about the loss—"It's really not like her," he said at the time—he now at least knew for certain that he had a true partner in the political process. In many ways, the loss made Dorothy and the rest of the family stronger and more determined than ever to win that Senate seat for Prescott in two years' time. It was pretty much decided right then that he would run again.

Prescott's Big Win

After his loss, Prescott Bush returned to Brown Brothers Harriman & Co., but now that he and his family had had a taste of politics, they weren't going to let it go. He would spend the next two years traveling around Connecticut and unofficially campaigning for the Senate seat he'd previously lost. He would also be adamant in his criticism of both Truman and his predecessor, Roosevelt, for "the chaos these men have caused in this country."

It was at this time that Prescott also became a big supporter of General Dwight Eisenhower, commander of NATO forces in Europe, encouraging him to run for President during his highly visible visit with him in November 1951. He vowed to campaign hard for Eisenhower should he decide to run. Moving about in such circles kept the Bush name front and center on the national stage. Prescott soon began to feel sure the 1952 Senate nomination would be his, and he was anxious to compete against William Benton again, up for reelection. "He's a shoo-in," Dorothy told her friends of Prescott's chances. "It's pretty obvious, isn't it?"

She was a bit premature. When the Republican governor of Connecticut, John Davis Lodge, decided that Prescott wasn't ready for the seat and instead supported William A. Purtell in his campaign, it threw a monkey wrench into Prescott's plans. "In state politics the governor commands an enormous amount of influence because he controls the patronage," Prescott Bush Jr. recalled, "and as a result he was able to swing enough votes to Purtell to defeat my father at the Republican convention that summer. At that point my father said, 'Well, okay, that's it. I've given it two chances and the party thinks somebody else can do it better.'"

The family was bitter. By this time, they felt Prescott had been cheated out of the seat—twice. He had raised millions for the Republican Party, and this is how he was to be repaid? "That's it, I'm done," he decided. Dorothy wasn't so sure. She said she needed to sit down in a quiet place, read the Bible, and pray about it. A couple of days later, she decided Prescott was right; the family really was better off without politics. She suggested they let it all go, saying she now feared politics had changed them, and that some of the changes weren't for the best. She would later write, "I felt that the political world was at odds with what we as a family held in our hearts as personal standards. It would take time to square politics with our own convictions. But I would wager this is a challenge faced by many political families, that is if they've lived as we Bushes have with an eye toward living good, charitable lives." Soon, however, her family would be dragged back into the political game.

The sudden death of Senator Brien McMahon in July 1952 created another seat vacancy. A special election was called and, as a result, now there would be *two* U.S. Senate races in Connecticut. In the Republican primary, Prescott would face off against the formidable Clare Boothe Luce, not only a politician but also the critically acclaimed writer of *The Women*. She'd shattered so many preconceived notions of what women were supposed to be like in the 1950s, she perplexed a lot of men, including Prescott. "Clare, I've always been a little frightened of her," he admitted, "because I don't deal easily with women who are severe or terribly determined. I've always been afraid of women who are pithy and sharp and sarcastic." This was an ironic statement considering the personality of his wife, but then again, Prescott didn't always "deal easily" with her either, did he? In the end, though, he easily won the nomination over Luce with 412 delegates to her 50.

After Luce was out of the picture, Prescott went up against the Democrat Abraham Ribicoff in November 1952, and, this time with religious concerns not an issue, he won handily by more than 37,000 votes. Meanwhile, William Purtell won the other Connecticut Senate seat. However, because Prescott had won the seat vacated by Senator McMahon's passing, he would be sworn in immediately, whereas Purtell would have to wait until January. Therefore, Prescott became the *senior* senator from Connecticut. "This was a big win for our family in so many ways," reflected George H. W. Bush many years later. "I think winning that Senate seat meant more to my father and mother than anything else. In many ways, I think it was the beginning of everything for this family."

Dorothy was elated. The week after the election, she and Prescott hosted a party and welcomed into the Bush home politicians and people of high society to help celebrate the victory. "The best man for the job won," she told one reporter at the gathering. "It was a long and difficult climb, but Prescott believes in government and in its ability to make people's lives better, as do I. I'm just glad voters saw it." To another journalist, though, she was perhaps too open about what she viewed as the secret agenda of some of the guests present at the gathering. Dorothy had lately begun to believe that a few of the people in Prescott's life were transparent in their quest for power. She hated what she viewed as their false deference to him, and she suggested as much to the writer. "People are close to the levers of power when they're near Prescott," she said, "and it makes them think they actually have influence. But they don't. It's not supposed to be about puffing yourself up, anyway. It's supposed to be about being of service."

By this time, as a function of his work with Brown Brothers Harriman and Co., Prescott was deeply associated with—and his coffers thereby further enriched by—a number of lucrative companies, such as Columbia Broadcasting (radio and television), the Vanadium Corporation of America, Dresser Industries (oil well supplies), Prudential Insurance, the U.S. Guarantee Company (a casualty company), Simmons Corporation (beds and bedding), and Pennsylvania Water and Power. Few other sitting senators had so many ties with big business. "I think it's good to have in Congress men of affairs who know what it is to operate business or practice law," he said. The bottom line for a lot of people, though, was that Prescott was making an awful lot of money, and some had to wonder if he was using his seat in the Senate as a way to profit from so many businesses. He denied it, but he also didn't divest himself from all these concerns, and many more to come.

Prescott would serve until January 1963; among the committees he chaired was the Joint Congressional Committee on Atomic Energy, a top secret commission dealing with America's nuclear capabilities. He took the confidentiality of the job so seriously, he wouldn't even discuss the particulars of it with Dorothy. He would go on to distinguish himself in many ways as a senator, not the least of which was his support of civil rights legislation and the work of the Peace Corps, as well as flood and hurricane protection.

Family Secret

Prescott Bush's life, as full as it was, apparently did take quite a toll on him, as evidenced by his increasingly heavy drinking. Today he would no doubt be considered an alcoholic. "Back then, you just accepted that the man drank a lot," said Myra Delcot, whose mother, June, was a close friend of Prescott's trusted chief of staff, Margaret Hampton, and who, by extension, was also close to Dorothy. "My mother told me that Pres was almost always a little drunk, that it was just sort of his personality to have a few drinks in him at all times. His younger brother, the much-married James [four times], also had a serious drinking problem. It was a different world back then, though. People drank to excess and not much was thought or done about it."

Myra Delcot recalled one afternoon when she, at the age of about fifteen, and her mother were visiting with Dorothy and enjoying a high tea lunch. "I remember everything was lovely with tea and finger sandwiches and Mrs. Bush looking very put together in a silk skirt with white pearls. A maid would bring out a serving and we would watch and wait until she finished, and then Mrs. Bush would say, 'Thank you. That will be all,' and the maid would dart away nervously. We were seated at an enormous table in the dining room, just the three of us, and it somehow felt very, I don't know, *big*, I guess."

Suddenly, they heard a loud noise in the foyer and the voice of a male shouting out, "Goddamn it. Who put that umbrella stand there?"

"What in the world?" Dorothy said as she rose from her chair. She walked out of the room and to the entry hall.

"Then, from the foyer, we heard a sort of whispered discussion," recalled Myra Delcot. "I wouldn't call it an argument; it was more like an urgent conversation. Finally, I heard Mrs. Bush say, 'Okay, fine, Prescott. Go upstairs now. I am entertaining. I'll be up soon, dear.' She was gone for a few more minutes and my mother finally said, 'Myra, go make sure she's okay.' I walked into the foyer, and there was Mrs. Bush sitting on the stairs and, much to my surprise, crying. When she saw me, she jumped to her feet, quickly dried her tears, and said, 'I'm sorry, sweetie. It's been a hard day. I'm fine. Let's go find your mommy.' She and I walked back into the dining room. She sat down, smoothed out her dress, composed herself, and said, 'Now, where were we?' as if everything was just fine. She was very fidgety, though. She kept drumming her fingers on the table as if she couldn't wait for us to leave. I was only fifteen, but I was very sad for her. Clearly, her husband had had too much to drink."

An important priority for Dorothy was to protect her children's image of their father. She always wanted them to view him with the greatest of respect. Therefore, if she couldn't get him to stop drinking—and, apparently, she couldn't—she didn't want him to appear to be inebriated when he was in the presence of their children, especially when they were younger. To that end, she insisted he not drink in the house. Instead, he would have cocktails at one of his favorite country clubs, like the Hartford Club, an exclusive men's organization in Connecticut. Still, though, he would almost always come home in his cups. It got to the point where Dorothy could tell just from the way he unlocked the front door whether he'd had too much to drink. She then had to find that fine line between being angry at him or, for the sake of their children, acting as if everything were copacetic. It was exhausting, but for a good number of years while they were raising a family, finding this balance would be a big part of her life. Dorothy also had another concern. She knew that Prescott's work in the Senate was not only important to him but also a sacred responsibility. She worried that he wouldn't always be in his right mind to make the right decisions for his country.

Myra Delcot vividly recalls a conversation her mother had with Dorothy while she, still aged fifteen, sat obediently in a chair listening. "I have never doubted Pres's commitment to us or his sound governance of this family," Dorothy said. If she sounded oddly formal, that was her way from time to time. The observation opened the door for June to begin complaining about her own marriage to a prominent attorney in Greenwich, Myra's father. He was always at work, preoccupied with his job, never available to her and their children, she said, and on and on she went, criticizing him. Dorothy was taken aback. For her, complaining was anathema. Or, as she once told someone who had pushed her to the limit, "Stop whining. Whoever told you life is fair was lying to you."

At any rate, June ended her harangue by saying, "I make do, but it's not what I had hoped for. But then again," she concluded sadly, "it never is, is it, Dotty?"

Dorothy, shaking her head, said, "Well, maybe *you* make do, June. But *I* don't." She added that if June's marriage was flawed it was up to her to do something about it, and not wait for her husband to magically change. She said she was surprised at her and reminded her it was 1952, not 1922. Women now had choices, an interesting observation from Dorothy considering that a lot of people didn't quite see it that way, at least not yet. She suggested that, if all else failed, June should "pray more. God can help you. He always does."

By 1953, the Bush family was on its way to true distinction, not only by virtue of Prescott's growing influence on the political landscape, but because the family was thriving in other ways, too.

By this time, Prescott Jr.—known in the family as "P2"—now thirty-one, had graduated from Andover (1940) and had attended Yale. He dropped out in 1943 to work for Pan Am Airlines in Brazil during the war, and then in their office in New York. A staunch Republican, in 1944, he married

Elizabeth Kauffman; they would have a daughter, Kelsey. In 1952, he joined Johnson & Higgins, a New York insurance brokerage firm of which he would soon become a partner. He commuted back and forth to Greenwich every day, just as his father had done before him. He was also his father's great confidant, someone with whom the senator could plot out political strategies.

It was surprising that Prescott Jr. didn't become a politician, especially given that he seemed on his way when he was elected to the Republican town committee and filled the seat in which his father had sat for more than fifteen years. President of the Greenwich Country Club, he also worked with the Red Cross and a number of other charities and was nominated Man of the Year by the Greenwich Junior Chamber of Commerce. In thirty years' time—1982—Prescott would also embark on a brief campaign for the Republican Senate nomination, but his heart wasn't in it. A serious but quiet and even contemplative man, he wasn't cut out for the often vicious nature of politics.

George, who was twenty-nine at this time, was making a very good living with the Zapata Oil Corporation. This was the beginning of the amassment of a real fortune for his family as he and Barbara raised their children, George, seven; Robin, three; and Jeb, an infant.

Nancy, twenty-seven, had graduated from Vassar (1946) and was now married to Alexander Ellis Jr., an executive at the Fairfield and Ellis insurance firm. Breaking with the family's politics, she was a liberal Democrat and activist in her own right. She would go on to become a top fund-raiser for the New England branch of the NAACP and also worked with the New England Medical Center and the Boston United South End Settlement House. Her politics were always dismaying to her staunchly Republican family members—Prescott Jr. once referred to her as a "political maverick"—but Nancy held her own and refused to acquiesce to anyone's influence.

Nancy and Ellis lived in Massachusetts and would have three sons and a daughter: Alexander, John, Josiah, and Nancy. Her marriage was a strong one, but only after one serious indiscretion. In the late 1950s she would embark on an extramarital affair with the historian Arthur M. Schlesinger Jr., one of JFK's advisers. The family was disappointed in her, so much so that Prescott refused to even acknowledge that it was happening. During that time, Nancy's marriage suffered. It would take real commitment on both her part and Alexander's to put things back together again, which they did for the sake of their children. From all accounts, Nancy never strayed again. Once was enough. It hadn't been worth risking everything, and she had deep regret about it for a long time.

Nancy and her mother, Dorothy, had a good relationship; Dorothy often counted on her to cohost parties for government officials at the Bush home. She was effervescent and seemed able to sweep even the stuffiest of senators off his feet with her charm. Dorothy considered her a "secret weapon," in that she knew that if Nancy was cohosting with her, the event would be a success. "Nan was gorgeous," recalled one relative, "slim with short dark hair, great eyes. Very bubbly personality, but also well-read and smart, which I think was the aspect of her character her mother thought of as her so-called 'secret weapon.' A Supreme Court Justice, for instance, might think she was just another pretty face in the room, that is until he started conversing with her. Then he would see that she was just as smart as any man, but she demonstrated it in a disarming way. She was never a show-off. She knew what she was doing, in other words, when it came to meeting those old goats at their own level. I always thought she could have been a great politician."

As Dorothy's only daughter, Nancy knew her mother had certain expectations of her, and she went out of her way to not only satisfy them but exceed them. She was a people pleaser, or at least that's how she's been described by family members and, said one, "Nan came from a mother with exacting standards, someone who could be quite critical. She also came from a mother with a strong core. Nancy was tough like Dotty. She was nobody's pushover."

Jonathan Bush, twenty-two, was, as he once put it, "a different kind of Bush." He was artistic and musical, got very good grades in college, and made it clear from the beginning that he wasn't interested in politics.

William Bush—Bucky—was just fifteen and attending Hotchkiss School, a private college prep boarding school in Lakeville, Connecticut. He was a fun-loving youngster, or as Dorothy put it, "he's a spirited boy and I like that. I do wish he gave more thought to his future, though," she concluded to one friend of hers. "But I suppose there's time for that."

PART FIVE

Robin

A Devastating Diagnosis

While Prescott and Dorothy Bush thrived in their new life political life in Washington, their son George and daughter-in-law Barbara were in Texas with their three children and about to face their greatest challenge thus far.

In March 1953, Barbara noticed a dramatic change in the behavior of her three-year-old daughter, Robin. Ordinarily a happy and active child, it was as if she'd changed overnight. Suddenly, she seemed listless and even exhausted. At first, Barbara thought it was nothing more than what her mother used to call "spring fever," a phrase used to describe lethargy once thought to occur during the first days of warm weather. Trying not to overreact, Barbara let it go for about a week. She was focused on newborn Jeb, who had just come into the world a few weeks earlier. Meanwhile, little Georgie was in the first grade at Sam Houston Elementary School. After about a week, when Robin seemed no better, Barbara decided to have her examined by the family's pediatrician, Dr. Dorothy Wyvell.

While examining the little girl, Wyvell observed black-and-blue marks on her legs, which Barbara hadn't previously noticed. The doctor would later say she had her suspicions but didn't want to venture an opinion. After she drew blood, she suggested that Barbara take Robin home and return later in the day with George for a consult. This didn't sound good to Barbara.

She called George and asked him to meet her at the doctor's office that afternoon.

Dr. Wyvell looked stricken as she sat down with the Bushes, her eyes even reddened. She slowly explained that Robin had the highest white blood count she'd ever seen in a child, and it was clear to her that the girl was suffering from leukemia. "There's really no hope for recovery," she said. The Bushes' puzzlement was apparent on their faces; they knew nothing at all about the disease. Most people didn't. When George asked exactly what the doctor meant by "no hope," he was told, according to his later memory, "It means that it's not likely she can live many more weeks longer." The best course of action, they were told, was to just take their daughter home and wait for her to pass away peacefully, probably in just three weeks. Dr. Wyvell also suggested that the Bushes not tell many people about Robin's illness for fear of their reactions panicking the youngster. "It was just unfathomable," Barbara later recalled. "One day she was fine, the next she was dying? I couldn't believe it. I wouldn't believe it."

When George called his mother to tell her the terrible news, Dorothy refused to accept it. "With God, all things are possible," she told him, and that included a cure for her granddaughter. She also suggested that she and Barbara take Robin to New York for a consult with her brother, Dr. John M. Walker. He had been recruited by Memorial Hospital in New York a year earlier; later, he would serve as president of the medical institution, known today as Memorial Sloan Kettering Cancer Center. Dorothy had all the utmost confidence in him and was certain he could help. She said she believed "God works through doctors"; the right one could make all the difference in the world, and she was sure that was her brother. The very next morning, Barbara and George took Jebbie to one friend's home and Georgie to another's, and then boarded a plane with Robin, headed to New York.

John Walker was well acquainted with suffering. He'd been an athletic man until he was struck by polio in 1950. Though now in a wheelchair, he refused to give in to self-pity and, instead, devoted himself to the complex emotional needs of his patients, not just their medical concerns. Also, the fact that both his daughters had Down syndrome had imbued him with a kind of compassion that often eluded his colleagues. "You have no choice," he told Barbara and George. "You must do all you can to keep her alive." He felt they'd never be able to reconcile allowing Robin to just die without at least trying to save her. "But aren't we just dragging out the inevitable?" Barbara asked, crying. Maybe, answered the doctor, but he told her that if Robin were his daughter, he wouldn't give up on her. He recommended a radical treatment that would likely hospitalize her for as long as six months. "You have to realize," John Walker told Barbara in answer to her question as to how such a thing could happen, "that every well person is a miracle. It takes billions of cells to make up a person, and all it takes is one bad cell to destroy a person." In that moment, as she would later recall it, Barbara was suddenly conscious of the true miracle of human life, and how astonishing it was that anyone was ever able to live a long life considering the odds of something terrible occurring. It would give her a new appreciation of things . . . but that would come later, much later. For now, her only thought was saving her daughter's life.

Once the decision was made to treat Robin in the aggressive manner recommended by Dr. Walker, Barbara was determined to see it through. Dorothy sent a nurse named Marion Fraser down to Texas—she had once helped Dorothy raise her own children—to take care of her grandsons. With that responsibility now off her mind, Barbara moved to the apartment at 1 Sutton Place owned by Dorothy's parents, Bert and Luli, just a few blocks from the hospital. Meanwhile, George would fly back and forth from Texas.

"What else can I do to help?" Dorothy asked once Barbara was settled into the apartment. She was worried about the emotional toll Robin's illness would take on Barbara, and said she couldn't imagine trading places with her. If one of her own children was ever so desperately ill, she said, she didn't know how she would cope, other than to just pray. She was almost as worried about Barbara as she was about Robin. After all, Barbara was only twenty-seven, and the diagnosis was devastating. With her mother gone, Dorothy felt a responsibility to her. Barbara appreciated it and said she was determined to be strong. Since marrying into the family, she said, she'd learned that Bushes rely on faith and never feel sorry for themselves. She was one of them now, and she would strive to be just as strong.

Though a Bush by marriage, it would turn out that Barbara was really the strongest of them all during the ordeal that followed. With Robin's life on the line, she was determined to take care of her *her* way. "It was tough on Barbara," George recalled, "I guess the toughest assignment a mother could have . . . someone had to look into Robin's eyes and give her comfort and love, and I'm afraid I didn't have the guts."

Robin's grueling treatment involved painful bone marrow tests, heavy rounds of chemotherapy, and seemingly endless blood transfusions. For the next six months, Barbara decided not to allow anyone near her bedside who was unable to control his or her emotions. She felt there was no way forward other than to be strong and stoic and to refrain from desperation or hopelessness. Plus, she didn't want Robin to be frightened. "I just won't have it," she told relatives who came to visit and would subsequently burst into tears. She tried to be patient with her husband, but that was difficult; George was so devastated he could barely stay in the room for more than a few moments without becoming emotional. Seeing little Robin lying in bed with tubes coming from her limbs, looking sick and drained, and then seeing the photos of Georgie and Jebbie, which Barbara had taped to her headboard, was usually more than George could handle. Barbara propped him up as best she could, but her focus had to be on Robin. "If you cry, you have to leave," she told George as plainly as she could, and she meant it.

Dorothy came to agree with her daughter-in-law that there was no upside to demonstrations of dramatic emotion from anyone. She would sit at Robin's side and say the rosary, or read to her even if she didn't think her words were being heard. While it was devastating, she knew how to control herself.

Barbara wanted to be for Robin what Pauline hadn't been for her: a comforting presence, one that could be relied on, or so she told her friend Martha Tillerson. Louise Fraser, Martha's daughter, recalled, "My mother said Barbara said her own mother didn't have it in her to be a good mother. 'I have that chance now with Robin,' she said, 'and I'm not going to let it pass me by the way my mother did.'"

Barbara's ill will for her mother was still so strong, she couldn't see what was apparent to others, which was that now she had something in common with her parents, too. Both had seen their son Scott—Barbara's brother—

through a debilitating illness that had lasted for seven long years. "My mom thought Barbara may have been able to gain some strength from her father in talking about those difficult years with Scott," observed Louise Fraser, "but I think because he was such a strong memory link to a mother she felt had let her down, she just couldn't see it."

Resting Place

On a blustery day, bright and cloudless, in September 1953, two lone figures walked with great purpose through the Putnam Cemetery in Greenwich, an older man with a young woman. As they spoke, he'd sometimes reach over and take her hand. "Look at that mausoleum over there," Prescott Bush said as he pointed to a monstrous structure. "I knew the guy in there. He sure thought highly of himself, didn't he, Bar?" Barbara Bush smiled. One thing she knew about her father-in-law was that he despised boastfulness. He had raised his children to understand that along with wealth and privilege came responsibility. Now that he was in politics, should any of them choose public service it was to be viewed as an honor; there was no glory to be found in it, just responsibility.

Barbara had a warm relationship with her father-in-law, perhaps because she was never intimidated by him. Early in her marriage, she had been sitting on the stoop of the big house in Kennebunkport enjoying a Newport cigarette. Prescott came over and sat right next to her. Looking at her with disapproval, he said, "That's not a very nice habit for a woman." She took a puff, exhaled slowly, and said, "Well, I smoked before I became your daughter-in-law, so there's no use lecturing me about it now." He nodded, sat down, lit a cigar, and joined her. George W. Bush's version of this same story is that his grandfather said to his mother, "I didn't give you permission to smoke, did I?" to which she responded, "Well, I didn't marry you, now, did I?"

Now, a couple of years later, Barbara and Prescott were walking toward a bucolic hillside and then up a steep incline, at the top of which they stopped. He motioned before them to a small, modest granite headstone, about three feet tall and four feet wide, upon which was engraved just one word: BUSH. A lilac tree had been planted on one side of it, a dogwood on the other. "What's this?" Barbara asked, looking down at the stone. "Well, you never know," Prescott said with a faint smile, "I may end up here or, someone else . . . who knows?"

Barbara suddenly understood the purpose of their visit: Prescott had purchased a plot for Robin.

The two stood in front of the tombstone and took in the wide vista before them, the green, sloping lawns with gravestones, mausoleums, and other memorial sites as far as their eyes could see, all below a sky of the palest blue. It was peaceful. Barbara would later recall being quite conscious of the serenity. Prescott then held her hand as they slowly walked away from the BUSH gravestone, knowing only too well they would be returning to it soon.

Crumbling Inside

On a Monday morning in late September, Barbara Bush found herself standing in a stall in a ladies' room, completely unable to catch her breath. So overwhelmed was she with emotion, she could barely manage to stay on her feet. She was panting, her face and neck damp with perspiration. She felt frantic. As she struggled to compose herself, she heard a voice from the other side of the stall door: "Mrs. Bush, are you okay?" What a question. Of course she wasn't "okay." She hadn't been "okay" in months. "I'm fine," she managed to say. As her throat tightened with emotion, she added, "Please leave me alone."

Earlier, Robin, now bald from chemotherapy, had been getting a blood transfusion when she began to convulse. At just that moment, George walked into the room, blanched, and began to cry. Barbara's face darkened. "Don't you dare, Poppy," she said. "Not here." He bolted from the room. It was harsh, and she knew it. Feeling contrite, she went after him, but by the time she got into the hallway, he was already gone. That's when she took refuge in the ladies' room and tried to pull herself together.

Not surprisingly, Robin's condition had only worsened with the passing of not much time. Now she was perilously close to death, and some doctors thought another surgery was necessary because of internal bleeding. Dr. Walker was dubious and recommended against it; maybe, he suggested, the time had come to end Robin's suffering. When he and Barbara called George in Texas to discuss it with him, he agreed that it was time to stop treating her; it was time to let Robin go.

Years later, in 1989, Barbara had a different account. In an interview for a biography of her by Donnie Radcliffe, she said that she actually agreed to that final surgery on Robin. "Our uncle-doctor, whom we love more than life, really thought we should let her go," Barbara told the author. "The doctors at Memorial really wanted to operate. I opted to go with the doctors. She was very, very sick. She never came out of the operation. But they asked me to do it. I just felt they were killing themselves to save a child and we ought to cooperate. I don't care what anybody says, where there's life, there's hope."

In her 1994 autobiography, Barbara didn't mention her decision to allow a final surgery.

In 2019, thirty years after the Radcliffe book, the surgery was also omitted from Barbara's account of this time in an exhaustive biography of her, *The Matriarch* by Susan Page. Page wrote: "Barbara and the doctors called George Bush in Texas to discuss one more operation. 'I said, "No, we've done enough to her,"' Bush told them. There was nothing more that could be done. 'We thought it was time to let her go.'"

This omission of this crucial operation on Robin does seem odd. Had Barbara stopped referencing it because she felt guilty about having authorized it? Only she would know the answer to that question, and she never addressed it.

After the call to George in Texas, he immediately got on a plane headed to New York. By the time he got to the hospital, his daughter was in a coma.

On October 11, 1953, a couple of months shy of her fourth birthday, Pauline Robinson Bush drew her last breath. "Her death was very peaceful," Barbara would remember. "One minute she was there, and the next she was gone. I truly felt her soul go out of that beautiful little body. For one last time I combed her hair and we held our precious little girl. I never felt the presence of God more strongly than in that moment."

There would be no funeral, just a memorial service. Robin's body was then donated to Memorial Hospital for science—"We said, do with it what you will," Barbara recalled—and then cremated.

Laid to Rest

One morning shortly after Robin's death, Dorothy Bush walked through the graveyard in Greenwich holding a small box. At her side was her son's good friend Thomas Ludlow "Lud" Ashley. It was a gorgeous day; the sun was shining bright and the sky couldn't have been more blue. Dorothy, now fifty-two, seemed smaller and somehow more frail. The two walked very slowly to a grave site, the same one her husband, Prescott, had shown to Barbara a few months earlier.

When Barbara had called her to tell her that Robin had died, it was everything Dorothy could do just to not break down on the telephone. Like her daughter-in-law, she too had suppressed her deep emotion about the battle Robin had faced, and once it was all over she felt overwhelmed by a tidal wave of grief. After she hung up, Dorothy went to her bedroom and stayed there for the rest of the day, just praying and thinking. She then wrote to Barbara that she was "heartbroken," and she added, "Having faith is easy in good times, but it's in difficult times such as these that we need it most of all." She vowed to always be there for her, "no matter what you may need, dear," and said that she knew she could never replace Pauline, "but I am here for you always, and this is my promise to you for as long as we two draw breath. We will get through this," she wrote. "You are like a daughter to me, Barbara, and I *promise* you we will get through this."

Once Barbara was back in Texas with George and the boys, she called Dorothy to ask for a favor. Would she go to the hospital in New York to collect Robin's ashes, and then have them buried at the grave site Prescott had selected? Dorothy said she would do so and said she would be "honored." After she hung up, though, she collapsed into a chair. How would she ever get through such an ordeal?

Dorothy asked Prescott to accompany her, but he said he couldn't face it. He said that if it had been a funeral with all the family members present, he would've felt buoyed by the united support and love from their grief. However, the idea of just him and Dorothy in a graveyard with little Robin's cremains? He was tough, but not that tough. Even for Dorothy, he couldn't bring himself to do it. He regretted his lack of resolve. "This isn't the time to fall apart," he lamented. "No," she said, "I disagree. In fact, I think this is *exactly* the time to fall apart."

Though Dorothy accepted that Prescott couldn't accompany her to the cemetery, she was still determined to do what Barbara had requested. After praying about it, she decided to ask Lud Ashley to accompany her. (In about a year, Lud would be elected to Congress and would go on to serve thirteen terms.)

Dorothy and Lud approached a small hole in the ground, next to which stood a man with a shovel. With trembling hands, she handed the small box to the worker. For a moment, she wouldn't release her hold on it, as if maybe it felt wrong to give Robin to a complete stranger. The man soon bent down and gently placed the box into the hole. It would be here that Robin would rest for the next forty-seven years before eventually being moved to the grounds of the George H. W. Bush Presidential Library.

As Dorothy and Lud looked on mournfully, the worker slowly covered the box with dirt. It took just a couple of shovelfuls before it was completely buried. Dorothy then knelt down and made the sign of the cross. She stayed on her knees, and she prayed.

"Even If It Hurts"

Two days after Robin's passing, little Georgie, now a second grader at Sam Houston Elementary School in Midland, was carrying a Victrola from his classroom to the principal's office when he spotted his parents' car in the parking lot. He told his teacher he had to leave because his mother, father, and sister had just arrived, and he wanted to see them. "I run over to the car," George W. Bush recalled, "and there's no Robin." That was when Barbara told him she was dead, all the details coming forth in a torrent while there in the parking lot. Something about it seemed cruel. A stricken expression settled in the little boy's eyes. "Why didn't you tell me?" he asked, upset. *"Why didn't you tell me?"* One of his schoolmates, John Kidde, remembered George later saying, "You think your life is so good and everything is perfect; then something like this happens and nothing is the same."

"I fell apart," Barbara would recall. "There's no other way to put it. I just fell apart."

In the weeks and months to come, Barbara found herself in the grips of such despair she could barely function. For six months, she'd been the strong one, determined not to lose her composure for fear of starting a chain reaction that might affect Robin. Though she had terrible moments of privately breaking down, she was able to stay distracted by the endless list of things that needed to be handled for her daughter. Now that she was gone, it was as if there was nothing left for Barbara to do but fully experience her grief. It came upon her like a fierce storm, brutally washing over her.

"It was all just so devastating," said one of her relatives who sat with Barbara in her kitchen in Texas and tried to help her come to terms with it. She would recall Barbara's face as being devoid of expression, her eyes dull and lifeless. "I can't do this anymore," Barbara told her. "I want out of this, I really do." She wasn't crying. It was as if she couldn't even weep, she was just that numb. When told she was stronger than she thought she was, Barbara disagreed, saying, "I used to be. But I'm not strong anymore." When told that she should lean on George, she also resisted that advice, saying, "Poppy can't handle it. He just can't."

Over the previous six months, Barbara had so convinced herself of George's fragility, she was now certain he couldn't be there for her. It was true that George was just as devastated. However, he seemed better able to focus on his day-to-day activities in his oil business, and he wanted to try to help his wife do the same with her own life. Dorothy had warned him that these kinds of crises can often tear a marriage apart if the couple isn't careful to guard against it. George, not wanting this to happen to his marriage, promised Barbara they'd endure. He found a way to be sympathetic and supportive, even on those days when Barbara did everything in her power to push him away. He tried to make her laugh or at least get a smile. "I think eventually, Mother began to see that she didn't need to be alone in it," their son George recalled many years later. "She's tough. She's the one people lean on. It was hard for her to reverse that. I know my father had to work on her to wear her down. Mother doesn't yield easily."

Six months of a painfully slow process passed. "Two steps forward, five backward" is how Barbara would put it to nurse Marion Fraser, who stayed on for a while after Barbara returned to Texas. One turning point, which Barbara talked about often in years to come, was when she heard little Georgie say that he couldn't go out and play with a friend because he had to take care of her. He was just a child, and he was taking care of her? Barbara said she knew in that moment that she shouldn't allow him to miss out on his childhood because of her grief. She resolved to pull herself out of her slump.

According to a memory of Martha Tillerson's, handed down to her daughter, Louise Frasier, one spring morning Barbara walked into the kitchen with what seemed like a little more color to her complexion. She stood in front of a window and gazed out at her vegetable garden and, beyond that, to a sea of red and yellow columbines and lavender bluebonnets. She opened the window and looked up at a bright blue sky filled with golden sunshine. She took a deep breath and closed her eyes. It must have smelled fresh . . . clean . . . new.

"Did you sleep?" Marion asked her.

Barbara nodded. "I dreamed of Robin," she said.

"Oh, I'm so sorry, Mrs. Bush."

"No," Barbara said with a reassuring smile. "It's okay."

"You'll get over this," the nurse told her.

Barbara thought it over for a second. "I hope not," she finally said. "I think I want this pain with me," she concluded, "even if it hurts."

PART SIX

The Senator's Wife

"Call Me Senator"

Dorothy Bush may have been ambivalent about politics at first, but within about a year she found real purpose in being the wife of a senator. Sylvia Jenkins was ten years old in 1953 when her mother, Ivy Jenkins, was hired for a brief time to work for Dorothy as her personal secretary. She has indelible memories of the times she spent at the Bushes' new home in Georgetown, Washington, D.C., a quaint brick town house that they rented on Volta Street. They would continue to keep their estate in Greenwich until selling it in 1963 and moving into a smaller home in the same neighborhood at 21 Pheasant Lane.

"After the senator was elected, the Bush home in Georgetown became sort of a hub of social activity," recalled Sylvia Jenkins. "It was a somewhat smaller house than one might imagine, but lovely and well-appointed. In the back of it was a lovely, walled-in garden, which was Mrs. Bush's pride and joy. There, she and the senator would host cocktail parties, weather permitting, for all sorts of big shots. In the spring, summer, and fall it was ripe with color—dogwood, azaleas, verbena, phlox, alyssum, and hyacinths. Mrs. Bush would also have tea parties there with the wives of politicians.

"I also remember her older sister, Nancy, was always around. I noted that there wasn't much warmth between her and Prescott, and when I asked my mother about it, she said, 'Nancy doesn't have a life of her own, so she takes up a lot of her sister's time. Prescott doesn't like it.' I was only ten, but I thought, my goodness, that's too bad."

Actually, Nancy Walker's life wasn't as tragic as some might have assumed if just based on her single status at her present age, which was fifty-six. She did a great deal of traveling, had gone to France and the United Kingdom several times recently, and had also visited Italy, Spain, and Germany several times. She'd also been volunteering as a so-called Pink Lady at Roosevelt Hospital for many years, tending to patients' personal needs and keeping them company. Seeming not at all embittered or disillusioned about being alone, she was also known to be a matchmaker at the hospital, always eager to find mates for others; eight of her matches resulted in marriages. She lived in a large apartment in Manhattan—often, when they were younger, Dorothy, Prescott, and the children would stay with her while in the city— and spent her summers in her cottage on Walker's Point. She also had no money troubles, benefiting from a family trust. Her nieces and nephews called her "Flash"—actually her nephew Prescott Jr. came up with the nickname because somehow it seemed as if Nancy always had the latest news. "Whenever she would walk into a room," he recalled, "she would always start with, 'Did you hear that . . . ?'"

"Nancy was the family's most colorful character," Christopher Walker, her great-nephew, recalled. "She wore bright red lipstick no matter the occasion and big flowery dresses. I can still see her in the back of a limousine looking like a little painted doll in a fur wrap. She is definite proof that the women in our family are far more interesting than the men."

"You don't have to marry and have children to be happy," Nancy Walker once told a friend of hers, this at least according to the daughter of that friend. "I think Nan was a feminist long before anyone knew the meaning of the word," said that source. "My mother admired her because Nan never let society dictate who she was or who she should be. My mom used to say, 'I like her clarity.' She was like Dotty in that respect. Dotty was sometimes a little envious of her. After all, Nan could just pick up and go and do whatever she wanted without having to worry about a husband or children or, really, any responsibilities at all. Dotty used to say, 'What a life that one has; we should all be so lucky.' With that being said, Nan did cling to Dotty. However, Dotty did to her, as well. They were extremely close and, yes, I'm sure it did sometimes annoy Prescott, because he was known to be pretty territorial where Dotty was concerned."

Meanwhile, with Prescott now in office, he was becoming known for his ability to reach across the aisle in search of bipartisan solutions to problems. Now that Eisenhower was president, Prescott would always align himself with his policies, and Dorothy would follow. "It's a wonderful life with a Republican in the White House for the first time in twenty years," she wrote in a letter to one friend. Both Bushes had been earnest critics of Roosevelt and Truman and, as she wrote, "Prescott and I are quite pleased to see the backs of them and all of those like them."

Because Prescott wasn't so wedded to strictly Republican concerns, he was viewed as a moderate face of the party. "I suffer with him," Dorothy once wrote about her husband's stance on matters that put him in opposition to other senators, such as when he opposed a pay increase for his colleagues. "But I am always just especially a little more proud of him when he takes an unpopular stand because, in his heart, he feels that that is best for the country."

In his personal life, Prescott still wasn't necessarily viewed as a particularly warm presence in the lives of his progeny, and perhaps nothing suggested this more strongly than the announcement he once made while standing in the middle of a drawing room filled with relatives. "From now on, I think all of you should call me Senator, no longer Dad, no longer Gampy." Later, some of those relations would explain that it wasn't a question of vanity for Prescott as much as it was his wanting them to show respect for the office he now held. Dorothy was a little taken aback by it, though. She didn't say anything in the moment, but after everyone was gone she told him she wasn't sure it was a good idea. She was afraid it would scare the younger ones and make them fearful of their grandfather. Also, the fact that he'd come up with it on his own without discussing it with her annoyed her. They did have a deal, after all: no important decisions without mutual consent. However, the deed was done, and there was no way Prescott was going to change his mind about it. Dorothy decided to let it go. "Senator" it was.

Maybe it wasn't surprising that, at times, "the Senator" would become so immersed in his work, he'd tend to neglect his children. It wasn't purposeful as much as it was just the lapse in attention of a man with such a heavy workload. Dorothy wouldn't tolerate it for long. She monitored it closely. For instance, she might ask him, "Have you spent time with Bucky?" or "Did you call Nancy?" Such queries might have seemed random to Prescott, but the reason for them was usually because Dorothy knew his children were missing him. One relative recalls her telling Prescott, during a bit of a disagreement about his work while at a family dinner, "You want to be a public servant? Fine. But you'd darn well better serve this family, too." She understood the pressure he was under, however, because she too, even if to a lesser degree, was stressed. At this time, she wrote to her friend Anne Morrow Lindbergh, the wife of aviator Charles Lindbergh, that "Life gets so hectic that I feel I am constantly in a jet plane whirling through space. I am more determined than ever to let nothing interfere with our quiet little time for reading and prayer together each morning before Prescott goes to the Senate."

As long as she felt the family wasn't being ignored, Dorothy was sure to fully support her husband. He appreciated it too, often telling people, "I don't do this alone, you know? Dotty is the foundation upon which we have built everything." The sight of the two of them walking into his Senate office together on those days when Dorothy accompanied him was memorable. Prescott was always exceedingly well-dressed, usually in a pin-striped suit, tall and handsome with a wide smile. "He looked more like a senator than any senator I've ever met," said William Hildenbrand, the former secretary of the Senate. "He would never come on the Senate floor unless looking impeccable. He was the kind of guy who probably put out the garbage in pressed pajamas, or wore black tie to bed. He carried himself with all the confidence of an aristocrat."

Dorothy was about a foot shorter than her husband, always elegant in her stylish ensembles. She never walked even a step behind him, always at his side and sometimes appearing to struggle to stay there because of his steady gait. She often visited the Senate gallery, watching as legislation crawled its way through the system, especially excited whenever Prescott had the opportunity to speak. Sometimes, Dorothy took Nancy to the gallery to watch her father debate on the floor. "You never forget a thing like that," Nancy said. "That's your father? And this is what he does? You leave with such a sense of pride, it just fills you up."

Dorothy Realizes a Dream

The social aspect of Prescott's work in the Senate appealed to Dorothy in that there was always one interesting event or another on her busy schedule. Much greater than just mingling with fascinating people, though, was the urgency she began to feel to apply herself to something truly worthwhile and maybe even patriotic. For instance, she wanted to be able to represent Prescott by giving speeches when necessary, but she wasn't sure she had the presence for it. Typical of her drive and determination, though, Dorothy decided to take elocution lessons and devote herself to them until she was number one in her class of fifteen. Soon, she could stand before an audience and talk for as long as thirty minutes before ever having to refer to her notes. It felt good, but she wanted to do more. To that end, she soon became a member of the Ladies of the Senate, also known as the Senate Ladies Red Cross Unit or Senate Wives. The organization was founded in 1917 to aid the allied cause in World War I, with all of its members being wives of current U.S. senators. Eventually, wives of former senators were also invited to join. "It feels good to belong," she would write of the organization, "and it feels good to do something for others, especially the less fortunate. It's what I have always tried to impart to my children."

Dorothy usually felt invigorated by her duties as a senator's wife. However, back in the spring of 1953 when her granddaughter was so ill, she had fallen into a depression uncharacteristic of her. Despite the fullness of her days, she still felt joyless. She wasn't used to such melancholy, yet she couldn't seem to pull herself out of it. Would Robin live or die? It was the only thing on her mind. Though already so busy, she felt maybe she needed something new to distract her, but what could that be?

Dorothy had always enjoyed writing, going all the way back to her school days in New York. An avid reader as well, nothing used to thrill her more than the assignment of a book report. When a high school instructor once paid her the compliment of telling her the synopsis she wrote of a book was better than the book itself, she began to wonder if she might one day have a career as a journalist. However, when she approached her father with the idea, he was, not surprisingly, discouraging. "That's not a job for a woman," he told her. Dorothy abandoned the idea. However, she always had a nagging regret about this dream deferred, and, especially as she got older, she couldn't help but resent the fact that it was because of her father.

One evening, Dorothy and Prescott were guests at a charity fund-raiser in Boston. This was a grand affair held at the mansion of a wealthy philanthropist who'd contributed millions of dollars to build a wing at Massachusetts General Hospital. The Bushes arrived in a chauffeur-driven white Rolls-Royce, which was sent for them by the host of the party. When they exited it, they were met with a burst of bright flashes from the cameras of paparazzi. "This is an awful lot of fuss for just us," Dorothy was heard saying as they walked from the car to the manor. She seemed to enjoy it, though. In photographs taken that night, she's wearing a gown that was more striking than anything else she'd ever been seen in at any social event. It was decorated with what appear to be bugle beads, the color lost to the ages since the pictures are in black-and-white. The design's halter-neck bodice featured various size emeralds; the next day, one of the papers described the look as "cut velvet on silk chiffon." Her salt-and-pepper hair was styled in a short, wavy fashion; she looked so dignified, she appeared to be downright royal. Prescott, proudly at her side, was in a sharply tailored tuxedo with a crisp white shirt and matching bow tie.

This was an unusual look for Dorothy, who, just as in her younger days, very rarely dressed to the nines. It had always been Nancy who most enjoyed couture. Dorothy would call it "the la-dee-das" when she felt people were putting on airs. "She never worried about how she looked and never had any fashion sense," says her daughter, Nancy Bush Ellis. "My grandmother, Luli Walker, was very fashionable; she had lovely suits made to order in New York, and beautiful shoes. Mom never went to New York to shop if she could possibly help it. She would order something from Macy's." When Dorothy did have the occasion to dress up, though, she sure seemed to enjoy it.

At this same event, Dorothy became involved in a lively conversation with a doctor, who'd once treated Prescott for a hernia, about why his first bid for the Senate had failed. The two disagreed on just about every point. That was fine with Dorothy; she firmly believed people had a right to their opinions regardless of how wrong they were. As they talked, Dorothy changed the subject to Robin's illness. She wondered if the physician had ever heard of a deadly cancer in someone so young. He said it was unfortunately far too common. Dorothy then said she felt she needed to do something to take her mind off the upsetting struggle. She could only do so much for her daughter-in-law, she said, before she would inevitably find herself obsessing over worst-case scenarios. The physician came up with an idea. "Dorothy! You should write a column for the newspaper," he exclaimed. "You have strong opinions, and I think you could do it. Who do you know who might be able to help you with that?" Dorothy was intrigued. "Who, indeed?" was her response.

Within a few days, Dorothy had considered the doctor's suggestion and was fairly certain it was something she wanted to do. "Thank you for inspiring me to perhaps be something in this world that I always wanted to be ever since I was a little girl," she wrote to him. "When a person stirs one's imagination, it should not be taken lightly but rather with gratitude and appreciation."

When Dorothy brought up the idea to Prescott, he didn't like it. First of all, he pointed out, the biggest problem Dorothy once said she had with politics had to do with invasion of privacy. Now she wanted to bare her soul in a newspaper column? It made no sense to him.

She wasn't about to "tell all," Dorothy explained. However, she did wish to share certain aspects of her life and that of her family, and she felt she had the right—and maybe the talent and, who knows, but maybe even the obligation—to do so. More important, she said, as the wife of a senator she could provide a glimpse into political life, to which outsiders might not ordinarily be privy. "I want to bring people closer to politics," she said, and by doing so, she explained, she could perhaps further the public's understanding. She had learned a lot about the political world in recent years and she thought that her way of giving back, of being of service, could be to write about it. She already had a title for the column: "Washington Life as Seen by a Senator's Wife."

Why, Prescott demanded to know, would Dorothy have gone ahead and named a column he hadn't even given her permission to write? Dorothy didn't entertain the question. She'd always supported Prescott in his goals, even when she had her doubts. Why couldn't he now do the same for her? She was fighting a losing battle, because even greater than any question of privacy was Prescott's core belief that women shouldn't work. A big part of his reticence also had to do with Dorothy getting paid to write. Maybe if she was going to be doing it gratis it wouldn't have been as much of an issue for him. Another problem was that because of the way he felt the media had ruined his first Senate run, he now thought of the press as adversarial and something that needed to be controlled, not encouraged. For his own wife to now ostensibly want to become a member of the fourth estate rubbed him the wrong way. He didn't want her to do it, and he was clear about that.

When he felt he was getting nowhere with Dorothy, Prescott decided to call in reinforcements, namely his two eldest sons, Prescott Jr., thirty-one, and George, twenty-nine. The brothers were in alignment with their father in the way they viewed their own wives.

For about the last ten years, Prescott Jr. had been married to Elizabeth Kauffman. She was very happy with her life raising their two children, and it was probably for the best that she didn't have other ambitions, because he wouldn't have supported them. He was "old school," just like his father, and never wanted his wife to work or focus on anything other than her household duties. Moreover, like his brother George in the way he treated Barbara, he rarely asked for her opinion about anything substantive going on in their lives. The pressure he and George could bring to bear on their mother was the best chance Prescott had to change her mind. The brothers would give it their best shot—especially not easy for George at this time given that he was so consumed with his little girl's illness.

Over the course of about a week, Prescott and George actually did make a dent in Dorothy's steel resolve. She started to waver from the idea of the column, thinking that maybe they were right, perhaps she should beg off—that is until her daughter, Nancy, intervened.

Nancy, twenty-seven, was like her mother in many ways: She was very involved in philanthropy, not interested in exclusively staying at home, and she often went up against her husband, Alexander, with the debates between them lively. Though he respected her opinion, it had been tough going at first. Like her mother had done with her father, she had to break him in slowly to the idea that he should respect her. Also, Nancy was a Democrat in a family of die-hard Republicans and vociferous about her views, too. She had a mind of her own, which her mother admired about her.

"Why are you letting Father, Pressie, and George get to you?" Nancy asked Dorothy. She reminded her that this wasn't the way Dorothy had raised her; she'd always told her to find a way to express herself outside of her relationship and had assured her that doing so was the key to a long and happy marriage; Nancy and Alexander would be married for forty-three years, until his death in 1989.

Nancy urged her mother to write the column, telling her that she had a lot to offer and that she shouldn't refrain from doing so just because of opposition from some of the men in the family. Dorothy knew Nancy was right and was even a little annoyed with herself for having almost folded. Her daughter believed in her, and that meant the world to her. She would go forward.

Racking her brain to come up with a plan, Dorothy then remembered that Prescott had an old friend named Bernie Yudain in the newspaper business. She didn't have his number, though, and wasn't about to ask Prescott for it. She did a little nosing around and eventually was able to get his contact information from his secretary. It was now time to move forward with her idea.

Dorothy Becomes a Journalist

Veteran newspaperman Bernie Yudain was the former managing editor of *Greenwich Time* now working in the Washington office of Time, Inc. He and Prescott had history; back in 1945, Yudain was the twenty-seven-year-old journalist who broke the story that the United Nations Organization was trying to take over a forty-two-square-mile area of Greenwich for its headquarters, which was projected to be called "The Free City of the United Nations." He got that tip from Prescott, who was working on Wall Street at the time. "I have to say I think it is the biggest news story in the modern history of Greenwich," Yudain told *Greenwich Time* years later in 2003. "The town, the physical town, and the whole notion of Greenwich as a community was at stake. I don't know anything else that came close to it."

Prescott recalled of the venture, "There was going to be a new airport, a hotel, new churches and schools, a hospital as well as fire and police stations, as well as a twelve-story administration building for the U.N. that was to be modeled after the Pentagon. Needless to say, the town went into an uproar. Thank God the Rockefellers donated land in New York City, which is where the United Nations ended up, and which was fine and good as far as Connecticut was concerned."

Yudain was more than happy to meet with Dorothy Bush. According to the family history, she went into his office, sat across a desk from him, and gave him every reason why she felt she would make an excellent columnist. When she finished, she added, "There is only one reason this won't work." When he asked what it was, she answered, "Because you refuse to give me a chance." Then, leaning over the desk and taking both his hands into her own, she added with great earnestness, "Please don't let that be the reason, Bernie." How could he turn her down?

After some discussion over the next few days about the column's format, it was decided it would be a column in which Dorothy would have free rein to describe the social events she and Prescott attended as well as her personal philosophies about the political arena, and even some insight into her family life in politics if she liked. Basically, she was given great latitude to write about anything she felt appropriate. She couldn't ask for more than that.

As planned, the column would be called "Washington Life as Seen by a Senator's Wife by Mrs. Prescott Bush." Many years later, she would reframe its origins by saying in an interview, "I agreed only because he [Yudain] said it would help Pres." That wasn't true. However, it was very much like Dorothy to not want to do anything to take the public spotlight away from her husband.

After a slow start, the column would end up being syndicated in newspapers all across the state and in some nearby states, as well. When the first one appeared in early 1953, as the story goes, she brought it into their parlor and placed the paper on Prescott's lap as he lay on the couch. She didn't say a word. He looked down at it. He gazed up at her. "You did it anyway?" he asked.

"Well, it certainly looks that way."

Naturally, he was upset. He jumped up off the sofa, bolted from the room, and slammed a door somewhere else in the house. It would take him a few days to get over it. He still didn't like being defied, though he was certainly used to it by now where Dorothy was concerned. He was also disappointed with Prescott Jr. and George; he'd given them an important task, and they'd failed miserably at it.

One thing was always true about Prescott, though: He could be gracious in defeat, especially where his wife was concerned. As earlier stated, he would give her as a present the Underwood typewriter she'd later use to write her columns. Also as earlier stated, Dorothy could barely type. Sylvia Jenkins, whose mother, Ivy, was Dorothy's secretary at this time, recalled, "My mother was an excellent typist; she'd been a Kelly Girl secretary before working for Mrs. Bush, and she taught Mrs. Bush how to type. Mrs. Bush looked at it as she might have a sporting challenge; she was going to learn to type faster than any person ever had in the history of typists, and she was going to be better than my mother at it, too. Sure enough, I would say that within about two months' time she had it down. Even though she'd peck away and certainly didn't remember anything about 'home row,' she was fast. No one was to disturb her when she was writing. When my mother would have questions about the calendar and peek into the study, Mrs. Bush would glare at her over her bifocals. She knew that this meant to get out while the getting out was good.

"Every week, Mrs. Bush would walk a couple blocks to Morgan's corner drugstore to buy ink ribbon for her typewriter. They could be delivered and my mother would often say, 'Let's just call them and have them send some over.' But Mrs. Bush insisted that the brisk walk to the store to purchase the ribbon was part of the discipline of writing. Therefore, she would insist on doing it herself."

Dorothy's column was sometimes outspoken, sometimes chatty, but always engaging and informative. Foremost, she delighted in writing about Prescott: "Every personal contact with that man increases my respect for him, if such a thing is possible."

Often, she wrote about her high-society friends: "Monday night, we attended a lovely dinner party given by the Arthur Krocks at their home in honor of Lord and Lady Caccia. If anyone is beautifully equipped to promote the friendship that must exist between the English-speaking world, it is Lord Caccia, the British Ambassador, as he is so natural, so friendly, such a completely genuine person."

In another column, she wrote: "I went to play badminton at Mrs. Hugh D. Auchincloss's with Martha Krock, wife of Arthur Krock of *The New York Times*, and several other girls. Mrs. Janet Auchincloss is the mother of 'Jackie' Kennedy, wife of the nice young Senator from Massachusetts, who has been laid up so long with a bad back. I was delighted to hear from her that after this last operation, he seems to be recovering rapidly."

In about ten years' time, Dorothy would further write about Mrs. Auchincloss: "Last Monday, I lunched at Margaret Walker's with Janet Auchincloss. It was the first time I had seen Mrs. Auchincloss since the Inauguration, and when I told her that I thought her daughter, Jackie Kennedy, looked beautiful and so queenly and dignified throughout, she said, 'You will make me cry.' Such a genuine motherly reaction—don't you always feel like crying when someone says something nice about one of your children. I do."

Most of Dorothy's columns were more substantive, though. Often, they had to do with critical issues, such as when the Supreme Court ruled school prayer to be unconstitutional in 1963. Dorothy wasn't hesitant about expressing her views: "The six judges who concurred in that decision seem to completely ignore the fact that we are a nation founded under God. The first thing the Pilgrim Fathers did when they landed on the bleak Massachusetts coast was to kneel and give thanks to God. This country was founded so that its citizens could be free to practice religion. Are we going to weaken our country by denying our children their rightful heritage?"

In another column, she devoted at least ten inches to a fulsome explanation of how the Senate works: "What is going on in the Senate is almost a daily question. So in case any of you are equally confused I will try to explain in a few words . . . a legislative day is the time from which the Senate convenes until it adjourns, be that one day, one week, one month or what have you . . . If at any time one of the Senators says, 'I suggest the lack of a quorum' and upon the call of the roll 51 Senators do not respond, the Senate is forced to adjourn and a new legislative day begins all over again."

In yet another column, she expressed her concern about the education of America's youth as it relates to government. "Sometimes I wonder how our government ever functions, at all," she wrote, "what with everyone butting into everyone else's business. While it's a slow moving machine, I urge people, as does the Senator, to learn as much about it as possible. I fear that our children glaze over in school when attending classes in which the levers of power are fully explained. Let's not allow our children to be ignorant to how our country works! I sometimes fear the Senator is boring our grandchildren with his orations in our parlor about his work. But I realize it's for the best. They must know. They simply must know!'"

Whenever she wrote about President Eisenhower, Dorothy's respect for him was evident, such as in her reporting of his speech at the Republican National Convention after suffering a heart attack in 1955: "It was a very moving moment. All the women clapped and screamed and waved, but the really touching thing was that after he had spoken, there was hardly a dry eye around me, and I'm not ashamed to say that my handkerchief was in use, too. There is just something so big and fine and noble about that man." Two years later, in 1957, she wrote of "the big moment," when the Eisenhowers made their appearance to the tune of "Hail to the Chief" during a biannual reception for United States senators, noting "the direct gaze of the President's blue eyes, the warmth of Mamie's greeting and the light in her face leaving each one of us with the fresh realization of what a great—truly great—pair we have in the White House."

Dorothy was at least partly responsible for the public's perception that Prescott and Dwight were inseparable friends who played golf all the time at the Burning Tree Country Club, just by virtue of how often she alluded to it in her column. While the two men were certainly friendly, they actually didn't play as often as Dorothy reported, and sometimes it was just once a year. Neither was Prescott "largely responsible," as Dorothy wrote, for Ike's decision to run for President in 1952. Many people in Eisenhower's circle had encouraged him to run, including Prescott. But as far as Dorothy was concerned it was Prescott who'd had the most sway. She knew it helped her husband politically for people to think he and Ike were close.

"But does it matter?" Dorothy asked Bernie Yudain when he challenged her on the exaggeration. At the time, the two were having a lunch at the Alibi Club. It was traditionally a men's club (of which Prescott happened to be a member), which Dorothy described in one of her columns as "an old, old house in downtown Washington filled with curios and cartoons of members from the Club's founding." Occasionally, members were permitted to bring women into the club for lunch, as was the case on this day. However, much to Dorothy's consternation, only Yudain was given a menu, from which he was to order not only for himself but her, as well. It unnerved Dorothy, she would later write, that the waiter never even acknowledged her presence. "Women have a long way to go in this world," she would later write. "A long way."

As the two dined, Dorothy reminded Bernie that the whole point of the column was that it was based on her personal views. When he asked, "But Dorothy, is it true?" Her response reportedly was, "Well, it's certainly true that this is how I see it." She didn't understand the problem. The veteran journalist explained that she had a responsibility to be truthful, not just opinionated. He called it a "sacred trust." Women in the male-dominated news business couldn't afford to make mistakes, he told her. That's how high the bar was for her and others like her in media, and she really was of the media now whether she realized it or not. His opinion gave Dorothy a lot to think about, and she never forgot the lesson. From that time onward, she would strive to be not only thought-provoking in her work but also as truthful as possible.

"Washington Life as Seen by a Senator's Wife by Mrs. Prescott Bush" would run for more than a decade; the title would eventually be shortened to simply "Washington Life" with her byline, Mrs. Prescott Bush, not part of the title. Dorothy would finally abandon it after Prescott's tenure in the Senate was over in 1963. In one of her final columns, she encapsulated her reasons behind writing it: "We shouldn't be afraid of politics. No matter what our affiliation, Republican or Democrat, we should educate ourselves about platforms. I think, and I know the Senator would agree, that the worst thing we can do as Americans is be ignorant of the world around us and how it works. Don't be afraid to have an opinion about it because whatever your views they are legitimate. That is what we do best in America; we express ourselves freely and without recrimination. I daresay this right is the most sacred of civil liberties. I know none of my little ramblings are memorable past the day they are first read in this column. I only pray that doing my little part brings people closer to their government. Knowledge leads to engagement which often leads to change."

PART SEVEN

Jenna Hawkins and Harold Welch

Laura Bush's Parents

Jenna, "True Daughter of West Texas"

T he Welches Announce Birth of Daughter," read the notice in the *El Paso Times* on November 14, 1946. "A daughter was born to Mr. and Mrs. Harold Welch of Midland on November 4," it continued. "She was named Laura Lane."

This announcement gave Jenna Hawkins—Mrs. Harold Welch—such great joy. When she gave birth to Laura Lane, she was filled with a sense of relief and good fortune. Though she'd wanted a baby for as long as she could remember, she feared it might be impossible given the personal histories of other women in her family. For instance, she knew her mother, Jessie Laura Hawkins, had a tragic history of stillbirths, one before she bore Jenna when she was twenty-one and two more after that. Jessie never talked about it, though. She remained true to the stoic nature of the West Texan woman who rarely complained about her lot in life but instead coped privately with whatever cards she'd been dealt. Jenna also knew that her maternal grandmother, Eva Louise, had suffered several stillbirths. Again, these painful losses were rarely discussed. There were other women too, cousins and relatives who'd also suffered in silence, their pain never addressed, never reconciled. Being as cautious as possible, Jenna was on doctor-ordered bed rest almost the entire time she was pregnant. While Laura's birth was difficult, happily, the baby was healthy. Jenna and her husband felt blessed beyond all measure.

Two and a half years later, Jenna would become pregnant again and, under strict bed rest orders as before, hoped for another miracle. However, this time she wouldn't be as fortunate; she gave birth to a son who died shortly after taking his first breaths. The baby's death was devastating to Jenna but, somehow, if even possible, more so to Harold, who'd so desperately wanted a son. They named their lost boy John Edward and buried him three days later in an unmarked grave, along with dozens of other babies like him who'd died in the small town of Midland, Texas, either at birth or shortly thereafter.

Jenna was a small-framed woman, barely five feet tall, with a face that somehow always seemed serene. Her presence could best be described as soft and comforting. People in the family gravitated to her when they were troubled. "She could make you feel good just by sitting with you," recalled one of her relatives. "She was the kind of woman who, if you had a lot of stuff going on, you could go to her house and sit with her and have coffee and just talk and feel better. You knew she'd had heartbreak in her life, but you also knew she was strong. She made people around her strong, too. She had the warmest hands, that's what I remember most about Jenna, those warm hands. She would hold your one hand within both of hers, and there was so much warmth and comfort there."

Jenna Louise Hawkins was born on July 24, 1919, in Little Rock, Arkansas, to Hal and Jessie Hawkins. She was raised from the age of seven in Canutillo, on the outskirts of El Paso and close to the banks of the Rio Grande. Many years later in her obituary, she would be described as "a true daughter of West Texas—a woman who loved its people, its wildlife and its land."

The summer before she and her parents moved to Canutillo from Taylor, Texas, they'd driven to California in Hal's little Model T to visit relatives. While there, Hal noticed "tourist courts" gaining in popularity because of the upswing in automobile sales. A tourist court usually consisted of small, one-room buildings in which passersby could, for a fee, spend the night and use a communal bathroom before continuing on with their journey; it was basically a precursor to the motel. When they got back to Texas, Hal bought seven acres of property and opened his own tourist court, which he called the New Way Auto Court and Camp Diner, as well as a lumberyard, Nu-Way Lumberyard.

Jenna would often talk of the Great Depression, which hit the country when she was ten, and she had memories of a great exodus on Highway 80 as Texans fled their state for California in search of a better life, sometimes ending up at her father's facility. "When the Depression started, all the Arkies and Okies were moving to California," she recalled in an interview with El Paso Inc. in 2005. "There was a lot of movement about that time, people from Oklahoma, mainly, coming through. And then, of course, after twenty-nine and the Crash, there was more of that. We were the only tourist court between Las Cruces and El Paso, and they had to stop somewhere. I remember there would be so many hitchhikers coming by my dad's little tourist court, and they wouldn't have had anything to eat. My dad had a little grocery there in connection with the tourist court, and he'd always fix baloney and cheese sandwiches to pass out to them.

"I'm sure my parents just held on by their fingertips in those days, though," she said. "But I guess they didn't take time to feel sorry for themselves. If they did, I wasn't aware of it. Everyone else was in the same shape. Everyone was struggling."

As a young girl, Jenna was an excellent student, curious about the world around her. She loved to hike with a friend along the foothills of the Franklin Mountains, taking in nature all around her and looking for arrowheads.

"Being an only child, I couldn't wait to get back into school in the fall," she recalled. "I went to little Lone Star Elementary, [which was] seven grades. I . . . stayed out of high school a year or two because there wasn't transportation. I was young anyway; I had started school early. So when they did have buses that took us into town, I went to El Paso High. But a lot of Canutillo children didn't go on to high school." Her favorite subject was always English: "I loved to read and I loved my English teachers. Didn't like math. But I liked everything about the school. I loved El Paso High."

When Jenna decided she wanted to go to college, her parents weren't supportive of it. They worried she was setting goals too high; after all, she was "just a country girl" in their eyes, and they felt she should marry and settle down with a family. However, Jenna very much wanted a higher education. Somehow she convinced Jessie and Hal to allow her to apply to the Texas College of Mines and Metallurgy (now the University of Texas at

El Paso). Once she was accepted, Jessie couldn't believe it. "A college girl, in *this* family?" she said, filled with pride. Jenna would drop out after two years, though. "The war was on by then and I thought I'd rather work," she later explained. "I'd studied journalism in high school and college, so I got a job in the advertising department of the Popular [Dry Goods Company in El Paso]. It was a wonderful education. It was the biggest department store in the area. The wife of the President of Mexico would send up there for clothes. And while I was working at the Popular, I met my husband, Harold Welch."

One day Jenna looked down from the window of a second-floor office at Popular just as a man happened to be looking up. Their eyes met. "It was love at first sight," recalled Jenna's friend Adair Margo, who as a child had lived next door to the Adolph Schwartz family (third generation), who owned the Popular Dry Goods Company.

That's not the entire story, though. Their eyes did meet that day and Harold Welch was taken by Jenna Hawkins. He then made some calls in an attempt to figure out who at Popular might be a mutual friend of his and of the woman on the upper floor. He eventually located such a person, and then asked her to encourage Jenna to go on a blind date. Jenna was reluctant but decided to do it. They settled on a location. When Jenna got to the restaurant, she found Harold sitting at the table, smiling at her. *Then* it was love at first sight.

Harold

Harold Welch was never an easy man to figure out. Not only did he always seem to have some kind of secret life but he also compartmentalized things in such a way that his friends from one circle never knew those from another. His friends used to say that only when he died would all his secrets be revealed, because that's when his survivors would finally have a chance to compare notes at his funeral.

Harold—often referred to as "Hal" by friends and family—grew up in the Dust Bowl of Lubbock, Texas, a little more than a hundred miles north of Midland. His parents, Mark and Lula Welch, both from Arkansas, had married late in life when both were forty and then moved to Fort Worth and, finally, Lubbock. Mark had died by the time his son met Jenna Welch. Laura Bush once recalled her paternal grandmother, Lula, who would die at the age of eighty-four when Laura was eight, as "a big, sturdy but very elderly woman with heavy, black lace-up shoes."

Harold had one brother, Mark, a doctor in Little Rock. "He was the one who got to finish college," said one relative, "because he was in med school, and having a doctor in the family was sort of incredible. Mark had somehow put himself through school working jobs and taking loans, whereas Hal had to drop out of Texas Tech [Technical College] after two years and take care of their sick and widowed mom. He didn't think that was fair, but that's the way it was. That was the first of many disappointments in his life."

Seven years Jenna's senior, Harold was good-looking, with piercing blue eyes and the solid physique of a football player. Always in some sort of trouble, he was known as one of the town's biggest mischief makers. He seemed a tad old, in his late twenties, to not take life seriously. He went from one job to the next until finally enlisting in the army.

Jenna's parents felt she could do a lot better than Harold. "No ambition, no future, no nothin'" is how Hal summed him up. However, Jenna knew what she wanted and, like many young women of that time and place, felt pressured by the war to get on with her life with Harold. She had a real connection with him and it seemed right, though she'd never had a serious relationship in the past against which to judge it.

Jenna and Harold were married on the grounds of Fort Bliss in its Post Chapel on Saturday, January 29, 1944, a chaplain named Jefferson Isbell officiating. Harold was about to turn thirty-one; Jenna was twenty-four. In a post-wedding announcement in the *El Paso Herald-Post*, Jenna appeared significantly older than her years, her brunette hair cropped short and wearing studious, wire-rimmed glasses. The paper noted that "only relatives and a few close friends were present" and added that "the bride wore an aqua crepe gown with wide-brimmed, black velvet hat and black accessories. Sergeant and Mrs. Welch will leave tomorrow for Shreveport, La., stopping en route in Lubbock and Dallas. Sergeant Welch is stationed in Shreveport, with the Anti-Aircraft Artillery."

"He had volunteered for the Army," Jenna later recalled of Harold. "He later said everything he ever did in the Army was a mistake, and the first [one] was that he'd ever volunteered. He had a high draft number and he supported his mother, so he probably could have stayed out for a while. But he joined under the Volunteer Officer Candidate program. Well, he flunked out of Officer's School, so they just put him in a line outfit, antiaircraft, and he went to Europe."

Harold would be gone for two years, during which time he was part of the assault on Germany and among the U.S. forces to liberate the Nazi concentration camp at Nordhausen. Meanwhile, Jenna went back to work at Popular and lived with a friend whose husband was also serving. "Every night after dinner we sat down and wrote our letters to our husbands," Jenna recalled.

Apparently, Jenna also tried to stay busy with social activities. In October 1944, when a friend named Marian Brooks Cocke, who had been Jenna's maid of honor, was to be married, Jenna offered to host a "coffee" at which would be made the formal announcement. As a result, she found herself written about in the society section of the *El Paso Times* with the headline: "Mrs. Welch Will Give Coffee to Reveal News to Friends." The paper noted, "News will be revealed with cleverly painted mortarboard caps [tasseled headwear worn by school graduates] which, when opened, will bear the inscription graduating from Miss to Mrs." It also specified that Jenna wore "a gown of aqua crepe," which was the same dress she wore on her wedding day.

When he was discharged, Harold took a job in El Paso at the Universal CIT Credit Corporation, which he'd also had before the war, extending credit for car loans. Daily, Harold would make his way to car dealerships far and wide in a vehicle battered by hot sand blowing in from the surrounding dry lands ravaged by years of drought. Paradoxically, he would never take out a loan himself. He was too practical to ever do so and wouldn't think to spend money he didn't have. A child of the Depression, he was notoriously thrifty, never even buying Jenna Christmas presents. He was always fearful of never having money and kept at least a hundred dollars handy, sometimes hidden away in the house, for emergencies . . . or, if the mood hit him, for gambling. He loved to gamble and would spend most of his adult life either owing bookies or having them owe him, another contradiction for a man given to financial worries.

Eventually, Harold's job saw him and Jenna relocate to sleepy Midland with its population of about twenty thousand, where the oil business had just begun to boom. Little Laura came along shortly thereafter in November 1946.

When Harold returned from the war, he was a different man. He'd been a real rabble-rouser when Jenna first met him, but now, as a vet, he was quiet and sullen. Or maybe he was just sad, the horror of war sticking with him. "On one hand, he was proud to have served," explained Donald Lane, whose father, Fred, was a friend of Harold's; the Lanes also lived in Midland. "He was patriotic and loved his country. But on the other, he hated what he saw while serving and wished he hadn't seen any of it. He never let on how he felt about things, though. Bad memories were never talked about by men like Harold Welch. They buried them deep in order to get on with things. They were survivors—oil men, cowboys, cattle ranchers, and other hardworking Texans whose jobs now kept them confined to office work or, in his case, driving across West Texas for hours at a time."

"Hal's [Harold's] father had been a builder in Lubbock, and so he was also interested in building," said Todd Southern, another friend of the family's. "The big oil strike of '46 saw a huge influx of people moving into Midland and Odessa and not enough accommodations for them. Hal saw a need and filled it by deciding to quit his job and go into the construction business for himself. He was a self-made man. Honest. Forthright. He was mostly self-taught by taking the little knowledge he had gleaned from two years of college to learn how to draw plans. He wasn't someone who could handle a hammer or nails. He was more a thinking guy who could draw up blueprints.

"He starting taking out loans to buy parcels of land, and then hired a couple guys to do the work. He'd build a house and move Jenna and Laura into it for a few months. Then it would sell to someone else, and he'd move his family into the next house he built. Jenna once said it was like playing a game of leapfrog along the block.

"The structures were small ranch homes situated right next to each other, so close you could hear your neighbors talking through the walls. Harold got really busy, though. I remember him saying, 'I'm busier than a one-legged cat in a sandbox.'"

Even with all the moving about from one house to the next, it was an easy and comfortable life, at least at first. "Folks living in Hal's homes bonded to one another," said Laura McKinney, whose parents had bought a home across the street from the Welches. "We all knew each other's business, sometimes being too intrusive but always lending a helping hand, celebrating achievements, being encouraging during hard times. There were six houses on our street and they were small and tight; we were packed into that block like sardines. Holidays at each other's homes was a big deal: 'Y'all have Thanksgiving at our house and we all will have Christmas at your house.' That sort of thing. It was all about family. Or, as Jenna used to say, '*Our* family, *your* family, *their* family. The one thing we all have in common is . . . family.'"

Within about a year, the pressure of owning a successful construction business apparently began to wear on Harold, because he began drinking more than Jenna would have liked. Even though Midland was a dry county, buying liquor on its outskirts was never a problem. "For all its neighborly virtues, Midland wasn't an easy place to live," said Donald Lane. "It was a small town where the weather was brutal. It wasn't pretty what with all the structures being flat and one-story—had to be, though, because of tornadoes. Even with the twisters, Midland was always in a drought. It was hot and dry. There were oil storage tanks everywhere, and these darn things would catch fire and blow up and cause holy hell.

"The closest town was Odessa. Everything else was a couple hours away. You lived in Midland, you had no choice but to get along with people because you were in it together. But it was good, don't get me wrong," he added. "If you were from Midland, like me, you were proud of it and still are today. First of all, you know you're tough-skinned. Secondly, you know you're bighearted. That's Midlanders for you: tough-skinned and bighearted."

The Mystery of Harold

Maybe it was because her marriage to Harold Welch was always strained that Jenna began to develop so many outside interests. Harold just wasn't very solicitous of her. While he didn't openly mistreat her, he wasn't exactly warm or affectionate, either. The older he got the more brooding he became; he was always argumentative and defensive for seemingly no good reason. Jenna tried to dismiss it by calling him "a big grouch" or "an old coot," but she did have to wonder why he was always in such a bad mood. After ten years of marriage, she finally got to the point where she stopped trying to figure it out and just accepted it.

Most days, it was the same routine: Harold would come home from work seeming irritated by one thing or another. He would go to the refrigerator and pop open a cold one. Then he would go into the backyard and collapse into a lawn chair with his beer, where he would chain-smoke in silence. Sometimes he would open the hood of his truck and putter around in there, fixing this and that and whiling away the time. Or he would take out his golf club and hit balls over the roof and into the street in front of the house. Sometimes he would look after his garden of onions and chilies. The idea of actually having a conversation with Jenna about his day or hers didn't seem to interest him much. When they did speak, he tended to contradict her. If she said it was too hot, he disagreed and felt it could be warmer. If she liked a certain kind of food, he hated it.

Donald Lane recalled a story his father once told him that might help explain Harold. According to Donald, his father was sitting in a bar in Midland with Harold, who'd had a few beers in him and was feeling them. "'Guess I gotta accept that the worst time of my life was the best time of my life,' he told my father," said Donald Lane. "He said that when he had to drop out of college while his brother went on to become a doctor, his self-esteem took a real hit. Enlisting, though, made him feel like he had real value, as a soldier. As much as he hated the war, being in the service was the most important thing he'd ever done, and he never surpassed it. 'Those were my best days,' he said. Since his discharge, it'd been all downhill for him, and now he felt like his life was sort of wasted.

"My old man was surprised," continued Donald Lane. "He started talking about how lucky Harold was to have Jenna, who loved him, and Laura, who thought the world of him, not to mention his business, which was booming. He was just an unhappy person. The death of the babies added to it. Maybe he had depression, who knows? Back then, the treatment for depression was four or five beers, one right after the other."

Harold was nothing if not paradoxical. He could have dramatic mood swings. There were days when he would walk into the house after work whistling his favorite tune, "Up a Lazy River," causing Jenna to wonder, *Who is this man?* On those days, Jenna knew he was in a good mood and she'd bask in it. He'd have a humorous story to tell about his job, and the two would laugh while sitting at the table having dinner with Laura. Jenna would serve up one of her specialties—such as a casserole of squash, green chilies, and Velveeta cheese—and, for those hours together, all would be right in their little world.

An Independent Life

Rather than dwell on trying to understand Harold's unpredictable nature, Jenna Welch decided to focus on her hobbies. For instance, she had always loved reading books, and doing so occupied a lot of her time. Laura would recall coming home from school to be "greeted by the soft rustle of book pages" and finding her mother in a corner with a good book. She loved it when Jenna read aloud to her; *Little Women* was among their favorites, which mother and daughter had started reading when Laura was about seven. They also went to the library and spent hours reading about Snow White and Pinocchio and exchanging ideas about these fantasy stories in which Jenna always found deeper meaning. Eventually, as Laura got older, they began to enjoy the writings of authors such as Somerset Maugham and John P. Marquand. Because Jenna was very nearsighted—so much so she was almost legally blind—reading close-up was more comfortable for her than looking into the distance. Laura would inherit her poor vision and, as a result, wear thick glasses from the second grade onward; she would be fitted with contact lenses when she was thirteen, but for the rest of her life she would always have severe vision problems.

Jenna also began studying naturalism at the local library, especially the area of botany. She'd spend hours there while Laura was in school and soon ended up with stacks of binders full of notes about Midland's wildflowers, every one of which she could identify. She also studied birds in all their many varieties. Soon she joined the Midland Naturalist Society, called the Mid-Nats. (The society was not named after Midland, Texas, incidentally; its origins were out of England.)

"Jenna once shared with me that she would always have a pair of binoculars handy so that she could spot a rare bird at a moment's notice," said Adair Margo. "Midland was on the migratory route of many different species. If she spotted a special bird in their backyard, oh my gosh, what a moment that would be for her. She'd then summon her fellow bird-watchers and they'd all come over to the house and file through the living room and into the breakfast nook to look out in the backyard. Everyone would jump up and down and hug each other, so excited that they'd seen this rare bird with their very own eyes. Harold would walk in and say, 'I can't believe all the fuss y'all are making over some gosh-darn bird.' And Jenna would say, '*Shhhh*, you'll scare it away.' I loved that story. Just imagine it, the simple joy of seeing a beautiful bird and how much it meant to her and her friends." Chuckling, Adair added, "She also told me that she once found a very rare bird in her backyard and the poor thing was dead. 'I didn't know what to do with it,' she told me, 'I was just so heartbroken, and I knew I couldn't leave it out there.' So she wrapped it up in some soft towels and put it in the freezer. It stayed there for a while until she or her husband buried it."

With the passing of the years, Jenna continued to look for ways to expand her horizons within the confines of her difficult marriage. Not only did she immerse herself in her books but she also became a Girl Scout leader (she was Laura's leader when the girl got her "bird badge"), a student of Bible class studies, and later a Sunday school teacher at the First United Methodist Church in Midland. Soon, she ended up taking a number of extension courses in astronomy at Midland College. She was an excellent student there and found great satisfaction in her studies. As a result, she was able to name any star in any constellation, and she was known for that for pretty much the rest of her life.

Jenna's Dream for Laura

W e're just two specks in this big universe," Jenna Welch would tell her daughter, Laura, when she was eight. On any balmy West Texas summer night, the two could be found lying on a wool blanket in their backyard, gazing up at the vastness of space. "You can have any kind of life you want," Jenna would say wistfully. She would remind her daughter that she really didn't have to stay in Midland. She could do anything, go anywhere she wanted.

While her own mother, Jessie, had encouraged Jenna to settle down, marry, and raise children in West Texas, Jenna at first fought it. She couldn't shake the feeling that there was maybe more to life than just living in a small town where everyone knew everyone else's business. Jenna had always loved reading, her imagination stimulated by literature, her view of the world expanded by it. She wanted her own daughter to have more in her life than what West Texas could offer. Or, as she told one relative, "Midland is so great. I love it here, don't get me wrong. But do I want Laura to live here for the rest of her life? I don't think so. I want her to see more, and then she can make up her mind as to where she wants to live, and maybe it will be Midland."

Laura loved it in Midland, she would tell her mother, and didn't want to go anywhere else. "I felt my greatest sense of contentment lying on the couch in our den," she recalled. "I had no desire to stray too far from home or from Mother and Daddy."

Jenna would say that the decision was all hers, as long as Laura realized that she did have a choice. Then, Jenna would point out what she thought were the best, most splendid stars—Polaris, Antares, Vega, Canopus—and even the planets, Jupiter and Venus. "The whole universe is at your fingertips, Laura," she would say dreamily. "There are no limits."

Midland Girl

From all accounts, Laura Welch was a happy child. Small and delicate, her best features were her preternaturally blue eyes, which were almost turquoise and always inquisitive. Though her father was often distracted, she didn't feel unloved by him. She relished those little pockets of affectionate time with him, such as when Harold would allow her to crawl into his lap. He would make up stories for her off the top of his head, silly little tales having to do with cowboys and Indians that suggested he had hidden imagination and humor. She would laugh and nestle up close to him as he ran his fingers through her soft hair. He really did love her, and she had no doubt about it.

Because she was an only child, she felt lonely at times, but she got used to it and found ways to compensate. Adair Margo recalled, "Laura and I often talked about how rich our childhoods were because we had been so interested in reading. She told me that when she was little her mother would pack a picnic lunch for her, and then she'd go across the street all by herself and eat while reading a book. 'Why, Laura, that sounds so sad to me,' I told her. And she said, 'Oh, no, it really wasn't, Adair. It was a great adventure. I treasured those moments so much.'

"She also told me that sometimes her mother would put her on a train; this was when she was about seven. Jenna would pack a little lunch for her and send her to El Paso to visit her grandparents. Laura would know El Paso was near when she'd see the silhouette of the Franklin Mountains in the distance. Those were the mountains her grandparents lived at the floor of, on the west side. When she got there, her grandmother would be waiting for her at the station. This was such an adventure for her, so exciting for a little girl, to be on her own like that. You could never do it today, I guess, but back then, yes, of course."

Little Laura could also be somewhat obsessive-compulsive. As an adult, she would be known by her friends as a "clean freak." No doubt, this penchant for sanitation had its roots in her childhood, when all the way through the second and into third grade at North Elementary in Midland, she would suck her thumb and be chastised by Jenna for doing so. Laura was warned that the habit provided a breeding ground for germs. Therefore, before dinner, she would scrub her hands as clean as possible and then, with both of them in the air as if she were a nurse about to go into surgery, she'd walk to the dinner table. If she so much as brushed a wall on the way, she'd quickly turn around and race back to the bathroom to wash up again. A sort of mania for cleanliness would stay with her the rest of her life.

As Laura grew up, her father's construction business continued to flourish, especially after Harold partnered with a man named Lloyd Waynick. The two purchased as many lots as they could from farmers and ranchers and then quickly built homes on them to satisfy the growing population. In time, Welch and Waynick began making strong connections with other businessmen as well as local officials. As they networked their way through the small town, they even started to fancy themselves as Midland power brokers. After building dozens of homes in the small town, they did know just about everyone, and everyone knew them. "Yeah, those two began to boss others around, acting like the local big shots" is how one former Midlander put it.

"Harold began to hang out with some pretty unsavory people," said one relative. "Once, the FBI showed up at his front door asking him questions about a bookie Harold had done business with. That really scared Jenna and Laura, but he told them not to worry about it. There was another time the police showed up asking questions. Harold told Jenna and Laura to go into the back bedroom and close the door. Who knows what that was about? There was a lot of mystery about the guy."

By the time Laura finished with second grade, the Welches moved to a bigger house built by Harold in a more upscale part of town. Even given the lack of warmth and communication in their marriage, Jenna and Harold continued to try to have more children. When Laura was eight, Jenna became pregnant again. Though due in September, she went into labor in July and, tragically, the baby died.

This latest death was almost more than Jenna could bear. So devastated was she, Harold thought it best that Laura not be around while her mother was in such a fragile emotional state. They had already planned to send her to Girl Scout summer camp—Camp Mitre Peak, outside Alpine, Texas—so the timing was right. She left about a week after Jenna lost the baby.

Laura was miserable at the camp for about a month. When she sent a letter home and it was returned (because she had misaddressed it), she got it into her head that her parents had abandoned her. Harold was right, though; it was for the best that she be away. Jenna had the worst time coming to terms with this latest loss. "She really went deep inside herself," said one Welch relative. "It was a terrible time. I think maybe the only thing that saved her was knowing that she had a daughter who loved her and couldn't wait to be picked up at the camp. Then, for the next six months, at least, Jenna had to work hard to conceal her sadness. Harold tried his best to be there for her, but he didn't know how to do it. He needed someone to be there for him. I'm not sure they could do that for one another, though, which made it all the more difficult."

Laura's Rebellion

By the time she was thirteen, Laura Welch had grown to be a lovely young girl, her dark hair framing her face and falling to her shoulders, her blue eyes no longer obstructed by large, thick glasses thanks to the recent fitting of contact lenses. She, like most of her peers, was now interested in boys, and the "Daddy Date" was the newest craze. This was the term given to a date where the boy's father drove him and his girl to the movies or wherever else they wanted to go during their time together. Laura's first "Daddy Date" was when she was thirteen with a boy who was the brother of someone who would introduce her to George Bush some twenty years later.

"Jenna told me that when Laura discovered boys, that's when things started taking a different turn at the house," recalled Adair Margo. "It was nothing unusual in that the arguments Laura started having with her parents were typical of what teenage girls have with their moms and dads. But because Laura had always been so easy, this was a new and different dynamic in the household."

At particular issue was Laura's driving. Back then, youngsters got their licenses at thirteen. Laura, though, started driving at twelve before she even had her license, sometimes sneaking out with her best friend from San Jacinto High, Regan Kimberlin (later Gammon). They would take Regan's older sister's Thunderbird or her mother's Nash Rambler and just take off, she and Regan in the front seat with maybe three other youngsters in the back. "I remember one time we had just gotten back from the drive-in movies. 'Quick, switch seats with me,' Laura told Regan," recalled one of their friends. "'If my mom sees me driving, she'll lose it.' But apparently Jenna had been looking out the front window at the time waiting for Laura to get home, and she saw her pull up. She was upset. I remember her running out the front door in her bathrobe, this little woman in big glasses, and hollering at Laura, 'You're twelve. *You're twelve.*'

"'You are not to drive until you have your license, and even then maybe not,'" Jenna told Laura, according to the source's memory.

"Mother!" Laura exclaimed, raising her voice. "You're embarrassing me in front of my friends."

"*You're* yelling at *me*?" Jenna asked. "*I don't think so.*"

"After the two went into the house with me following," recalled one of Laura's friends, "I remember her dad, Harold, saying, 'Well, Jenna, this *is* West Texas, you know? I started driving when I was ten.' Jenna said, 'Some good example *you* are,' and left the room pretty upset. So, there I was, standing alone with Hal in the kitchen. After an uncomfortable moment, he said, 'Both of them got sand in their gears, looks like,' and just shrugged his shoulders and walked out."

Though this rough patch with her parents started when Laura began to assert herself around the age of twelve she never recounted any such incidents in any of her memories of this time, even in her autobiography. "Because of some things that would happen when she was a little older, I think she always felt bad about the start of these rebellious years," said Ethan Marshall, a friend of Laura's at this time who would remain one for many years after. "She would gloss over them to the point where I think she actually began to forget them. Once, I asked her, 'Do you remember this or that . . . when we were fourteen? And she would say, 'No, Ethan. That never happened.' When she got older, she totally blocked out any unpleasantness between her and her parents." In her memoir, *Spoken from the Heart*, Laura writes, "I was a classic only child who never wanted to disappoint Mother and Daddy." Maybe from her perspective that was true, but there's ample anecdotal evidence to the contrary.

"I was sitting in the kitchen of their home having grilled cheese sand-wiches with Laura and Jenna and some other friends of ours when the topic of discussion turned to Laura's smoking," said Ethan Marshall. "Laura was adamant that she wanted to smoke even though her mother was against it. 'Don't start a war with me over this, Missy,' Jenna told her. 'You won't win it.' To my memory, Jenna never smoked, though Harold did, a lot. As mother and daughter were discussing this smoking issue, Harold came in and be-came upset because he felt Laura's dress was too short and too tight. 'Pull that dress down,' he told her. 'Dang, girl! I can see clear to the promised land.' At that, Laura ran out of the room, embarrassed in front of us, and Harold followed her, leaving us alone with Jenna. 'This is just that age, I guess,' she said, shaking her head. 'Here we go, I suppose.'"

Whereas Jenna used to spend a great deal of time with Laura as "best friends," Laura naturally now just preferred to be with her friends. Jenna understood she was going through a normal phase for a teenage girl, but it hurt just the same. Then, when after some bad decision was made by Laura, Harold would bellow, "Did you see what your daughter has done now?" Jenna would feel more alone than ever.

Where the matter of Laura's driving was concerned, Jenna didn't want the discord to continue; she decided she'd teach Laura. The two went to the Midland Cemetery and drove along its winding concrete pathways. "It was perfect because it was so empty," Laura recalled. She then studied for her written test and passed it and the driving examination when she was fourteen. Now that she had her license—and her freedom—Laura wanted to take advantage of it. She would sometimes sneak out and take Jenna's Ford Fairlane without asking permission, causing both Jenna and Harold to again wonder how things in their family had gone so off the rails so quickly.

Once, Laura and Regan snuck off in Regan's car to a place called Mr. X's on the south side of town, where neither girl was allowed to venture, just to eat fried chicken livers. They met a couple of guys who were about seven-teen and arranged a date for a later time. Somehow, Jenna and Harold found out about it. Naturally, they were upset. "What do these boys do?" Jenna asked Laura. Being flippant, Laura answered, "They drink beer, smoke cig-arettes, and fix cars in the backyard. Isn't that what everyone does around here?" Jenna couldn't believe her ears. "No, ma'am," she said. "You don't get to talk to me that way. No, ma'am, you do not." At that, Harold put his foot down and grounded Laura for a week. Laura said that was fine with her as long as her parents agreed to just leave her alone.

When Laura was about fourteen, Jenna got pregnant again. This wasn't a joyous occasion. There was a lot of fear around it given Jenna's history. Therefore, just like the last time, the doctor ordered immediate bed rest. Laura put her teenage grievances aside and did everything she could think of to make things easier on her mother, even sometimes skipping school to be available to her. It was during this time that they had a bit of a détente. Laura would crawl into bed with Jenna and the two would talk for hours, just as they used to in the backyard while staring at the heavens. As much as they were often at odds, they had never stopped loving each other. Jenna would sometimes say of Laura, "I envy her. I wish I had her spunk when I was her age." She'd say that when she was a teenager never would she have had the nerve to do some of the things Laura did; she would have been much too frightened. This didn't mean she approved of every one of Laura's decisions, it just meant she knew she was raising a headstrong girl. She also knew this temperament would bode well for Laura if she ever did decide on a life bigger than the one they all had in Midland.

Around Easter, Jenna lost the baby; it had been another boy. Like the previous tragedies, this latest one hit her hard. Rather than cry or be emotional, though, she just sort of collapsed into herself again, like the last time. Laura was gravely worried about her. "I don't think she'll get over this one," she said. Hal was also upset, especially since the loss had been another boy. He seemed to not be in any condition to help Jenna; as usual, he would sit in the backyard on his lawn chair under the stars, drink beer, and chain-smoke cigarettes late into the night.

With the environment in the household so tense, Laura couldn't wait to leave as soon as she got home from school. "Or, sometimes if it got too late, we boys would go over to her house and sneak her out her bedroom window," recalled a friend of hers named Harold Kelly. "Hard to believe it now all these years later, but yeah, I used to sneak Laura Bush out her bedroom window."

On weekends during the summer, she and her friends would lie in the sun at the Ranchland Hills Country Club, where the parents of one of their friends belonged. She would then come home late at night, again after both Jenna and Harold were asleep. Sometimes Laura would go to Regan's house and the two of them would play until Regan's mother would finally insist that Laura go home. She'd then drive back to her house, let herself in, and tiptoe past her parents' bedroom into her own. It was as if Jenna and Harold were just too distraught from the recent loss to even realize it. From all other accounts, it sounds like it was a lonely and sad time.

A Midland Life

Rather than attend Midland High after San Jacinto Junior High as she had anticipated, Laura ended up at Robert E. Lee High School, and all because the family had moved again—under the strangest of circumstances. As the story goes, one day a real estate agent showed up at their front door and offered to buy the house for a client. It wasn't even for sale. Still, Harold felt the price was a good one and couldn't be turned down. He made a deal right there on the spot to sell, without even consulting Jenna. "You did *what*?" she demanded to know, as angry as she was hurt. Years later, there would be a rumor that Harold had actually lost the house to a bookie in a gambling bet.

Jenna had no choice; she begrudgingly began to pack. Harold then made quick arrangements for the three of them to relocate to a new house.

Laura, too, was unhappy about the prospect of moving. Most of her friends were on their way to Midland High, but because the new house was out of the school district, she wouldn't be attending with them, which is how she ended up at Robert E. Lee High. It didn't seem fair.

Besides not wanting to leave her friends, the fact that the new Robert E. Lee High School was named after a Confederate commander troubled Laura. Though Laura and her friends were by no means political, they were bothered by the fact that racism existed in Midland. As in most of Texas, and indeed most of the south, the schools weren't integrated. There were still water fountains for "Whites Only" or marked "For Coloreds." At the time, Laura didn't have any black friends. But how could she? Where would she have met them? African Americans kept to themselves in their own little pockets of neighborhoods. They went to Carver High, which was all black, and it was clear that they were thought of as being "different." "If you saw a black person, there was a weird sort of wonder about it," said Ethan Marshall. "You almost didn't know what to make of him or her. While there were racists who were just out-and-out bigots, most of the racism was more subtle. It was there, though."

Laura once recalled, "At Lee, they played 'Dixie' at the football games and we were expected to sing when we heard the first chords." "Dixie" was and still is considered a minstrel song to be performed primarily by white actors in blackface. It's considered by many an anthem of the Confederacy and what the Confederacy stood for, the very reason most southern states seceded: slavery. "It bothered me," she recalled. "It bothered me from the moment I went [to Lee]."

By the time Laura was in high school, attending the weekly football games on Friday night was the dominant social activity for just about everyone in town. All of Lee's home games—most of which were against the Odessa schools, Permian High and Odessa High—were played in the cavernous new Midland Stadium, which had been built adjacent to Midland High School in 1958. The players on the football team were local heroes and their coaches practically viewed by the townsfolk as gods. "Everything in Midland—and I mean *everything in Midland*—revolved around football during the season," Laura once observed. "Football wasn't just our pastime. It was our *lives*. You might even say it was our religion."

Throughout high school, Laura continued to enjoy life in her beloved Midland. She made good grades in school, her love of reading, cultivated by her mother, a true asset to her education. While she wasn't one of the most popular girls in school, she was well-liked. She was pretty, her dark hair parted on the side with a flip, but not remarkable in her beauty or, as one of her friends put it, "She was just *any* girl."

Harvey Kennedy, a tall and lanky kid, was her first boyfriend; "a strong fart in a whirlwind would blow him right away," Harold Welch used to say of him. "I was a junior, seventeen, and she was a sophomore, sixteen," Harvey recalled. "We got together on a double date with my best friend, Todd Southern, who was dating Laura's best friend, Regan. We hit it off right away.

"Was I her first kiss? I doubt it. As kids, we all went to kissing parties, so I'm sure she'd been kissed before me. She liked taking me to recitals, upscale, classical. I enjoyed it but I wasn't an aficionado. I was a rock guy; that was okay with her. We'd get together with a bunch of kids and hang out at Luigi's Italian restaurant in downtown Midland or maybe Agnes's drive-in. I remember once we went to the house of one of my friends whose parents were out of town and we drank all of their Mogen David wine. You know, teenage stuff. I spent a lot of time at her house, had many meals there. [Harold] Welch liked to keep her close to home if he could. I got that, her being an only child. He and Jenna were protective, but she had a mind of her own, and she made sure they knew it.

"One thing about Laura was that she made it clear that she didn't like being contradicted," Harvey Kennedy recalled. "She would raise her voice and tell me, 'Do not contradict me.' I had to wonder about that. Made me wonder if she'd heard her mother say that to her father, or where the heck that came from, because she was pretty serious about it. I can still hear her saying it: *'Do not contradict me.'*"

"As she got older, she became more grown-up, more thoughtful," added Richard Pendleton, one of the Welches' neighbors. "Not the best driver, though. We fellows would be out in the front yard playing football and here would come Laura speeding around the corner on two wheels. She would drive in pretty fast and then come to a screeching halt in her driveway. It was kind of a joke we had—oh boy, here comes Laura Welch."

PART EIGHT

Laura's Crucible

Pauline Robinson Pierce with her children, James, Scott, Barbara, and Martha, 1936. (GEORGE H. W. BUSH PRESIDENTIAL LIBRARY AND MUSEUM)

Dorothy Walker Bush at the age of fourteen, 1915. (GEORGE H. W. BUSH PRESIDENTIAL LIBRARY AND MUSEUM)

Barbara Pierce (*middle*) with her parents, Marvin and Pauline, on her wedding day, January 6, 1945. (GEORGE H. W. BUSH PRESIDENTIAL LIBRARY AND MUSEUM)

Barbara with her groom, George Herbert Walker Bush (*left*), and his parents, Prescott and Dorothy. (George H. W. Bush Presidential Library and Museum)

Pauline Robinson Pierce with her first grandson, George Walker Bush, in 1946. (George H. W. Bush Presidential Library and Museum)

Barbara and little George W. in 1947. (George H. W. Bush Presidential Library and Museum)

George H.W. and Barbara pose with their children George and Robin at the rodeo grounds in Midland, Texas, in October 1950. (George H. W. Bush Presidential Library and Museum)

Barbara with daughter Robin, who would tragically die of leukemia at just three years old. (GEORGE H. W. BUSH PRESIDENTIAL LIBRARY AND MUSEUM)

Dorothy and son George H.W. pose with little Robin and George W., in April 1953. Robin would be gone in six months' time. (GEORGE H. W. BUSH PRESIDENTIAL LIBRARY AND MUSEUM)

Dorothy and her grandson John Ellis Bush, aka Jeb. (GEORGE H. W. BUSH PRESIDENTIAL LIBRARY AND MUSEUM)

Barbara, Dorothy, and Prescott with (*left to right*) Neil, Doro, Jeb, and George. (GEORGE H. W. BUSH PRESIDENTIAL LIBRARY AND MUSEUM)

The woman behind the man: Dorothy and her husband, Senator Prescott Bush. (GEORGE H. W. BUSH PRESIDENTIAL LIBRARY AND MUSEUM)

Harold and Jenna Welch, shortly after their marriage in January 1944. In two years' time, they would welcome a daughter, Laura Lane Welch. (GEORGE H. W. BUSH PRESIDENTIAL LIBRARY AND MUSEUM)

Laura Welch's graduation picture from Robert E. Lee High School in Midland, taken in 1963, the same year as the tragic accident that would change her life. (GEORGE W. BUSH PRESIDENTIAL LIBRARY AND MUSEUM)

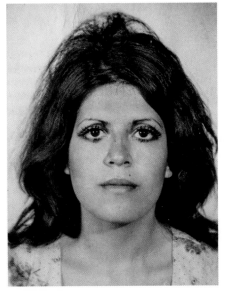

Columba Bush, at eighteen, a couple years before marrying into the Bush family as Jeb's wife. (RETRO-PHOTO)

Congressman George Bush and Barbara Bush pose with their children in front of the United States Capitol in Washington in 1966. *Left to right:* Doro, Marvin, Neil, Jeb, and George. (GEORGE H. W. BUSH PRESIDENTIAL LIBRARY AND MUSEUM)

Left to right: Dorothy Walker Bush and her son George H. W. Bush, along with Barbara Bush and her son George W. Bush and daughter-in-law, Laura Bush, together on George and Laura's wedding day, November 5, 1977. (GEORGE H. W. BUSH PRESIDENTIAL LIBRARY AND MUSEUM)

Christmas 1979 with the Bush family. *Left to right, back row:* Doro, George H.W., Barbara, Columba, Laura, and George W. *Front row:* Marvin, Noelle (Jeb and Columba's daughter), Jeb, George P. (Jeb and Columba's son), and Neil. (GEORGE H. W. BUSH PRESIDENTIAL LIBRARY AND MUSEUM)

Barbara would endure Jennifer Fitzgerald's involvement in her marriage to George for more years than she would care to remember. Barbara is behind George in this photo, Jennifer sitting next to him. (WALLY McNAMEE/CORBIS/ CORBIS VIA GETTY IMAGES)

George H.W. announces his run for the presidency on May 1, 1979, at the National Press Club with his family joining him on-stage. He would go on to lose to Ronald Reagan in the primaries. *Left to right:* Jeb, Columba, Marvin, Margaret, George H.W., Barbara, Dorothy, Laura, and George W. (GETTY IMAGES)

George and his mother, Dorothy, share a moment during his second presidential campaign in Miami, Florida, in March 1988. (GEORGE H. W. BUSH PRESIDENTIAL LIBRARY AND MUSEUM)

It was when she moved into 1 Observatory Circle as the wife of the VP that Barbara had the greatest of epiphanies about her life… and her marriage. Here she is in that great home on April 6, 1981. (PHOTO BY VIRGINIA MADISON)

When Jeb Bush announced his candidacy for the 2016 Republican presidential nomination at Miami Dade College on June 15, 2015, his wife, Columba, and mother, Barbara, were fully in support even though Barbara did have her doubts. (UPI/ALAMY)

Barbara Bush would die on April 17, 2018, followed by her husband of seventy-three years, George, on November 30, 2018. She was ninety-two; he was ninety-four. (GEORGE H. W. BUSH PRESIDENTIAL LIBRARY AND MUSEUM)

Even after two difficult terms as President and First Lady, the bond between George and Laura never once weakened; theirs has been an incredible marriage. Here they are at their ranch in Crawford, Texas. (GEORGE H. W. BUSH PRESIDENTIAL LIBRARY AND MUSEUM)

A Tragic Accident

November 6, 1963. It only takes a second for a person's entire life to change, as young Laura Welch, who had just turned seventeen two days earlier, would discover while driving with her friend Judy Dykes along a dark, backwoods country road in Midland. Judy and Laura had known each other for almost two years; they'd met just before their junior year, both in the same English class at Robert E. Lee. Their fathers had known each other from back in their Lubbock days; Harold later built the Dykeses' home in Midland.

Laura might not have been the best driver, but her real problem was her poor eyesight. On this Wednesday night in November, Laura was behind the wheel of a Chevrolet Impala owned by her parents with Judy in the passenger seat. Thursday was to be a school holiday, so the girls were out enjoying themselves with no concern about having to wake up on time the next morning. They were headed to a drive-in movie and, on the way, found themselves on a dark and dusty road. Though this was a place outsiders might call "the middle of nowhere," to Laura and Judy it was just a thoroughfare on the outskirts of town. They knew where they were; they weren't lost. Sometimes kids would race their cars on this very same street because it was so isolated, but it was also very dark.

As Laura approached the intersection of Farm Road 868 and State

Highway 346, Judy noticed a stop sign. It was off to the side of the road in a field about twenty feet to the right of the vehicle, certainly not entirely visible. Laura didn't seem to see it. "Laura," Judy said, her tone even, "there's a stop sign right there." Years later Judy recalled, "It was like it just came out of nowhere. Suddenly there it was. I remember purposely trying not to scare Laura by shouting out. She didn't stop, or maybe couldn't stop."

Laura kept on going, her Impala sailing right through the intersection. It smashed right into the side of a 1962 Corvair Monza sedan, a popular compact sports car that was all but dwarfed by the much larger Impala. The horrible sound of crushing metal and glass shattering all around them would haunt both young women for the rest of their lives. There wasn't even enough time for them to scream out. Seat belts were not required in vehicles at this time. Judy was shoved down into the footwell. "I think I bent my knees, which kept me from just flying through the windshield," she recalled. Disoriented and frightened, she heard a small voice in the distance calling out her name. It was Laura.

Laura was thrown from the car, violently thrust through the driver's-side door, which had been jarred open during the tumult. The force of the impact was so powerful that she was thrown clear of the car and onto the ground beside the road. She later had no memory of landing. Judy's recollection was also always spotty; "some things are vivid," she later said, "some things are not."

As if in slow motion, the scene played itself out in bits and pieces: the sounds of anxious people running . . . the wails of approaching sirens . . . the sobs of one woman and the screams of another. As Laura slowly came to consciousness, she felt arms enfolding her, a person who had happened by and was now attempting to comfort her. Someone else was doing the same to Judy, who was now sitting on the curb next to Laura. "I saw what I thought was maybe a body laying on the ground in the distance," Judy recalled. "And I was staring at it thinking, is it a body? Or . . . what is it?"

Out of the corner of her eye, Laura noticed a man she knew, Bill Douglas, the father of a good friend of hers named Mike. He seemed upset as he paced in front of the crushed car she'd hit. He then leaned over a heap in the middle of the road, something Laura wasn't able to make out. Was it an animal? A dog, perhaps? Like Judy, she squinted, trying to make out what was before her, but she couldn't.

"I think that man is maybe the father of whoever was in the other car," Judy offered.

"No," Laura said, shaking her head. "That's Bill Douglas, Mike's dad. But what's he doing here?"

The only thought Laura recalls having as she was being loaded onto an ambulance was a desperate prayer: *Please God. Please keep the other person alive.*

For the rest of her life, the next hour or so would remain a confusing jumble in Laura's mind. However, she does remember being in the emergency room waiting to be stitched up by a doctor when, from the other side of a thin curtain, she heard the sound of a woman talking. Laura recognized the voice. Her heart tightened and the woman then began to sob hysterically. It was Jane Douglas, the mother of her good friend Mike.

No More Laura Welch

The night of the accident, a dazed Laura Welch lay in her bed at home while a steady stream of school friends wandered in and out of her bedroom to check on her. After a few hours, she'd been released from the hospital with bruises and contusions on her face and a deep cut on her knee. It was surprising that she hadn't been killed considering the way she was thrown from the car. "Don't tell her anything," Jenna said to her daughter's friend Regan Kimberlin when she arrived. Harold added, "She doesn't know it was Mike."

Everyone liked Michael Dutton Douglas, a young, good-looking kid who was just seventeen, like Laura. He had short-cropped dark hair, big ears, and a great smile. One of the star football players in Midland, he was funny and full of personality with a memorable boyish, gap-toothed smile.

"He was my best friend," said Midland's Benjamin "Ben" Franklin of Mike Douglas, "a heck of an all-around guy. We'd known each other since junior high. We played sports together, hunted, camped, fished. He was smart and interesting. Mike and his parents, Bill and Jane, lived outside of Midland on a little farm on Solomon Lane. Bill was in the oil business, but in the service industry aspect of it, a salesman for oil field chemicals."

Mike and Laura had been good friends all through high school, often spending hours on the telephone late into the night. She had been a passenger in his car many times over the years. People have claimed they'd even dated, but Ben Franklin says that wasn't the case. "I knew who he dated," he says, "and it was never Laura. They were just friends. Actually, at the time of his death, he was dating her friend Peggy Weiss. He was on his way to a date with her at the time of the crash. He'd once also dated Regan Kimberlin."

Ben Franklin was at a local drive-in movie with his girlfriend, Karen Fury, when his brother, John, tracked him down. He tapped on the window of his Volkswagen. "Mike Douglas is dead," he shouted out, upset. Ben couldn't comprehend it. John repeated: "Mike! *Mike is dead.*" Shocked, Ben immediately took Karen home and then drove over to the Douglases'.

"Mike's death was nothing more than a cruel twist of fate; he was just in the wrong place at the wrong time," said Ben Franklin. "Making matters worse, his father, Bill, came upon the accident shortly after it happened. Bill had been following him at a distance in his own car. He was on his way to see his nephew, his sister's baby who suffered from a disability. So, yeah, he saw the wreckage and realized it was Mike's car. He was with his kid when they took him to the hospital with a broken neck, but Mike was already gone.

"Once I got to the Douglas home, I saw that there were a lot of people there consoling Bill. I believe Jane was at the hospital. Bill told me Mike had been hit by two girls who may have been drinking. That was the word, anyway. He said he didn't know who they were. He figured maybe they were driving sixty or seventy miles per hour to have T-boned Mike like that and caused so much damage." (The speed Laura was traveling was illegible on the two-page police report, though some have suggested it was noted as fifty miles per hour, which was five miles slower than the speed limit. Also, there was never any finding that Laura was drinking, and she has made clear that she was not.)

"Just as I was leaving the house," Ben Franklin continued, "someone whispered in my ear that it had been Laura Welch and Judy Dykes in the car. I was shocked. I thought to myself, 'Holy shit. *Holy shit.*'"

While Laura was being treated at Midland Memorial, Judy Dykes telephoned her parents to tell them what had happened. They, in turn, contacted Harold and Jenna Welch, who immediately came to the hospital. Within about four hours, both girls were released, Judy with a sprained back, Laura with a deep cut to her knee and other contusions.

"I went to the house and there were a lot of people there," recalled Ben Franklin, "about a dozen of us gathered around Laura, who was in bed. I asked her, 'What happened, Laura? What the heck happened?' She was dazed and not able to talk about it."

Apparently, Laura did talk to her friend Regan after everyone else had left the room. "I'm so worried about the person in the car I hit," she told her, according to her own memory. "I hope he or she is okay." But according to her later account, she was already certain the victim had been Mike. She just didn't want to believe it. Not sure how to respond, Regan tried to calm her friend while also not giving her any information, which left, as Laura recalled it, "this horrible, unspoken truth hovering in the air."

After Regan departed, Harold and Jenna went into Laura's room to confirm that the victim had been Mike Douglas. Not much is known about this difficult conversation; the three never spoke openly about it.

By this time, Laura had amicably broken up with her first boyfriend, Harvey Kennedy, now a student at University of Texas at El Paso. "At UTEP, I got a call from Regan telling me that Laura had been in a horrible car accident," he remembered. "She asked me to go and see her. Of course, I wanted to. I hightailed it to her parents' home right away, and they showed me to Laura's bedroom. She was bedridden and in disbelief. 'Mike was a lifelong friend of mine,' she told me, crying. She was devastated. I was just a kid, what could I say? I certainly wasn't prepared for this kind of thing. I sat with her, held her hand, tried to comfort her as best I could. Right after, I went to Judy Dykes's house and we two tried to process things. We were worried about Laura. 'How in the world does a person ever get past a thing like this?' I asked Judy. We just didn't know."

The next day, the headline on the front page of *The Odessa American* had to do with Nelson Rockefeller formally announcing his candidacy for the Republican presidential nomination, challenging Senator Barry Goldwater. Directly below it was another headline: "Midland Boy Dies in Crash—2 Teen Girls Injured." The article referred to the accident as "a grinding two-car crash." It said that Mike Douglas had been alive at the scene but that he died in an ambulance en route to Midland Memorial. It noted that he had been "voted 'Most Popular Boy' of his junior high class and was recently nominated as a candidate for the 'Mr. Howdy' award at school." It added that "injured in the wreck were Laura Lane Welch, 17, and Judy Dykes, 17" and confirmed that it had been Laura who was driving. "Douglas was lying on the pavement near his wrecked auto when police arrived at the scene," it read. "However, officers were unable to say whether he was tossed from the car or was removed by a passerby."

Someone had brought the *Odessa American* newspaper to the Welches' home that morning; they'd never know who, but it would have to have been one of the many visitors. It was neatly folded on the kitchen table. When she saw the story on its front page, Jenna had to steady herself. She and Harold couldn't believe their eyes. It was as if the headline somehow made the tragedy more real to them. They immediately decided they had to visit Mike's parents, Bill and Jane. The Welches found the Douglases in shock, as were Mike's sister and other relatives. According to one of those family members present, Jenna took Jane in her arms and held her for a long time while Harold spoke in a sorrowful voice to Bill.

The funeral was to be held on Saturday, November 9, at St. Mark's Methodist Church in Midland. Mike would be buried in Austin later that day. Two of Laura's friends recall being at the Welch household and sitting at the kitchen table with her and her parents as they discussed the services. "What time should we leave?" Laura wanted to know. Jenna glanced nervously at Harold. He then said that he and Jenna had discussed it and decided that Laura would *not* be going to the funeral. Laura protested and said she felt she had an obligation to go. At that point, Jenna got up and stood behind her daughter, placing both her hands on her narrow shoulders for support. "Look here, Laura, you need to stay as far away from the Douglases as you can, you hear me?" Harold said. They didn't yet know whether the Douglases would press charges or file a lawsuit. He didn't want Laura around any of them until he knew for certain what would happen next. At that point, according to the witnesses, Laura began to weep.

"Should I at least call the Douglases?" Laura asked. No, her father told her.

In the end, Laura did what she was told: She didn't go with her parents to the funeral and she never contacted the Douglases. Judy Dykes also didn't attend the funeral. Laura, traumatized and confused, felt powerless to disobey her parents. As she got older, though, she would always regret not having extended her sympathies to the family. She'd also feel ashamed. She probably should have seen a therapist to help her cope. "But this was West Texas in 1963," observed Judy Dykes. "You didn't go to a psychiatrist. You just never talked about it, that's how you dealt with these things. Laura suppressed it, as did I. I don't think we two ever spoke about it again, not in detail, anyway. We may have alluded to it from time to time as 'the accident,' but that was it. It was too painful.

"Two weeks later, JFK was assassinated in Dallas, and then that became the thing we talked about. That became our focus, not Mike."

For the next couple of weeks, Jeanie Pendleton (now Bohn), who lived across the street, brought Laura her homework assignments so that she wouldn't fall behind at school. "I just tried to keep her spirits up," she recalled. "I knew she would get through it. She had a resolve about her. I remember thinking, 'Okay, this is awful for her, but somehow I think she'll survive it.'"

After almost two weeks, Laura went back to school. She found that she wasn't ostracized by her friends; they rallied around her. While there were memorials as Mike's friends grieved for him, they tried not to bring him up in Laura's presence.

Laura had changed. She no longer wanted to go out with friends after school; she just wanted to stay in her bedroom with the door closed. She would also admit, many years later, that she'd lost her faith. She said that before she knew it was Mike who'd been killed, she'd prayed harder than she'd ever prayed before for the victim to survive. However, that prayer had gone unanswered. It would be many years before she would come to terms with the God she believed had abandoned her when she needed Him the most.

Within about a month, a grieving Jane Douglas began calling Jenna and, according to Richard Pendleton, Jeanie's brother, "haranguing her, telephoning her in the middle of the night, crying out, 'Your daughter killed my son. Your daughter killed my son.' That was horrible. Jenna was such a sweet, gentle woman."

Harold was consumed with worry that the Douglases might file litigation or, worse yet, that the authorities might file charges against Laura. "Hell yeah, the Douglases wanted to file a lawsuit," recalled Ben Franklin. "But not for money. For answers. Every time they asked the Department of Public Safety for answers or for records, they kept getting the runaround. They kept hearing that Harold Welch was working behind the scenes to make sure the lid was kept tight on this thing.

"I remember hearing my parents talk about it and my dad saying he'd had some conversations with Harold and that he and Jenna were worried about a lawsuit and how they'd ever be able to afford one. My dad was president of three local banks at this time, and Harold was trying to figure out how to get some money. I remember my father saying, 'My God, this is very serious for the Welches. It's going to be a big financial blow to them.'"

Jane's calls shook Harold profoundly. "The accident had a big impact on him, for sure," said one relative. "They'd had tragedy in their lives, the loss of their children. But this was just so awful. It caused Harold to become very protective of Jenna and Laura. You had to go through him to get to them. We saw a real change in the way he treated both."

People who knew Harold well back then insist he used his connections with the local police department to make sure no charges were filed against Laura. She wasn't even ticketed for running the stop sign. Had she even been given a sobriety test at the scene of the accident? Laura has never said so one way or the other. If so, the results vanished. "How is it that she didn't even get charged with manslaughter or reckless driving?" asked Harold Kelly. "Don't get me wrong. We all liked Laura and no one wanted to see her punished. But still, we had to admit it was a little strange."

"Harold did have a lot of influence," said Ben Franklin, "so much so that I believe the original police records having to do with the accident were expunged at his hand. I believe this because Mike's father, Bill, told me so. In my opinion, knowing Welch and growing up in Midland, it felt like a cover-up."

Some people also insist that Harold paid the Douglases a monetary settlement. "I did what I had to do for my family" is all he would say when asked about it by a cousin. Whatever he did—if anything at all—it worked. The calls from Jane to Jenna stopped. There was no litigation. There were no charges.

In the months after the accident, Jenna and Harold encouraged Laura to continue to be active in school in clubs like the Student and Junior Councils and the Physiology Club, but it was clear to them that she was just going through the motions. Mike's death would have lasting repercussions on Laura.

"You can look at Laura's life in two parts: before the accident and after the accident," concluded Richard Pendleton. "Before? Screeching around the corner in her car and jumping out with her schoolbooks in her arms, smiling and waving at me and hollering out, 'Hi, Richie.' After? No more driving. Her mom and dad would drive, or a friend would drop her off and she would get out of the car wearing a head scarf with big sunglasses like Jackie Kennedy, looking down at the ground. No more 'Hi, Richie.' It was so sad. I thought to myself, *Oh man. No more Laura Welch.*"

A Chilling Experience

After Mike's death, Laura clung to some of the friends they had in common. For a time, she and Mike's best friend, Ben Franklin, remained close. But it proved difficult. Whereas Laura was trying to figure out how to move on, Ben, who'd been a pallbearer at Mike's funeral, sought closure for himself and for the Douglas family.

One weekend evening, Laura and some friends, including Ben Franklin, were tooling around Midland. As the friends drove toward the outskirts of town, Ben whispered to the driver to take a turn. It was pitch-black, no streetlights. Before anyone in the car realized where they were, they were parked on Solomon Road across the street from the Douglases' farm, about a mile from where the accident had taken place. Ben turned around to face Laura, who was in the backseat with two female friends. "Okay, look, I want you to go with me across the street to see Mike's parents," he told her. "I'll be right there with you. You need to apologize to them, Laura. You need closure, and they need it, too. This is the moment, Laura. You will always remember this moment."

Completely taken aback, Laura began to cry. The other two girls began to protest.

After a few moments, a frustrated Ben got out of the car and ran up to the farm, about fifty feet from the road. He knocked on the door; Mike's mother,

Jane, answered. Ben told her he had someone in the car down the road who wanted to speak to her, and he just wanted to make sure she was home. "Would you maybe come to the car and talk to her?" he asked. She said yes. He then told her to wait and he'd return to get her. He turned around and ran back down to the vehicle while Jane stood by the door, inside the house.

By the time Ben got back, Laura was so upset she couldn't seem to speak. She clenched her hands together in her lap as if trying to get ahold of herself. Looking trapped, she said in the smallest of voices that she wanted to be driven home, immediately. "Look, Laura, you've taken somebody's life," Ben told her. "It was an accident. But don't you think you might want to at least tell his mother how sorry you are? You need to do this." He said Jane Douglas was willing to come down to the car. All Laura had to do was get out and talk to her.

By this time, the other two girls sitting in the backseat with Laura were also crying while vehemently protesting. Ben realized he'd probably taken things too far and it wasn't going to work out the way he had hoped. He got out of the car, walked back up to the farm where Mike's mother was still waiting, and told her, "Never mind. Sorry to bother you." He left her confused and standing in her doorway. "Then I went back down to the car," he recalled. "We turned around and took Laura home, dropping her off at her house.

"She was angry and hurt, as was I. That was it for our friendship, too. I think she realized it was impossible for her to have many of Mike's friends in her life, and some of us couldn't have her in ours, either. It was too painful.

"I look back on all of this now, more than fifty years later, and I think, okay, well, that had to have been very traumatizing for that poor girl," concluded Ben Franklin. "Maybe I could have handled it better. But at eighteen, what do you know? We were all just kids trying to sort it out.

"I still feel that Laura should have talked to Jane Douglas, though. I'm sorry, but I will always feel that way, and I'll bet Laura, today, agrees."

Trying to Find Her Way

By the summer of 1964, Laura Welch, about to graduate from high school, was still in a state of deep despair. It would seem, at least based on the recollections of close friends and family members, that she was experiencing post-traumatic stress disorder. "She had a dazed quality about her," said Richard Pendleton. "She was distant, disengaged, nervous, with the slightest sound behind her making her jump. In the Robert E. Lee yearbook, she was designated as the girl with the best smile, which seemed ironic because her smile was gone."

During this time, Laura made the decision to attend the conservative Southern Methodist University in Dallas. Prior to her acceptance, mother and daughter took the trip to Dallas to tour the school, which gave them an opportunity to have some time to themselves. Jenna would later remember exploring the campus and feeling relieved that Laura was getting out of Midland.

Laura began attending the university in September, majoring in education. Laura's enrollment gave her the opportunity to live on campus in a sorority house after pledging to Kappa Alpha Theta. She stayed in the background for the most part, had a small circle of close friends.

While at college, Laura began dating her old friend Ethan Marshall from Midland. Ethan noticed that Laura seemed to wear only the colors blue and gray, sometimes black. "She never wore colorful clothing," he recalled. "I was once in her room and the closet was opened and I noticed all of the same colors—blue, gray, black—and everything was hanging in a way that was color coordinated. I figured this was how she kept control in her life, nothing left to chance. She always had the same things when she ate, a chicken salad sandwich, a cup of coffee . . . the same Danish. She had a large era-appropriate microwave oven in the kitchen in which she would cook the same frozen dinner every night. Nothing was left to chance, everything the same."

Shortly after she graduated from college in 1968, Laura began teaching third grade in Dallas. "I walked to that school," she told biographer Ann Gerhart. "It was an older neighborhood, and the children there went to private school. They bused in my children from around Parkland Hospital. It was a predominantly African-American school, and it was a really good school. . . . My favorite part was the reading. After lunch, I would read stories to them. . . . And they had a really great time, and I did, too."

After about a year, Laura moved to Houston because she was feeling lonely. She ended up teaching at John F. Kennedy Elementary School, which was also mostly African American. "She hadn't been exposed to any black culture in Midland, and I felt she was drawn to it for that reason," said Ethan Marshall. "She taught second, third, and fourth grades at JFK. It was hard work. A lot of the kids had problems and were disadvantaged."

Laura moved to a large apartment complex with six swimming pools called the Chateaux Dijon and began dating Jimmy McCarroll, a Houston stockbroker with the Eastman Dillon firm. He was four years her senior. He and Laura often enjoyed lively debates about politics. "She was liberal," he recalled. "I was conservative. So we had some pretty good arguments. She would get frustrated with me, for sure.

"The closest she ever came to opening up to me was when she once said, 'Something happened to me that was supposed to be life changing. But nothing changed.' I was intrigued and tried to push a little. 'What do you mean?' I asked her. 'Oh, never mind,' she said. 'It's not worth it.'"

After teaching for a year, Laura decided to go to graduate school at the University of Texas and get her master's degree in library science. Jenna had mixed feelings about it. She felt Laura was retreating into a world of children and books in order to maybe avoid committing to a future. She would often say, "Acting like you're healing isn't the same as actually healing. I just want you to push away the pain," she would tell her, "and replace it with something good."

After she got her graduate degree in 1972, Laura started working as a librarian in the McCrane-Kashmere Gardens Library in Houston. She soon moved to Austin, where her friend Regan now lived with her new husband. There, she ended up employed by the library of the Mollie Dawson Elementary School, in a run-down barrio neighborhood in the southeast part of town. "She was drawn to working with the underprivileged," said one friend of hers. "The neighborhood was tough. It wasn't an easy place to live, and none of us could figure out why Laura wanted to work there. I asked her, 'Laura, why there? I mean, it's so hard. And she said, 'Because they need me.'"

"A librarian in a run-down school in a terrible part of Austin" is how Jenna viewed Laura's choice in life at this time. Therefore, Laura decided to invite her to the school so she could see for herself that her work there was important.

On the day Jenna arrived in Austin, she and Laura went to lunch at a popular diner in East Austin called Cisco's on East Sixth Street. It wasn't a fancy place, more like a greasy spoon, but its Tex-Mex food was top-notch—still is today. They were accompanied by MaryAnn Colton, who had occasionally worked as a substitute teacher at Dawson and had become friends with Laura. "Laura asked me to join them because, I believed, she was anxious about being alone with Mrs. Welch," MaryAnn recalled. "She had a sense her mother wasn't very happy about things. She was right."

"Laura, I just don't think where you're living and working is the place for you," Jenna said as she picked at her *migas*, a dish made with crushed tortilla chips, scrambled eggs, tomatoes, chilies, onions, and cheese. She said that if only Laura had a man in her life about whom she was serious, she—Jenna—would be able to relax knowing someone was looking out for her. Instead, she was "hiding away in a library in a bad part of town, all by your lonesome."

"Mrs. Welch had this sort of frozen smile on her face as she spoke," MaryAnn recalled, "as if she was determined to keep things as light as possible. Laura sighed and said something like, 'Oh my God. You just want me to get married and settle down, don't you?' Jenna became flustered. She felt Laura was being unfair. She reminded her that from the time she was a little girl she'd been telling her that she could do or be anything she wanted, anywhere she wanted, with no limitations. All she was now saying was that she and Laura's dad were worried about her. 'Is that so wrong?' she asked. Then she turned to me and said, 'Is that so wrong?' Finally, Laura very gently said, 'Okay, Mother, I get it. I understand.' She reached out and placed her hand on top of Jenna's. 'So, how's Daddy?' she asked, changing the subject. 'No change there,' Jenna answered."

Jenna then spent the rest of the day with Laura as her daughter worked with underprivileged kids in the library. Jenna began to see that Laura's job was actually influencing young people and coaxing them into a relationship with books. How could Jenna argue with that?

"Mrs. Welch was impressed," said MaryAnn Colton. "I saw her before she left, and she told me and a friend I happened to be with, 'You know, all I ever wanted was to give her the perfect childhood.' She told us she never tried to push her into marriage. She was still a little hurt by that comment. I told her not to let it bother her. Laura loved her so much. She smiled and—I'll never forget it—she said, 'Well, there's nothing wrong with sharp elbows. I raised her to think for herself, you know?' Then she wrote her number on a sliver of paper. 'Call me if you think my little girl ever needs me,' she told me, and with that she was off. As she walked away, I thought, *Wow, now, that's a pretty great mom.*"

PART NINE

Long Days and Short Years

Bush Family Matters

By the end of the 1950s, things were moving very quickly for the Bush family due to the good fortune of George H.W.'s company, Zapata, finally striking oil at Jameson Field in Coke County. Never again would he and Barbara face financial difficulties. He later wrote, "It was my big break in the business world and the thing that permitted me to finance our kids' education and gave me the financial base to risk going into public life." In all, he would only be in the offshore drilling business for less than a decade (though he would have substantial and lucrative interests in the oil business for many years to come). Oil would definitely pay off big-time for George H.W.

Despite their good fortune, Barbara couldn't shake the sadness she still felt about Robin's death. Her mother-in-law, Dorothy, couldn't help but notice it every time they were together, which wasn't as often as she would've liked. Dorothy thought of Barbara as a daughter and just wished she didn't live so far away. "Lucky, lucky are mothers who have their daughters nearby," she once wrote.

At times, Dorothy even publicly lamented not being closer to Barbara. "If we have been short-changed in visits by any one member of the family, it is by our daughter-in-law Barbara," she wrote in her column at the end of 1956. "I remember so well last summer when she flew right over us coming and going to Maine for a 10-day vacation without stopping at all! At that time, the Senator wrote her: 'All right for you, Barbara, if you won't come and see us, we will come and see you.' And we did at Thanksgiving go to Midland. Maybe that was too much, though."

By this time, Barbara and George's two boys, George and Jeb, were joined by Neil, born in 1955, and Marvin, in 1956. Perhaps Barbara had felt overwhelmed during that holiday dinner. Dorothy wrote that she'd been "so remote," she fretted that she and Prescott had inconvenienced her with their visit. Also, Barbara seemed to not be very interested in anything having to do with politics, which Dorothy found off-putting. Of course, because it had taken her time to warm up to politics, she understood. She'd grown a great deal since Prescott became a senator, though, and lately had been talking to her relatives about the political landscape in Washington with great enthusiasm. Therefore, determined to not only forge a better relationship with her but also maybe expose her to her world, Dorothy invited Barbara to spend a couple of days with her, without George and the boys, in January 1957.

Dorothy didn't waste a moment. As soon as Barbara showed up at her door on Monday morning, January 19, "we were off to the races," she recalled. Indeed, Barbara hadn't even unpacked her bags when Dorothy whisked her off to the Pan-American Union for the first of a series of meetings held by the new Secretary General, Jose Antonio Mora Otero, to promote better understanding among the countries of the Western Hemisphere. The speaker that day was Dr. Milton Eisenhower, brother of President Eisenhower, who was introduced by Vice President Richard Nixon. "He pleaded for greater friendship between our peoples," Dorothy recalled of Eisenhower, "the establishment of the common market on the South American continent, and investment of more U.S private capital to augment our government investments. It was inspired, and I turned to look at Barbara and she seemed transfixed."

That night, the Japanese ambassador to the United States, Koichiro Asakai, hosted a dinner for the secretary of defense, Neil Hosler McElroy, and his wife, Camille. Though Dorothy and Prescott had accepted the invitation a month earlier, Dorothy couldn't bear the idea of going off and leaving Barbara. Therefore she called to see if perhaps Barbara could take her place at Prescott's side. However, Asakai suggested that Barbara tag along. "We were then thrilled to have Barbara have the experience of dining at one of the big embassies and of meeting two such charming representatives of their country as Ambassador and Mrs. Asakai," Dorothy wrote, "both of whom speak beautiful English."

On Tuesday, President Arturo Frondizi of Argentina addressed a joint session of Congress, and Dorothy took Barbara to the Capitol to witness it. Then, on Wednesday, they attended opening arguments of a session of the Supreme Court. This was thrilling for Barbara. Though she'd been on tours of both the Capitol and the Supreme Court Building, this was the first time she'd ever attended any official sessions. She was impressed.

On Wednesday, Dorothy took Barbara to the Smithsonian National Museum of Natural History and then to lunch at Martin's Tavern, one of Georgetown's oldest family restaurants. They were joined there by Dorothy's friend Kay Summersby, who had been Major General Dwight Eisenhower's personal secretary during the war. There had always been rumors that the two had had an affair, though Summersby was now married to a Wall Street stockbroker. It was an enticing story, though. Barbara and Dorothy couldn't help but spend, as Dorothy put it, "many hours speculating about something we knew was likely just idle gossip."

On Wednesday night, George showed up from Texas. That evening, Dorothy and Prescott invited four of his classmates from Yale, including Lud Ashley and Billy Moorhead, both of whom were in the Democratic majority of the House, to their home for a steak dinner.

By the time Barbara left on Thursday morning with her husband, Dorothy felt the brief visit had been a great success. "I can't remember any four days that were more fun for me in Washington," Dorothy later recalled.

Barbara had to agree. On January 25, she wrote to her mother-in-law that the experiences they shared had broadened her thinking where politics were concerned. "As you know, I have never been much for politics," she wrote, "but I see now that there is so much I don't know and so much I, as an American citizen, should know." She thanked Dorothy for opening her up to new thoughts and ideas and said she would never forget the visit. She concluded that she would love to host her and Prescott again next Thanksgiving, "and this time I won't be so jittery."

Another thing that impressed Barbara about her mother-in-law was her attention to detail as she took copious notes about every experience they enjoyed, which she would later use to write her columns. For instance, Dorothy would always ask for the spelling of people's names and wanted to make sure she completely understood the political ramifications of everything she would eventually report. Barbara later said she had no idea how much work went into Dorothy's columns. She was impressed. Indeed, Dorothy Walker Bush *was* impressive.

In 1959, when Zapata Off-Shore split from Zapata Petroleum Company, George H. W. Bush took over the Off-Shore company, and the family prepared to move from Midland to Houston. At this same time, they were overjoyed when a daughter came into their world. Dorothy—known as Doro—was born on August 18, 1959, now six years after Robin's death.

While Barbara was overjoyed to have a little girl again, there was also something frightening about it. Gazing at the infant in her bassinet, she couldn't help but wonder about the fate of her newborn. Also, at this same time, she sank into another depression over leaving Midland.

Barbara loved Midland. Her friends were there—her *life* was there. She would get up in the middle of the night feeling nauseated about leaving and vomit in the bathroom. "Then don't go, Bar," Dorothy told her, even though she had to know this wasn't realistic advice. Dorothy had never believed her daughter-in-law should suffer in silence. However, she wasn't about to get in the middle of their marriage—especially when Barbara defended it, saying "We're complicated." At any rate, the die had been cast, and the Bushes left Midland for Houston.

Distraught and at her wit's end with five children, one of whom was an infant, Barbara needed help, especially when the family's longtime housekeeper had to leave. Barbara was about to contact an employment agency when she saw an ad in the paper soliciting work, and she answered it. This was when Paula Rendon came into her life.

Consuela Diaz, one of Paula Rendon's cousins, recalled, "Paula arrived at the Bush home in Houston from Mexico. She had been abandoned by her husband and left with three children. It had been everything she could muster to come to America with three little kids and start a new life. When Mrs. Bush met her, she was impressed partly because she figured out pretty fast that Paula had nerve. Paula, who was stout and not even five feet tall, was much smaller than Barbara. Still, she wasn't intimidated by her. 'I do things my way,' she told Mrs. Bush at the job interview. Her English was very bad, but she still managed to communicate. Basically, she said she had a way that worked and that if she was allowed to do things her way she would be happy to work for the Bushes. It was almost as if she was doing them a favor, and Mrs. Bush liked her moxie. She hired her right away. Paula would end up staying with the Bushes for fifty years."

"Paula is like a second mother to us," Doro Bush confirmed. "She took over when my mother was busy helping my dad. She fed the five of us, cared for us, and taught us Spanish—all while raising her own family at the same time." George W. added, "She loved me. She chewed me out. She shaped me up, and I have grown to love her like a second mom."

By this time, George W. had just finished the seventh grade at San Jacinto Junior High; he was class president that year. He then went to Kinkaid School in the upper-crust suburb of Houston called Piney Point Village. He was an instantly popular student there, always able to make friends easily. As the eldest son, he also became a bit of a surrogate parent to his four siblings. "We came to him with our problems sometimes before we'd go to Mom and Dad," said Doro Bush. "Plus, to be honest, he was just a lot of fun, full of mischief."

After the family moved to Houston, George H. W. Bush began to actively pursue a new interest in politics that was influenced by the success of his father, Prescott. In February 1962, George decided he wanted to run for Harris County Republican Party chairman. "I got this itch to do something bigger than just be concerned about my own income, my own success. Now that I had achieved a certain amount of security, I felt the time was right to look at the bigger picture. I was like my father in that respect. He never wanted to be in politics until he was sure he was financially secure. I took a look around and thought maybe I could be of some help as the Harris County Republican chairman."

Before throwing his hat into the ring, George surprised his wife by asking for her opinion. Was he aware that Barbara was already so depressed about leaving Midland, the last thing she needed was him making another life-altering decision without her?

Barbara saw that George really wanted to run. Reluctantly, she agreed. "I understand that he's a man who was raised with one rule in mind," she said at the time, "which is: you must achieve *something* in your life." She had one proviso, though: "This family still has to come first." Like George's mother, Barbara felt that there was nothing more important than family. He agreed. Barbara and baby Doro then went off to visit Dorothy and Prescott. "Then, when we got back, George was in the meanest political battle of his life," Barbara recalled.

It was a tough race, though he would certainly face tougher in years to come. George was thought of as being not quite as conservative as some other Republicans. He was moderate, but he had strong views that bent to the left in some areas, especially on foreign policy. Undaunted, he traveled to the county's more than 210 precincts to campaign with Barbara at his side. She wanted to be with him and was happy he wanted her along, but she realized early on that campaigning wasn't for her. She was turned off by the phoniness and duplicity of many of the people she met along the way. "I could see right through them," she would say. George could, too, but he knew how to play the game. Barbara didn't want to learn. "I don't play games," she said, and no four words ever summed her up better.

Barbara began to feel that George had reneged on his promise to her not to neglect their family. He was out of town a great deal, spending time away from her and the children. They started arguing about it. "What is it you want from me?" he would demand. "If I have to tell you, then I don't want it," she would counter. The couple had entered a stressful period in their marriage, one that Barbara would later admit caused her "pain and jealousy."

It was obvious to everyone that Barbara and George had their problems, and no one recognized it more clearly than Dorothy. Once, at Kennebunkport, she very pointedly asked George, "Are you making decisions *with* your wife or *for* your wife?" According to a relative who witnessed the conversation, he looked at his mother with surprise and asked if Barbara had said something to her. Dorothy said no, but that she could plainly see her daughter-in-law wasn't happy. He must talk to her, Dorothy told him, and not dictate to her. George seemed a little embarrassed. "Yes, Mum," he said obediently.

George was a man of a certain time when many fathers often had little to do with the raising of their children; they expected their wives do the heavy lifting at home. In the case of the Bushes, it fell to Barbara to herd the kids together for long and difficult cross-country trips to Kennebunkport for the summer. It wasn't easy, and she wasn't always happy doing it.

"This was a period, for me," Barbara said, "of long days and short years; of diapers, runny noses, earaches, more Little League games than you could believe possible, tonsils, and those unscheduled races to the hospital emergency room, Sunday school and church, of hours of urging homework, short chubby arms around your neck and sticky kisses; and experiencing bumpy moments of feeling that I'd never, ever be able to have fun again; and coping with the feeling that George Bush, in his excitement of starting a small company and traveling around the world, was having a lot of fun." In another interview, she recalled being "jealous of attractive young women out in a man's world . . . and I'm sitting home with these absolutely brilliant children who say one thing a week of interest."

George wasn't much help. Once, when she was at the end of her rope, Barbara called him on the road to vent. "I said, 'I'm desperate, I don't know what to do,'" she recalled in 1989. "'Your son's in trouble again. He just hit a ball through the neighbor's upstairs window.' And George said, 'Wow. What a great hit.' And then he said, 'Did you get the ball back?'"

In 1961, Barbara and George decided to send young George W. to Phillips Academy in Andover, once attended by his father and grandfather. George would enjoy his time at Andover, though he wasn't intellectually curious; he'd do just barely enough to get by in school. He preferred sports to academics. He was competitive and an outstanding athlete, especially in soccer, baseball, and basketball. Well-liked, he was known for his sense of daring and good humor.

Barbara was frustrated with him. As the oldest, she felt he had a responsibility to set an example for his siblings, and he didn't seem up to the challenge. She was tired of arguing with him about it. There seemed no way to convince him to apply himself. "I give up," she said. "He's not his grandfather and he's not his father, and I just have to accept it." George tried to convince her that their son still had a lot of growing up to do, and that there was no telling what he might later achieve. "Well, I'm not going to hold my breath," Barbara said. She had a lot on her mind at this time, which may explain some of her impatience. As well as any concerns about her son, she was worried about the future.

When George H.W. won the Harris County chairmanship in 1962, Barbara realized that this was just the beginning for her husband in politics and that she'd either have to change her attitude or be left behind, especially after George made it clear he wanted to run for Senate, just like his father.

Two years later, in 1964, George won the Senate nomination. However, he lost the general election to Democratic senator Ralph Yarborough. George had supported the war in Vietnam and opposed civil rights legislation. Though stung by this loss, two years later he decided to run for Congress.

This time George waged a successful campaign. After selling off his share in Zapata to avoid any conflict of interest, he ran against Democrat Frank Briscoe and was elected to a seat representing the Seventh District of Texas, winning 57 percent of the votes cast. He would be the first Republican congressman to represent his hometown Houston district.

With George now a congressman—and he would serve two terms—the Bush family had to relocate again, this time from Houston to Washington. While she packed up the house yet again, Barbara stayed behind while Neil, Marvin, and Doro went ahead with their father to Washington. George W. was now at Yale, and Jeb was finishing up high school and soon to start Phillips Academy. Soon the Bush family would move into their new home on Hillbrook Lane in Northwest Washington.

By this time, Barbara knew what was expected of her. She understood that little in her life ever would have much permanence. She also tried to resist the anger she felt at having so little control.

As usual, Dorothy didn't agree. She did believe she and her daughter-in-law had an absolute duty to support their husbands' political aspirations. However, to be silent? To not voice an opinion? To be complacent? No. That wasn't who Dorothy had ever been in her marriage to Prescott, and not who she wanted Barbara to be in hers to George—even if he was her son.

Dorothy's Namesake, "Doro"

By fall of 1971, Doro, Dorothy Bush's namesake, was a pretty twelve-year-old girl with brown hair, large brown eyes, and a small, cherub-like face. The only girl in a household with four older brothers, she often felt outnumbered but easily made friends in the neighborhood and seemed quite self-sufficient with a sweet disposition. Her relationship with her mother, Barbara, was complex, though. Barbara loved her, but everything Barbara learned about being the mother of a daughter she'd learned from the unfortunate example set by her mother, Pauline.

Consuela Diaz, a cousin of housekeeper Paula Rendon's, recalled visiting the Bush home in October 1971. She was twenty-two at the time. "It was tense," she recalled. "Barbara was out of sorts, upset, and no one knew why. She would burst into tears for no reason. She had a hair-trigger temper, too. Her words could really cut. One time, I was sitting in the living room and she came in and said, 'That's Pop's chair—meaning George H.W.'s. Who told you you could sit there?' She seemed so angry, I was immediately scared. I jumped out of the chair. 'No one told me I couldn't sit here,' I told her. 'Yes, but did anyone tell you you *could*,' she said. I apologized and ran from the room, crying."

Consuela says that Doro had put on some weight when she was twelve, nothing unusual for a prepubescent child, but enough for Barbara to be concerned. "Eat it today, and wear it tomorrow," Barbara would tell Doro—the exact same warning Pauline used to give her. "I went through the same thing when I was that age, and it was very upsetting to my mother," Barbara said while knitting at the kitchen table. "We need to cut back on the junk food," she told Paula.

Paula, who was standing at the stove making her special jalapeño jelly, disagreed. "We shouldn't focus on it," she said. "It will just make Doro self-conscious." She then returned to her work at the stove. "You're giving up awfully easy, aren't you?" Barbara asked, seeming surprised. "Either you have convictions about this thing or you don't," she told Paula. "So, do you have convictions?" Paula walked right up to Barbara and, standing mere inches from her, looked down at her with hard eyes. "Do I look like I have convictions?" she asked. Barbara backed down. She had met her match in Paula.

"Later Paula told me Mrs. Bush was upset most of the time about one thing or another, and you just had to let it go," recalled Consuela Diaz. "She said she meant well, but 'she's very high-strung.' Paula later made some pretty dresses by hand that fit Doro beautifully. Mrs. Bush was happy about it. 'I don't know, but maybe I'm just better with boys,' she told Paula. But Paula wouldn't accept it. 'No. You're good with girls too,' she told her. 'Just keep trying. You're very good with Doro.'"

"Your Life Is His Legacy"

It was 1972 and Prescott Bush, the revered patriarch of the Bush family, was not well. The last ten years had been very difficult for him, especially given his severe arthritis. While he rarely complained about it, the stooped posture of his six-foot-four frame had caused family, friends, and colleagues to wonder if he was really worse off than he was letting on.

In June 1961, Dorothy had felt she had no choice but to put her foot down. Prescott, who was now sixty-seven, looked gaunt and thin. She said the time had come for him to retire from the Senate.

Prescott had served in the Senate for ten years, and, regardless of health issues, he fully intended to run for reelection. However, his doctor was discouraging of the idea, going so far as to tell him he would be "crazy" to run and that if he did he "might not live to see Election Day." Prescott felt the physician was overreacting. Still, when he discussed it with Dorothy, she agreed with the doctor. A few weeks later, Prescott made the difficult decision; his office announced he wouldn't run for reelection. When the deed was done, he sat in his office in Georgetown and wept over it. His term expired on January 3, 1963.

Prescott returned part-time to Brown Brothers Harriman just to fill the hours, but his heart wasn't in it. By the summer of 1972, he was nothing like the man he'd been ten years earlier. He'd spent the last decade trying to find purpose in his life, but there was just nothing that seemed to interest him, not even his son George's political career. "He was always bitter about that decision to retire," recalled Prescott Bush Jr. "He was simply miserable after he left the Senate. He was bored and felt that he'd made the biggest mistake of his life in leaving."

"All that summer, Dad was ill," recalled his daughter, Nancy Bush Ellis, of the summer of 1972. "Mom would wrap him up in a blanket and say, 'He's just got a cold.' But you could sense Dad wasn't doing well."

In late August, the family received his terrible diagnosis: Prescott, now seventy-eight, had lung cancer. Dorothy's brother, Dr. John Walker, suggested that Prescott go to Sloan Kettering in New York for treatment, which he did in September. The cancer was fast moving, though, and there was nothing that could be done. Dorothy took a suite at the Waldorf while Prescott was in the hospital, and family members then started flying in to be with him in his final weeks.

On October 8, 1972, Prescott Bush passed away. It was devastating to the entire family, but no one suffered as much from the loss as his wife of fifty-one years. "I wish I had gone with him," Dorothy said.

The funeral was at Christ Episcopal Church in Greenwich, the place of worship for Prescott and Dorothy for more than forty years. Dorothy told family members not to wear black at the service; she wanted them to wear bright colors to celebrate Prescott's going to heaven. As difficult as it was for her to do so, she also wrote a stirring eulogy saying that Prescott had given her "the most joyous life that any woman could experience." She praised him as a father, saying that "As the children grew older he respected each as an individual, ready to back any decision thoughtfully reached and giving advice only when sought."

Prescott's grave marker at Putnam Cemetery in Greenwich is embossed with his name as "Prescott S. Bush." His birth year is inaccurate: It says 1895; the year is actually 1894. The rest of the marker reads: LEADER, ATHLETE, SINGER, SOLDIER, BANKER, STATESMAN, CHURCHMAN, COMPANION, FRIEND, FATHER, HUSBAND EXTRAORDINARY.

After Prescott died, the family hired a woman named Virginia Mason* to act as a caretaker to Dorothy, who was now seventy-one. "I was just twenty at the time," she recalled. "My mother had been a good friend of Mrs. Bush's, and I was in nursing school. I had no real, practical experience and was told that Mrs. Bush was spry and lively and didn't need someone watching over her for physical reasons. Emotionally, though, I heard that she ran hot and cold. Her grown children felt she needed to be supervised in that respect. So I was brought in by Mrs. Bush [Barbara] who, after interviewing me, arranged for me to have lunch with Dorothy Bush at the Sulgrave Club, an elegant, private women's club she belonged to in Washington. Since she was going to be in town to meet with attorneys about her late husband's estate, we met there.

"The first thing she said to me after we sat down was, 'I don't need help. To humor my daughter-in-law, I'll allow you to live with me. But the first time you tell me what to do will be the first time we have a problem.' We then enjoyed a nice lunch during which we had a lively debate about which was more beautiful, the Lincoln or the Jefferson Memorial. She preferred the Lincoln and spoke in-depth about how marvelous she thought it was that its sculptor, Daniel Chester French, had been able to capture in Lincoln's eyes such concern and love for his country. While we spoke, many people came by the table to say hello. Mrs. Bush held court with these well-wishers, many of whom had tears running down their faces over Prescott. I was impressed with how generous she was with her time, how composed she was, and how she wanted to speak to each and every person. I thought, My goodness, she could have been a politician, too. As we got up to leave, First Lady Pat Nixon came over to say hello. She really became undone while talking to Mrs. Bush about Prescott. 'He was very much loved,' Mrs. Nixon said as she and Mrs. Bush embraced.

"After that day in the winter of 1972 I would be at Dorothy Bush's side for the rest of her life. I learned right off that she was wracked with guilt over her husband's final years."

"I'm so mad at myself," Dorothy told Virginia one day over tea with her

---

* I am using a pseudonym for this source since she asked to not be identified.

daughter, Nancy, and her daughter-in-law, Barbara. She said Prescott felt it had been selfish of her and his sons to force him into retirement, and he never got over it. She said he let it all but ruin the last ten years of their life together. Her hands were trembling as she spoke, so much so that Nancy took the cup from her and gently placed it back on its saucer. "But maybe it was for the best," Virginia told her, trying to comfort her.

"Yes, maybe," Dorothy said, "but we always made each other stronger. And for him, being strong meant working in the Senate. Why didn't I see that?" Overcome with emotion, Dorothy then rose and left the room. Nancy followed.

Barbara, concerned by her mother-in-law's state of mind, asked Virginia if Dorothy was always so distraught. Then Barbara took a look around and noticed all the framed pictures of Prescott on the walls and the others placed on various pieces of furniture. She suggested that Virginia take down at least half these mementos, put them in boxes, and store them in the attic. Virginia agreed.

The next day, after Virginia did as she was told, Dorothy became agitated when she noticed so many of the keepsakes missing and said she wanted the photographs returned to their right places. "I didn't tell her it was her daughter-in-law's idea," Virginia recalled. "I didn't want there to be any kind of wedge between them because I knew Mrs. Bush [Dorothy] needed her now, more than ever."

Later that week, George H.W. and his sons George, twenty-six, and Jeb, nineteen, and his daughter, Doro, thirteen, paid a visit to their grandmother. By this time, George was ambassador to the United Nations; nominated for the position by President Nixon in 1970 and speedily confirmed in 1971, he would serve for two years.

As Virginia Mason supervised, a lunch was served to Dorothy and her family by a butler. The first course was something called "Dotty's Cold Spinach Soup"—spinach, cream, and eggs with a quarter cup of vermouth.

During dinner, Dorothy reminded her family of their duty. "Your life is Prescott's legacy," she told them, directing her comments to George and Jeb. "Whatever you both do from this moment on reflects on him. Don't forget it."

Moved with emotion, George H.W. rose and went to his mother and put his hand on her shoulder. She brushed it away and told him to sit back down.

"She didn't want a sentimental moment," recalled Virginia Mason. "She had something she wanted to say, and she wanted to make sure they heard it. 'Your father,' she said, looking at George H.W., 'and your grandfather,' she said, looking at George W., Jeb, and Doro, 'was very proud of the four of you just as he is of all his family. You have to now do *him* proud.'"

PART TEN

Columba and Jeb

The Wild Card

Jeb Bush, like his older brother, George, gave his parents more than a few headaches over the years, especially during his adolescence. At the age of fourteen in late 1967, he enrolled in Phillips Academy in Andover like many of his other male relatives. By this time, he was a tall and lanky six feet—he would grow to be six foot four—with a thick mop of brown hair never combed neatly, and a dismissive attitude not unlike a lot of young men his age. He began to misbehave in surprising ways. At Andover, for instance, he quickly became known for selling pot to other students. Indulging in hashish and drinking, he wasn't a serious student. He was bright enough, but, like George, he just didn't want to apply himself, and he hated the school. "I was a cynical little turd at a cynical school" is how he once recalled it.

After his first year of poor grades at Andover, his parents feared Jeb would be expelled. When he went home on a break, there was nothing short of pure war between Jeb and his mother. He promised he'd try harder to get good grades during the next semester. "As usual, you're underestimating me," he said. "Jebbie, I actually don't think that's possible," she shot back. Even his grandmother Dorothy laid into him about his grades, telling him, "Jebbie, my faith in you is less than full right now."

A big challenge for Jeb were the constant comparisons between him and his younger brother by two years, the blond and blue-eyed Neil. Neil also

struggled in school but had good reason for it. He was diagnosed with dys-
lexia. He worked hard in school, though, and if he often failed his parents,
at least they knew he tried. Jeb didn't.

In 1970, when he was about seventeen and in his senior year at Andover,
Jeb started teaching English as a second language and also became involved
in the school's two-month student exchange summer program, which was
called "Man and Society." Soon, he found himself helping to build a cinder-
block schoolhouse in Ibarrilla, a village on the outskirts of León, Guanajuato, Mexico. His friends had ribbed him about making the trip. "Jebbie's
going to save the world," one said at a going-away party. "Yeah. One im-
poverished country at a time," Jeb joked. When his friend asked, "Are your
parents proud?" Jeb rolled his eyes and answered, "Oh yeah, they're over
the moon."

It was in Mexico where Jeb would meet the young woman who'd soon
change his life. Though she was only sixteen, there was something about
her that seemed much older. She was just five feet tall. Jeb towered over
her, but she had an outsized personality. Her eyes were dark and piercing
and she favored heavy makeup with false eyelashes. Her lips were full and
usually painted a vibrant red. She had a mane of straight, jet-black hair. She
comported herself with determination—not a shrinking violet. She was a
real beauty, and Jeb was smitten.

Columba

Despite her youth, Columba Garnica de Gallo (pronounced Co-loomba) seemed like a grown woman, perhaps because she'd never had it easy. Her maturity was born of struggle and hardship in her life story.

Columba's father, José María Garnica Rodríguez, born on February 5, 1925, was the oldest of four brothers raised in a small mud-brick adobe house in the village of Arperos, about 250 miles north of Mexico City. His father, Hilario Garnica, herded chickens and sheep and grew corn and avo-cados in a small ranch comprised of just a couple of dilapidated buildings. They had no running water or electricity. The Garnicas were proud, never thinking of themselves as poor or disadvantaged. They just knew they had to work hard to get through a tough life.

In 1947, when he was about twenty-two, José María—known to his friends as *"Bajito,"* or *"Shorty"*—snuck across the Mexican border in search of a better life in the United States. After the war, it was common for immi-grants to cross the border without proper paperwork in order to work. For the next two years, he would work illegally in the fields of Arizona, earning about thirteen dollars a day, if he was lucky, by picking fruit. Eventually, he returned to Mexico with a couple hundred bucks in his pocket, and that was when he met Josefina Gallo Esquivel, twenty-nine. She hailed from a family that was a little better off; her father was a successful businessman in León, Mexico.

Josefina, born in 1922, was a dark-haired beauty who, at twenty-nine, was already considered an old maid. She'd been raised in extremely religious León, where Catholic mass was held every day and all the townsfolk were expected to attend. Primarily brought up by her very strict godfather, she attended a strict parochial school. "My mother's godfather was selling lamp oil to a man from a nearby town," recalled Columba. "This man had a son—José María—about the same age as my mother. They thought it was a good idea to arrange for them to marry. I don't think she was ever really in love with him. She just said, 'Okay, well, I'll try my best.'"

Josefina and José María were married on February 10, 1949. Ten months later, in 1950, Josefina gave birth to a son, Francisco José, followed by a daughter, Lucila, in 1951, and then Columba, on August 17, 1953.

José María continued to go back and forth to America for work. With the money he earned in America combined with that of her mother's family, Columba was able to attend the Instituto Mayllen, a private school in León. Her parents' marriage was in trouble, though. José María had become jealous of Josefina, convinced that while he was in America working she was seeing other men. Though she hotly denied it, he wasn't convinced. Eventually, he began to hit her in front of their children. Columba says that remembering this time in her life brings forth "the most painful memories. My father made my mother's life hell." She says he often beat Josefina, and once even fractured her, Columba's, knuckles with a belt buckle.

Columba's stepmother, Antonia Morales Garnica, José María's second wife, recalled that it was when José María started raising his hands to Columba that Josefina drew a line and filed for divorce. "Columba was battered by her father and this was one of the main reasons for the divorce," she said. "He would come back from work tired and frustrated and smacked Columba. That caused problems between him and Josefina to the point where she had no choice. She had to to leave. It took everything in her to do it, though."

Somehow, Josefina was able to conquer her fear of further retaliation by José María and leave the marriage. He didn't make it easy, however. He tormented her by showing up unannounced and threatening her. How she mustered the courage to go through with the divorce was a mystery to even her closest friends.

Columba was ten when her parents finally split in 1963. "The end of my parents' marriage was a big blow to their families and friends," she said. "What I admire about my mother was that she didn't run away. She didn't leave town. She was strong with such resolve, and she said, 'Fine. It is what it is. I'm sorry it happened but I will stay here and I will go to church and I will live my life just as I had before, and I am not going to care what people say about any of it. I have my children and I will live my life with my head held high and be proud. I will do it for them to show them how it's done.' That was my mother."

José María died in November 2013 at the age of eighty-eight; his daughter Columba did not attend the funeral.

By 1970, Columba was sixteen. Her sister, Lucila, met a young man named John Schmitz from Andover who was part of a high school exchange program. One Sunday night, as the two drove down the streets of Guanajuato in Lucila's car with Columba sitting in the backseat, they came across some of Schmitz's friends, including Jeb Bush. Soon, Schmitz brought Jeb over to Lucila and Columba's home for a meal. There was obvious chemistry between Jeb and Columba, and four days later he asked her out on a date. "It was a very old-fashioned courtship," Columba recalled. "For the first two weeks, he didn't even hold my hand."

After a few dates, Columba had some doubts about Jeb. While he was tall and good-looking and had a bright personality, he also had a streak of what she later called *"chico malo"*—the bad boy—about him. She wasn't trustful of men anyway, and this was one she really had to wonder about. Was he just a rich playboy? When she found out how poorly he was doing in school, she became convinced that he wasn't for her. It wasn't so much his bad grades as it was his lack of commitment to education. *"Si eres estúpido, bueno, así es como es y tal vez, tal vez, podría aceptarlo,"* she said in her native tongue. *"Pero si solo eres vago. No, no puedo aceptar eso en un hombre."* Translated, it meant: "If you're stupid, that's just the way it is, and maybe I could accept it. But if you're lazy, no. That, I cannot accept in a man." She told him that if he could prove himself able to commit himself to his education, she might believe he could also be committed to her. Rather than leave Mexico with his friends, Jeb took Columba on a trip to Acapulco. Then he went back to the States, determined to make Columba proud.

When Jeb returned to Andover, he was a different man. He applied himself and finished his last quarter on the honor roll. His parents were astonished. Meanwhile, Jeb continued his courtship of Columba as pen pals, the two of them writing to each other every day. For the next couple of years, they would see each other only occasionally when Jeb would visit her in Mexico. His parents knew nothing about her.

After Andover, Jeb decided to pass on Yale, not wanting to have to compete with his grandfather, father, and brother and their grades there. Instead, he enrolled at the University of Texas, where he remained dedicated to his studies and excelled on the tennis team.

In the winter of 1973, with more good grades at the university under his belt, Jeb finally told his parents about Columba Gallo. Barbara and George figured it was just a teenage romance. If it had motivated him in school, all the better. However, the relationship was much more serious than they knew. When he went to Mexico for the holidays that year, he proposed marriage to Columba. "Maybe you should finish school first," she suggested. He didn't want to wait that long. She would marry him, she decided, but not right away. She gave him a peace-symbol ring to seal the deal. Jeb then called his parents to give them the good news. It did not go well.

Accepting Columba

S orry, but that's not going to happen" was Barbara's reaction to Jeb's surprising announcement that he planned to marry a nineteen-year-old girl he'd met in Mexico. "Oh, hell no" was his father's. Jeb was finally on his way to becoming a serious adult with good grades in college, and they didn't want him distracted.

"Is she pregnant?" Barbara wanted to know, according to one account. "No, she isn't," Jeb answered. "But if she were, would it make a difference?" Barbara said, "The only difference would be that now you get to continue to live, whereas if she was pregnant, you would not."

At this same time, 1973, George H.W. held the position of head of the Republican National Committee, appointed back in January by President Richard Nixon. George hadn't wanted to leave the United Nations but felt strongly that a public servant should do whatever asked of him by a President; it was just a matter of country and honor for him. Barbara disagreed. "I felt the RNC position would be a terrible experience," she recalled. "Party politics are dog-eat-dog." But then George wrote to Nixon, "My initial 'no' has changed after a sleepless night to a happy 'yes.' The shock has worn off, and Barbara will see that it makes sense."

As was his way, George did what he wanted to do, but at least Barbara had made her opinion known to him. Had he been able to predict what lay ahead in the next twenty months of his service, maybe he would have listened to her.

About a month into his tenure, the Watergate scandal broke out. President Nixon denied involvement even though it was quickly becoming clear he was guilty. A loyalist, George remained supportive of him. Soon, though, he would change his mind about that. Much later, in August 1974, he would end up being the one to formally ask for Nixon's resignation.

The last thing George needed at this time was his son coming home with the surprising news that he wanted to get married. "Congrats, son," he said when Jeb told him. "I'm sure you and the missus will be very happy." He actually thought Jeb was joking. When he realized he wasn't, he reportedly said, "Over my dead body." He pointed out the obvious, that he and Barbara hadn't even met Columba, and said no wedding was going to take place.

However, he and Barbara had to admit that they really could see a difference in Jeb ever since Columba came into his life. "That's because she sees me and helps me see myself," Jeb explained. "What does that *mean*, exactly?" Barbara asked. "Speak English, Jeb." What he was trying to say was that because Columba believed in him, it made him want to try harder. It was because of Columba, he insisted, that his grades had improved. At this, according to what Jeb later told his friend Laurence Jeffrey Edmonds, his mother said, "What you're saying she brings out of you is already there, Jeb. It's the way we raised you." Still, Jeb's mind was made up about Columba. He also promised he'd continue in school with the same good intention moving forward that he'd demonstrated since meeting her. However, his father remained resistant, especially after Jeb admitted that Columba barely spoke English. According to Edmonds, "The old man insisted that the first marriage in the family wasn't going to be to a teenager from Mexico they hadn't met yet who didn't speak English. 'Not gonna happen,' he said. Then, I guess because he was wrapped up in the Nixon imbroglio at that time, he told Jeb, 'Thanks for making a bad day even worse.'"

What could they do, though? Jeb was twenty-one. At least he seemed serious about someone, unlike his older brother, George, who made it pretty clear that his two priorities in life were, as he put it at the time, "cold beers and hot women." Barbara and George had no choice but to bless the marriage.

Once committed to something, Barbara usually went all the way with it. If she was going to agree to support Jeb, she'd follow through. About a week later, she took him to Boone & Sons, where the two bought an engagement ring for Columba. Barbara then had her paternal grandmother's wedding ring fitted to Columba's size. "I am praying that he'll be as happy as Grandmother Pierce was and I am," she wrote in her diary. "How I worry about Jeb and Columba. Does she love him? I know when I meet her, I'll stop worrying." Barbara wrote that she hoped she could be as strong and resolute as her mother-in-law would likely be in the same circumstances. "I am praying to be like Dotty Bush," she wrote, "but it will be hard."

After the holiday, Jeb took his mother to Mexico to meet Columba. Though Barbara thought she was charming, she was a little puzzled as to how Columba had gained so much influence over her son. She didn't even make it up to his shoulder. She didn't speak English and seemed incredibly shy and awkward. She also seemed terrified by the prospect of meeting his mother. Also, the language barrier made it difficult for Barbara to connect with Columba, who understood English better than she spoke it. In seeing her with Jeb, though, Barbara did sense that Columba truly loved him and that he felt the same way about her.

Columba didn't know what to make of Barbara. She thought she liked her, but she couldn't be sure. A smoker since she was a young girl, she lit one in front of Barbara, who then looked at her with such strong disapproval there was nothing left for Columba to do but take it out of her mouth, flick it to the ground, and grind it out with her stiletto. When Barbara looked down at the butt with even more disdain, all Columba could do was bend over, pick it up, and find a trash can. Barbara then told her that she'd stopped cold turkey about five years earlier after decades of smoking. In other words, Barbara wanted Columba to quit smoking. Columba said she would try.

George H.W. didn't meet Columba until the night before the wedding at the rehearsal dinner. "Better late than never, I guess," is how Barbara later put it. In the end, he shared Barbara's opinion: Columba was sweet, but what did Jeb see in her? Though he didn't get it, he accepted it. "He was gracious and accepting even though I placed this burden on him of not even knowing the love of my life until the night before the wedding," Jeb recalled.

The wedding took place on February 23, 1974, in a chapel at the University of Texas. It was a small affair with just Columba's mother and sister; Jeb's parents, grandmother, siblings . . . and the family's housekeeper. Jeb was twenty-one. Columba—who would now be known in the family as "Colu," pronounced Coo-loo—was nineteen, the same age Barbara had been on her own wedding day. Jeb's younger brother Marvin was responsible for memorializing the event with his camera. Unfortunately, he botched the task and double exposed every single negative with shots of Frank Zappa from a recent concert in Richmond, Virginia. If not for the fact that Barbara managed to get one picture with her Kodak Pocket Instamatic, there would be none at all of Jeb's wedding.

"It is a wonderful day," Columba was overheard telling Barbara. "Thank you, Mrs. Bush."

"Oh, maybe you can call me Mother now," Barbara offered.

"Yes . . . Mrs. Bush" was Columba's response. For many years to come, she would call her "Mrs. Bush."

Relatives also remember Dorothy Bush taking both of Columba's hands into her own and trying to have a conversation with her, asking her one question after another in an effort to get to know her. However, Columba's grasp of English made it difficult for Dorothy to understand the answers. Still, she gazed at her with encouragement. As Columba spoke, Dorothy nodded and smiled, determined not to let the difference in their cultures come between them. Later, Jeb, who had observed the whole thing, went over to his grandmother, kissed her on the cheek, and said, *"Gracias."* Dorothy smiled sweetly at him. *"De nada,"* she said with a wink.

PART ELEVEN

Challenges

"It's Complicated, Mum"

In the months after Jeb and Columba's wedding, the Watergate scandal came to an end when President Richard Nixon resigned. George had hoped his successor, Gerald Ford, would reward his loyalty to Nixon with an offer to be the new Vice President. It wasn't meant to be, though, because Ford felt he needed someone who had no connection whatsoever to Watergate. He chose Nelson Rockefeller, the former governor of New York. George then gave up his post as chairman of the RNC and accepted Ford's offer to become chief of the U.S. Liaison Office to the People's Republic of China. He told Barbara they were moving to China, and she started packing, no questions asked—not that he gave her a chance to ask any. In a letter to his friend Paul Dorsey, George explained, "Because I keep my business and politics separate from my home life—usually that is. She [Barbara] is not informed on issues and intrigue—perhaps this is selfish on my part but we have a close, close relationship with the kids, et al, and I just want to have that oasis of privacy."

In October 1974, the Bushes were off to China, but maybe there would be a bright side to it for Barbara. "His previous work schedules hadn't allowed much time for each other: first back in Texas, when he worked so hard to build his business; then in Washington, keeping up with the hectic life of a congressman; and finally as RNC chairman during Watergate," their daughter, Doro, recalled. "In China, they would be alone for the first time since George W. had been born twenty-eight years earlier."

But something else was going on at this same time, something more troubling. Barbara started hearing that George had become fascinated by a woman he'd just hired as a personal assistant, Jennifer Fitzgerald. At first she didn't believe it. It was impossible to imagine that he would ever stray. When would he even have the time?

Jennifer Fitzgerald, at forty-two, seven years Barbara's junior, was pretty and petite with blond hair, which she wore in a short, stylish fashion. George had hired her to be his "special assistant" just as he was preparing to go to China.

She was born Jennifer Ann Isobel Patteson-Knight in the United Kingdom in 1932; her mother, Frances Patteson-Knight, was from a wealthy Boston family; her father, Brigadier General Douglas Henry Patteson-Knight, an English military officer. Jennifer attended private schools and Mount Vernon College. In 1955 she married U.S. Army private Gerald FitzGerald, separating from him a year later and then divorcing him in 1959. (She subsequently dropped the capitalization of the *g* in "Fitzgerald.") George was introduced to her while he was chairman of the RNC by his friend Dean Burch, the former Federal Communications Commission chairman. Jennifer had been Burch's personal assistant.

About a week before Jennifer was scheduled to arrive in Beijing, Barbara asserted herself and said she didn't want her working for George. The couple had a heated argument about it; he denied that anything was going on and expressed dismay that she'd ever think otherwise. According to what we now know, Barbara wanted to believe him. However, many people in their circle who were not particularly known to be gossips had serious concerns about Jennifer. It didn't help that George seemed to depend on her for so many fine details relating to his new position, whereas he wasn't as reliant on Barbara. This would be the case, though. Jennifer was his personal assistant; Barbara, his wife. Still, something about it didn't sit well with Barbara. Therefore, after an argument with George about Jennifer, Barbara decided she needed to get away to think.

At the end of November 1974, Barbara made quick plans to go back to the States, ostensibly to visit her children for the holidays. She would, many years later, write in her memoir that this trip home had always been planned, and that the reason she went alone was because George couldn't leave his new post so soon after taking the assignment. "But they would not have planned a trip back to the States for just Barbara," said one person who knew the Bushes well at that time. "There was no way they would ever purposefully plan to be apart for Christmas. The truth was that Barbara decided to put some space between herself and her husband."

This would be the first Christmas George and Barbara would spend apart in thirty years. It would be the only Christmas they would ever be separated in seventy-three years of marriage. "It is right that Bar be there with the children but boy do I miss her," he wrote in his diary on December 4, 1974.

At this time, George W. was studying to earn his master's at Harvard. He had applied without telling anyone in his family just in case he didn't make it; he'd earlier been rejected from the University of Texas School of Law. Marvin and Neil were in boarding school, and Doro, fifteen, was in the tenth grade at Miss Porter's School in Farmington. Meanwhile, Jeb had just graduated from the University of Texas with honors and a degree in Latin American studies. He had done what he'd set out to do; Columba was proud of him, as were his parents.

At the time, there were only two flights in and out of Beijing per week. However, wanting out of China immediately, Barbara hitched a ride on an air force jet reserved for the visiting Henry Kissinger and his family.

The day after Barbara left China, George and Jennifer took off for twelve days, first to Honolulu for the Chief of Missions Conference, where diplomats from around the world gathered for seminars. They weren't alone; there were dozens of people traveling with them. Some reported back that George made important contacts in Hawaii, meeting and greeting diplomats and, while doing so, depending on Jennifer in a way he rarely did Barbara. One aide noticed that Jennifer could handle, "a million important things at once."

George also had numerous telephone calls with President Jimmy Carter. It was clear to observers that he thought Carter was a weak President but that he tolerated him. He was also preoccupied with the energy crisis which had plagued the Western world, particularly the United States, and he had numerous meetings to discuss how the crisis had affected oil prices. The boon to his own oil businesses, which he continued to run but in a low-profile manner, was tremendous and he was elated about it. In fact, Bush said he was making more money than ever thanks to "this gosh darned energy crisis thing. I'm rakin' it in," he boasted.

"I think that's where it happened, in Hawaii," continued the source. "Prior to Hawaii, it had just been a flirtation. In Hawaii, I believe it turned into an affair, first at the Sheraton Waikiki and then at an apartment Bush leased in Kahala. A lot of people were perplexed by it, wondering why George would choose this particular time, when Barbara was already so suspicious. You couldn't picture it in your head. Old, conservative George, with his receding hairline and those big glasses, being intimate with a younger woman. It seemed odd. But he had power. It was what it was. No one would ever confront him about it, though. It wasn't anyone's business."

After Hawaii, the contingent then went to Tokyo. George wrote in his diary: "Again sponged off of Jim Hodgson [ambassador to Japan] at the Embassy. He and Maria put Jennifer Fitzgerald and me up for the afternoon."

George and Jennifer returned to China on December 17, 1974. "Flew back to Peking on Iran Airlines," George wrote in his diary. "Jennifer and I alone in first class. Four or five others in the whole rest of the 707 and a crew of about 8 or ten. The food was fantastic . . . we arrived very tired but well fed on the finest Iranian caviar."

While they were gone, George's mother, Dorothy, who was now seventy-three, heard the rumors. She was at Kennebunkport with her caregiver, Virginia Mason. Mason recalled, "Mrs. Bush didn't believe the stories. 'It's preposterous,' she said of George and the other woman, 'completely preposterous.' Then she said, 'Get my daughter-in-law on the phone.'"

After Virginia did as she was told, Dorothy and Barbara had a brief conversation, which, according to at least Dorothy's side of the call overheard by Virginia, didn't seem to amount to much. "I gathered that Barbara Bush said she was fine," said Virginia. "'But why are you home?' I heard Mrs. Bush ask. Then, she said, 'I know he's a big boy, Bar, and that he can be in China by himself. But why are you not with him?' I took it that Barbara didn't want to discuss it. That made sense to me. She wouldn't have discussed a marital issue with Dorothy Bush; that wouldn't have been in her character. In the end, Mrs. Bush [Dorothy] decided to wait for her upcoming trip to China to talk to her son firsthand. She was concerned. 'These things have a way of getting out of hand,' she told me. 'You have to nip them in the bud.' She then had me change the tickets and move the trip up by almost a week. I booked three first-class tickets, for me, her, and her sister-in-law, Marge." (Marge Clement was Prescott's seventy-five-year-old sister.)

"I then spoke to Jennifer Fitzgerald in Hawaii and told her we had moved our trip up. She seemed a little concerned. Five minutes later, George called to speak to his mother. She wasn't available and so I gave her the message. When she called back, I assume Jennifer answered because I heard Mrs. Bush say, 'This is George Herbert Walker's mother. Who is this? I want to speak to my son.' I know he then tried to convince Mrs. Bush not to change the plans, to just keep the original arrival date, which was, if I recall, December 24. She said no. She was coming early. So, in the end, we arrived in China on December 18."

In his diary on December 18, George wrote: "Mother arrived on a beautiful day. Gave her a nice 20 minutes or so to shape up and then we took a long bicycle ride down past the Great Hall of the People. You should have seen the people stare at old momma on the bicycle . . . the kids were openly incredulous, but she cycled majestically . . . doing beautifully in her PLA hat, teenage looking ski outfit and did just great."

"After we had a day or two to acclimate to our surroundings, Mrs. Bush had a chance to actually see Jennifer with her son and then she knew what was going on," said Virginia Mason. "I did, too. You could sense it.

"Mrs. Bush was clear," continued Virginia. "'Fix it,' she told him. 'Otherwise, these stories will follow you forever.' He said, 'It's complicated, Mum.' She said, 'Phooey. Is that really the hill you want to die on, son?' He said, 'It's not what it looks like,' to which she angrily responded, 'It's *always* what it looks like.' At that point, they realized I was still in the room. I actually wished I had been anywhere else, to tell you the truth. It was incredibly awkward for me. Mrs. Bush glared at me. "That will be *all*," she told me.

So, I eagerly left to give them their privacy. But this was the first time since I started working for Mrs. Bush that I thought, okay, well, now I know who calls the shots in this family."

Though she wasn't present for it, someone close to the family told Virginia that when George continued to protest that Jennifer was just his secretary, Dorothy told him, "That's weak, George. Don't be weak," repeating what had also been Prescott's admonition to his son.

"I sensed that it wasn't just his marriage she was worried about," said Virginia Mason, "it was also any political ramifications down the line. After all, who knew what his future might hold?

"The next day, Mrs. Bush said to me, 'You should not have been present for that conversation, and this is not a topic for you and I to discuss. This is between me and my son, and you are never to bring it up. Do we have an understanding?' I told her we did."

That same day, December 19, 1974, George told Jennifer it was over between them. It would appear, based on this timeline, that the affair lasted less than two weeks. "He said it had been a very bad idea," recalled one source close to H.W.'s son W. "She accepted it. He also promised that she'd always have a job with his organization. For that, she was grateful. That was the end of it."

"That same night, there was a dinner with the ambassadors of Australia and Argentina," recalled another source. "Jennifer was there, and she seemed fine. George seemed fine. Everyone was just . . . fine, even Dorothy. I figured whatever had happened must not have been so bad because, apparently, everyone had accepted it and had quickly moved on, or at least it appeared that way."

"George and Dorothy spent Christmas together, bicycling," said Virginia Mason. "We then had turkey and cranberries and stuffing for dinner, very traditional, with Peking Dust for dessert, which is a chestnut and heavy cream dish. There were probably fifteen people at the table, including Jennifer Fitzgerald. However, Mrs. Bush kept her distance from Mrs. Fitzgerald. I never saw her have a conversation with her.

"The next day, the twenty-sixth, we all went to the Great Wall and had a picnic.

"On the twenty-seventh, Mr. Bush was deathly ill with a fever and his mother had a chance to nurse him, which she loved doing. That night, he somehow rebounded and they had dinner with Qiao Guanhua, the Minister of Foreign Affairs of the People's Republic of China. Mrs. Bush acted as hostess; I could tell her son loved having her there.

"The next day, Mr. Bush was sick again and Mrs. Bush spent the day bringing him food on trays and making him eat. It was cute watching her fuss over him. 'He's still a mama's boy,' she told me.

"When we left China on December 30, Mrs. Bush felt it had been a very good trip and that she had done her part to straighten things out with her son. She was quite pleased. 'All's well that ends well,' she said."

Barbara was gone for about six weeks, returning to China at the end of January 1975. There was a misunderstanding, though. She thought that when George told her that Jennifer was no longer a problem, he meant it was over between them. If this was the case, and many people in her life attest to it, it would also suggest that he had admitted to something more than a platonic relationship. As soon as she got to China, though, and then to his office, there sitting behind the desk in the reception area was Jennifer. George clarified that they'd reached an understanding, but that this didn't mean she would not be working for him. He said he promised her she would always have a job, and he meant it. There was nothing Barbara could say about it. Apparently, she just absorbed the hit and went on.

In the weeks and months to come, things did seem much better between Barbara and George. While her discussions with him about Jennifer remained private, it seemed clear from the way she and George interacted that she'd made a decision to move forward and not allow anything to ruin her marriage. "That's pretty much all there is to say about it," said a source. "She wanted to put it behind them, and he wanted that, too."

From this point on and for more than a year in China, the Bushes did seem happier. There was no television at that time in Beijing, no radio, no English newspapers or magazines and few phone calls from the States at sixteen dollars a minute. Therefore, there were few distractions, which was fine with Barbara because it just meant more time with George. At one point, her friend Nancy Hamon, a wealthy philanthropist from Dallas, came to visit with her husband, Jake, an oil man, and Barbara told them she and George had never been happier.

Meanwhile, the Bush children, George, Doro, Marvin, and Neil, were able to visit China that summer of 1975, arriving on June 12, their father's fifty-first birthday. George W., who would celebrate his twenty-ninth in China, was now talking about getting into the oil business after graduating from Harvard. He was starting out a little later than his father had, but as George H.W. wrote of his suspicions in his diary, "If he gets his teeth into something semi-permanent or permanent, he will do just fine." Jeb had taken his first job as a loan officer at the Texas Commerce Bank in Houston and later at a branch in Venezuela. He hadn't been able to be with his siblings when they visited China in the summer of 1975. Also, Columba was now pregnant.

In all, George and Barbara were in China for fifteen months, from October 1974 to December 1975. At that point, President Ford asked George to return to the States for yet another new job: director of the CIA, an organization whose reputation had been seriously compromised during Watergate. Returning to Washington wasn't going to be easy for Barbara, though. She had been happier in China than she'd been in some time. Maybe it was being away from American politics that had made a difference, or maybe it was because she'd had so much alone time with George. Whatever the case, Barbara had felt more settled in China. Regardless, George accepted the new job.

The Bushes left China for Washington on December 10, 1975, after which George was quickly confirmed by the Senate, which was the good news. Maybe the bad news for Barbara was that Jennifer Fitzgerald also came back to the States with the team, her job intact as George's assistant. The rumors had never died down, so people couldn't help but remain curious about her. Veteran *New York Times* reporter R. W. Apple said at the time, "her name is known everywhere, and it is not used."

One night, soon after their return to the States, Barbara and George were coming out of a restaurant in Washington and ran into Jennifer, who was going inside with a date. According to a witness to the scene, Jennifer was very composed. When she expressed surprise that this particular restaurant was on George's schedule that evening, Barbara gave her a hard look. "Let's just have a nice night, shall we?" Barbara said as her smile slipped into a grimace. George stood at Barbara's side looking a little sheepish as Jennifer nodded and walked away. "She's too relaxed, if you ask me," Barbara said once Jennifer was gone. "I hate her presumption."

Black Cotton

I t was April 1976. As Barbara Bush drove her car down a busy highway in Washington, she was crying about something, as was usually the case these days. The headlights of an oncoming vehicle appeared, first as two small bright dots in the distance. As they got closer, nothing separated her and these beams of light except maybe common sense and self-preservation. She wondered what would happen if she just let it all go, if only for a few seconds? What if she swerved into the other lane? She'd collide with that other vehicle and it would all be over. As she took her last breath, she suspected she'd probably be relieved, maybe even happy.

Barbara stared at the headlights as they got closer. She could feel her hand on the steering wheel turn ever so slightly to the left. *Do it,* a voice inside her commanded. *Do it.* But at the last possible second, she refused to listen and, instead, made a sharp turn to the right. Brakes squealing, she pulled over to the side of the road. She then burst into tears.

How had things gotten so bad?

Barbara had loved being in China with George, but now they were home. When they returned to the States and after he was confirmed, he went full throttle into his new position. He began to work hard to redefine the CIA after the battering it had taken during Watergate. Meanwhile, Barbara tried to stay busy in Washington, working as a volunteer in a nursing home as well as giving lectures relating to her experiences in China, complete with a slide-show. She was very social and did what she could to enjoy her present life and not think too much about the past in China and how much she missed it. Something was still wrong, though, and now she felt it more keenly than ever. She would wake up feeling more and more the absence of joy in her life and closer and closer to the idea of wanting to end it.

Was it just that she'd felt so invisible in her marriage for so many years, it had finally gotten to her? Or maybe it had to do with menopause: She was fifty-one and the time was right for it.

Or maybe Barbara's malaise had to do with the women's movement?

Barbara had begun to feel that the new breed of feminism being pop-ularized during the 1970s had it right and she had it all wrong. Perhaps she should've been aspiring to more in her life than just her role as her husband's greatest supporter. Every time she turned on the television and heard newly empowered feminists discussing the growing movement, she found herself becoming more and more depressed. She even started to envy her housekeeper, Paula Rendon. At least her life seemed to work for her.

Or maybe she was concerned about Jennifer Fitzgerald. The fact that George refused to cut ties with her remained troubling. Two months earlier, in February, he had taken Jennifer to meet Frank Sinatra at the home of his brother Jonathan Bush.

Sinatra had indicated through mutual friends that he wanted to some-how work with the CIA. It seemed like a far-fetched idea, but even George Bush couldn't resist having drinks with Sinatra. So a meeting was arranged at his brother's. George didn't tell Barbara about it, though.

"It was a great evening," recalled Tomas DiBella, a friend of Sinatra's from New York who was present. "Frank genuinely wanted to help the CIA in any way he could. He said he had the contacts with people like the Shah of Iran and different royal families, and he could keep an eye on things, or so he said. Bush didn't take him seriously, I could tell. He just humored him, but was still excited to be talking to him. Sinatra had that effect on people. Mean-while, I had my eye on this dame sitting next to Bush. Attractive, middle-aged, doting on his every word, nice enough, pretty, she kept reaching over, touching his hand, that sort of thing, making eyes at him. George said she was his secretary. She didn't have no steno pad with her, though."

Barbara found out about it; Jonathan's wife told her the very next day. Naturally, she was upset. First of all, why did George take Jennifer, and second, why did he feel he had to hide it? When she confronted him, he said it had all been CIA business and that he needed Jennifer present in her official capacity as his assistant. The reason he hadn't told her, he explained, was that much of his job at the CIA had to be confidential, including these kinds of meetings. That justification seemed suspect to Barbara. George didn't want to discuss it any further, though. He shut it down, and that was the end of it. (When he chaired the Joint Congressional Committee on Atomic Energy in the mid-1950s George's father, Prescott, had also cited confidentiality concerns as being the reason he couldn't share details of his work with Dorothy. Most certainly, though, he wasn't using his work as a cover for a personal relationship.)

"All I knew was that I was very depressed, lonely and unhappy," Barbara would later recall of this time. She said she had a sense that life was passing her by. She also couldn't escape the feeling that many of the moments she'd shared with George had been somehow false. She was also impatient with herself and wished she could be stronger in the face of marital disappointment. Or, as she told one relative, "You know what my mother used to say? She used to say, 'When you get married, you learn a lot about yourself. And some of it's not good.'"

Making things worse, George was also talking about maybe one day running for President. Barbara dreaded the idea, but she also knew it didn't much matter how she felt about it. The fact that the children were all out of the house also added to her despair. "I felt ashamed," she would recall. "I had a husband whom I adored, the world's greatest children, more friends than I could see—and I was severely depressed. I hid it from everyone, including my closest friends. Everyone but George Bush. He would suggest that I get professional help, and that sent me into deeper gloom."

Today it's clear that Barbara was suffering from a textbook case of clinical depression and probably an anxiety disorder as well. As George apparently suggested, she should have sought professional help. This was nothing new for her, though; she'd had similar bouts several times over the years. However, she seemed to be getting worse, hiding her despair from her friends and, especially, her children. It would be many years—decades, really—before her children would learn about it.

One of her relatives on her mother's side of the family recalled a time the two were sitting in Barbara's parlor having tea when Barbara suddenly became emotional and seemed on the verge of tears. She said she felt she was losing her mind. Everything around seemed dimmed or blunted, she said, as if she were "surrounded by black cotton." She further said she vacillated from feeling emotional about everything to not feeling anything at all. She was really coming apart, and she knew it. Her relative suggested that she see a doctor, but Barbara said that whatever was going on with her would probably pass. "It always does," she said with resignation.

In November 1976, the Democrat Jimmy Carter was elected President. George Bush thought he was a good man, but he also thought he could do a much better job as commander in chief and that getting a Republican back in high office needed to be the party's mandate. He was talking about running, and now with more focus. He had 1980 in his sights.

It helped during this time that George wanted the family to have a home in Houston again. That idea kept Barbara busy as she tried to find one and then furnish it. George hadn't even seen the house when he cosigned the purchase documents in January 1977.

As soon as they moved in, the Bushes entertained King Hussein of Jordan, as well as many other notables, including Vice President Nelson Rockefeller. For a time in the spring of 1977, Barbara felt a little better about things. It would take a lot more time, though, for her to get over her latest dark spell. She would later say six months, but others in her life say it was more like two years. Others aren't sure she ever really got past it. It helped that two grandchildren appeared during this time, born to Jeb and Columba: George Prescott Bush in April 1976 and Noelle Lucila Bush in July 1977.

In the fall of 1977, Barbara and George returned to China, this time as guests of the government. The day after she and George got back home, their son George W. showed up with a new woman at his side and announced that he wanted to marry her. Again? Another son wanting to marry someone his parents didn't know? Barbara wasn't sure if she should be happy, sad, or angry. She just felt dead inside.

PART TWELVE

Laura and George W.

Complacent

It was now 1977, almost fifteen years after Laura's accident that had claimed Mike Douglas's life. In those years, Laura had become a very insular person. She wasn't much for parties, had a few good friends, and was really a loner. She had moved to Austin from Houston, where she'd been working as a librarian. She was living by herself in a small apartment on the second floor of a dilapidated house close to the University of Texas, where she'd recently gone to graduate school in its library science program. She was working, again as a librarian, now for the Mollie Dawson Elementary school in a Hispanic urban neighborhood of Austin. She had a cat, a black-and-white shorthair named "Dewey" for the Dewey decimal system. She'd dated a few guys, hoping one might make her happy, and stockbroker Jimmy McCarroll came close, but in the end none of these romances lasted.

Laura was in a rut and she knew it. Hers was a safe, easy, and orderly kind of life she could control, an escape from the terrible event that had so devastated her. She had found a way forward that made sense to her all these many years after the most painfully uncontrollable event of her life. "My life had found its routine: work in Austin, visits to Midland a few times a year," she recalled. "My summer vacations consisted of a week or two of visiting Mother and Daddy and trips around Texas to visit friends. I was back on the flat asphalt highway between Austin and Midland, bisecting the geography of Texas, the Big Empty, as it is often known. And I was thirty years old."

Things might have continued that way for many more years to come if not for a friend of Laura's named Jan Donnelly O'Neill, with whom she had gone to grade school and with whom she had also roomed at the Chateaux Dijon in Houston. Jan had married a man named Joey O'Neill in 1972. For the last year, the couple kept talking about someone they referred to as "Bush Boy." Jan said she realized George and Laura were opposites in some ways, but that these differences might be the glue to cement a good relationship. That didn't make sense to Laura. "If he's so different, what could I possibly have in common with him?" she asked Jan. "You'll find out if you'll just meet him" was her answer. She suggested a blind date.

When Jan mentioned that this man—this "Bush Boy"—had just announced that he was running for Congress, it was but one more strike against him as far as Laura was concerned. She liked politics, of course, but not necessarily politicians, and the fact that George was a Republican wasn't helpful, either. She was a Democrat, always had been, and remained progressive in her views. "But they were both well read, well educated," Jan O'Neill recalled. "I just thought they would have fun together. They both have a great sense of humor. It's like any other blind date you put together— you don't expect it to work really, but they're your good friends and you want to get them together."

"Bush Boy"

Now thirty-one in 1977, George Walker Bush was "still a good ol' Texas boy," or so he once described himself. He was good-looking, six foot two, slim, with brown hair that always seemed tousled. He had mischievous glint in his eye. He was sexy, but in a naughty kind of way that might've concerned any parent. In other words, he seemed like trouble. His rakish, devil-may-care attitude worked for him, though, and he'd lost count of how many women he'd had in his bed. Some potential suitors saw his irresponsibility as a sign of immaturity, but, as he himself said, "that don't bother me none." He didn't try to impress. He knew who he was. In some ways, he *was* impressive, with degrees from Yale and Harvard Business School. But despite his education, he didn't seem like a serious person.

He had been in the Texas Air National Guard as a pilot, though he'd scored very low on a pilot aptitude test. Serving in the Air National Guard had the benefit of allowing him to avoid Vietnam. He was even suspended from flying for failing to take a required physical; most people believed then and still do that he had ducked out because he didn't want it to be revealed that he had drugs in his system. The highest honor he would ever receive was an honorable discharge in 1970; he never saw combat in any form, nothing at all like what his father had seen in the war. It felt like a real failure.

Certainly everyone knew H.W. was disappointed in his namesake and would have been prouder if he'd served his country in Vietnam.

Throughout these years, George would drink to the point where he'd pass out, and it had happened more times than he cared to remember. He had a DUI under his belt, from back in October 1976 in Kennebunkport; it made all the papers in Maine at the time. His father was furious with him. Barbara didn't want to speak to him for weeks. It took some time for things to settle down in the family. There was another incident when George, drinking too much, crashed into some trash cans with Jeb in the car. When confronted by his father, it became more clear than ever that George had a lot of pent up resentment toward him; he even had the temerity to challenge his father to a fistfight! George H.W. could not have been angrier or more disappointed. Never would he have disrespected Prescott in that way. But H.W. had quietly lived up to his father's expectations without complaint, even if he did feel pressure and was unhappy about it. W. was more emotional and, it might be argued, maybe even more in touch with his feelings—and his anger.

George also did cocaine from time to time and was known to joke to friends about it, saying, "That's how cowboys put hair on their chests." For years, he would successfully dodge what became known in the press as "the cocaine question," never actually denying he'd imbibed but also not confirming it. For instance, during the presidential primaries in 1999, eleven out of twelve candidates in both parties denied ever using cocaine. George was the only one who refused to answer the question. "What I did as a kid?" he observed. "I don't think it's relevant."

"He drove his mother crazy with his irresponsibility," said Laurence Jeffrey Edmonds, a friend of Jeb's from these early days who occasionally went bar-hopping with Jeb and George. He recalled the time he and the Bush brothers returned to George's home after an all-night bender and found Barbara sitting in the kitchen waiting for her sons. She had let herself into his house. "I need to get that spare key from you," an annoyed George told her. "Oh, yeah?" she said. "Well, lotsa luck with that." As soon as Jeb saw his mother, he made a beeline for the bedroom in order to avoid her.

Edmonds recalled, "Barbara was upset that we'd been out drinking.

She reminded George that his father and grandfather had both been inde-
pendently wealthy by the time they were thirty-one. George said, 'But they
were sharks and that's not me. Besides, lots of people hate Dad,' he told
her. He said he'd been hearing stories for years about land the old man had
stolen, gushers that shouldn't have been his, money he'd overcharged for
property and for oil. 'Dad ain't no saint, Mom,' he said. But Barbara didn't
want to hear it. She popped him on the side of his head with the palm of her
hand and told him, 'Maybe it wouldn't hurt to have a little more in you of
whatever he has in *him*! After all, we're family.' To which George said, 'You
make that sound like it's a good thing.' She was fed up with him. 'The world
isn't fair, son,' she said. 'You're just learning this?' He started to leave but
she stopped him, kissed him on the cheek, and gave him a look that said,
Shape up, buster."

Barbara then apologized to Edmonds for the scene. "She told me George
was a Bush through and through," he recalled, "and she worried that he'd
have to carry the weight of that name. She said it wouldn't be easy on him.
She knew this because his father, H.W., had to live with the same high expectations. "I really do believe in my son, though,' she told me. I was surprised
because I knew George didn't think so. 'You do?' I asked. She smiled at me
and said, 'Of course I do. I'm his mom.'"

By the time he was thirty-one, George W. Bush was still living a reckless
life, and perfectly content doing so. He was now back in Midland, where
he'd spent much of his youth. He'd just started his own oil company, called
Arbusto Energy—*arbusto* is Spanish for "bush"—and managed to convince
some of his relatives to invest in it, including his parents. He had just recently bought a new house on West Golf Course Road. But the oil business
wasn't working for him. Despite all his father's connections and the fact that
the old man had previously been so successful at it, George just foundered.
He needed something else to do, something that would distinguish him.

On July 6, 1977, Representative George Mahon announced his retirement from Congress after twenty-two consecutive terms of service representing the Lubbock-based nineteenth congressional district. George decided
to declare his candidacy for that seat. Though the decision seemed to come
out of the blue, it made some sense. After all, he had participated in three of

his father's campaigns and seemed to enjoy it. Also, he had been involved in Gerald Ford's presidential run in Midland in 1976 and had also worked for Republican candidates in Alabama and Florida. He now felt he could make a difference, and felt he maybe had what it took in terms of charisma and likability, traits that could take a politician far. Just as important, though, he wanted to duplicate his father's success, and if it wasn't going to be in oil maybe it would be in politics.

His parents were astonished that George wanted to run for office. "They were a little confused about why I was doing this," George later admitted. Barbara, in particular, had to wonder if her son's new political ambition was just a lark or serious business. In front of family, she cringed when he announced he was running. "I thought you'd be happy," he told her. She said she *was* happy, but also concerned about repercussions should he lose. "It would be bad for the family," she said, "and could hurt your father politically."

It was interesting that Barbara expressed concern about her husband's political future given her well-known ambivalence about politics. She recognized, however, that George H.W. had worked hard in government for many years and that he had future aspirations which she didn't want to see jeopardized. It was also true that she and George H.W. would have preferred it if Jeb had been the one going into politics. Even though he'd had a rocky start in education, he seemed, in their minds anyway, to be a much more serious person than his older brother. "They had their eye on Jeb," is how Charlie Younger, a childhood friend of George's, put it, "not George."

In late July 1977, Laura Welch returned to Midland to visit Jenna and Harold. They had settled into a place where they were comfortable together. While Laura was home, her friends took it as an opportunity to finally introduce her to George Bush. The O'Neills hosted a small barbecue in their backyard; it was just the four of them—Jan, Joey, George, and Laura. This was the blind date Jan had been talking about.

George was immediately taken by Laura, while she was more cautious about him. Besides her obvious beauty—she was still rail-thin with brunette hair cut short, dazzling blue eyes, and that iridescent smile—she was also intelligent and well-spoken. George liked intelligent women. His mother and grandmother were well-read, thoughtful, and deeply feeling women, so he gravitated toward those same qualities in the few women he'd seriously dated. That night, he stayed later at the cookout than he'd intended. He was interested in Laura.

Once they started talking about their lives, they quickly realized they actually did have something in common: Midland. His family had moved to Midland when he was three and stayed there until he was thirteen, in 1959, and Laura had grown up there.

A quick courtship followed. In George, Laura saw someone with great potential, a man she suspected had been underrated by a lot of people in his life. While on the surface, in speaking to him about his worldview and how he wanted to help the disenfranchised, she realized he had good intentions. She felt he actually did want to be a better person and not just a "Good-time Charlie," but maybe kept getting in his own way. He *was* trying, though. She also recognized his family's low estimation of him and couldn't understand the reason for it. "It's because excess is never enough when it comes to achievement in this family," he told her.

Considering that he was raised with such wealth, Laura thought it admirable that George was able to understand and empathize with so-called kitchen table issues concerning everyday Texans, such as taxes and education. Unlike her father, he seemed to respect the women in his family. And George cared about her views. Also, he had introduced passion and sexual excitement to her life like no one before him. He was wild in bed with plenty of experience, and she'd never known anyone quite like him. He was exhilarating. Still, it wasn't easy for her to open up to him. It would take a real leap of faith for Laura to give in to emotional intimacy him.

"He's a little rough around the edges, sure," Laura said a couple of weeks after meeting George. "But he knows who he is, and I like a man who's strong in who he is." She and this friend were splitting a pizza at Luigi's, an Italian restaurant in Midland. "Do you think he's the one?" her friend asked. Laura said she didn't think she believed in the romantic notion of "the one," but pragmatically concluded, "I like him, though. I like him a lot. If he's not *the* one, he's definitely *a* one."

On their third date, Laura finally confided in George about the accident that had claimed Mike Douglas's life. He was sorry she had gone through such an ordeal. He also reminded her of the many years that had passed since the tragedy and suggested it was time for her to move on from it. His heart went out to her, though.

Laura asked George not to tell his family. He agreed. They found out anyway. It took about a month before an aide of George H.W.'s came to him with the information, armed with news clips, the police report, and even photos of the scene. Shortly thereafter, George H.W. asked his son to fly to Houston to discuss what he called "a personal matter." When George arrived, his father laid it all out for him, all the details of the accident, saying he wanted him to be aware of it. George said he already knew. So what was he going to do about it? "Nothing," George answered, "absolutely nothing." George H.W. took him in for a moment, studying his face. Then he shook his head, smiled, and said, "Good for you. That's my boy." George, according to this account, asked if his mother knew about it. George H.W. smiled and said, "What do you think?" Barbara knew. However, they had both decided, he told his son, that they would never mention it to Laura, not unless she brought it up first. That was the end of the discussion. It took no longer than about five minutes.

Meeting the Parents

In late September, while they were at her small apartment in Austin, George Bush asked Laura Welch to marry him. The next night, he went to meet Jenna and Harold, neither of whom was quite sure what to make of him. He was polite, which went far with Jenna, but the well-connected Harold had already checked around and learned of George's reputation as a ne'er-do-well. However, Jenna saw a marked difference in Laura in the few short weeks George had been in her life. She seemed lighter, happier. "She always looked like she had the weight of the whole world on her shoulders before she met George," Jenna would say. She decided that George might be just what Laura needed. She reminded Harold that they, too, met on a blind date, and had been together ever since. Her only fear was that George might blow it because he was pushing so hard. "Laura usually didn't like it when guys were pushy," she recalled, "and I wanted to say to him, slow down, because I really wanted it to work."

Jenna told a relative that, in her company, George said to Laura, "I love that you believe in me." Laura froze. Maybe it seemed too soon for that kind of emotional intimacy. Even though they were engaged, it was as if she still felt they barely knew each other. She was leery.

Still, if he was going to be in his daughter's life, Harold was going to work to get to know George better. "He loved sports and enjoyed putting down a wager or two on football," George recalled of him. "His hangout was Johnny's Barbecue. The locals called it the Sick Pig because of the awful wooden pig on top of the restaurant. One day Laura's dad introduced me to his friends at the Sick Pig, including Johnny himself. I think I passed muster, because I was offered a Screwdriver. I turned it down. It was nine o'clock in the morning."

On a Sunday in early October, Laura finally met George's parents at the home of his brother Jeb. George H.W. and Barbara had just gotten home from a visit to China and he'd recently taken a position as the chairman on the executive committee of the First International Bank of Houston. Barbara was just happy he was out of politics—for now, anyway. The occasion for the Bushes to come together was the christening of Jeb and Columba's daughter, Noelle. George had warned Jeb that he was bringing Laura to the christening, and that he had asked her to marry him. "Really?" Jeb asked. "But you've known her for, what? A couple months? I've had beers in the fridge longer than that," he quipped.

When Barbara first met the senior Bushes back in the 1940s, she found herself wondering if she'd ever be able to fit into such a close-knit family, with all its history, camaraderie, and inside jokes and competitive spirit. She never forgot, though, how Dorothy had extended herself to make her feel welcome. Barbara had tried to do the same with Columba, but the two had never seemed able to gel.

Columba was always sweet, but the fact that she wouldn't call Barbara "Mother" and instead continued to call her "Mrs. Bush" was still off-putting. It was as if she didn't really want to be close. Or maybe it was just cultural? Barbara wondered. Now, when she looked at Laura Welch, at first blush she saw a tentative young woman whose eyes were as big as saucers. Another lost lamb in the woods, just like Columba? *Here we go again*, Barbara may have thought.

George's entire immediate family was together when Laura first walked into the house, and it had to have been intimidating for her, especially when the comedian of the bunch, Jeb, fell to one knee, took Laura's hand in his own and, turning to his brother, joked, "So have you proposed to her yet, old boy?" Of course, he already knew the answer. Without missing a beat, Laura gazed down at Jeb and said, "Why, yes, he has. And I accepted." Her surprising response was met with stunned silence. When everyone realized it was true, they all broke out in cheers. "She just jumped right in and met us at our own level," Barbara said later. "It was like Audrey Hepburn walking into the Animal House," said George's younger brother Marvin. "Here was this bright, cerebral, lovely human being—a very serene-type person—coming into this chaotic environment known as the Bush household."

George and Barbara weren't sure that their son was serious. He'd had a previous failed engagement back in January 1967 to a Houston woman named Cathryn Wolfman, a college graduate who majored in art and literature. This sudden relationship with Laura felt impulsive to Barbara, especially given that they said they wanted to be married before the end of the year.

Before she'd left for this most recent trip to China, Barbara had had a visit with George that did not go well. He was clearly inebriated when, again, she let herself into his home. She was angry about it and, once again, told him he had to pull himself together. "You are *such* a disappointment," she told him. As usual, George didn't just take it without question; he challenged his mother even though he was in the wrong. "By the time I get back from China, you'd better be straightened up, mister," Barbara had told him.

Now she had returned, and instead of presenting her a new version of himself, he presented a new girlfriend he wished to marry. Though Barbara wasn't happy about it, she did her best to be gracious. "At least it was a commitment of *some* sort," she later told one relative, "and I just wanted him to be committed to something other than playing around."

Unlike Barbara, George H.W. sensed that this was the real deal for his son. He took out his pocket calendar and started reviewing the family's plans for every weekend that coming fall. Eventually, the family settled on a date for Laura and George: November 5, 1977.

Uniting Two Very Different Families

This second wedding in the Bush family was an exciting time. Barbara and George felt more relaxed about things than they'd been when Jeb and Columba married. When Jeb wondered if maybe George was being impulsive, George reminded him that at least he had the good sense to introduce his fiancée to their father before the wedding day. The two always had a push-and-pull kind of rivalry going between them, especially as they got older. "It's hard not to be competitive when you were raised in a family like mine," Jeb has said.

The rehearsal dinner for George and Laura was held on Friday, November 4, 1977, in the basement of the Hilton Hotel in Midland. The meal served was a basic chicken-and-rice dish. Barbara and George hosted, and this would mark the first time they'd have an opportunity to meet Laura's parents, Jenna and Harold Welch.

One might imagine that George and Harold wouldn't have found much common ground given their completely different stations in life, but George could get along with anyone. It would take him less than three minutes to find common ground with a person; he and Harold got along just fine, as did Barbara and Jenna. When Barbara and Jenna met, it was as if they'd always known each other. Barbara took her in her arms and held her for a long time. From their children, they were aware of each other's tragic stories, the many babies Jenna had lost, the young daughter Barbara had buried. It had been many years ago for both women, but they still carried with them all the pain and sorrow. They would always have a certain kind of understanding.

Keeping it light, Barbara was overheard complimenting Jenna on the way she had raised Laura, and she asked about her secret. She had a daughter, she told her, and her own way of doing things, but she wondered about Jenna's. Jenna thought for a moment and said, "Well, to be honest, I spent most of the time just assuming I had no idea what the heck I was doing, and then I went ahead and did it anyway." Barbara looked taken aback. "My God, that's exactly what I did," she exclaimed. "You hit the nail on the head, Jenna. You really did."

Jenna then confided in Barbara that she was embarrassed because the meal she had planned for tomorrow's wedding reception at the Midland Racquet Club was . . . chicken and rice. She hadn't thought to ask Barbara what her menu was to be for the rehearsal dinner. Barbara laughed. "Well, you know, I could have just as well called you to tell you, and I didn't think to do that either," she said, letting Jenna off the hook. "I'll tell you what, though," she said, wrapping her arm around Jenna's shoulder. "You can never have too much chicken and rice. Right? So don't worry about it." The next day at the wedding reception, chicken and rice was served again.

A mere three months after she met him, on Saturday, November 5, 1977—the day after her thirty-first birthday and a day before the fourteenth anniversary of the accident—Laura Welch became George Bush's wife in a small ceremony at the Methodist church in Midland. There hadn't even been time to have formal wedding invitations printed; Jenna just wrote them out by hand. Laura didn't want a formal wedding with a traditional white wedding gown and, as George put it, "all the trimmin's." Instead, she bought a very simple ivory silk skirt and blouse right off the rack. She had gardenias in her hair and carried a bouquet of the same flower. There were no groomsmen, no bridesmaids. Perhaps seventy-five family members and friends attended.

After the ceremony, Dorothy was heard telling Laura, "One thing I can promise you, my dear, is that you will never be bored in this family. My son may run for President one day, did you know that? It's going to be all hands on deck. Are you ready to pitch in?" It was a strange thing for Dorothy to say. After all, George H.W.'s intentions weren't that widely known. Unless George had told Laura about them, there was no way she would have been aware. According to a witness, she just said, "My, my. Isn't that nice, Mrs. Bush. You must be very proud."

Laura was also heard telling Barbara she hoped her marriage to George would be as happy as Barbara's was to his father. Barbara took the compliment graciously, even though she may have had a few private thoughts about it considering what had lately been going on with George.

It was at about this time that Barbara looked across the room and her eye caught George talking to an attractive woman in a corner. She squinted to look more closely until, much to her astonishment, she finally realized who it was: Jennifer Fitzgerald. Apparently, George had invited her to the reception—not the wedding—and hadn't put her name on the guest list. Was this omission intentional in that he didn't want Barbara to know she was coming?

Prior to the wedding, Laura Welch had packed up her apartment in Austin and then watched with anticipation as the movers loaded her small stash onto a truck and drove away. Then she and her cat, Dewey, got into her car and began the five-hour drive back to Midland. It was difficult to believe she was going back to the country town she had so loved as a child. Then again, though, somehow it made perfect sense.

The car accident when she was seventeen had laid waste to all Laura had cherished in Midland. She had left Midland, desperate to be somewhere—anywhere—people didn't know her. For the next seventeen years, she had wandered aimlessly as she tried to find purpose in her life and lose herself in her work. It took the right man coming into her life before Laura began to once again feel good about the world around her. George saw her for the good person she was, and he wanted to be there for her. He then helped her fulfill a dream she'd long harbored: He brought her back home.

Reclaiming That Lost Girl

Once the newlyweds returned from their honeymoon on Cozumel, Mexico, to their home in Midland at 1405 West Golf Course Road, a single-story, 2,500-square-foot, two-bedroom brick ranch home, it was time to get to work. George was running for Congress in the nineteenth district. A lot of people were still surprised. Harold Welch, who actually liked his son-in-law, put it this way: "I think he's got less sense than you can spread on a gnat's ass with a butter paddle." Still, George knew what he wanted, and Laura would get her first taste of politics by canvassing all over West Texas in George's Oldsmobile Cutlass. A lot of the campaigning was in small neighborhoods in the homes of farmers, where George would shake hands with a handful of people and then sit down at a kitchen table and have coffee and pastries with them. It was a grassroots effort, to say the least. Because the district had been traditionally Democratic, George knew he had his work cut out for him.

They got along so well, Laura couldn't believe her good fortune. All her new husband seemed to want was to make her happy, and he constantly expressed his gratitude for just having her at his side. Laura also knew he valued her opinion. Right before the two began campaigning, she had a conversation with her mother-in-law, Barbara. "What would you suggest in terms of our campaigning together?" Laura asked. Certainly, Barbara had a great deal of experience in this regard. "Just don't criticize his speeches," Barbara told her. She explained that politicians need all the emotional support they can get in order to stand before an audience and be persuasive, and that it has to start with the wife. Something about that advice bothered Laura, though; it just seemed so old-fashioned. No, she decided. Maybe it had worked for Barbara, but it wouldn't work for her. She knew she needed to speak her mind, and she didn't want to be in a marriage where she'd feel constrained from doing so.

At one point in the campaign, after a speech in Lubbock, George asked Laura how he'd done. He knew it hadn't gone well, and he suspected Laura felt the same. He kept pushing for compliments during the drive home. Laura was evasive. She didn't want to pile on; she knew he already felt badly about the speech. However, he wouldn't let up; he really wanted to know her feelings, or maybe he was just fishing for a compliment. He stayed on the subject, refusing to let it go. As they were pulling into their driveway, Laura finally turned to him and said, "Okay. You know what, George? It wasn't good. Okay? You could do better." George was so surprised, and maybe even a little bit delighted by her moxie, he turned to look at her and, in doing so, lost control of the car as they were pulling into the garage. He ended up smashing right into the back wall. They'd joke about it publicly for years, with Laura saying she learned not to criticize his speeches, or maybe George saying he'd learned not to ask her opinion. Neither was true; that's not the kind of relationship they had. They spoke their minds, and when Laura had an opinion, George listened even if he didn't always agree.

George began to wonder if Laura might be an asset to him on the campaign trail. After all, she was charming and personable; people seemed to like her. She lacked confidence, though, and sometimes it showed.

One day, George said he had a scheduling conflict and wouldn't be able to give a speech in the small town of Levelland. "You'll have to pinch-hit for me," he told her. She looked at him as if he'd lost his mind. "Me?" she asked. "No way. I can't get up in front of people and speak. That's just not me, George." He wanted her to take a chance, though, and said he believed she could do it. It would be a small crowd, a good testing ground for her. If she failed, maybe a dozen people would know about it. But if she was a success, she would know it, and it might make a huge difference in her life.

Laura knew that George was far too organized in his campaign to ever have a scheduling snafu. He'd orchestrated a scenario for her to be able to rise to the occasion. She was afraid, but she also wanted to do it. She saw it as potentially a giant leap forward in her recovery, and she also knew that if she could pull it off it would make George proud of her. Therefore, she agreed.

George didn't tell Laura that his rivals—two Democrats and two Republicans—would be right up there on that stage with her, sitting in folding chairs behind her. Their presence certainly raised the stakes. It was one thing to humiliate herself in front of twelve people she didn't know and would never see again, another to do so in front of other politicians vying for the same seat as her husband, all of whom she'd run into again on the campaign trail.

It was mid-March 1978, and Laura Bush stood on a small makeshift wooden stage in front of a flat, one-story building in the middle of an empty parking lot in a small West Texas town. This was the Levelland Courthouse, and Laura faced a small group of people who seemed only mildly interested in what it was she had to say.

"I'm standing here before you," Laura began, "to talk about . . ." She faltered. "Well," she said, "to, um . . . to kind of . . . well, to talk about you . . . I mean to talk to you about . . . my husband." For a second she seemed to even forget his name. Then she smiled and said, "George. George Bush." She added, "A few months ago, he promised me that I would never have to give a political speech. Well, so much for that promise, I guess, because here I am." A few people chuckled, but the joke landed with a thud. She would later remember feeling deflated. Reading from handwritten notes, she then talked about George's commitment to the people of West Texas to "make a difference in your community, and people are excited about what he wants to do. I know I am." She spoke in generalities. Maybe it wasn't an impressive speech. However, there was something about her that drew people in, and it could have been her vulnerability, or maybe just her sheer honesty. She genuinely did believe in George, and she wanted others to do so as well.

Laura spoke for about five minutes. A few people applauded, some smiled at her, some seemed to have listened. However, this day would mark the beginning of a new age in the life of Laura Bush. It felt good to take on such a challenge, and even if it hadn't been a great speech, it had been hers and it had been delivered with everything she had in her. "When I finished speaking, I wasn't particularly eager to do it again, but it also wasn't nearly as bad as I had anticipated." It felt right, and it felt to her like she could do it again one day. She knew that if given the chance, she could be better.

In the end, George won the Republican primary, and Kent Hance the Democratic primary. Unfortunately, George ended up losing to Hance, but, at 53 percent to 47 percent, only by about 6 percent of the vote. The heartening news was that he had gotten more than 75 percent of his hometown Midland's votes; that meant a lot. George was disappointed, of course, as was the family. However, Barbara felt gratified that he had handled himself well throughout the campaign. He hadn't been an embarrassment, anyway. She started seeing in her son shades of his father's eagerness to be of service and to do something meaningful for others, which had always been his grandfather's attitude as well. "I started thinking, Okay, maybe I had misjudged him," Barbara would admit, "and I started thinking I needed to be more supportive of George. It gave me a lot to think about, actually."

After losing the election, George returned to his work at Arbusto Energy while Laura tended to the business of setting up house for them in Midland. "I'm all name and no money," he complained during these lean times. But after the loss at the polls, things seemed different for both of them, and they sensed it. "We were disappointed," Laura later said, "but not devastated. It was a leap forward, I think, for both of us—for me as a public person and for George as a public servant. I began to feel excited about our future in politics, and it would never have occurred to me before George Bush to ever have imagined being in public life. He was opening my eyes to a whole new world. The wonderful part was that I knew it while it was happening. It's not as if I have had to look back on it to realize it. I knew it then, which made it all the more exciting."

PART THIRTEEN

VP

What to Do About Bar?

During the summer of 1978, George H. W. Bush invited allies and confidants to Kennebunkport to discuss the possibility of his running for President in 1980 in an effort to unseat Jimmy Carter. Politics was still not something Barbara enjoyed. She felt her son had been treated unfairly in his run for Congress. She thought he'd not been given enough credit for the hard work he'd put into mapping out his policies and had, instead, just been painted with a wide brushstroke as an entitled rich kid whose life had been one of lucky breaks. However, she knew she had to support her husband's ambition to be President, even though every time she opened her mouth with a suggestion, he shot her a look that said, *Not now, Barb. Not now.*

Barbara also knew George had been antsy ever since leaving the CIA. He was too ambitious a man at fifty-four to just sit back and watch life pass him by. While he took an office at the First International Bank in Houston and was on its executive committee, what he really wanted was to make a difference in the world. Meanwhile, now that his CIA assignment was over, Jennifer Fitzgerald had finally left George's staff. He arranged for her to be a special assistant to former Yale University president Kingman Brewster, who was the U.S. ambassador to the United Kingdom. Because her ongoing presence had caused a lot of stress in George's organization, most people were happy to see Jennifer go, including Barbara.

"He is uniquely qualified, and I am more than willing to tell people why," Barbara had written to her friend Frances Hammond. "He knows what it means to meet a payroll, work with all government rules and regulations, and he also knows how to wrestle with tough problems and make it work. When you add his business experience to his many government jobs that he did well, it just adds up to the right person at the right time for the job."

During the Kennebunkport summit, George was smart and focused and had great ideas about policy. Several pros and cons to his candidacy were discussed. It was theorized that he didn't have much name recognition despite his many years in government. If he were to run, George would have to build a strong coalition by spending the next year traveling the country and generating support in each state. He wasn't a great speaker, lacking in charisma. He readily agreed he would work on it. The manner by which he had held the party together during Watergate, it was also decided, would definitely bode well for him. "The country is in trouble," he said. "Jimmy Carter has made a mess of things. Unemployment is sky high. The energy crisis is out of control. I know how to straighten it all out." His experience with foreign intelligence was also a plus, as was his vast work in so many other facets of government. As it happened eventually, his campaign's motto was: "George Bush: A President We Won't Have to Train."

George's presumed opponent for the nomination, Governor Ronald Reagan of California, was viewed as somewhat of a lightweight, a former Hollywood actor. Reagan was a Democrat turned Republican, whereas Bush was, as he later put it, "a dyed-in-the-wool Republican."

The die was all but cast: George would try to win the nomination. However, according to what Barbara later recalled, he never had a real conversation with her about the decision. She later said that if she'd had any objections, she would have voiced them. But based on the couple's history, one has to wonder about that.

One thing was certain in Barbara's mind: If she was going to one day be at George's side as First Lady, she wanted to make certain she had a real purpose. As has long been the custom, the First Lady is supposed to have a platform, something she believes in to which she will dedicate herself during her husband's administration. Jackie Kennedy sought to restore the White

House, for instance, whereas Lady Bird Johnson dedicated herself to the beautification of America. Betty Ford had become invested in combating arthritis. This platform usually has to be thought out prior to the White House because it's helpful to use it as a talking point during the campaign.

Barbara settled on literacy and education. She'd long believed education to be key to alleviating many societal problems. Even though she didn't know a lot about the specifics of promoting literacy and realized it was a larger issue than just telling people they needed to read more, she would work to inform herself and figure out ways to get her message across.

After George formally announced his candidacy, he and Barbara hit the road. Barbara would later talk about one stop in particular, a press conference at the Waldorf Astoria in New York, where she was asked to pose with the wives of the other candidates: Nancy Reagan, wife of Ronald; Joy Baker, wife of Senator Howard Baker; Jackie Fernandez, wife of Ben Fernandez; and Elizabeth Dole, wife of Bob Dole. They weren't asked to speak, just stand next to one another and smile. The moment hit Barbara hard: The other women were all so thin and beautiful, at least in her eyes. Compared to them, she felt unattractive and overweight. "In a beauty contest or best-dressed contest, I didn't stand a chance," she later wrote. She got through it, though, and vowed to at least try not to compare herself to others or have a critical self-view lest she fall back into a real depression. It wasn't easy. Almost always, she could feel the pull of that ubiquitous black hole; it was everything she could do to just not sink right in, especially when she felt people pushing her toward it. Recently, at a rally in San Antonio, she had been standing next to her husband and a photographer shouted out, "Will the woman in the red dress standing next to George Bush please get out of the photo?" She recalled, "I looked down at my dress and I thought, My lord, it's me."

Shortly after the campaign began, Barbara heard from her sister-in-law Nancy Bush Ellis that a topic of discussion among some of the women in the family over a recent dinner was: "What are we going to do about Bar?" In other words, how were they to make her presentable as a serious candidate's wife? Maybe they should encourage her to dye her hair? Or lose weight? How about hiring a stylist? It was all so hurtful; Barbara couldn't believe such critique was coming from within her own family. It made her cry with despair. Though she knew that, especially these days, she had to be tough and not sensitive, she couldn't help it. This kind of criticism tapped into all her insecurities—"Eat up. *But not you, Barbara*," her mother had said, and she could still hear those words ringing in her ears. She also knew that some people they'd met recently actually thought she was George's mother, not his wife. That, too, was painful. Though George assured her she shouldn't change a thing, especially her white hair, which, by now, had become a true signature, she had to really go within and pull herself together just to get past the fact that there were those in her own family who thought she, just as she was, wasn't good enough.

When Nancy told her mother about the catty criticism of Barbara, Dorothy was outraged and wanted to know specifically who was responsible. Nancy didn't want to start a family war, however, by naming names. A couple of days later, Dorothy called Barbara. She told her that whatever she had heard from the rumor mill, she should completely disregard. She was deeply ashamed of her family, she said, and added that as far as she was concerned, Barbara was "a remarkable woman." Anyone who couldn't see that, she said, "has no eyes, and," she concluded, "to heck with them, Bar. To heck with them."

Tucking Away Her Sadness

During the campaign, George Bush decided to return Jennifer Fitzgerald to his staff. She'd only been gone a couple of years, but now she was back. This decision was difficult for Barbara to reconcile. She had told many people she was happy Jennifer was gone, and now she had to just accept that she was back. It was embarrassing. Shouldn't the fact that she didn't want Jennifer around count for anything? "But George had promised Jennifer she would always have a job with him," explained one source. "He was sorry he wasn't able to find something for her when he left the CIA. But during the campaign, he needed an assistant and he thought of her. He assured Barbara there was no affair, that it was strictly business. End of story."

Apparently, Barbara found a place in her heart for any hurt relating to Jennifer, and she worked hard to keep her sadness tucked away separate and apart from everything else. Perhaps she didn't think Jennifer was worth blowing up her whole world over. "Plus she loved her husband," said one source, "and she wanted to believe in him." Also, something else always came into play when Barbara weighed the terms of her marriage, and that was the way she and George had shared their sorrow over the death of little Robin. That tragedy so many years ago had bound her so tightly to him she always came back to it when trying to decide how she felt about things. In June, Barbara turned fifty-four, and a note from George to commemorate that milestone perhaps also explains why she was willing to look the other way where Jennifer was concerned. "I love you very much," George wrote. "Nothing, campaign separations, people, nothing will ever change that. I can't ever really tell you how much I love you." He signed it, "Pop."

Barbara's daughter-in-law Laura had heard the stories about George and Jennifer, just as had most people in the family. She didn't know whether to believe them, and certainly would never have asked Barbara. She was fairly new to the family and none of it was any of her business anyway.

One day Laura was in the Houston office when she and Barbara spotted Jennifer. According to one of the Secret Service agents charged with protecting George (most candidates had such protection), Barbara was in the process of giving Laura some good advice. She told her that if a reporter ever put her on the spot, she mustn't "spit and sputter like an old Buick running low on gas." She suggested she be firm, because otherwise the media would walk all over her. She then offered to let Laura shadow her as she did an interview later that day with the *Houston Chronicle*. While holding both her hands, she assured her that she, Barbara, wasn't adept at giving interviews, either—she was actually very good at giving them—and so maybe they could help each other out. At that point, the two noticed Jennifer standing in a corner trying to look busy, reading from a clipboard. Was she eavesdropping? "Mrs. Bush did a double take and then stared Mrs. Fitzgerald down," recalled the agent. "Mrs. Fitzgerald gave her a sort of embarrassed smile, turned on her heels, and walked down the hall. Mrs. Bush then said, 'Just look at that one, Laura. The light's on, but nobody's home.' Laura started giggling, 'Well, God bless her little heart, then,' she said. They had a laugh."

The agent continued, "But then Mrs. Bush realized I'd overheard them. She walked right up to me and hit me on the shoulder with a steno pad. 'Hey. You. Stop being such a busybody,' she told me. 'Don't you have something to do? Go guard somebody!' I had to laugh."

When George's campaign manager Jim Baker had had enough of the stories that continued going around about Jennifer, he told George that either she would have to go or he would. It was only then that George reluctantly told Jennifer to pack her bags and leave for New York, where she could work from the office there; George then paid her salary out of his own pocket.

There was little time to worry about anything other than campaigning. It was hard work, flying from one city to the next, shaking hands, trying to be personable, especially when Barbara and George were exhausted. Beyond the public relations of it all was the need to articulate George's policies, which he continued to fine-tune and present in a thoughtful way—issues relating to the economy, energy, or defense. He also spoke of the deregulation of industry, the boosting of America's influence in foreign affairs, and what he felt was "a decline in U.S. credibility and certainly a mounting perception of weakness."

Barbara and George had decided that it made more sense to be in Washington during this time than in Texas, so they rented a home there, on Lowell Street. Meanwhile, the entire family came out to work hard for their patriarch.

George W. and Laura campaigned as much as possible, both eager to chip in.

Jeb and Columba had been living in Venezuela, where he had a job as a bank manager. He decided to leave his position and return to the States to work for his father. He would later become key to the campaign in Puerto Rico, which, at the time, was holding its first primary (which George would win). It was tough on Columba, though, who was not a political animal.

Marvin, a senior at the University of Virginia in Charlottesville, took a year off to stump for his father and work in Iowa. About a month before the election, he would announce his engagement to Margaret Molster, who was also a student at the university. Margaret, born and raised in Richmond, would marry Marvin in June 1981.

Neil was also very involved in the campaign and became engaged as well at this same time to Sharon Smith, a spunky schoolteacher and real estate agent who he'd met while working in the New Hampshire campaign. They married in the summer of 1980 in Kennebunkport at St. Ann's Episcopal Church. Though Barbara said she was "lovely," no one ever witnessed a warm moment between them when Sharon first came into the fold. Maybe that was because the family was too busy to celebrate; "the girl must wonder what kind of family we are," George H.W. fretted in his diary. An uncomfortable moment occurred on the wedding day when a photographer asked for a family portrait. Barbara thought what he wanted was a shot of the immediate family. When the bride got into the frame, Barbara said, "No, I'm sorry, Sharon. We don't want you in the picture." Barbara, always direct, probably didn't mean to hurt Sharon on her special day, but Sharon would never forget it.

When Doro, who was twenty, said she wanted to drop out of Boston College for a year and join her father's campaign, George surprised her by saying she needed to contribute something other than touting herself as the candidate's daughter. She didn't understand why it was okay for his sons to just be his sons, but she had to bring a special skill set to the campaign. It's just the way it is, he told her. Barbara agreed. "Women have to work harder," she told Doro. "We always have to do more." To that end, Doro enrolled in a nine-month course at Katherine Gibbs to learn to type, and that's what she ended up bringing to the campaign headquarters in Boston—her typing skills. She was also extremely personable and well-spoken. People seemed to love her.

Doro's first speech on behalf of her dad was at a Republican women's club in a small Massachusetts town. The audience was comprised mostly of elderly people who seemed, as she looked out from her lectern, to be the friendliest group she ever could have asked for. It didn't matter, though. She froze, the words just not coming forth. "I literally experienced the sensation of choking," she recalled. "By that, I mean not being able to breathe. I opened my mouth to try to talk about my dad, but was so overcome by emotion and fear that nothing but a few unintelligible sounds escaped my lips. So I had no other choice but to sit down. Thus went my very first speaking engagement."

Later, she and her sister-in-law Laura would commiserate about the difficulties of public speaking. Eventually, both would excel in this arena, but their early days were challenging. "Speaking for myself," Doro said, "you just can't think about it. It's the same as anything you're dreading but know you must do. The more you think about it, the worse it is. My grandmother used to say public speaking was like anything else in life that just had to be done. 'You take a deep breath,' she would say, 'and maybe you close your eyes. And then you just plunge in and hope for the best.'"

A Surprising Turn of Events

As the weeks turned into months, George Bush's popularity soared and he was consistently up in the polls. The enthusiasm for him really grew, especially once the press began to take a turn from being dismissive of him to really giving him a fair shot. However, some cynics did feel he wasn't "Republican enough" in his views, which often did tend to be more liberal than the party would have liked. He wasn't as conservative as Reagan. He was against abortion, for instance, a very Republican stance, but for it in the cases of rape and incest, which pitted him against some in his party and much of his constituency.

As it would happen, the subject of abortion was a major one during the primary season, and Barbara was clear about her view in that she was pro-choice. However, she also maintained that abortion shouldn't be used as a contraceptive. Moreover, it should only occur in the first trimester. That said, she felt it was a personal issue that should not be legislated. She and George didn't talk about it much, though. "There was no point in discussing it every time it came up," Barbara later noted.

Much to everyone's excitement, all the hard work and family unity paid off when George won the Iowa caucus, 31.6 percent for Bush to 29.5 percent for Reagan. It was beginning to feel as if he had a real chance. But then morale took a nosedive five weeks later when Reagan prevailed in New

Hampshire, 50 percent to Bush's 23 percent. Some felt that the ongoing Iranian hostage crisis and the Soviets' recent invasion of Afghanistan helped the governor, who appeared a much more hawkish alternative to Bush.

There would be a few more primary wins for George, but mostly losses. Then Reagan won the Nebraska primary, which changed everything because that victory gave him the number of delegates he needed to seize the nomination. "I fear we are very near the end of this long quest," Barbara wrote in her diary. "Will I be able to cope with the letdown George will feel?" Then, with her insecurity maybe showing, she added, "Will I be enough?"

On May 26, 1980, George dropped out of the race in what he would say was "the toughest decision of my life." He then vowed to do everything he could to support Reagan in his effort to defeat Jimmy Carter.

Though most people thought it was over for George H. W. Bush, his mother had a sense that maybe it wasn't. Dorothy said she remembered when Prescott lost the Senate race and they all thought they were finished. They weren't, though. They got pulled right back in when they least expected it. "These things do happen," the very prescient Dorothy Bush concluded.

Immediately after Dorothy's son dropped out, people began talking about the possibility of him being added to the Reagan ticket as his Vice President. At first, George wasn't interested in the role, and neither was Barbara. Both had been laser focused on winning the presidency, and coming in second place held little interest. Besides, no one, in their view, cared much about the Vice President post. Vice Presidents were usually capable statesmen ultimately neutered by the nature of the job. Primarily, as President of the Senate, the Vice President's official duty is to cast the tie-breaking vote in the case of a deadlock in the Senate. Also, he presides over the vote count of the electoral college. Beyond that, he just shows up at certain events and functions and on diplomatic missions overseas and basically appears presidential until the day comes when there's a vacancy in high office by removal, resignation, or death. At that point, according to the Twenty-fifth Amendment, the Vice President ascends to power. The last time this chain of events occurred was pretty recently, in 1974, when Richard Nixon left the presidency in disgrace and was replaced by Gerald Ford, who just eight months earlier had taken over from Spiro Agnew after he resigned in the wake of criminal charges relating to tax evasion. That was recent enough to make the job feel a little more significant.

Ronald Reagan felt he needed a politically moderate Vice President to perhaps satisfy voters who felt he was too far to the right. He also needed someone with more experience in Washington politics. In polls conducted at this time, Bush seemed to be the front-runner for the job, with Gerald Ford second. The problem was that Reagan was angry at Bush, still stinging from some of the criticism lobbed his way during the campaign. He was more interested in Ford for the position.

On July 13, 1980, the Bushes arrived in Detroit for the Republican National Convention and checked into the Hotel Pontchartrain. They didn't know what to expect of Reagan, only that an announcement of his vice presidential pick would soon be made. Gerald Ford, who was staying at the Detroit Plaza, was scheduled to address the convention at the Joe Louis Arena. In his speech, he suggested that he'd be open to joining the Reagan ticket. Suddenly, the bizarre idea of a former President becoming the nation's Vice President actually seemed like a real possibility.

The next day, Reagan appealed to Ford to take the job. George was discouraged when he heard about the offer; Barbara kept her mouth shut and just decided to wait and see what would happen next. Then, after a great deal of private and public discourse about whether Reagan would somehow end up in a strange kind of "co-presidency" with Ford due to his previous Oval Office experience, the governor decided against him. Later that night, the phone rang in the Bush suite: Reagan calling.

"Out, out, out!" Barbara told everyone in the packed room; the place was vacated in seconds. Ronald Reagan asked George Bush to be his Vice President. George was elated. He'd hoped for the presidency, but Vice President wasn't so bad, especially to a President as advanced in years as Reagan. At sixty-nine, he would be the oldest man ever elected; maybe George really *was* just one heartbeat away from the seat of power. It didn't take him long to adjust to the idea, which was very much in character for George Bush. He wanted to serve, and if it was to be as Vice President, he would make the best of it, as would his wife. "You're not going to be sorry," Barbara told Reagan the next morning at breakfast before the press conference to announce his decision. "We're going to work our tails off for you."

On November 4, 1980, America voted Ronald Reagan in as the fortieth President of the United States. The Ronald Reagan–George Bush ticket had prevailed over Jimmy Carter–Walter Mondale in a landslide. The Bushes were ready for the next phase of their lives; as George told Barbara at the time, "I have a feeling things are about to get real interesting."

1 Observatory Circle

It was December 1980. Against the dreary backdrop of a steady rain on a frigid Monday morning, a black Cadillac proceeded slowly up an incline in an affluent neighborhood of Northwest Washington, D.C., called Observatory Circle. As it traveled along the verdant grounds of the United States Naval Observatory, it was followed by another vehicle just like it and then another behind that one, all three meandering along at a funereal pace with their red and blue lights flashing. The first car pulled up to a small guardhouse, one of five on the property. A sliding door opened and a uniformed security guard exchanged a few words with the driver.

As the two men spoke, one passenger in the car, Barbara Bush, reached over and anxiously grabbed the hand of the other, her friend Mary Ann "Andy" Stewart. Andy was the wife of Supreme Court Justice Potter Stewart, who'd sworn George in as the director of the CIA back in 1976; Stewart would retire in a year's time to be replaced by Sandra Day O'Connor, the first woman to ever serve on the court.

After being cleared, the three cars drove single file up to two polished black wrought-iron gates. These gates yawned open to reveal a stately Queen Anne–style brick-and-wood-framed mansion towering in all its majestic glory, painted a gleaming white and accented with sage green shutters. The lawns surrounding it were lush, manicured and dotted with ancient tall trees and small bushes that would flower into a sea of red, pink, and magenta later in the season. This was 1 Observatory Circle, NW, Washington, D.C., home of the Vice President of the United States, just outside historic Georgetown. While practically every American is familiar with the President and First Lady's White House residence at 1600 Pennsylvania Avenue, this place was—and remains today—not as well known. Ask almost anyone where the nation's Vice President lives, and you'll likely be met with a blank stare.

In the past, because the office of the vice presidency had been deemed so irrelevant, few even cared where he lived. The Vice President and his wife were put up in apartments in Washington, or in small homes and even hotel rooms. For instance, Vice President Harry Truman lived in an apartment with no servants; he and his wife, Bess, prepared their own breakfasts and did their own laundry. Later, Hubert and Muriel Humphrey resided in a modest house in Maryland before moving to a condo in Washington. Gerald and Betty Ford lived in a humble colonial home in Virginia, where they did their own cooking and housework.

It was finally decided that makeshift accommodations for Vice Presidents were undignified, especially when people remembered that at any moment the Vice President could end up President, as had happened after Lyndon B. Johnson took over for the fallen John F. Kennedy in 1963. In 1966, a committee was formed to address the minimal money the federal government had customarily provided for the housing of Vice Presidents and their families. Finally, in 1974, after requisite hearings and plenty of red tape, this twelve-acre site on the U.S. Naval Observatory property of seventy-two acres was dedicated to vice presidential housing, with four acres specifically dedicated to the main house itself. Previously, the property had served as the residence for the chief of Naval Operations, and before that the home of the superintendent of the Naval Observatory. It's also where the Master Clock, or Atomic Clock, is, which provides the official and most accurate standard of time for the entire country.

After being cleared by security, the cars moved slowly past them and up a short driveway to the front door. The house's bay windows of different sizes glittered in the morning light. White smoke curled from its chimneys. In typical Queen Anne architecture, the most striking element was its prominent turret, on top of which was perched a weather vane. A welcoming veranda wrapped halfway around the structure.

It was surprising that Barbara was nervous about this visit. After all, she'd been to the home several times in the past when Nelson Rockefeller was Vice President under Gerald Ford, from 1974 to 1977. Though he was the first Vice President to have the opportunity to live here, he'd opted against doing so and just used the place for entertaining purposes. Jimmy Carter's Vice President, Walter Mondale, and his wife, Joan, were the first ones to actually reside here. The Bushes would be its second full-time occupants.

Stepping forth toward the car from a pillared porte cochere was a petite brunette woman. "Joan," Barbara exclaimed as she stepped out of the vehicle. She reached for Joan Mondale's hand, took it in her own, and squeezed it tightly, after which she introduced Mary Ann. The women were all acquainted; as Second Lady for the last four years, Joan had been very social. A dedicated patron of the arts, she was lovingly referred to as "Joan of Art" and, at this time, served as chairperson of the Federal Council on the Arts and Humanities. She was known for the vitality and energy she brought to her passion for the arts.

After a few pleasantries, the three women walked up to the house and went inside. Barbara stood in the foyer and took in her surroundings while soft chamber music played in the background. It was a big house—about ten thousand square feet with twelve-foot ceilings and thirty-three rooms—but somehow it still felt intimate. Barbara took a look around, a faint smile flickering on her lips. Joan then took Barbara on a tour of the well-maintained place, which had been designed back in 1893 by architect Leon E. Dessez.

On the first floor, they walked through a large reception hall, the living room, sitting room—which Joan called the library—and garden room with a sun porch. There was also a pantry and dining room. On the second floor could be found two very large bedrooms, including the master, along with a study and dressing room, which would end up being George's, and a family sitting room. The third floor boasted three more bedrooms, one very large and two that were quite small, one of which was to be housekeeper Paula's. Barbara also would have an office on this floor, which doubled as a gym with a stationary bike and a treadmill (which, at the time, the Bushes called "a running machine"). The view from this floor was pretty spectacular; to the east could be seen the Capitol and the glistening Washington Monument. To the west was the Washington Cathedral sitting atop Mount St. Albans. To the north was the Naval Observatory, the Atomic Clock, and the tennis court and helicopter pad. The kitchen was in the basement—meals were brought to the main floor by use of a dumbwaiter—as was the laundry room and the quarters that housed the navy stewards who helped run the place as well as offices for the Secret Service.

Finally, Joan, Barbara, and Andy made their way back to the library. Once there, they stood in front of a green-tiled fireplace with its white lacquered mantel. On either side were six shelves, each shelf displaying books about the office of the vice presidency, as well as framed pictures and other small pieces of art. However, many of the books were on shelves so high, they couldn't be reached. What was the point, the ever-practical Barbara couldn't help but wonder, of books too high to be accessed and read?

Barbara felt the house was comfortable but, as she later put it, "out of whack." Contemporary pieces of art hung from most of the walls, which seemed incongruous with the otherwise traditional setting. Joan had turned the home into a showplace for modern art; there were paintings and photographs hanging everywhere by Louise Nevelson, Ansel Adams, Robert Rauschenberg, and Edward Hopper. However, Barbara thought the art was, as she later recalled it, "hideous." She also admitted that it wasn't so much that Joan had terrible taste as much as it was that she, Barbara, had none at all when it came to modern art. "George will last about five minutes with most of the pieces in this house," she recalled thinking to herself.

Barbara's critical assessment of the home's décor didn't much matter in the bigger scheme of things because something else happened that day, something that would turn out to be transformative, due in large part to Joan Mondale. What happened was that Barbara, perhaps for the first time, realized she had a role to play on her own.

Joan looked like a Vice President's wife. She was slim with short but stylishly cropped, chestnut-colored hair. On this day, she was fashionable in a jaunty bright red skirt and wool turtleneck sweater and small diamond earrings. She was breezy and full of personality. Her eyes were so large and expressive, they seemed to take over her entire face, yet they were also steady and, somehow, peaceful. Barbara was used to sizing up people, and Joan seemed happy and content. With her dark eyes flashing, she told Barbara that she was now being given a very special opportunity as the wife of the Vice President, and "I promise that you will love every second of it."

Joan proudly noted that things had changed where the office was concerned, and that this transformation was largely due to her husband. After Jimmy Carter was inaugurated in 1977, Walter Mondale emerged as a real power player in his administration, determined to redefine the role. He would pioneer what later became known as "the Mondale Model" for Vice Presidents, Walter became instrumental in helping Jimmy shape policy. He made America's second-in-command a relevant figure for the first time. (Much later, Vice President Dick Cheney under George W. Bush would redefine the role even more, to a point where some wondered if he was actually running the country.)

Joan also told Barbara that with the growing importance of the VP, his wife had also begun to be taken more seriously, and that this dynamic might actually bode well for Barbara's literacy platform. Joan said she needed *four* secretaries just to keep up with all the action. The work was exciting, she said, involving overseas travel, too. The way Joan spoke about it was infectious. It seemed less a political job than a diplomatic one, which made it even more attractive to Barbara. The fact that Joan was a Democrat and Barbara a Republican didn't matter at all, at least not between them. The idea of being truly happy and content while also being of service to the country was what really mattered.

It was on this day that it finally hit Barbara that the time had come for her to stop living her life through her husband. She was fifty-five. How much longer was she going to allow herself to be unhappy?

"As cliché as it sounds, I think she started to get it that it was time for her to start loving herself," said Joan Mondale in her oral history. "When I look back on it, I think maybe her visit to the house that day sort of inspired Barbara Bush to reach out and be, really be, who she knew she could be as the wife of the Vice President. I'm very proud of that. I thought she was an absolutely fabulous woman, and I knew she would do great things in her new role. I knew I would miss playing the part, but I knew Barbara would be magnificent."

"You're responsible for your own happiness," Barbara's grandmother Lulu once told her mother, Pauline. "Take a look around. You've got it made! Be happy about it." And then, as the story goes, Lulu turned to her granddaughter, pointed at her, and said, *"And you too, Barbara."* It was as if now, all these years later, the message was finally received.

Things wouldn't change overnight for Barbara Bush. However, there would be a definite sea change in her attitude, and it would commence at the end of the year 1980.

Out on the far horizon, the first rays of sun shimmered through scudding white clouds just as Joan Mondale walked Barbara Bush away from 1 Observatory Circle.

PART FOURTEEN

Family Geography

Laura's Emotional Roller Coaster

Throughout her childhood, Laura Bush had watched as her mother struggled not only with infertility but also with the devastating sorrow of giving birth to babies who didn't survive. She had long wondered if she'd have to endure similar heartache. "Maybe it's just karma," she told one close friend. Even without elaborating, her friend knew exactly what Laura meant. Perhaps she didn't deserve to be a mother because she had, so many years earlier, robbed another woman of the opportunity to see her son grow into adulthood.

George Bush had never met someone who deserved to be a mother more than Laura. He, too, desperately wanted to be a father. He had four siblings, had thoroughly enjoyed his own childhood, learned a lot about parenting from his folks, and knew he'd be a great dad.

After losing the congressional race in 1978, George had devoted himself to his Arbusto oil company and was still depending on the investments of friends and family members. He set up shop in a three-room office and paid himself $75,000 a year. (That's around $300,000 in today's money.) For the next few years he would try in vain to find an oil well that would set him up for life. By the spring of 1982, he would decide to capitalize on his family name, especially now that his father was in the White House, and rename the company Bush Exploration. It wouldn't help; he'd keep drilling dry holes. Eventually, all his investors would lose their money.

By 1980, George and Laura were real celebrities in Midland. Everywhere they went, people pointed at them and singled them out because not only had George run for Congress, but his father was now Vice President. Also, the couple had a great many friends and family members in Midland, and their life there was a happy one, no surprise considering how much they had always loved the West Texas town. The only thing missing was the one thing they wanted more than anything else: a baby.

George had told Laura not to worry about it; he felt she'd get pregnant right away, maybe even on their honeymoon. After about three years of trying, though, Laura was still unable to conceive. This was heart-wrenching for both of them. Finally, they decided to adopt. While it wasn't an easy decision to abandon the idea of having a child of their own, giving a baby in need a real home still felt right to them, and they knew they'd love an adopted baby just as much as they would if he or she was their biological child.

In the fall of 1980, George and Laura applied at the Gladney Center for Adoption in Fort Worth. Jenna took a picture of them to send along with the application, and looking at that photograph today one can't help but note, first of all, how lovely a couple they were, but also, from the expression of longing on their faces, just how much they yearned to be parents.

After George told his folks of his and Laura's plans to adopt, Barbara suggested that the biggest impediment to becoming pregnant was worrying about whether it would happen. She said she believed with all her heart that George would be a father. She also knew Laura's mother felt the same way about her chances. She was all for adoption, but she still wanted them to try to have their own baby. Barbara then did some research and was able to recommend a fertility expert in Houston, Dr. Robert Franklin.

Betty Wagner was a nurse in Dr. Franklin's office; he passed away in 2018 at the age of ninety after battling Parkinson's disease. "I remember the day George and Laura walked into the Women's Hospital of Texas—of which Dr. Franklin had been one of the founders about five years earlier," she said. "We specialized in endometriosis and fertility. While the Bushes were celebrities in Texas, Dr. Franklin was world-renowned in his field. People came from all over to be treated by him. He had been contacted out of the blue by Mrs. Bush [Barbara], which was impressive. So, yes, he really wanted to help.

"I walked them into Doc's office—his nickname was 'Doc.' It was a lovely, light space filled with books from the floor to the ceiling on one shelf after another. We three sat on one side of his giant mahogany desk; he was on the other. I took notes, and I still have them today. Those notes tell me it was February 18, 1981, when we all met, at ten in the morning.

"Laura and George were the cutest couple; I remember she called him 'Bushie.' I also knew in the span of a heartbeat that she was at the end of her rope. The first thing she said was, 'I'm in my mid-thirties. That's too old to have a baby, isn't it?' Back then, some did consider that age to be risky for a first-time mother. 'But there are no rules to this,' Doc told her. 'The key to having a child under these circumstances is to continue to try but with no attachment to the outcome. And if it's meant to be, it will be.'

"Laura shook her head in dismay. 'No offense, Doctor, but that doesn't do me any good,' she said. 'I've heard that a million times before, but hope for the best and stop thinking about it means nothing to me. Again, I don't mean any disrespect.'"

According to Betty Wagner, George then said, "Well, look, Laura, I'll be goddamned, but that's exactly what Mother told me."

Dr. Franklin laughed. "You tell Mother to come work for me, then," he said. "I could use a gal like her."

"Doc was trying to lighten the mood, but Laura was too distraught to even crack a smile," recalled Betty Wagner. 'I know you want a baby more than anything,' she told George with tears in her eyes, 'and I want to give it to you.' I'll never forget what happened next. He reached over and held her hand and said, 'I want *you*, Laura. Anything else is just more of a blessing, but I already have what I want.' I felt, my God, this is a man so in love with his wife, he can get right to the heart of things with her. I found myself full of respect and admiration for them both."

In the days to come, the doctor suggested hormone replacement therapy for Laura, and he also began giving her a fertility drug known to sometimes result in multiple births. It didn't work. "After that drug failed, Laura really lost hope," said Betty Wagner. "One day, she came in with her mother and she was crying. Mrs. Welch said, 'My daughter can't keep coming here because it's too painful seeing all these women in the same boat. She said it's like a lottery; maybe one will get lucky, but what about the others? She wants to just wait for the adoption. My heart aches for her. Please. Can you talk to her?' I could see that a lot had been going on in a short period of time; emotions were running hot. Laura looked at me and said, 'I can't bear this. Truly.' I held her hand and I told her not to lose faith. 'If God wants you to give birth, you will, Laura,' I told her, 'and if not, you can bear that, too. I think you're a lot stronger than you know.'

"By coincidence, Doc's wife, Mary, was passing through the office. She took Laura in her arms and said, 'Look, I've seen this a million times, Mrs. Bush, and every single time, my husband has been able to figure it out. Doc's brother is a priest, and I'll call him today and tell him to say a rosary for you on Sunday, okay?' Laura wiped away her tears; I could tell she felt better. Mrs. Welch held her tightly, and by this time we were all crying."

One day soon after, while Laura was in the hospital having more tests, she received a surprise telephone call from George's grandmother Dorothy. She hadn't had a lot of exposure to Dorothy, but she liked her very much and knew the feeling was mutual. Virginia Mason recalled, "George had called his grandmother and asked her to call Laura. He said she was very sad and that if anyone could prop her up it would be Dorothy."

"I was in the room when Mrs. Bush called Laura," Betty Wagner recalled. "I would say she spoke to her for about thirty minutes. Laura later told me Mrs. Bush said she'd suffered a miscarriage in her youth—Laura said she didn't know that—and that she understood the anxieties of wanting to be a mother. She told Laura she mustn't give up. She said she believed Jesus's story for her and her grandson was that they have kids, and that this had always been His plan. 'So, write that story now,' she told her, 'and make that story your story.' Laura told me it was very much like Dorothy Bush to frame things in that way. 'You must hang on, Laura,' she told her, 'because your day is coming.' I know Laura was very inspired by those words."

A few days later, Laura and George had a home visit scheduled by the adoption agency. It was standard practice. "Laura later told me," recalled

Betty Wagner, "that about an hour before the woman from the agency was supposed to show up, George told her, 'Say, why don't you go into the bathroom and take a [home pregnancy] test. Just to see.' She said, 'But why? We can wait.' And he told her, 'I just have a feeling, Laura. Do it now before this woman shows up.' So she did. And, my goodness, who could have believed it, but lo and behold, the test came back positive! They were elated and dancing around the living room with joy when the doorbell rang: the woman from the agency. 'Um. . . . we may be putting the adoption off,' George said. 'We just found out that maybe Laura is pregnant.' The agency woman was so overcome, Laura told me, she collapsed into a chair and started to cry."

The next morning, Laura went into Dr. Franklin's office, and he confirmed that she was pregnant. She was given a sonogram, which at the time was a fairly new technology. The radiologist examined the images on the screen and gave the Bushes the good news: "I see two babies here." Laura and George were overwhelmed. One was a girl, they were told, and the other? The radiologist wasn't sure. Likely, she said, it's a girl as well. "You don't know what it means to hear you say that," Laura exclaimed.

"Throughout her pregnancy, Laura was filled with so much anxiety I think it was difficult for her to enjoy the experience," recalled Betty Wagner. "She woke up every day fearing she would lose the babies. She told me she decided not to set a room aside in her house as a nursery. She was afraid it would jinx things. She didn't want a baby shower, either."

While Dr. Franklin was Laura's fertility specialist, her obstetrician was Dr. Charles Stephens in Odessa. Laura's father, Harold, drove her to every appointment. In early October, when Laura was about seven months pregnant, she was diagnosed with preeclampsia, marked by high blood pressure and swelling in the hands, feet, and face. She was quickly admitted to Baylor Hospital in Dallas where her uncle, Mark—Harold's brother—was a doctor. For the next seven weeks, she would be hospitalized under complete bed rest. This was difficult. Though friends and family came and went from her room, it was still a bleak, lonely time for her.

On November 24, 1981, George, who was in Midland, got a phone call from one of Laura's doctors at Baylor. He was going to take the babies five weeks early because Laura's blood pressure was so low her kidneys might fail. The time had come. The next morning, she was given a caesarean section; George was in the operating room with her when the twins came into the world. They were both girls. One would be named Barbara after George's mother, and the other Jenna after Laura's.

A few days later, Betty Wagner visited Laura and met her daughters. "I held one in each arm," she said, "and what a moment that was. Laura looked at me with tears in her eyes and said, 'You and Doc mean more to me than you'll ever know. In my darkest moments, you gave me hope. Thank you for my family.' We both had a good cry, and that was the very last time I ever saw Laura Bush. But I will never forget her."

Come to Jesus

During Laura's pregnancy, her father, Harold Welch, began complaining of muscle and bone pain in his left shoulder. As someone who'd been very active throughout his life, he was certainly used to aches and pains. However, this was persistent and had been troubling him for at least six months. When he and Jenna flew to Dallas to meet their new granddaughters in the hospital, Harold mentioned the problem to his brother, Mark, a doctor. Mark said that he recently had a patient diagnosed with lung cancer whose first symptom was shoulder pain. It was unlikely that Harold was suffering from the same disease, he said, but best to rule it out. He immediately sent him to radiology for a chest X-ray. Sure enough, Mark detected a spot on the film that was later revealed to be lung cancer. He would have to have surgery to remove a section of his lung.

A day earlier, George had asked a friend if his private jet could be used to fly Laura and the twins home from Dallas to Midland. Now Harold and Jenna were on that same plane, being dropped off for Harold's stay at Baylor. Everyone was crying.

Harold, now sixty-nine, was frightened. He'd changed a lot in recent years, mellowing with age. All he wanted now was more time with Jenna, to live to see his granddaughters grow up, and maybe even put right some of his more questionable choices of the past. "This is my come-to-Jesus moment," he said at the time. None of whatever happened in years gone by mattered to Jenna, though. All she wanted was for Harold to be restored to good health so that they could have more years together.

Happily, Harold pulled through the surgery, though it was a slow, laborious recovery. Jenna was at his side the entire time. Meanwhile, Laura and George had a few challenging months of their own trying to cope with the twins, both of whom spent most of their time crying at the top of their little lungs. It wasn't easy for two parents with no experience to suddenly find themselves responsible for two infants. Things settled down eventually, and the Bushes fell into a happy rhythm with Barbara and Jenna, both of whom started walking by the age of one.

Eventually, George and Laura moved from the house they lived in on West Golf Course Road into a larger home at 910 Harvard Avenue. Life was good. Though Laura hoped and prayed for more children, it didn't happen. However, she was eternally grateful that Dorothy's prophecy had come to pass; her story as a mother had only just begun. Something was still missing for her, though: Barbara's approval.

"Does Bar Not Like Me?"

While Laura Bush was in the hospital expecting the twins, Barbara Bush flew into town to make an appearance at a charity event and took that opportunity to come by and say hello. It was a pleasant if also short visit that felt to Laura as if it had just been tacked onto a trip already planned by Barbara's office. Couldn't she just take a plane to Midland any time she wanted to visit her pregnant, bedridden daughter-in-law? Why did it have to be so scheduled?

After Barbara left that day, Laura had time to think, and she began to wonder why George's mother hadn't been more present for her during this difficult time. Certainly, her own mother was at the hospital every day, as was her father. True, Barbara had recommended the fertility expert Laura consulted and was happy when George gave her the news of the pregnancy, but she never called Laura. George always made excuses for his mother, saying she was very busy with her Washington duties, and that was true. But, still, something about it didn't sit well with Laura. "When I married George, I had thought that I would be embraced by his mother every bit as much as he was embraced by mine," she would recall. "I had planned on being more a daughter than a daughter-in-law, but Barbara Bush had five children of her own. She was their defender first. What I came to see ultimately as our bond was that we both loved George, and the depth of our love was what we had in common. Beyond that, we had little contact."

When Laura would telephone Barbara and then, two days later, receive a call back from a secretary asking her to please be specific about what she wanted, it hurt her. When George would call his mother to ask why she hadn't personally returned Laura's call, Barbara would become exasperated and explain that she had a lot on her plate. Somehow, it was Laura who was the insensitive one.

The members of the Bush family were generally not very open with one another. They didn't know how to express their love. The most intimate anyone ever was with them was when George H.W. wrote long and moving letters to them. In this correspondence, the depth of his emotion was on full display. "We didn't need the reassurance of verbal professions of love and affection," he would say. "It's easier in a letter to tell someone what's in your heart."

"I was never a touchy-feely kind of person with my kids, either," Dorothy once told Barbara during a barbecue at Kennebunkport in 1987. "And Prescott wasn't either. And our kids turned out just fine, and their kids are just fine. I think we should all stop watching Phil Donahue," she concluded. "He's messing us all up."

It was ironic that when she first married George, one of Barbara's chief complaints about him was that, like her own mother, he wasn't more openly demonstrative. With the passing of the years, she had begun to mirror that same behavior, but without the outlet of writing touching letters to express her feelings. As George H.W. got older, he would become more expressive, crying at the drop of a hat, as would his son George W. But not Barbara. She would always be much more reserved, almost embarrassed to shed a tear.

"Maybe I'm just being hormonal," Laura told her friend Ethan Marshall when he visited her at Baylor, "but it bothers me, Ethan. I mean, does Bar not like me?"

He felt she was probably overreacting. He had a sense that Barbara Bush had troubles of her own, and that she just wasn't thinking about Laura—which, said Laura, was precisely the problem. When he asked Laura what George's opinion was on the matter, Laura said he had told her she was probably fortunate that Barbara wasn't a bigger part of her life. "He says she can be tough, and that this is why they call her 'The Enforcer,'" Laura said with a smile, "and that she's better in small doses. But I don't know. I guess I just want her to like me. Is that ridiculous?'"

Laura also mentioned that a couple of years earlier, in 1978, after George lost his congressional bid, Barbara called to ask a favor. George's brother Neil had moved to Midland to help George with the campaign. When it was over, his belongings were still there while Neil went back to graduate school in Houston. Since Laura lived in Midland, Barbara asked her to pack up all Neil's belongings and ship them to him in Houston. Really? How, Laura wondered, was it her responsibility? Still, Laura decided she might win some points with Barbara. It was hard work, and she was angry. It didn't seem like it should be her problem. When it was finally all done, she waited for Barbara to call to thank her. That call never came. Neil phoned, but it wasn't his approval she hoped to win, it was his mother's.

It was in the telling of this story that Ethan realized just how much Laura craved Barbara's approval. "She said she could count on one hand the times she and Barbara Bush had had a real conversation, just the two of them, since the day she and George married," he recalled. "'It hurts being cast aside by her,' she told me."

When Laura talked to her own mother about Barbara, Jenna felt that Laura shouldn't hold anything against her. She had a feeling that Barbara's nature had something to do with the death of her little girl, Robin; that when she died a part of Barbara died with her. She told her daughter that a mother is never the same after losing a child. She may go on with her life and raise other children, but always there's a hole in her heart. Barbara deserved all the love and understanding in the world, Jenna said.

Laura knew Barbara had a great capacity for love, and she saw it the few times she was with her twin grandchildren. She would recall that when they were about two and a half, "Bar Bush made a rare stop in Midland. Jenna and Barbara ran out of the house with their arms held out to greet her, calling 'Ganny,' the name all Bushes give their grandmothers, and she looked up at me and said with gratitude, 'Thank you for teaching your girls to know me.'"

Just Like Mother

Barbara Bush never liked standing next to Nancy Reagan. In her mind, the contrast just wasn't flattering. Barbara was five foot eight; Nancy Reagan five foot four. Barbara weighed 140 pounds; Nancy, about 105. Barbara's hair was snow white; Nancy's was colored a reddish brown. On an early morning in the beginning of 1980, the two were standing together in front of a scrum of reporters and photographers, Nancy wearing her trademark color of red and Barbara in hers, which was blue. Nancy looked stylish; Barbara, conservative and traditional. Both were animated, their radiant smiles not leaving their faces. If you didn't know them, you'd probably think they were enjoying the attention.

Soon, both women were whisked away by their handlers and rushed into a waiting car in a caravan. However, there were so many people standing in front of the convoy, the vehicles weren't able to move. As Secret Service agents attempted to clear the way, the First and Second Ladies sat side by side in the backseat at what maybe they viewed as a safe distance from each other. Through the half-opened car windows, it could be seen that one was looking to her left and the other to her right. As they waited, they continued to stare out their windows, not speaking. Finally, when Nancy realized they were being watched, she raised her tinted window. Seconds later, Barbara did the same. The car then pulled off.

Barbara never wanted a contentious relationship with Nancy. Even at her moodiest, when it came to dealing with people of influence, Barbara always avoided conflict. But Nancy had it in for her and George from the very moment her "Ronnie" considered him for the vice presidency. "I always knew that Nancy didn't like me very much, but there is nothing we can do about all of that," George would write in his diary. "I feel sorry for her, but the main thing is, I feel sorry for President Reagan."

Happily, Bush was immediately off on good footing with Reagan, especially after writing him a note a couple of days after the election in which he pledged to "never do anything to embarrass you politically" and suggested he "call me if I can lighten the burden." George did everything he could do to be of service, and in return Ronald treated him with respect and made sure he knew that his opinions mattered.

Prior to the election, Barbara and Nancy had met a few times over the years and were fine with each other. It was only when George and Ronald were pitted against each other for the nomination that trouble with Nancy started. Ever loyal to her husband, she couldn't get past what she thought were personal shots George took at Ronald relating to his age and experience. She also never got over the fact that George had demeaned her husband's fiscal plans by calling them "voodoo economics." She had wanted Nevada's senator and Reagan campaign chairman Paul Laxalt, not Bush, as her husband's VP. Not only was he a good friend but she felt he also deserved the position. "I did not like George Bush," she later plainly stated in her memoir.

During an interview the day after the Republican National Convention, Barbara was asked how she and George got along with the Reagans. Trying to be diplomatic, she answered that they didn't really know them that well yet. "We're sort of like new dogs, sniffing each other out," she said. When Nancy heard Barbara's remark, she gasped and covered her mouth with her hand. "How is that appropriate?" she asked one of her staff.

Later, a reporter asked Barbara what the biggest difference was between her and Nancy. "Well, Nancy is a size four and I'm a size forty-four," Barbara quipped. Most people thought it was a funny line, typical of Barbara's self-deprecating nature. Nancy didn't like it, though. "Why would a woman of her status make fun of herself like that?" she asked. "That makes no sense to me." When Barbara heard about Nancy's reaction, she concluded that she just didn't understand her humor. If she got to know her better, Barbara figured, it could only be to the advantage of both of them. So, in July 1980, she invited Nancy and Ronald to the Bush home in Houston.

Because the Bushes hadn't been in Houston for at least a month, Barbara called ahead and had the place tidied up—"spic-and-span clean," as she put it—and an assortment of colorful flowers brought in to help show off the place. She also hired a local caterer to organize a luncheon.

When the Reagans showed up, the couples got along beautifully as they dined on the veranda. The main course was a rich Senegalese soup, thick with fresh lobster. There were also salmon, crab, and other seafood pâtés. A tasty compote of blackberries, raspberries, and melon followed. Then enormous servings of cold Grand Marnier soufflé were dished out for dessert. "Don't be embarrassed, Governor," Barbara said, according to what she recalled of the day to Virginia Bohlin for *The Boston Globe,* "you don't have to eat all of that." He wolfed it down, though, saying he loved nothing more than a good dessert. Nancy didn't eat much of anything, explaining that "I rarely eat," which Barbara found a little odd. However, Nancy was cordial, talkative, and in good spirits.

After lunch, George took Ronald out on his speedboat for mackerel fishing; they would return with about fifty of them. Reagan looked sunburnt but was relaxed and happy.

While the men were out on the water, Barbara and Nancy spent time getting to know each other. It turned out they did have things in common. Both were born in New York hospitals—Nancy four years earlier—and thought of themselves as overweight youngsters; Nancy said she was also sensitive about her legs, which she thought shapeless, and her ankles, which she judged too thick. Barbara had her own self-esteem issues, and she then said she liked to make fun of herself before others had a chance to do so; it was a good opportunity for her to explain her earlier remarks. Nancy seemed to understand. Both women attended Smith College, Nancy graduating in the spring of 1943, before Barbara's term began.

Nancy also talked a lot about her mother, Edie Davis, who was now ninety-two. She had a close, if tricky, relationship with her. She explained that Edie had been an actress—primarily on radio, but also in the theater—and had been married twice. Now she was suffering from Alzheimer's, but prior to the disease she'd been an effervescent, high-spirited, funny woman and chairman of the Chicago Community Fund. Especially as Nancy got older, she said, she worshipped her mother, but even in her youth she had wanted to be just like her. But Alzheimer's had taken over her mother's personality. Barbara's heart went out to her. She then talked a bit about Pauline and her tortured relationship with her. Commiserating about the one thing almost all women have in common—their mothers—did seem to bring the two a little closer.

It was a pleasant afternoon; Barbara thought she'd made some real progress with Nancy. When they parted, they embraced and expressed their hopes that the election would go their way, which it did.

Things were quiet until Inauguration Day, when a little snafu relating to fashion was happily avoided.

George had said he was tired of hearing about how frumpy Barbara had appeared during the campaign. She tried not to let his criticism of her personal style hurt, but it did. George suggested Barbara go to New York and purchase designer clothes suitable for her new position, as well as something stylish to wear to the inauguration. While in Manhattan, Barbara settled on a purple dress and a red coat. A couple of days later, Nancy sent her a message saying she was going to be wearing red at the inaugural. In other words, Barbara should stay away from that particular color, which she did; she wore blue instead. Barbara didn't complain. But after Reagan was installed, Nancy thought the Bushes were generating too much press. She told mutual friends she wished "the Shrubs"—as she derisively called them—would keep a lower profile. *That* Barbara found insulting. After their pleasant afternoon in Houston, why would Nancy say such a thing about them? And why not just call her and talk to her about it herself?

On the morning of Tuesday, January 20, 1981, George and his mother, Dorothy, took coffee out to the mob of press waiting in front of the gates of the

Bush rental home in Washington. They were asked how they were thus far enjoying their new life. "It's only been a day," Dorothy said, "but so far so good." George and Dorothy were still speaking to the press when two moving trucks arrived to move the Bushes' furniture out of the rental and over to 1 Observatory Circle.

President Ronald Reagan was inaugurated later that morning. At sixty-nine, he would be the oldest person to assume the presidency until Donald Trump in 2017, who was seventy. Chief Justice Warren E. Burger administered the presidential oath of office to Reagan. Prior to that honor, Supreme Court Justice Potter Stewart had sworn in George H. W. Bush as Vice President. After the ceremony, there were the usual celebrative festivities at the White House, including a luncheon with the Reagans. Everyone in both the Bush and Reagan families were on their best behavior.

Afterward, George and Barbara were driven to 1 Observatory Circle. By this time, all their clothes were already hanging in the closets and the furniture was all in place. Barbara had also brought an assortment of orchids, which she'd directed to be planted in the gardens. When they arrived, the gardeners were in the process of doing just that, under Paula Rendon's supervision. Many of Barbara's children and grandchildren would also converge at the VP's home that day, and plenty of food would be laid out for everyone. They then all used the residence to get ready for the nine glamorous inaugural balls that were to take place that evening.

About a week later, on January 26, 1982, Ronald Reagan gave his first State of the Union address. As is customary, George sat directly behind the President, next to Tip O'Neill, the Speaker of the House. That night, as soon as he got home, Dorothy was on the telephone wanting to talk to him. She said he had been very rude to the President during his speech. He couldn't understand why she felt that way, and she explained that he had been talking to Tip O'Neill and not listening to Reagan. "But, Mum," George said, "Tip O'Neill turned to me, once, and said, 'This is a great speech, isn't it?' And I said, 'Yes.' And that was it." It didn't matter, Dorothy said: "You were rude to talk during a speech by the President."

About two weeks later, on February 13, 1982, George and Barbara invited the Reagans over for dinner at 1 Observatory Circle; for the occasion, their chef, Ariel De Guzman, would prepare his special marinated pork tenderloin with mustard sauce and, for dessert, baked peaches flambé—a longtime family recipe concocted by Dorothy Bush's sister-in-law, Grace.

Dorothy was present for the evening, wearing a soft cast on her arm. A few months earlier, she had been bicycling when she hit a rock and flew off her bike at the age of eighty. She broke her arm. Six weeks later, she was back on the bike. However, it still hadn't healed properly, thus the cast.

She didn't dine with them, but she did socialize with them afterward in the parlor. Her caretaker, Virginia Mason, recalled, "Mrs. Bush [Dorothy] told me that because they knew that Mrs. Reagan wasn't a particularly effusive woman, she and the other Mrs. Bush [Barbara] tried to mirror her and not be too forward with her. 'I'm afraid she misinterpreted it,' Mrs. Bush told me, 'and thought we were being very standoffish.' Mrs. Bush said, 'It was difficult. Finally, Barbara just shut down completely. I looked over at her and she was staring into her after-dinner drink.'"

When the couples parted company, Barbara said, "It was a pleasure to have you both." Nancy, with a frozen smile, responded by saying, "Yes, I'm sure it was." Barbara just stared at Nancy. "Finally," Dorothy remembered, "it was I who broke the silence by saying, 'Indeed, it was a pleasure for *all* of us,' and, blessedly, *that* was the end of *that*. Afterward, Barbara was upset. She asked me, 'Did Nancy really say what I think she said, or did I imagine it?' 'No, dear,' I told her, 'she really said it. Now, you must forget it and not let her get to you.'"

A few days later, she telephoned Barbara from her home in Greenwich and said she had been mulling over how Nancy Reagan had acted and wanted to discuss it. Barbara wasn't open to it. "Fine," Dorothy said, not wanting to push it. "I just want to say this to you, dear: Mrs. Reagan does not get to tell you who you are. Only God can do that." She added that Barbara now had a chance to make a real difference, and she shouldn't allow anything as inconsequential as the pejorative opinions of others to stand in her way.

"Nancy does not like Barbara," George Bush wrote in his diary. "She feels that Barbara has the very things that she, Nancy, doesn't have, and that she'll never be in Barbara's class . . . Bar has sensed it for a long time. Barbara is so generous, so kind, so unselfish, and frankly I think Nancy Reagan is jealous of her."

Barbara's problem with Nancy was a little more complex. It was clear to anyone who knew Barbara that Nancy reminded her of the one woman in her life who'd caused her the most pain—her mother, Pauline. Both were slim and gorgeous and didn't seem to have to try hard to be that way, either. Both enjoyed spending money on designer clothing. More important, Barbara couldn't help but feel the constant sting of Nancy's judgment. "That woman," she noted to an assistant once, "she's only, what, a couple years older than me? But she's my mother all over again. Look at the way she stares at me. No one has looked at me like that since I was twelve."

During their eight years with the Reagans, Barbara and George were always invited to state dinners at the White House; that was just protocol. However, in that same period of time, the Reagans only invited the Bushes up to their private residence at the White House twice. They never invited them to Camp David. "When Barbara and George would meet with a high-level state delegation, they were shoved over to one side of the room and never even saw the visitor," said Al Haig, Reagan's secretary of state. "Barbara was treated like dirt. And Barbara cried, and believe me, it's hard to do that to Barbara."

An incident in the spring of 1981 did cause Barbara to become emotional. A rumor circulated that George was having an affair with the widow of a former congressman. Barbara was particularly sensitive about this story because, at about this same time, Jennifer Fitzgerald had made yet another return to Washington.

Jennifer had been working in the New York office. However, as soon as George was installed as VP, he sent for her. An interesting thing about Jennifer now was that, with the passing of the years, she had put on a little weight, had cut her hair short, and looked as if she could've been Barbara's sister. Now she was George's chief lobbyist, ensconced in an office on Capitol Hill with two secretaries. She was also given free rein in the White House in Bush's West Wing VP office. Involved in all his meetings, she organized trips for him, accompanied him, and was, again, ubiquitous. "My understanding is that Mrs. Bush suspected that the affair was back on but didn't know for sure," said Virginia Mason. "Mr. Bush continued to deny it. However, by this time, all of us in the inner circle knew better than to even bring up the name Jennifer Fitzgerald. I could tell that the other Mrs. Bush [Dorothy] was concerned. However, she had made it clear that this topic was not up for discussion. I was in her presence, though, when one of her daughters-in-law broached the subject. 'No, I will not talk about that,' Mrs. Bush told her. 'I will not add to the upset and neither should you.'"

One of George's political operatives, Rich Bond, tried to draw a line in the sand about Jennifer, not wanting her around. But George wouldn't hear of it. "Jim Baker made me make that choice once before," he said, referring to when he banished Jennifer to New York, "and I made the wrong choice." Bond then decided to resign.

A Secret Service agent reported that he was standing just outside Barbara's study in a small alcove between that room and the hallway when he overheard her having a heated discussion with her husband. It sounded like it was about George's infidelity. The agent came in at the tail end of it, just long enough to hear George say, "Bar, if you're doubting my integrity, I can't indulge that, I'm sorry." Bush then left the room and, as he did, noticed the agent standing in the alcove. The agent froze. But George just nodded and walked right by him. Meanwhile, Barbara—this, again, according to the agent—collapsed into a chair, seeming undone.

"She wasn't crying, but she was obviously upset, so much so that I was afraid to move for fear that she would realize I was there and then both of us would be embarrassed," he recalled. "So there I stood, frozen in the hallway, holding my breath, filled with apprehension." He says that after about five minutes, Barbara took a compact from her purse, dabbed her eyes, touched up her lipstick, and composed herself. When he felt it was safe, the agent took a deep breath to steady himself and knocked on the doorframe. He asked if she needed anything. Barbara was surprised. "Oh. I didn't know you were there," she told him, seeming self-conscious. "Sorry, ma'am," he said. She gave him a small, thin smile. "Oh, that's okay," she said. "I'm just fine. Thank you for asking."

From that time on, anytime Barbara would see that agent, she would smile and lower her eyes. "She was always nice to me," he recalled, "and I went out of my way to make sure she was taken care of. I witnessed just a few seconds of fragility in her and, I don't know . . . it was as if it affected us both."

Barbara didn't know what to make of this new story about a congressman's widow, and to this day it's not known if the affair was real or not. When she did some digging, though, Barbara was dismayed to learn that the rumors were likely being spread by Nancy Reagan. Nancy was known to like to gossip. But what could Barbara do about it? Confront her? That just wasn't going to happen; she knew it would only make things worse. Instead, she decided to engage Nancy in a wide-ranging, general conversation about the hurtful nature of rumors, and she just hoped Nancy would take the hint.

This estrangement between Barbara and Nancy was particularly unfortunate in that they could have been so helpful to each other. After all, both understood the challenges for women in politics and how one was often forced to sublimate her own goals and aspirations to those of her husband. Many people in their circles would try to bring them together. Barbara was open to it, but Nancy wasn't. Once she didn't like a person, there was really no changing her mind about it. She had that in common with Barbara. It was maddening, though. But Barbara also understood Nancy more than the First Lady maybe realized.

"One time late in the administration's first term, I watched as Mrs. Reagan so obviously snubbed Mrs. Bush during an affair in the State Room," said a woman who worked as one of Nancy's assistants at that time. "Nancy turned and walked away from Barbara in mid-sentence. It was as if she'd spotted someone more interesting across the room."

The assistant went over to Barbara and put her arm around her shoulder. "She's something else, that one, isn't she?" she noted of Nancy. "But believe me, she means no harm. That's just the way she is."

Barbara nodded. "Well, look," she said, "she's built a wall around herself to keep people from getting close enough to hurt her."

"Then why do you keep trying?" the assistant asked her.

Barbara smiled and answered, "Because I can relate."

Linked to History

For Barbara Bush, despite any palace intrigue with Nancy Reagan, the four years of the Reagan administration seemed to fly by. During that time, she stayed extremely busy as the wife of the VP and, in the process, became quite popular with the American public, admired for her down-to-earth manner. She was happy during this time, too. "I think I was just tired of being unhappy," Barbara would later admit, "and I think I remembered my grandmother telling my mother that it was a choice to be unhappy, and to stop making that choice."

Others felt that maybe Barbara's mood had shifted because she was now able to spend so much more time with George. Plus, welcoming new grandchildren into the world was always sure to bring a smile to her face. During the first four years of Reagan-Bush, Barbara's son Jeb and his wife, Columba, had their third child, John Ellis Bush—"Jebbie" Jr.—born on December 13, 1983, and Neil and his wife, Sharon, had their first child, Lauren, born on June 25, 1984. Then Doro and her husband, Billy LeBlond, had their first of two children together, Sam, on August 26, 1984. They would have a daughter in two years' time: Nancy Ellis, known as Ellie.

Even though she had bad memories of her childhood, Barbara was still sentimental about her past and didn't want to forget it. For instance, when she was invited to speak at the Marysville Alumni Association banquet in

Ohio, she jumped at the chance. Her hosts were a local attorney named Dorothy Pelanda and Bob Parrott, the president of the Union County Historical Society.

"As soon as she arrived, she reminded us that she wanted to visit the graves of her parents and grandparents," Dorothy Pelanda recalled. "We had found them in advance and had vases of peonies placed on the burial sites so that they could be located easily. However, just as we were getting ready to leave, the Secret Service started giving Barbara a hard time about going, saying they couldn't secure the location. Barbara wasn't having it, though."

The agent told Barbara, "Ma'am, you can't—" before Barbara cut him off and said, "I *what*?" She then pointed to a nearby vehicle, indicating that she wanted the agent to get into it with her. He did. "You need to stop assuming that you know me," she told the agent, according to his later memory. "And furthermore, you need to stop dictating to me what I can and cannot do." When he protested that he was only doing his job, she said she understood but "enough is enough." She also suggested he watch his tone with her.

Barbara actually had great admiration for the agents; every year she would host a picnic at Walker's Point for the U.S. Secret Service Bush Protective Detail Division as well as the Special Officers Division assigned to Walker's Point, and all their families. Still, she usually didn't like it when the agents tried to enforce limitations on her. "By now you should know that when I really want to do something, I'll do it," she told the agent. "Are we clear?" When she was finished, she tapped on the vehicle's window. Another agent came and opened the door for her. She got out; meanwhile, the agent she'd reprimanded remained in the car for another few moments, maybe letting her words sink in.

"Barbara then came over to me," said Dorothy Pelanda, "and said, 'Don't worry, Dorothy. He works for me. I don't work for him. And we *are* going to the cemetery.'"

At that moment, another agent spoke into his walkie-talkie and said, "Snowbank is on the move," using the Secret Service's code name for Barbara. After an eye roll, Barbara gave Dorothy a wry smile and "off we went," Dorothy recalled, "and it was lovely and touching at the cemetery. She also wanted to drive by her grandfather's law office, and we did that as well."

The day after the event, Barbara summoned the Secret Service agent she had taken to task. He would recall that as soon as he heard she wanted to see him, he feared another scolding. He walked into her office with trepidation and found her sitting behind her desk on the telephone. She raised a finger to indicate she'd be finished soon, and then pointed to one of two chairs in front of her. After she ended her call, she stood up and walked over to the chair next to the agent and sat down. Looking at him with sincere eyes, she said, "I'm sorry about what I said to you yesterday. I didn't mean for it to come out that way. You're someone willing to take a bullet for me, and for that you deserve nothing but my gratitude. So I just want to say thank you."

Taken aback, the agent told her, "Duty doesn't require thanks, ma'am."

"Maybe," Barbara said. "But for what you've chosen to do with your life, you deserve my appreciation. Not my bad mood."

The 1984 reelection campaign wasn't a particularly contentious one for Ronald Reagan, a popular president running for a second term against former Vice President Walter Mondale and his running mate, Geraldine Ferraro, the first woman to campaign for Vice President in a major party. Of course, Barbara liked Walter's wife, Joan, very much; the two had stayed in touch in the last four years. In one letter sent to 1 Observatory Circle, Joan told Barbara, "What a job you are doing, Barbara. I knew it! You should be proud." They would always have a warm relationship. Barbara didn't feel the same way about Geraldine Ferraro, though. Simply put, she felt Ferraro got special treatment for one reason and one reason alone: because she was a woman.

By the mid-1980s, Barbara most certainly agreed that women had a place in all aspects of society. She would wholeheartedly endorse the Equal Rights Amendment as she would the right to choose, the latter more quietly so as not to be in opposition to her husband and son. However, she was also adamantly against the idea of a person being, in her view, treated with deference simply because she was female. She felt there should be no double standard for women.

There was one memorable incident where Geraldine Ferraro was late for an event because her dress had been left behind on a plane. Everyone had to wait to sit down for dinner, including President Reagan and Nancy Reagan, until finally they went ahead with the event. Geraldine soon showed up late, wearing a short dress to a formal event. Barbara was annoyed and said Geraldine was "playing by women's rules." In the "real world," she said, "if she was a man she would've shown up on time, apologized, said her bags had been lost and that would have been the end of it. Because she was a woman," Barbara said, "Geraldine got away with keeping everyone waiting and not acknowledging it."

Later, after campaigning in a shipyard, George was overheard repeating a longshoreman's sign: "George, You Kicked a Little Ass." After it was picked up on a television microphone, Geraldine went on the record as saying she thought it was a sexist expression. Barbara was irritated. She'd raised four boys and knew exactly what the longshoreman meant, she said, and it had nothing to do with sexism.

But there would be yet another incident, and this one was much more serious, or at least it felt that way to Barbara. She was flying on Air Force Two en route to New York for the Columbus Day parade with two reporters with whom she felt comfortable, Ira Allen of United Press International and Terence Hunt of the Associated Press. She was annoyed on this day because Ferraro kept bringing up the Bushes' wealth and needling them about it. This upset Barbara all the more because she had read that Ferraro and her husband, John Zaccaro, were worth at least $4 million.

"Well, you're not exactly paupers," Hunt teased.

Barbara didn't find it funny. She said she and George never tried to hide their wealth, unlike that "four-million-dollar . . . I can't say it, but it rhymes with 'rich.'"

"Shocker. End of conversation," recalled Terence Hunt. "The Bushes went to their compartment, and I sank back into my seat and marveled over what had just happened, playing it over in my mind. *'Rhymes with rich.'* Allen, the other reporter, ended my reverie. 'What are you going to do with that?' She must have thought conversations on the plane were off the record, I reasoned. But there was no such rule. So, we decided to report it."

Barbara was mortified, not so much because she was afraid she'd hurt

Ferraro's feelings but because she thought she may have in some way damaged her husband's campaign. She put out a statement of regret and then
called Geraldine to apologize and, fibbing, said she really did mean "witch,"
not "bitch."

The press wouldn't let it go, though, and the snippy comment followed
Barbara for some time. She later said, "at the time, it was agony."

Barbara really wasn't cut out for this kind of controversy and sank into
deep despair over it. "I just can't believe I did that to your brother," she
told her sister-in-law Nancy. "I've been crying for twenty-four hours and I'll
never stop. How could I have done it?"

Reagan-Bush won a second term, and that would mean four more years
at 1 Observatory Circle for Barbara and George. However, the writing was
now on the wall: surely George would want to run for President in four
years' time. Barbara didn't think she could bear it. "George is obviously the
most qualified person for the job," she wrote in her diary. "Do I want him
to run? *Absolutely not!*"

During the next four years, as the world around them changed, Barbara
and George found themselves traveling across the country and around the
world on diplomatic missions. The Iran-Contra scandal—the administration's trading of arms to Iran for hostages in the Middle East with the
proceeds then going to finance Nicaraguan Contras in Central America—
threatened to taint the Reagan presidency for good. Though George publicly claimed to know little about the operation, his writings in his own diary
would suggest otherwise. "I'm one of the few people that know fully the
details, and there is a lot of flak and misinformation out there," he wrote in
a November 5, 1986, entry, adding, "It is not a subject we can talk about."
In fact, this particular controversy would shadow his reputation for years
to come.

Besides the controversy of Iran-Contra, many aspects of the Reagan administration were considered a success, with inflation dropping to 4 percent
from 12, interest rates cut by 50 percent, and unemployment at its lowest in
fourteen years. There were other problems, though, such as the President's
stance on gay rights. "My criticism is that [it] isn't just asking for civil rights;
it's asking for recognition and acceptance of an alternative lifestyle which

I do not believe society can condone, nor can I," he said. He also mostly turned a blind eye to AIDS as it pulverized the gay community.

George was always afraid of going up against Reagan when it came to AIDS, but Barbara was not; she would co-sponsor AIDS benefits and encourage more research into the disease. She would visit hospitals and hold HIV-positive infants in her arms and, in the process, educate people about the epidemic and their unfounded fears surrounding it. She did her part.

Things never did get better with Nancy Reagan, though. In November 1985, when Princess Diana and Prince Charles made their much-promoted visit to the White House (the one during which the princess famously danced with John Travolta), the guest list for that gathering was wide and varied but did not include two noteworthy people: the Vice President and his wife. When Michael Deaver, deputy White House chief of staff, told Nancy Reagan it would be in bad form to not invite George and Barbara, she responded, "Just watch me."

Cold Turkey

While Barbara Bush was busy with her duties as the wife of the Vice President in Washington, her daughter-in-law Laura had her own hands full with Barbara's son George in Midland. She was trying to get him to stop drinking.

Everyone in Laura and George's social circle drank wine, vodka, or beer whether at one another's homes or at barbecues or in restaurants. However, George always went overboard. He enjoyed what Laura called "the three Bs"—bourbon before dinner, a beer with dinner, and B&B after the meal. This regiment always followed an afternoon of cocktails with friends in the oil business. It was just part of the networking process to have long lunches in private clubs and discuss the ups and downs of the business with like-minded people. His grandfather Prescott used to do the same thing.

"After Prohibition was repealed, Midland County remained largely dry; residents repeatedly voted against allowing alcohol sales," Laura recalled. "But that only changed how people drank. For years, liquor and mixed drinks couldn't be served in restaurants, but private clubs could pour a drink straight from the bottle, so people joined clubs, especially country clubs, where their individual 'bottles' could be kept in their lockers. Those who didn't join clubs, like my father, simply drove to package stores at the county line and carried out their bottles in brown paper bags."

It wasn't as if Laura also didn't also enjoy her cocktails from time to time; after all, she was raised in a drinking family. "Every day at four o'clock you could set the clock for the Welch Happy Hour until about seven," recalled Richard Pendleton, who lived across the street from them. "Most people had their windows open to let the cool air in, so I could always hear laughter coming from across the street. I remember my folks chuckling, 'Looks like the Welches are having cocktail hour again.' But my dad was a drinker, too: Scotch. Everyone drank back then. It was the culture."

It would not be an exaggeration to say that George was at least a little drunk for the better part of every day from about eleven in the morning until he went to bed at night. Upon rising, he would jog, as he did every day, hoping to sweat out much of the alcohol from the night before, but in a few hours' time he would just replace whatever he may have lost. However, after the twins were born, Laura felt he should be more disciplined. Her own father had been the same way. Her mother never did anything about it, and Laura didn't want to repeat that pattern. She decided not to appeal to her mother for help. Instead, she went to Jeb to ask him to talk to his brother. He begged off, saying he didn't think it was his place. "Oh my God, these people," Laura said, frustrated. "Maybe they should try *talking* to each other for a change." She then went to Barbara.

It just so happened that mother and son were on the outs at this time because of George's drinking. Apparently, he had embarrassed her at a recent party when, feeling no pain, he turned to one of her closest friends and asked, "So tell me. What's sex like after fifty?" Barbara struck him so hard on his shoulder, she almost dislocated it. The next day, she had angry words with him about it, telling him, "You are a father, for goodness' sake. Set an example!" He was, as she later put it, "mouthy with me." She demanded an apology, but he refused, saying she was the one who should ask for forgiveness for having taken such a hard swing at him. After she complained to George's father, he called his son and said he needed to apologize to his mother. "Is that an order?" the son asked. "It's a gentleman's request," answered the father. Maybe H.W. would have fared better by making it an order, because W. still wouldn't apologize. He was just like his mother; neither ever liked asking for forgiveness. So Barbara would be of no help to

Laura. With an absence of emotion, she said she didn't know what to tell her; George was going to do what he wanted to do. She had already tried with him and gotten nowhere. She was done with it.

Perhaps the only sensible thing to do, Laura decided, was to stop drinking herself. She did so, hoping to lead by example. It wasn't hard for her since she didn't have a problem. George didn't follow suit, though, and it soon became an issue in their marriage. "I was disappointed," she recalled, "and I let him know that I thought he could be a better man."

"He would not get drunk and pass out," his childhood friend Charlie Younger has recalled. "He would get a little boisterous, a little loud, a little happy. He would get off-color. I never considered him an alcoholic. He was more of a binge drinker. He would tease Laura. He knew how to get under her skin, and he would do it. She would get a little upset with him. The next day I imagine she would speak with him. She would reprimand him a bit, and he would respond." His friend Robert McCleskey was a little more direct about the situation: "He could be a real asshole when he drank too much."

In July 1986, when George turned forty, Laura finally appealed to him in a way he couldn't ignore. There had been a birthday party, a real blowout, and he had, once again, embarrassed her. She was angry. George's father was the Vice President and might someday be President, she reminded him. How would it look if something were to happen to embarrass him and President Reagan, such as a drunk-driving charge? Though she has never admitted it openly, according to close friends, she gave him an ultimatum. The story had always been that she said, "It's Jim Beam or me." That's not true; she never made such a statement. What she did say was that he had six months to clean up his act, or she would leave him. It might have been an empty threat. She probably would never have gone through with it, not while raising twins. However, she was tired of George's boorish behavior and she wanted it to end. George said he didn't think he could do it or, as he put it, "I don't think I have it in me."

At this same time, Laura was feeling a strong pull back to her religious convictions. She had been Christian as a child, but after the accident in 1963 she'd felt so abandoned by God, she lost her faith. It was a hole in her life, but she had accepted it. However, when she had the twins against all odds, it felt to her as if a real miracle had taken place in her life. As Barbara and Jenna got older she felt such gratitude for them. Now that they were five, she was again going to church and to Bible study classes. She had rediscovered her faith after so many years, and she was happy about it.

For the last year and a half, George had also been attending Bible study classes in response to the oil business having taken a real hit when the First National Bank of Midland collapsed. Mark Leaverton, who was the founder of Midland's Community Bible Study, recalled, "That was really the beginning of a precipitous slide in the oil and gas business in Midland. As things started to slide, a lot of fear set in. Marriages broke up. People started having pretty serious emotional problems. It was a real wake-up call, as to what was really important in your life."

It was at this time that Leaverton founded what would eventually become CBS—Community Bible Study. George was raised devoutly Episcopalian; religion had always been an important part of his life as it was in that of his parents and grandparents, especially on his father's side. "And when he came," recalled Mark Leaverton, "I thought, Isn't that wonderful? Here's a guy who has so much in his life. And yet, he has a need, just like I do. Something was missing in his life, and some friends had told him, 'George, you need to come, check this out,' and he did."

It was Laura who then urged George to expand his vision of Bible study to include more than just coming to terms with business concerns. She suggested he appeal to God to help him stop drinking. He was open to it, which would suggest that he really did want to break his habit and felt the time was right. Eventually, he stopped cold turkey, not attending AA but using Bible study. After many years of drinking, he just stopped and never looked back. He would say it wasn't even that difficult. Once he made up his mind about it, it was done, which was typical of George's resolve.

When family members tried to credit Laura for George's new sobriety, Barbara was resistant to that idea. "George is a grown man," she said privately, "and I doubt that Laura had a lot to do with it. He makes his own decisions. Besides," she concluded, "Doro told me it was Bible study classes, not Laura."

Coping with Barbara

Barbara's reluctance to give Laura credit for George's decision to stop drinking wasn't surprising. The two had gotten no closer in recent years. By now, Laura knew she had to just get used to a family dynamic where she felt on the outside. It wasn't going to change.

This lack of true intimacy seemed to affect everyone who married into the family. Laura and Columba, for instance, were cordial when in each other's company, but Laura wanted more. She felt that she and Jeb's wife had a great deal in common. For instance, she knew Columba also wanted a better relationship with Barbara, who she still called "Mrs. Bush." Columba would say, "When I did something that she didn't approve of, my mother-in-law would give me 'the look' or would just by her attitude show her displeasure. I could feel it." Laura was also aware that Neil's wife, Sharon, and Marvin's wife, Margaret, felt the same way.

Laura thought it would be a good idea if she and Columba stuck together. They could help each other out whenever they had an issue with Barbara or, at the very least, commiserate with each other about it. As an only child, Laura had always wanted a sibling, and especially a sister. She thought maybe this was her chance. She and Columba made a pact to be there for each other when they had a problem with Barbara. But when Jeb learned that Columba had spoken to Laura, he—in his controlling way—wanted to know exactly what was said between them. Columba folded and told Jeb about the deal she'd made with Laura. Jeb then went to Barbara with the information. Who knows why?

The last thing Laura wanted to do was hurt Barbara's feelings. She also couldn't understand why Columba had betrayed her. When she told George, he wondered if maybe Columba had done so just to curry favor with his mother. While that made sense to Laura, she also thought perhaps there had been some sort of cultural misunderstanding with Columba. Occasionally in the past, Columba didn't fully grasp the complexities of the relationships in the family. In the presence of some family members at Kennebunkport, she had once noted that in Mexico relatives either liked each other or didn't, but they never did both at the same time. "Well, Colu, I would say life is messier here in America," Barbara told her.

Barbara's first response to the news that her daughters-in-law had an alliance was anger. However, after she had a chance to think about it, she became hurt. She felt they were ganging up on her. She also thought she had a better relationship with them, especially with Laura.

George thought the little fracas was silly. "We have a lot on our plates," he told Laura. "We don't need all this rigmarole." He was right; they were all busy. Barbara and George H.W., in particular, were public servants. Still, for Laura, nothing was more important than family, even politics. "Y'all can serve America," she would always say, "but not at the expense of serving each other." Laura's admonition echoed that of Dorothy Bush so long ago to Prescott when she said, "You want to be a public servant? Fine. But you'd darn well better serve this family, too."

It wasn't just the daughters-in-law who had trouble connecting with Barbara; her own daughter, Doro, was also often at a loss. In her memoir, Doro Bush admitted she had no idea her mother had suffered from such debilitating depression that she'd once contemplated suicide. It wouldn't be until Barbara wrote her own autobiography almost twenty years after that day she thought about driving into oncoming traffic that Doro finally understood the depth of her mother's despair. But how could she not have known? Barbara had suffered from depression since before Doro was even born, and it continued through Doro's entire youth and into her adulthood.

While it was one thing to know her daughters-in-law felt removed from her, it was another when Barbara realized Doro also felt that way. By around 1987, her marriage to Billy LeBlond was in trouble. Doro tried to keep it from Barbara for as long as she could, in part not wanting to upset her, but also because she didn't know how to talk to her about it. Barbara just waited for her to come to her. When she didn't, this omission acted as a sort of wake-up call for Barbara.

Doro was now twenty-eight, and the pattern of her relationship with her mother had been established years before. But when Doro didn't confide in her, Barbara felt she needed to do something about it.

Finally, Barbara called Doro and suggested they talk. As Barbara slowly urged her along, Doro reluctantly confided in her about the slow disintegration of her marriage. She felt terrible about it, and Barbara understood. She said that the important thing was that Doro never denigrate her husband to their children, no matter how contentious the divorce proceedings became over time. "He's a good man, and they need to know that and remember it," Barbara told Doro. Barbara said she once had a friend who criticized her ex-husband in front of his children and that when the children grew up they realized they'd been caught in the middle of a messy divorce and resented their mother for alienating them from their father. "Just be careful," Barbara warned Doro.

Meanwhile, at about this same time, Barbara's son Marvin was suffering from an illness that had been plaguing him for some time. Only his wife, Margaret, to whom he had been married since 1981, was aware of what was going on, but she'd been sworn to secrecy by her husband.

Margaret was a formidable woman. When she was only five, she was diagnosed with ovarian cancer, which had spread to her liver. Amazingly, she had survived, after having her ovaries removed.

Barbara was frustrated by the lack of information about Marvin's illness. Like Doro, he apparently didn't feel comfortable confiding in her, and apparently not in his father, either. Barbara really had to drag it out of Margaret. It turned out that Marvin had such a serious form of colitis he would have to have surgery and then wear a colostomy bag for the rest of his life. He was only twenty-eight at the time. He and Margaret had been on a waiting list to adopt, and he was afraid the illness might somehow interfere with that process. Happily, it didn't. They ultimately ended up adopting two children, a daughter, Marshall, and a son, Charles.

However, despite their differences, like most big families the Bushes understood one another and recognized their boundaries. In other words, they knew how to—and how *not* to—push one another's buttons. Every summer, they would all retreat to Kennebunkport, and it was there that they would reconnect, maybe have a few fights and a few reconciliations, but most of all remember who they really were to one another.

PART FIFTEEN

The Presidency

George H.W. Runs for President

George H. W. Bush announced his candidacy for presidency on October 12, 1987. He had been planning to run for at least the last four
years, and probably for some time before that. "I mean to run hard, to fight
hard, to stand on the issues," he told a cheering crowd in Houston. "And
I mean to win." The day was particularly charged with emotion in that it
happened to be the thirty-fourth anniversary of the death of his and Barbara's daughter, Robin. "I'm so happy for him because he's proven himself
already," his mother, Dorothy, told *Greenwich Time.* "I think he will be by
far the best candidate," she said. "He's got so much experience. But we'll
see if the people like him."

That same week, *Newsweek* put George on its cover with the headline
"Fighting the Wimp Factor," which, to those who knew and loved him and
understood his story, especially as a war hero, seemed completely unfair.
There was always a sense, though, that because of his mild manner he would
be a less than forceful President. "Bush suffers from a potentially crippling
handicap," journalist Margaret Warner wrote, "a perception that he isn't
strong enough or tough enough for the challenges of the Oval Office. That
he is, in a single mean word, a wimp."

The cover story hit the family hard, especially given that they'd fully
cooperated with it. Even Dorothy had given an interview, which was unusual;

George almost never allowed the press access to her. The journalist noted that Dorothy hadn't liked it when her young children were boastful, and quoted her as having told them, "I don't want to hear any more about the Great I Am." This was true. Warner also wrote that Dorothy had once telephoned George during a campaign to admonish him by saying, "You're talking about yourself too much." When George tried to explain that this was how politics worked, she said, "I understand that. But try to restrain yourself." The anecdote made him sound weak, sort of like a momma's boy. "Despite his ambition, Bush may never overcome his mother's injunction against the Great I Am," wrote Warner. "But unless he learns to project his inner strength, voters may overlook his fairness and sense of duty—and see instead a lesser man."

Everyone in the family was up in arms about it, but none more than Dorothy. She made a couple of telephone calls to family members to express her annoyance. When her son called her to tell her he felt she was being "too emotional," she took it as an affront. "I don't get emotional," she said. "I get angry."

If some questioned George's assertiveness, no one doubted Barbara's. Almost eight years as the Vice President's wife had seasoned her and given her confidence. She now realized how vital she was in George's life. She had once asked, "Will I be enough?" Now she *knew* she was enough. Whereas she had once hated politics, after living at 1 Observatory Circle, she now had a hunger for more. It's what Joan Mondale predicted would happen all those years ago during her gracious tour of the property.

During the 1987–1988 election cycle, Barbara logged visits to an incredible ninety-two cities in twenty-nine states, traveling more than fifty thousand miles while campaigning for her husband. She gave almost two hundred interviews and somehow managed to make each one feel fresh, as if it were her first. People loved her grandmotherly image, her silvery hair more a trademark now than ever before.

Barbara had started going gray in her twenties and dyed it for a few years. Why? Because her mother had told her to. Finally, she stopped when she was in her forties. Many years later, she would say she did so because she liked to play golf and her hair would turn orange due to the effect of the sun on the dyeing chemicals, or that she liked to swim and her hair would turn green because of the chlorine in the pool, "so I decided to go white." Apparently, George couldn't have cared less. "In a voice tinged with bitterness," wrote the author Gail Sheehy, who interviewed her later in 1988 for *Vanity Fair*, "Mrs. Bush said that when she stopped coloring her hair, 'George Bush never noticed. So, why had I gone through all those years of agony?'"

Things changed once George became Vice President and even more so as he began his campaign for President. For instance, when she told him to forget about the *Newsweek* cover story and said there were more urgent matters in the world than whether he was a wimp, he agreed to let it go. These days, she had a center of calm about her that hadn't been there before. She was also taking a tougher stance on other issues, such as the stories about George's infidelity. "We were always concerned about how she was going to respond, how to address it. How do you discuss this issue," recalled George's chief of staff at the time, Craig Fuller.

About two weeks before that insulting *Newsweek* story was published, Craig Fuller, along with campaign manager Lee Atwater, and political strategist Robert Teeter, met with George on the front porch of 1 Observatory Circle to discuss the infidelity issue, which they worried would be raised in the article. George was angry that it was even a subject up for discussion. He reasoned that as long as they didn't comment on it, the story would have no oxygen and would just wither away and die. The men disagreed. This had been the strategy for years and it simply hadn't worked. Fuller, who was previously President Ronald Reagan's White House cabinet secretary, had a strong relationship with the press and believed that if a politician was open and honest with the media, it would always work to his advantage. Issuing a statement and being definitive about it would likely be the best way forward for George, he said.

As the men were discussing this delicate matter, Barbara, who had been out for a walk, came up to the porch. "What's going on here?" she asked with an arched eyebrow. She must have sensed the tension. George told her what was being talked about, that his aides wanted to compose a statement about the rumors of infidelity. Barbara couldn't believe her ears. "No. That's absolutely ridiculous," she said, erupting. "The answer is no. Forget about it. Why are we even discussing this? Why are you men even here?" She was adamant that no statement should ever be made about any gossip, and that was the end of it for her, and for them, too. The meeting was adjourned.

"Rarer Than a Three-Eyed Owl"

When George H.W. asked his son George W. to move to Washington and assist him with his presidential campaign, George agreed to it. It was a tough decision, though, because he loved Midland so much, and he knew Laura did as well. However, the two of them sat down and thoroughly discussed all the pros and cons and decided that yes, they would make the move. Therefore, after many years of being happy in Midland—separately and then as a married couple—George and Laura sold their house, packed their belongings into a moving van, and left Texas for D.C. While Laura agreed to the move, she also had a bit of a hidden agenda relating to it. She hoped that maybe moving to Washington would help her in forging a better relationship with her mother-in-law. She still had not given up on it.

Laura and the twins arrived in Washington a day before George got there and spent their first night at 1 Observatory Circle with the in-laws. Barbara and George loved the opportunity to spend some time with their granddaughters Jenna and Barbara, and right away it felt to everyone that the decision to relocate was a good one. The next day, Laura, got up early to get ready for the day and, while primping in front of the bathroom mirror, accidentally washed one of her contacts right down the drain. Her father-in-law the VP had to save the day with his trusty wrench by taking off the sink trap and finding the missing contact. Then Laura left for the day to move into the new town house she and George had purchased on Westover Place near American University in the Northwest district. George then arrived, and everyone was happily reunited. Soon after, the twins, who were five, were enrolled in Horace Mann Elementary School.

As soon as he got to town, George got down to business helping with his father's campaign; he would be H.W.'s fiercest protector, not allowing the media access without his authorization. This would prove to be a seminal time in George's relationship with his father. H.W. began to trust him more, not look at him with such a critical eye, and George was eager to please. "Give me one good reason I should let you talk to George Bush," he would tell a writer. "Just doing my job," he said when confronted about it, "protecting the old man." When he met campaign manager Lee Atwater for the first time, George asked him point-blank, "How can we trust you?" Atwater, seldom at a loss for words, didn't know how to respond. "Listen, pal," George told him. "If you go to war for our family, we want you completely on our side. We love George Bush, and you better bust your ass for him."

Meanwhile, now that they were all living in the same city, the family had an opportunity to come together in a different way. George got closer to his parents and by extension Laura got to know Barbara better. It's what she'd always wanted, and finally it was coming to pass. At first it was touch and go, but soon she and Barbara began sharing their love of books and art and finding common ground. There were moments when Barbara would look at her and Laura could actually see what seemed like genuine affection for her in her eyes. She'd have to wonder if it was her imagination, she told intimates, but it seemed real to her.

"At last, I saw Bar for who she is," Laura would recall, "a funny, warm woman and a mother who is devoted to her husband and her children. Away from that overflowing Maine summer house and the conventions and inaugurations, those high-profile, high-pitched events where Gampy's political career was on the line, Bar and I came to know and love each other."

Also, in the months to come, many of George's and Laura's friends would drive up from Texas to spend time with them, which was fun. They had the opportunity to show them Washington, and everyone enjoyed it. At the same time, though, Laura knew better than to mix outsiders with her mother-in-law. Whereas the family knew full well how blunt "Bar" could be and that they shouldn't be sensitive about it, others were often taken aback. "She's managed to insult nearly all of my friends with one or another perfectly timed acerbic comment," Laura would say with a chuckle. She once asked George, "Is it really necessary for your mother to always speak her mind?" George looked at her as if she were out of her mind. The answer was obvious. *Of course* it was necessary.

Unfortunately, one problem that kept coming up was that Barbara didn't always approve of the way Laura raised the girls, and, no surprise, she wasn't inclined to be silent about it. Laura was more relaxed with Barbara and Jenna, whereas Barbara thought a firmer hand was sometimes needed.

"Typically, the Bushes were low-key in disciplining the girls," recalled Monica Gonzalez, who would become Laura's personal assistant. "I never heard them raise their voices, ever. Mrs. Bush once told me how hard she'd struggled to have children and, she said, 'I never want to forget how blessed I am to be able to have these girls.' Still, they could be a handful, those two. They were willful. I remember when Mr. Bush was fed up about something little Jenna had done and thought she was really out of line. 'Look, I don't approve, either,' Mrs. Bush told him, 'but, Bushie, I think we have to raise her to think for herself and stand up for herself. That's how I was raised and I turned out pretty well, didn't I?' [Mr. Bush] said, 'That's true. But she's not supposed to stand up to us. My mother would have killed me if I ever did.' Mrs. Bush said, 'Okay, I'll talk to her and see if I can reason with her.' He laughed and said, 'Okay, well, good luck with that, then.'"

Once, the twins were at 1 Observatory Circle and, while Barbara and Laura were having tea, started racing all over the living room playing tag. When one of them bumped into a table, an expensive Chinese lamp toppled over and smashed to the floor, breaking into many pieces. The two girls froze in place, looking fearful. There was a moment of silence as everyone held their breaths to see what would happen next.

Barbara bolted from her chair and became angry, raising her voice at the twins and demanding to know what in the world they were thinking. She had gotten that lamp in Beijing, she said, and it had cost a fortune. She was furious and it showed. Laura didn't like it. She jumped to her feet and told Barbara she was scaring the twins and that she would handle it. She chastised the twins, telling them to sit in a chair and not to move "until Mommy tells you."

"That's it?" Barbara asked Laura. "Sit there until Mommy tells you? *That's* their punishment?" Barbara then said probably the worst thing she could have said in that moment, something along the lines of: *It probably wouldn't hurt you to read a few books about raising children, especially if you refuse to listen to someone who has raised five of them.* That was all Laura needed to hear. She quickly packed up her daughters' belongings and got them out of there as fast as she could. She was upset, to say the least.

Laura kept waiting for an apology from Barbara that never came. When she told George she wasn't going to make the first move, George said, "Well, better get used to the way things are now, because the Barbara Bush apology is rarer than a three-eyed owl." He suggested Laura not dig her heels in too deeply because his mother never backed down.

At the end of two weeks, George wanted Laura to apologize to his mother. Apparently, Barbara had been complaining to him about the dispute and he didn't want to hear about it any longer. Laura became upset with him. Why would he take his mother's side against her? The next thing they knew, the two of them were having a fight about it. "It was just standard Bush family drama," said one of the family members. "The son sides with the mother because it's easier to argue with the wife than it is with the mother. Laura was really pissed off at him, but she knew the terrain by now. He was never going to give in either, just like Bar. 'These people are driving me out of my mind,' she told me. 'All I have ever wanted was for all of us to sit down in one place and have a real conversation about things, but that never happens, does it?' She was really frustrated."

Finally, at the end of about a month, Laura decided that the impasse was absurd and she was done with her part of it. The twins needed their grandmother and she knew Barbara needed them as well. Plus, to hear her tell it to intimates, she knew somewhere deep down that Barbara Bush loved her and that it made no sense to keep this quarrel going. "The love is there," she said, "even if she can't show it. I don't know . . . I can still somehow feel it."

Barbara and Laura soon came together with the girls on a Sunday afternoon to have another enjoyable day together. Their dispute was never again discussed.

Victory

In 1988, also up for the Republican nomination for President were Ronald Reagan's former secretary of state and President Nixon's chief of staff, General Al Haig; former Delaware governor Pierre "Pete" du Pont; New York congressman Jack Kemp; Kansas senator Bob Dole; and televangelist Pat Robertson. The Democratic contenders were Massachusetts governor Michael Dukakis; Senator Al Gore of Tennessee (who would become Bill Clinton's Vice President in four years and who would then run against George W. for President eight years after that); former Arizona governor Bruce Babbitt; Congressman Dick Gephardt from Missouri; the Reverend Jesse Jackson; former senator Gary Hart of Colorado; and Senator Joe Biden from Delaware (who would go on to become Barack Obama's Vice President for two terms). Biden and Hart ended up dropping out—Biden because he'd been caught plagiarizing parts of a speech and Hart because of an illicit relationship with a woman named Donna Rice.

All of the family came out for their father, traveling the country, campaigning hard. Barbara continued to be a strong presence. George eventually won the nomination. Dorothy, now eighty-seven, was present when he accepted it during the Republican National Convention in August at the Superdome in New Orleans. What a night this was for the entire family, but especially for its matriarch. She would never change, though; later, when

George had a contentious interview with Dan Rather—it's since become iconic footage because of the way Rather pressured Bush over the Iran-Contra affair and the way George pushed back—she called him and said, "Just because that other man was rude was no excuse for you to be."

The rest of the family also showed up in force at the convention, which had begun on August 15. On the sixteenth, thirteen-year-old George P., Columba and Jeb's son, led the proceedings with the national anthem.

The next day, Columba gave a nominating speech at the convention, first a long one in Spanish—which she read from cards she was holding—and then briefer words in heavily accented English. She had recently surprised the family with the announcement that she'd just become a U.S. citizen so that she could vote for her father-in-law. Now, looking fetching in a black-and-purple plaid ensemble with pearls and with her husband standing behind her for support, she stood up to speak before the audience. Surrounded by television reporters with cameras and excited people thrusting BUSH placards, all she had to say in the English part of her speech was: "With respect, with hope, and with love, I second the nomination for the President of the United States for one who has been like a father to me, an honest, intelligent, and capable man, my father-in-law, George Bush."

After her words, the audience broke out in cheers. She appeared delighted to have gotten through it. Jeb took her into a bear hug, proud of her; it also just happened to be her thirty-fifth birthday. A genuine moment occurred when she caught an image of herself on a television monitor and nervously ran her hand through her hair. Jeb continually massaged her shoulders, as the crowd cheered.

It was Barbara, though, who gave the most memorable, emotional speech, in which she spoke of the way her bond to George was strengthened by the death of Robin. "He simply wouldn't allow my grief to divide us, push us apart, which is what happens so often where there is a loss like that," she said. "And for as long as I live, I will respect and appreciate my husband for the strength of his understanding."

Then, Ronald Reagan gave a rousing talk, telling George to "go out there and win one for the Gipper." In his own speech, George called for a "kinder, gentler nation." He talked about "a brilliant diversity spread like stars, like a thousand points of light," and about taxes he famously said, "Read my lips: *no new taxes*." He would later come to deeply regret this promise, especially after he raised taxes.

In the end, the race was between George Bush and his running mate, Dan Quayle, the young senator from Indiana, against Michael Dukakis and his second, Lloyd Bentsen.

After a tough campaign, George H. W. Bush was ultimately elected forty-first President of the United States, taking it with 53 percent of the popular vote and 426 electoral votes. He won all but ten states: a real landslide. It was the first time since Martin Van Buren in 1836 that a sitting Vice President won the White House. Now George was finally commander in chief, and Barbara was no longer second in the country to Nancy Reagan or to anyone else, for that matter. She had earned her place as First Lady or, as she so adeptly put it at the time, "This isn't about me or anyone else in this family. It's about George and the fact that he is the best man for the job, and that he has put in years of service to get here. And in America, that's acknowledged, I'm happy to say."

The Matriarch Visits the Oval Office

No one was more excited and proud than Dorothy that her second-eldest son had been elected President. "I loved standing next to my eighty-seven-year-old grandmother, my namesake, sharing a front-row seat to history," Doro Bush would recall of the inauguration on January 20, 1989. "Dad later said how he regretted that his father wasn't alive when he became president," she added, "but the fact that Ganny was there made that remarkable occasion all the more special for all of us. As the sun pierced through the breaking winter clouds, I watched my father become the forty-first President of the United States. In one majestic moment, Dad was the leader of the free world."

At the White House that night, Dorothy slept in the high-poster, mahogany bed in the Queens' Bedroom, formerly the Rose Guest Room and renamed by Jacqueline Kennedy because it had been occupied by so many royal guests. She'd been to the White House many times over the years and had even written in-depth about those experiences in her newspaper column. "We wandered from room to room," she wrote in 1961 when Mrs. Kennedy invited her, "and Jacqueline explained the history so quickly and breathlessly I could barely keep up with my note taking!" This visit, however, would mark the first time Dorothy would spend the night there. "She seemed so small and tiny in that enormous bed," Barbara later recalled of her mother-on-law. The next morning she and Barbara watched with teary eyes as a huge crowd below her window sang "God Bless America" in tribute to the beginning of a new presidency. Later in the day, Barbara went to the Queens' Bedroom to check on Dorothy, and she wasn't there. She looked out the same window and, below, there was Dorothy in her wheelchair accompanied by her doctor, her nurse, and three Secret Service agents. She was surrounded by admirers, smiling and shaking hands with all the well-wishers.

To further honor his mother, George made certain she was his first guest in the Oval Office. Showing her the historic artifacts of the office gave George more pleasure, he would later say, than pretty much anything he'd ever done for his mother. Of his personal items, he had already placed a framed photo of Robin in a special place.

Mother and son sat together in the Oval Office for about a half hour and reminisced about the family's long, hard climb up the political ladder. He also showed her a letter from President Reagan on a memo pad upon which was emblazoned the words: "Don't let the turkeys get you down." Reagan wrote that he would "treasure the memories we share" and noted that he'd also "miss our Thursday lunches." He signed it "Ron." Dorothy was impressed; she'd always thought President Reagan was a good man, though she'd had her reservations about Nancy Reagan ever since that first awkward dinner at 1 Observatory Circle.

"You must always treat this place with respect," Dorothy told her son, and he agreed—so much so that he would make it a point to at least try to never enter the Oval Office without wearing a coat and tie. Before they left, according to Dorothy, she and George sat on a sofa facing his desk, clasped hands, and said a prayer of gratitude.

Afterward, George gave his mother her first full tour of the White House. Dorothy had been to there before, but never with such a thorough visit.

Dorothy's opinion of the White House was that the place was too big for family living. "They're never going to be able to make it cozy," she told her daughter, Nancy. She said she preferred the Vice President's residence, where she'd spent some quality time with the family and which she felt was "a better size for living," If it were up to her, she said, George and Barbara would continue to live there and just use the White House for official occasions.

On January 21, George's first full day in office, he gave a press conference in the Oval Office. Seated right next to him, wearing a lavender skirt with a matching long-sleeved jacket and white pearls, was his mother. She'd never looked prouder.

A few days later, Dorothy wrote to a friend, Luella Thompson, who lived in Los Angeles: "My son and I had to go about five blocks down the street from the White House, and you can't imagine the thrill of traveling in a procession of shiny black cars with red and blue lights flashing, flags waving and sirens blaring and concerned men on walkie-talkies being watchful. I have never seen anything like it, Luella. One might imagine it being easy to get used to this, but I never want to. Who can ever get over sleeping in a room called The Bedroom of the Queen [sic]? I just felt so honored and so humbled."

First Lady

Barbara Bush's four years as First Lady of the United States in her husband's administration proved to be among the happiest and most fulfilling of her life. Sixty-three when she began her term, she was a different kind of First Lady than Nancy Reagan. At one press conference immediately after George was inaugurated, Barbara affected an exaggerated, model-like pose for the press and said, "I want you to watch me all week and remember. Notice the hair, the makeup, the designer clothes, and remember. You may never see it again." To a lot of observers, this statement seemed as much a shot at Nancy as it did a self-deprecating sentiment. Barbara's White House would certainly be a more stress-free place, where state dinners and other important events had a more casual feeling. "Nancy was a perfectionist," Barbara said, "that's not me. I'm more relaxed and I think people are more relaxed around me."

"She was so much her own woman in the White House," recalled Franette McCulloch, who was a pastry chef at the White House for seventeen years, including those of the first Bush administration. "One morning, I remember she got up early and went into the kitchen of the private quarters on the second floor and there was the butler, as always, getting breakfast ready for her and the President. She went over to get the leash to take her dog, Millie, out for a walk. The butler took the leash from her and said, 'I'll take care of that, ma'am.' She looked at him and said, 'Seriously? Please. Thank you, but I can walk my own dog.'

"Every morning she would go out to the outdoor pool south of the Oval Office and go swimming, even if it was freezing. Once, I was walking down the second-floor hallway to the family elevator, and here comes Barbara. Her hair is wet and she has a towel over her head. She has a pair of flowery pants and a big ol' T-shirt. She has a pair of Keds tennis shoes, one is pink and the other is purple. 'Hi, Franette,' she says cheerily. 'I've been swimming.' I had to laugh. Having served with Nancy Reagan, I could tell you that she would never have been seen like that in the White House, or anywhere else for that matter. But Barbara was her own person. 'Oops, I forgot something, I have to go back down,' she says. So the elevator doors open, and standing there in a sharp black suit with a crisp white shirt and matching bow tie is Woody, the elevator operator. Barbara says, 'Morning, Woody,' and gets into the elevator wearing her get-up. What a funny sight, the two of them side by side like that."

Secret Service agent Denny Schlindwein recalled, "She really got mad if you treated her with deference. When someone would reference the Bush dynasty, she wouldn't like it. 'It's not a dynasty. It's a tradition,' she would say, 'a *patriotic* tradition.' I remember one time I was in an elevator with her and we were going to a function and somebody radioed me. She asked, 'What's going on?' I told her, 'They want me to hold you here a few minutes until everyone is seated.' And she said, "Oh, fiddlesticks. I don't care if everyone is seated or not. What am I, a queen? Let's just go now.' And we did."

Shortly after moving into the White House, Laura's daughters, Jenna and Barbara, who were about seven, didn't make it for dinner one night with the rest of the family. Barbara was babysitting the children for the weekend while their parents were out of town. "Where are the kids?" Barbara asked the butler. "They're down at the bowling alley [one of the features of the White House] and they ordered a couple of sandwiches to be brought down there for them. *"They're seven,"* Barbara exclaimed, getting up from the table. "They don't get to order sandwiches. What is this, the Waldorf?'"

As the two girls waited in the bowling alley for their sandwiches, they heard footsteps coming down the hall. They thought it was a servant with their meal. It wasn't. "Really?" Barbara said, bursting into the room. "*Really?* Let me tell you girls something," she said to both wide-eyed youngsters. "This is a house. This is not a hotel. And not only that, it's not even *your* house. So, no, you do not get to order room service here. You come down to dinner and eat with the rest of us. *Now.*"

Barbara kept a regimented White House, just as she did at Walker's Point. "She could be a little caustic sometimes, but only behind closed doors and only with people she truly loved and trusted," said one Secret Service agent. "Few, if anyone, ever betrayed Mrs. Bush to the media. She inspired loyalty because she was so fair and loyal. Her personal assistant, Casey Healey, would always say that if Barbara was on your side, she would always be on your side. Paula [Rendon], the housekeeper, was a good example. The Bushes brought her with them to the White House even though she had few duties there, such as sewing, some cleaning, and taking care of Millie, the dog. She was part of the family, though, so she moved in with them and had a little apartment on the third floor. There was a beauty parlor on the second floor; Pat Nixon had put it in, and Barbara used to joke with Paula that she was going to give her a makeover. Paula would shoot back, 'Oh yeah? You first.'"

Meanwhile, Barbara, as First Lady, continued to endorse the literacy programs that had so endeared her to the public. She raised millions of dollars for literacy programs for children, helped shepherd the National Literacy Act of 1991, and even encouraged her husband to continue to subsidize the Adult Education Act of 1966, which funded adult literacy programs. It was a subject dear to her, and one that even today remains closely associated with her.

Though she didn't have a lot of experience in foreign affairs other than as an observer of her husband's policies, she had great insight into people and into what pleased them as well as what didn't. She would find her ability to read people to her advantage as she forged relationships with women like the prickly and often contentious Raisa Gorbachev, Soviet Union President Mikhail Gorbachev's wife (who didn't get along with Nancy Reagan). Barbara wrote to her brother Scott just before the Gorbachevs visited Washington in June 1990, "One thing I can promise you. I am going to love her in spite of anything she does or does not do." Barbara knew what she had to do, not only for her husband's sake but for that of the country, and she would do it. She was never intimidated, always able to find common ground with people from all walks of life, entertaining many global leaders and their spouses at Kennebunkport.

That she was so successful in her new role despite the fact that she was facing serious health issues is a testament to Barbara's will and tenacity in the face of adversity. Shortly after George was elected, she was diagnosed with Graves' disease, a serious irregularity of the thyroid function, which caused a nearly twenty-pound weight loss as well as painfully distended and teary eyes. Her vision was also seriously compromised. Treatment for the disease was difficult, a matter of trial and error with the use of steroids and other drugs that caused her to experience terrible muscle and bone aches. Barbara would be forced to live with the disease for the rest of her life. "I confess I was in a lot of pain," she later admitted. No one outside her circle knew it, though. She never acted in any way enfeebled, always strong and robust.

In a strange coincidence, George would also, in fifteen months, be diagnosed with Graves' disease, which affected his heart and, at one point, even had him hospitalized.

The Bushes' first Christmas at the White House was memorable, if not also a challenging time for the staff. "Every year at Christmas it's absolute hell at the White House," recalled chef Franette McCulloch. "We'd have employees pass out from working so long and so hard, they were just so exhausted. After all of the parties for Congress, the military, and on and on—thousands of people we would have to feed—we'd have our staff Christmas party. This party was always on the first floor. The table with the food was set up in the State Dining Room, and then the rest of the floor was open to walk around. You'd bring your spouse and your children and they'd get a chance to see the White House, where you work. It was wonderful except for the fact that we'd always be so tired, we'd be on autopilot.

"Back during the Reagan administration," she recalled, "President Reagan was so adorable, he'd mingle with us and tell jokes. He was like the life of the party. But the only time out of the eight years we ever saw Mrs. Reagan at our

Christmas party was this one year when we were told to form a receiving line in the Red Room. We all just stood there in line stiffly, and Nancy came in, acting quite royal. She was escorted by the head usher, Rex Scouten, down the line. If she recognized you, she would nod and smile and you would nod and smile back. She walked right by me; didn't even give me the time of day. Then, when she got to the end of the line, she walked straight out of the room and went back upstairs. That was the extent of her participation in the staff Christmas party that year.

"Barbara Bush was with us every year for Christmas at the party, spending a lot of time with us and being very much a part of everything. She talked to each and every person, made contact with all of us."

After the White House celebrations, the Bush family spent the holiday at Camp David, as they would for every Christmas during the administration. Barbara and George loved the tranquility of Camp David, which is formally known as the Naval Support Facility Thurmont, as have most First Couples over the years.

Camp David is a secluded, two-hundred-acre country retreat for the President and his family about sixty miles outside of Washington in a mountainous region of Maryland. Most of the staff there is comprised of marines since it's a military installation. It was named by Dwight D. Eisenhower, who held his first cabinet meeting there in November 1955, after his grandson David. Since 1943, when Prime Minister Winston Churchill visited, Camp David has been used to host foreign dignitaries. The Presidents' quarters at Camp David is called Aspen, with four bedrooms, two bathrooms, and five fireplaces; it also has an enormous pool. Other cabins have names such as Birch, Maple, and Dogwood. There's a strict "no cameras" policy at Camp David, which these days is complicated by the use of cell phones.

Barbara loved the breathtaking views at Camp David and said that it was only there that she felt she was able to finally take a deep breath after whatever melodrama was currently being played out at the White House. Once, she broke her leg after careening into a tree while sledding at Camp David with Arnold Schwarzenegger and Maria Shriver. "No damage to the tree, though," George quipped.

The problem with Camp David was the many layers of security in place, which always upset the White House staff who had to come in and work there for special occasions. Just because one had a high-level White House security clearance didn't mean he or she would have immediate entrée to Camp David, and the guards there were perhaps overly conscientious. For instance, the Bushes' executive White House pastry chef, Roland Mesnier, complained that they hoisted his automobile up on jacks and took the wheels off, looking for bombs. "They treated us like terrorists," he said.

Christmas at Camp David in 1989 was melancholy. Doro, in particular, was troubled about her marriage and would spend nights crying to her father as he tried to console her. She was thirty at this time. Soon, she and her young children, Sam and Ellie, would move to Washington after the dissolution of her marriage in order to be closer to her parents. Eventually, she would settle in Bethesda, Maryland, and begin working for the National Rehabilitation Hospital in Washington in the communications department. Coincidentally, she would be working there when her father signed the Americans with Disabilities Act on July 26, 1990.

During the Christmas holiday of 1989, when her father told her not to worry, that "everything will be all right," it wasn't just empty optimism, it was actually prescient. Just a month later, Doro met Bobby Koch, who worked for Dick Gephardt, the Democratic House majority leader. The two hit it off quickly. The fact that he was a Democrat didn't bother Barbara and George, though it did some others. In February of 1991, at a state dinner for Queen Margrethe II of Denmark, Marilyn Quayle came up to him and demanded to know, "What are *you* doing here?" Barbara happened to be within earshot. "Bobby is our guest, Marilyn," she said, staring hard at her, "and we're *glad* he's here." In three years' time, Doro and Bobby would be married at Camp David, the very spot where she had mourned the end of her first marriage.

At this same time, George W. realized a childhood dream of his to own a baseball team when he bought the Texas Rangers and became its general manager. He and Laura and their two children, Jenna and Barbara, seemed to be in a good place. After H.W. was elected, they moved back to Texas.

"I settled into Dallas life," Laura recalled, "decorating our three-bedroom ranch house with a little converted garage for guests in the back. My days were filled with the girls and their friends and activities."

Though Laura's relationship with Barbara was still tricky, there were special moments between them now that she was in the White House. For instance, the two would sometimes walk the halls of the White House late at night, venturing into the many rooms, turning on the lights and admiring the paintings and furnishings. Sometimes they would flip on a light and shriek at the sight of a rat scurrying past them. There seemed to be rats everywhere. Barbara had even come across one while swimming in the pool one morning; when she screamed out, George rushed over, grabbed the rodent with a pool skimmer, and held it under the water until it drowned.

The two women would stand in the Treaty Room and marvel at the fact that Barbara was actually a distant descendant of the nation's fourteenth President, Franklin Pierce (1853–1857). His framed photo was right there on one of the bookshelves.

When she was growing up, no one talked much about President Pierce; Barbara would say she was "humiliated" as a child when she read up on him and learned that he'd been "one of our weakest Presidents." That kind of thing was relevant in a household where her mother was always reinforcing that appearances mattered and that what people thought of you mattered even more. Barbara didn't know back then about the tragic lives of Pierce and his wife, Jane. She'd later learn that they lost all three of their sons in childhood: Franklin Jr. lived for just three days, Frank Robert died at the age of four from typhus, and Benjamin, horribly enough, was killed when he and his parents were on their way to Pierce's inauguration and their train derailed and rolled over an embankment. He was just eleven. His parents found him nearly decapitated in the wreckage. Jane, grief-stricken and traumatized, fell into a depression that lasted the rest of her life. In so many ways, Barbara could now relate; she decided that George should have his own home office in this very same Treaty Room as President Pierce.

Barbara and Laura would also imagine the lives of the American women of note who'd been in these rooms. "To think that Eleanor Roosevelt once stood right here," Barbara would say, moved. She was also an admirer of

Pat Nixon's and felt she was grossly underrated as a First Lady, especially given what she had to put up with from her husband. Laura would agree that these women were special, never imagining that one day she would join their ranks.

For all her attributes, perhaps what Barbara Bush will most be remembered for during her time as First Lady is her emphasis on family values, even if sometimes things were strained with her own relatives. In her now historic commencement speech at Wellesley College in 1990, she urged students to "cherish your human connections: your relationships with family and friends. For several years, you've had impressed upon you the importance to your career of dedication and hard work, and, of course, that's true. But as important as your obligations as a doctor, lawyer, or business leader will be, you are a human being first, and those human connections—with spouses, with children, with friends—are the most important investments you will ever make. At the end of your life, you will never regret not having passed one more test, not winning one more verdict, or not closing one more deal. You will regret time not spent with a husband, a child, a friend, or a parent."

Dorothy's Reflection

A full-length gold gilt carved wooden mirror hung on a wall in a corner of Dorothy Walker Bush's bedroom. At the top of this enormous French Louis XV–style antique was an inset painting of four cherubs tugging on a vine of flowers and leaves. On opposite sides of the scene were two children on swings, both with small angel wings. This exquisite late-nineteenth-century piece had been gifted to Dorothy by her mother, Luli, for her twentieth birthday in July 1921. Certainly, this mirror had its own special story to tell about Dorothy Walker Bush, and every time she looked into it, she was flooded by memories, most of them joyful, of a life well lived. She'd spent the last seventy years gazing at her reflection, first as a young woman facing the challenges presented by married life, then as a middle-aged woman facing the challenges having to do with the raising her family, and now, as an old woman meeting the challenges of her own mortality.

Every morning, after Dorothy awakened, she would force herself to get out of bed, even on those days when she really didn't think it possible. She would take small, cautious steps—one hand on the mattress all the way to help with her balance—toward a small cabbage rose–upholstered chair. It was placed directly in front of the mirror, and once there she would stare at her image with a determined expression and begin her prayers in a whisper. Gazing intently at her reflection, she would compel herself to feel well, to have a better day than she had yesterday. This was her ritual, how she rallied for the day. Every morning for at least half an hour she would savor this time alone, during which she would collect her thoughts and set her intention.

The few friends Dorothy had around her own age hated getting old and complained about it incessantly. Not Dorothy. She didn't want to talk about her aches and pains, and she didn't want to hear about anyone else's. While there were certainly those days she could feel herself leaning toward self-pity, she never allowed herself to completely cross the threshold from determination to defeat.

"True to her competitive nature, she was resolute that she was going to get old better than anyone else had ever gotten old in the history of aging mankind," said Virginia Mason with a chuckle. "What bothered her most was that she could no longer do for others. She could no longer be of service. She used to always tell me, 'Giving well is the key to aging well.'" Indeed, in a 1960 column, Dorothy wrote of her mother, Luli: "For everyone who knows her, mother is the absolute ideal of how to grow old. Although eighty-five years in age she's younger than springtime in spirit. The secret of her triumph? She's always thinking of others and doing for others."

Though Dorothy was now in failing health, which seemed to be getting worse by the day, she refused to accept it. One morning, as she was being helped from her bedroom to the kitchen for breakfast, she told Virginia Mason, "God waits until you've experienced all of life's ups and downs, every one of them, before he presents you with your toughest competitor: old age. That's the biggest fight of all," she said, "and I will not give up the fight. So help me, I will fight it to the very last moment."

It was also obvious to both her caretaker and live-in nurse that Dorothy was sensitive about losing control. She often lamented the loss of independence. "Stop doing for me," she would tell her handlers. "I can prepare my own meals." She couldn't do so, but accepting this reality was almost impossible for her. "Mentally, she is as sharp as ever," one of her nurses reported back to her son the President in a note dated August 14, 1991. "She's a young woman trapped in a failing body. She's also more indomitable than any person I have ever known. I am proud to care for her, sir. Even if she does say to me, from time to time, 'You may remove yourself from my presence.'"

Getting Dorothy to take her medication was always difficult, especially since she had determined somewhere along the way that she really didn't need it. At one point, she took to slipping the pills under her tongue and then, after her nurse left the room, spitting them out and hiding them under her pillow. She would then forget they were there and the caretaker or nurse would find the tablets in the linens during the daily changing of the bed. "After that happened, I would have to stand before her and make sure she swallowed," said Virginia Mason, "and she was furious about it. 'I'm sorry, Mrs. Bush, but you have to take this medicine,' I would tell her, and she would respond with 'Says who?' I would say, 'Says your doctor,' and she would roll her eyes and say, 'Oh, please. What does he know?'"

As 1991 came to a close, Dorothy had to be hospitalized for congestive heart failure and pneumonia, which was the reason she couldn't be at Kennebunkport with the family for the holiday. After she was released, she didn't seem able to rebound. Barbara would call frequently to check on her, as would her daughter, Nancy, who telephoned at least twice a day. "Don't you dare give them any information about me other than I am well and having a good day," Dorothy would tell the women caring for her. She said she didn't want anyone, even family members, to have other details. "I don't need people out there thinking I'm sick," she said. "That does me no good. People should be thinking I'm well. *That* does me good." Virginia Mason would remind her that these "people" she was referring to were loved ones who should know the truth. "She would become frustrated with me," recalled Virginia, "and she would say, 'Read your Bible, Virginia. Jesus said, "It is done unto you as you believe." Well, I believe I am well, and I don't need people out there believing otherwise.'"

After the latest hospitalization, Dorothy was too feeble to make it to the mirror on her own. Her live-in nurse would have to help her from her bed and into a wheelchair. She would then push the wheelchair to the mirror and leave the room so that Dorothy could, once again, have her morning ritual. Soon, though, even that became too difficult and there was only one solution. Two of her young nephews lifted the incredibly heavy mirror off the wall and propped it up in a corner right next to the bed. Now, upon awakening, she would sit up and, buttressed by pillows, turn slightly to her left to catch her reflection. Only then would Dorothy Bush be able to begin her day.

"His Heart's Not in It"

By the end of 1991, the juggernaut that had propelled George H. W. Bush and his family from one political conquest to the next, going all the way back almost thirty years to his election as chairman of the Harris County, Texas, Republican Party, had finally begun to peter out. His Graves' disease continued to cause not only serious issues with his heart and lungs but also physical fatigue. Emotionally, he seemed to be flagging, too. Though he tried to give the 1991 campaign his all, he was slowing down and Barbara knew it. She began to suspect that he really didn't want to run for a second term at all and told family members, "his heart's not in it." She felt that he was compelled to do so because he was just so used to political warfare. Also, being a public servant still mattered to him. He was sixty-seven and Barbara was sixty-six; life was getting tougher for them, not easier.

The older they got, though, the tighter the bond became between Barbara and George. Barbara admired his confidence in himself, that he seemed always to achieve his goals in life, that he actually became President of the United States. When he began to slow down, she wanted more than anything to be his rock, and she would do whatever it took. Sometimes that meant shielding him from unpleasantness, such as the crisis facing their son Neil.

Neil Bush found himself caught up in a government investigation of the failing Silverado Savings and Loan in Denver, where he served on the board.

The U.S. Office of Thrift Supervision would eventually conclude that he'd engaged in a number of "breaches of his fiduciary duties involving multiple conflicts of interests." Though not brought up on criminal charges, Bush was the subject of a civil lawsuit brought by the Federal Deposit Insurance Company; he settled with fifty thousand dollars. In the end, Neil didn't even have to pay his legal fees of about a quarter of a million dollars. George H.W.'s friend Lud Ashley—the same Lud Ashley who had accompanied Dorothy to the cemetery to bury Robin's ashes—set up a fund for Neil, tapping many of the family's friends for contributions. The savings and loan failure of Silverado cost the government about $100 million. One can certainly conclude that Neil was lucky he didn't end up in prison.

The scandal got wide news coverage. Barbara and George felt Neil's problems wouldn't have gotten the attention they did had his father not been President. After all, eighteen savings and loans in Colorado had failed—why was Silverado the only one called to testify in front of Congress? It got to a point where George was so upset about it, Barbara had to monitor his exposure to the coverage. She wouldn't allow him to watch television news reports about it, and she told people not to bring it up to him.

It wasn't long before Neil was back on his feet with a new company, Apex Energy, which, unfortunately, would last barely a year. He and his wife, Sharon, felt ostracized by Denver society because of all the bad publicity and soon left that city for Houston. He then took a variety of jobs as a "consultant," in high finance, oil businesses, and computer technology, using his family name for leverage. But he was struggling and his parents didn't offer much financial help. George felt strongly that their children should imitate his work ethic but not expect to share in his wealth until after he was dead.

"I just had a hard time understanding how the President's grandchildren couldn't have enough food," Neil's wife, Sharon, later said in a sworn deposition. "I'd be at the store and buying groceries but then would tally it up in my head and realize I didn't have enough money, so then I had to put the food back on the shelves. Do you know how upsetting that is?" She said she felt the President should "maybe mail us some money so we could buy food for the children, because I assume we were in the spot because of his [Neil's] father being President. It was a political thing."

The economy was bad at this time, but still, one wouldn't think any Bush family member would be affected by it. Other Americans, though, were frustrated that the economy had taken such a serious downturn, and they blamed their President. On the other hand, he had many admirable and historic accomplishments while in office, such as Operation Desert Storm in 1991, the campaign to drive Iraqi invaders and Saddam Hussein out of Kuwait without destabilizing the Middle East. Whatever one thinks about the Persian Gulf War, the coalition led by President Bush was successful. Today it is viewed as his crowning achievement in office. As a wartime President, his approval ratings went through the roof. Also, with the decline and fall of the Soviet Union, the Cold War had ended during his presidency without a shot being fired. But his high approval ratings didn't last. It was as if the public felt President Bush had done all the really hard work abroad, and now Americans were bored with foreign policy and with him and just wanted to fix the failing economy at home.

The Republicans had been in power for almost twelve years, and the tide was turning, especially when Bill Clinton—young and vibrant at forty-two, the same age as George's eldest son, George W.—threw his hat into the ring. In his decision to run for President, Clinton kept referring to "the worst economy since the Great Depression"—which wasn't exactly true—and tapped into America's chief concern at that time. Also, some people wondered if Bush's Graves' disease was a factor they should consider in evaluating his suitability for office as he approached the age of seventy. He looked pale and not at all as robust as he had been even a year earlier, especially next to the vibrant Clinton. He would later tell his daughter, Doro, that he was, during this tough time, "maybe a couple of quarts low on charisma."

This time, Barbara would fight harder than George on the campaign trail; she was his biggest champion even as he seemed to be losing his spirit. Barbara felt George wasn't fully appreciated, not only by Americans but also by the media. She was growing weary of the constant uphill battle all Presidents face when it comes to public opinion. Also, she was dismayed that Bill Clinton became so popular so fast. After all, Clinton, who had received a student deferment to avoid the draft, stood in stark contrast to her war hero of a husband.

George now depended on Barbara more than ever. While she carefully laid out his suit for him in the morning—as she had done most mornings for as long as she could remember—the two had long conversations about the ways forward for him and for their family. She had a good eye for enemies. She could walk into a meeting and feel the temperature of the room and, after a quick perusal, know full well who was an asset to her husband and who was hurting his cause. She knew who was effective and who wasn't, and how much damage the latter could do. "Never underestimate the power of negative thinking," she would say. Just as her mother-in-law, Dorothy, once said back when Prescott was a senator, she understood how desperately people wanted to stay in proximity to power, and that often they didn't deserve to be there. She wanted John Sununu, Bush's chief of staff, to be relieved of his duties because she felt he was too divisive a presence and media coverage of him was out of hand; he had taken a military jet to visit his dentist, which did him no favors in the court of public opinion. Her son George also campaigned hard behind the scenes to have Sununu removed. A well-known story had it that Sununu once asked Barbara why people so instantly disliked him. She shot back, "Because it saves time." He was gone by the end of 1991.

"I have watched her grow," Dorothy Bush said of her daughter-in-law at this time. She was in bed watching her being interviewed on television. "She has many attributes that distinguish her," she told Virginia Mason, "but one thing I admire most about her is that she has her certainty, and it's a certainty that's been hard-earned."

A Family Secret Revealed

After George H. W. Bush became President, his long-term relationship with Jennifer Fitzgerald became more of a concern. Jennifer had been in the picture for almost twenty years. Barbara had accepted her as a fact of her life with George. One can never know the details of private conversations the couple had about Jennifer, but the fact that Jennifer was still around certainly seems to suggest that they'd come to some sort of understanding about it.

If Barbara was able to make peace with Jennifer's presence, she may have wondered why others couldn't do the same. For instance, George's executive assistant, Chase Untermeyer, had what he later described as "an intense conversation" with Barbara on Air Force Two about Jennifer. Afterward, Barbara wrote in her diary: "My own opinion is that Jennifer really does hurt George, but his eyes really glaze over when you mention her name. She is just what he wants, he says, and says the hell with it all."

Though her relationship to George was hardly a secret, having Jennifer in such close proximity to the President in the White House did seem risky. Therefore, after Bush was elected, she was sent to the State Department for a new job as deputy chief of protocol. Whether intentional or not, it was difficult to ignore *The Washington Post*'s sarcastic tone in its report of the new assignment when it noted that Fitzgerald "had served President-elect

George Bush in a variety of positions." When Dorothy heard about Jennifer's new role, she said to Barbara in front of others, "Protocol, huh? Ironic, isn't it, dear?" Barbara did not respond.

The story of George and Jennifer had been circulating under the surface for years. It was just a matter of time before it would become a national spectacle, and that time finally came in 1992. In an effort to divert attention from Bill Clinton's relationship with a woman named Gennifer Flowers, with whom he'd had a twelve-year affair, the Clinton campaign started feeding elements of the George and Jennifer story to the press, such as details of their trip to Hawaii, where they'd apparently consummated their relationship. Jumping on these leads, *Spy* magazine wrote about it, followed by *The Washington Post*. NBC and CNN then got into the act, as did *Newsweek*. George W. tried to keep a lid on it by telling *Newsweek*, "The answer to the big 'A' question is N-O." Barbara wasn't happy her son had injected himself by issuing a denial, because she felt it opened the door for further scrutiny. She'd later learn that her husband's strategist Lee Atwater had arranged for the statement, and she had words with him about it.

Things really came to a head when Hillary Clinton gave a troubling quote to Gail Sheehy at *Vanity Fair*: "I had tea with Ann Cox [Chambers, chairman of Atlanta Newspapers Inc. at the time], and she's sitting there in her sunroom saying, 'You know, I just don't understand why they think they can get away with this—everybody knows about George Bush.' And then Chambers launches into this long description of, you know, Bush and his carrying on, all of which is apparently well known in Washington. But I'm convinced part of it is that the Establishment—regardless of party—sticks together. They're gonna circle the wagons on Jennifer and all these other people."

It had become fairly impossible to contain the story, especially when on August 11, 1992, the *New York Post* published a front-page feature about it called "The Bush Affair." *The Post* managed to spin an entire story out of a mere footnote in a book called *The Power House* by former congressional aide Susan B. Trento. It quoted Louis Fields, a deceased U.S. ambassador to the nuclear disarmament talks in Geneva, as claiming that, back in the spring of 1984, he'd arranged for George and Jennifer to share a cottage house in Switzerland at Chateau de Bellerive on Lake Geneva, a castle owned by the

Prince Sadruddin Aga Khan. At the time, he claimed, Barbara was on a book promotional tour. In fact, her book *C. Fred's Story*, a whimsical memoir as seen through the eyes of her dog, C. Fred, was released by Doubleday in March of 1984. "It became clear to me that the Vice President and Ms. Fitzgerald were romantically involved," Fields supposedly said. "It made me very uncomfortable. I am not a prude but I know Barbara and I like her." He claimed the couple had been "staying in adjoining bedrooms" and that it was "so heavy-handed." The story was accompanied by photographs of George and Jennifer, who many observers felt bore a strong resemblance to a younger Barbara.

"There was never one piece of independent research or confirmation on the Fields assertion," recalled President Bush's press secretary at the time, Marlin Fitzwater. "But the Clinton campaign's political director, James Carville, sent fax after fax of the book reference to mainstream reporters, and they couldn't wait to get it in print."

At the time the story broke, George was meeting at Kennebunkport with Yitzhak Rabin, the new prime minister of Israel. This was Rabin's first visit to the United States since being elected, the purpose of which, the *Los Angeles Times* reported, was to "restore warmth to U.S.-Israel relations after a long chill during the tenure of Rabin's predecessor, Yitzhak Shamir." Prime Minister Rabin was scheduled to appear at a press conference with President Bush during which they would announce in principle $10 million in housing loans to Israel. Bush also hoped to use the opportunity to highlight his experience in foreign affairs in contrast to his opponent's, Bill Clinton's.

As news crews set up their equipment outside, Barbara, George, and members of his cabinet and a few other staffers (who asked to remain anonymous in the telling of this story) were sequestered inside the main house in a bedroom discussing the best way to handle the *Post* story. "Christ, Bar, I don't even remember this," George said. He pointed out that the event in question had supposedly occurred almost a decade ago, and the source for the story, Louis Fields, was dead. Barbara shook her head in annoyance. "Well, apparently he's figured out how to speak from the grave," she said. "Let's just get through this day," she added, "and deal with the rest of it later."

There was a knock on the door. Before anyone could respond, it flung open and ninety-one-year-old Dorothy, in her wheelchair, rolled herself into the room. "This is all Hillary Clinton's fault," she said, abruptly. She was quite worked up. Despite her recent health issues, she didn't seem at all frail. She added that Clinton had "stirred up" the controversy in the recent issue of *Vanity Fair*. "Did you see it?" she asked. Barbara concurred with her mother-in-law, adding that Hillary had obviously been trying to take the attention off her husband and Gennifer Flowers. She said her actions were "lower than low, about as low as you can get in politics." George concurred, but with a proviso. "I dislike Bill Clinton as much as the next guy," he said, "but what he does in his spare time is between him and his God." In response to that comment, Barbara took the *New York Post* off the table, rolled it up, and smacked her husband hard on the shoulder with it. "Between him, his God . . . *and his wife*," she said. She then left the room saying she had to tend to a matter having to do with Rabin's wife, First Lady Leah Rabin.

After Barbara was gone, Dorothy asked George if he recognized that such bad press could jeopardize his chances to be reelected in November. He responded by saying, "As of this moment, I'm still President, Mother, and I will handle it." He said he didn't want her to worry.

Though George didn't seem as concerned as the others, his aides were certain he'd be asked about the *Post* story; there was no way around it. One of his staff members had even suggested canceling the press briefing. However, George said it was too late. "How am I supposed to explain a last-minute cancellation to the Prime Minister?" he asked, to which his aide responded, "Sir, this is Maine. You ate a bad clam. Someone left your oysters out too long. Who cares, sir? Of all the days to have a press conference, to-day's certainly not the day." In the end, the strategy they agreed upon was to surround the President with family members, certainly unusual for a briefing with a foreign leader, in the hopes that maybe reporters would then be less inclined to ask personal questions. "All you have to do is stand there and smile," Barbara told her relatives. "That's it."

An hour later, the press conference commenced in front of the President's small, detached office cottage near the front entrance of the property. The President and Prime Minister were present, of course, as were Barbara, a few family members, such as Columba Bush, and a few Bush grandchildren, including Columba's fifteen-year-old daughter, Noelle. Some pets made an appearance as well. They even brought out Dorothy in her wheelchair. It was a true portrait of Americana with these family members standing off to the side and out of view of cameras, but in full view of the reporters.

During the subsequent press briefing, reporters on one side of a rope were eager to ask questions of Bush and Rabin standing on the other side at individual podiums. "I will let the Prime Minister, obviously, speak for himself," said George, "but I do not think he would object to my saying that we agree one hundred percent that our goal goes beyond that of ending the state of war. What we seek is real peace, codified by treaties, characterized by reconciliation and openness, including trade and tourism. It must be a comprehensive peace on all fronts, grounded in U.N. Security Council Resolutions."

The question-and-answer session relating to U.S.-Israel relations seemed to be going well until, after about twenty minutes, Mary Tillotson, CNN's White House correspondent, decided to go for the loaded question. Marlin Fitzwater later said he had a feeling she might be the one to worry about. He described her as being "aggressive and ambitious, clawing her way to success at CNN as the number-two White House correspondent."

"Mr. Bush, uncomfortable as the subject is," Mary began, "I would think it's one to which you feel the necessity to respond because you've said that family values, character, are likely to be important in the presidential campaign. There is an extensive series of reports in today's *New York Post* alleging that a former U.S. ambassador, a man now deceased, had told several persons that he arranged for a sexual tryst involving you and one of your female staffers in Geneva in 1984."

Barbara stared straight ahead, as did Dorothy. George was speechless, but not for long. "I'm not going to take any sleazy questions like that from CNN," he said angrily. "I am very disappointed that you would ask such a question of me, and I will not respond to it. I haven't responded in the past. I think it's . . . I'm outraged. But nevertheless, in this kind of screwy climate we're in, why, I expect it. But I don't like it and I'm not going to respond other than to say it is a lie."

"It's funny how kids understand this kind of personal challenge," Marlin Fitzwater recalled. "The grandkids started crying almost immediately. In fact, Noelle became so upset, Barbara escorted the crying teenager away from the press briefing and back up to the main house."

Things then spun out of control quickly, with other members of the media also demanding to know more about Jennifer Fitzgerald. "I was so stunned and so angry," Marlin Fitzwater recalled, "I simply could not speak."

Finally, someone changed the subject. Though the briefing went on for another five minutes, George never really recovered. Finally, he addressed a question as to whether America would pressure the Arabs in the Middle East peace talks. "No sovereign government is going to be pressured into reaching out and achieving peace," he said. "It just doesn't work that way. In any event, thank you all very much." Then, after that abrupt ending, he just walked away while reporters continued to shout out questions. The Prime Minister followed.

While members of the press began to disassemble, Virginia Mason wheeled Dorothy away. As she did so, they passed by one of the reporters—not Tillotson—on the other side of the rope. "Shameful," Dorothy said, looking up at the journalist with angry eyes. "Who raised you? Wolves?"

"The Bush family attitude toward the media hardened that day to granite," Marlin Fitzwater said, "and I didn't blame them."

"It was probably the worst professional day of my life," Mary Tillotson would later admit. "I so wish someone else had asked the question, but no one did."

An angry Fitzwater told Tillotson that what she did was "sleazy and despicable," which he claims caused her to burst into tears. He later even threatened that she would "never work anywhere around the White House again." In fact, CNN did pull her from that beat and, instead, had her host a show on the network called *CNN and Company*. The network said the decision hadn't been made because of any pressure from the White House.

Once it was all over, Dorothy Walker Bush took to her bed, upset. In speaking about Jennifer Fitzgerald back in December 1974, she had told her son to "fix it, otherwise these stories will follow you forever." Now, almost twenty years later, a reporter from a major television news network had the temerity to question him about "a sexual tryst" with Fitzgerald while in his own home surrounded by family. It was something Dorothy simply couldn't countenance. "Where is the respect?" she asked. "Where is the honor?" In her ire, she evoked the name of another famous family, one she'd always found somewhat lacking in personal morals as well as in humility. "Who are we now," she asked, "the Kennedys?"

Dorothy was used to a certain kind of political civility, an ideal that was now most definitely a thing of the past. She hadn't been happy for some time with the bitterness of political warfare shown not only by the other side—the Clintons in the case of the present presidential election—but also by her son's. She didn't blame George, though. She realized he had no choice but to fight strength with strength. In about a week's time, she would write to a friend, "I am distressed that conjecture is now so easily presented as fact. There's the way things look, and then there's the way things are, and the public is easily swayed and this matters not just for today but for history. I believe that the great Abraham Lincoln had it just right when he said, 'Public sentiment is everything.'"

But what was her present position on Jennifer Fitzgerald? "It appeared to me that she still believed that whatever had been going on, if anything, ended years ago and that people were now just being mean to her son for political purposes," said Virginia Mason. "The way Barbara handled things also had a lot to do with the way everyone else did. We took our cues from her. If she was okay, or seemed okay, so was everyone else."

But was Barbara "okay"? Dorothy didn't think so. The next day, she had a conversation with her during which she expressed her regret that she'd been embarrassed by the press briefing. However, Barbara said she'd survived worse. They'd been campaigning so hard for the last six months, she was certain that when it was time for Americans to go to their voting booths, "no one will remember any of this. I promise you." However, a witness to that conversation felt that maybe Barbara, who was wringing her hands nervously, was trying to convince herself as much as Dorothy.

Apparently, Dorothy wasn't buying it. She observed that with November right around the corner, voters would likely judge George as being no better than Bill Clinton in terms of morality. Since Clinton was the newer and maybe more exciting candidate, they might just cast their votes for him. "Mark my words," she told her daughter-in-law, "I've been around."

Barbara didn't want to accept it, though. She reminded Dorothy that George had been so victorious with Operation Desert Storm, there was no way America would vote him out now. She concluded, "We *will* get a second term, Ganny. You mustn't worry."

At that, Dorothy brought up *Time*'s "Man of the Year" cover," back in January. The magazine had named George "*Men* of the Year," citing what they called "A Tale of Two Bushes," a President who had proved himself strong on foreign policy but who had also all but wrecked America's economy.

Indeed, George had raised taxes in order to balance the budget, one of the most unpopular actions he ever could have taken given his oath at the 1988 Republican Convention: "Read my lips. No new taxes." Clinton had been able to seize upon George's economic missteps; Clinton strategist James Carville came up with the phrase "The economy, stupid," in explaining a major platform of their campaign. (In today's politics, it's often misquoted as "It's the economy, stupid.") After Operation Desert Storm, Bush had a 90 percent approval rating. Now, though, with unemployment hovering around 7.5 percent, it was at about 60 percent. It really got to George, which showed during the campaign. He was off his game in speeches, sometimes didn't make sense, calling people "crazy" and "nuts," and said of Clinton and Gore, "My dog, Millie, knows more about foreign policy than these two bozos." He also said, "Being called dishonest by Bill Clinton is like being called ugly by a frog." These kinds of derogatory statements were uncharacteristic of George H. W. Bush, who had always comported himself as such a gentleman. "If it's not that woman who brings us down, it'll be Clinton making hay of the economy," Dorothy said. Barbara actually couldn't disagree.

The next day, August 12, George went back to Washington without Barbara for an interview in the Oval Office with *Dateline NBC* reporter Stone Phillips.

Of course, considering all of the controversy that had been stirred by the news conference, Phillips had no choice but to ask the question, "Have you ever had an affair?" Again, George was upset. "I'm not going to take any sleaze questions," he said. "You see, you're perpetuating the sleaze by asking the question, to say nothing of asking it in the Oval Office, and I don't think you ought to do that, and I'm not going to answer the question."

Meanwhile, back at Kennebunkport, Barbara decided the family would have "Taco Day" to take their minds off things. This was an annual tradition for which chef Ariel De Guzman and housekeeper Paula Rendon would prepare a massive buffet of Mexican fixings so that Bushes young and old could make his or her own tacos, and then there would be a contest to see who could eat the most. Usually, one of the grandchildren would win. "You know Mexican girls aren't allowed to marry unless they can prove to their mothers that they can make a perfectly round flour tortilla," Paula told Noelle as she taught her how to do so at the stove. "I don't know that that's true, Noelle," Barbara said with a smile, "but I also don't know that it's false."

For the next few days in the world outside of Kennebunkport, it seemed as if all anyone wanted to talk about was that dramatic moment when the President blew up over a question about infidelity. It had actually been the first time he'd ever denied the affair on the record, which led to the headline in *The Washington Post*: "Bush Angrily Denounces Report of Extramarital Affair as 'a Lie.'"

Whatever her private feelings, Barbara's position didn't change in public. She said she and George had long admired CNN, but no more. "It's sick," she told the *Houston Chronicle*. "It was a lie. It was ugly. The mainline press has sunk to an all-time low and CNN gets the top of my list." She also criticized the author of the book that started the present controversy, Susan Trento, saying, "I don't know the person who wrote that sick book, but they ought to have their mouth washed out with soap and for the press to pick it up is even worse."

There were still people among George H. W. Bush's base who thought he still had a chance to win a second term, even as late as a week before the election. But then the other shoe dropped the Friday before Election Day when the independent counsel looking into the Iran-Contra affair, Lawrence

Walsh, indicted Caspar Weinberger for lying to the investigative committee, and a primary piece of evidence was a note suggesting that George Bush had known about Iran-Contra the whole time. Though it was something he'd long denied, his detractors were still able to weaponize it against him. The indictment, which seemed politically motivated, sucked whatever momentum was left out of the Bush campaign.

The Big Loss

On some level, maybe Barbara Bush always knew her husband would serve only one term. Back on April 28, 1989, fewer than a hundred days into his presidency, she happened to be in the usher's office looking at the computer log of all the First Family's daily activities. "That's very interesting, isn't it?" she remarked to Assistant Chief White House Usher Chris Emery. "Yes," he said, "and it's designed strictly for your family as a remembrance of your time here. It'll be given to you when you leave here eight years from now." She looked at him levelly and said, "*Four* years from now."

"This morning I am absolutely convinced that George is going to lose," Barbara wrote in her diary three years later on October 3, 1992, one month before Election Day. By this time, she pretty much had to agree that Dorothy was right; George's chances were slim. "It is wrong, but all the press are printing such negative things," she wrote. "I will miss the White House life . . . I would die for my George, who has been a superb president and will go down in history as a great leader for the free world. The momentum is so strong against him."

She tried to keep things light on election night as the entire family gathered to watch the returns. Barbara spent much of the time in her bedroom reading a book. Every few moments, she would appear in the living room and speculate about life after the White House. "Hmm . . . I wonder what it's like to drive a car?" she would ask deadpan, before turning around and going back to her room. "Hmm . . . I wonder how you buy an airplane ticket?" she would ask upon reappearing, and then again retreating. In suggesting that they'd all better get used to the real world again, her humor was pointed. It *was* all over, and there was nothing left to do as a family but try to laugh.

On Tuesday, November 3, 1992, William Jefferson Clinton was elected to succeed George Herbert Walker Bush as President of the United States. It was hard to believe that, even after Operation Desert Storm, Bush could still lose. It would take time for the family to accept it. George and Barbara agreed that third-party candidate Ross Perot ended up with many of Bush's votes, and history does bear out this theory. Clinton had won 43 percent, Bush 38, and Perot 19. If Perot's 19 had gone to Bush, it would have put him over the top.

Though leaving Washington would be difficult for George and Barbara after twelve years, first at 1 Observatory Circle and then at the White House, the time had come. Barbara was ready. "Let's start a new life," she told George. "In fact, let's start a better one."

Nancy Reagan Postscript

It would seem that Barbara Bush's White House experience couldn't end without at least one more salvo from her former adversary, Nancy Reagan. Apparently, Nancy had been unhappy about some of her friend Barbara Walters's reporting during the Clinton inauguration on January 20, 1993, and called in to the network, live on the air, to complain about it. She said she had *not* mistreated the Bushes as rumored. She was the one who'd been mistreated because she'd never even been invited to the White House for a state dinner during their administration.

When details of the surprising call from the former First Lady made it into *The New York Times*, she tried to call Barbara to explain. Barbara, with little reason to care about Nancy any longer, made herself unavailable. She and George were already sad about having to leave the White House and wanted to focus on the future; in other words, Barbara was in no mood for Nancy Reagan. The Reagans had just been at the White House less than two weeks earlier when Bush presented the Medal of Freedom to Ronald Reagan, so what was Nancy's problem? Finally, when the two women connected on January 23, Barbara let her have it in an outburst that had been a long time coming. She admonished Nancy for saying "those ugly things about me on the air." She said she was mystified as to why Nancy insisted on continuing to hurt her. It didn't matter, though, she said. It was time for them both to move on. She told Nancy to stop talking about her publicly, "and don't ever call me again." Then, in a move that must have felt as cathartic as it did liberating, she hung up on her.

Service of Gratitude

Three months after the troubling press conference at Kennebunkport that found her son ambushed by CNN, Dorothy Bush was still shaken by it. Some felt it had really done her in, while others felt she had already been failing.

A little more than a year earlier, in July 1991, the entire family had congregated at Kennebunkport for Dorothy's ninetieth birthday. Everyone was present—her children and their spouses, as well as her grandchildren. Dorothy was in a reminiscent mood. She talked about her newspaper column from decades ago and how much she'd valued doing her patriotic part by participating in the political conversation of the times. She had every article memorialized in a scrapbook, she said, and sometimes she would take it out and peruse her writings and remember those days. She spoke about raising her children with Prescott, and how much summer fun they all used to have at Kennebunkport. She had never stopped missing him, she said. She remembered their private study in their home, the inner sanctum in which the two would seek refuge from the outside world, cozying up to each other on the couch while sharing intimacies. "It all went by so fast," she said while cradling her little black poodle, Petey, "but what a wonderful time we had."

The Walkers and the Bushes had come together seventy years ago when Dorothy married Prescott in 1921, and it was as if from that moment on their lives were full of triumphs and victories, disappointments and losses, all of it memorable, all of it worthwhile. Listening to Dorothy talk in her soft, lilting voice, her face full of love, made some of her relatives despair; it felt to them as if the matriarch was now closing the book on her long, rich life. But her blue eyes still held the sparkle of her youth; her face, lined and creased, seemed ageless. As she spoke, Barbara held her hand, her thumb on Dorothy's palm as she squeezed it. She kneaded her knuckles nervously, seeming to not want to let go.

Over the course of the year after that party, Dorothy continued to fail. On November 18, 1992, she was struck by a severe stroke. Virginia Mason called the White House to have a message passed on to the President that she didn't know if his mother would make it through the night. She spoke to Paula Rendon, who was as emotional on the phone as if Dorothy were her own mother. "Do you think the President should go there now?" she asked Virginia. Virginia said she didn't know for sure because Dorothy could always rally, as she had in the past.

The Clintons happened to be at the White House the next day as Hillary took her first tour of the private quarters. George and Laura slipped away to get on the phone with Dorothy to tell her how much they loved her. However, Dorothy was so out of it, they doubted she'd even heard their words. An hour later, Barbara called again and asked to speak to her. However, the doctor now on duty said there was just no way. "Tell her I love her," Barbara then told Virginia Mason. "Just make sure she knows it, okay?" she asked. "Will you, please? And thank her for me, will you?" She was distraught and desperate. "Just tell her Bar said thank you, Ganny, for everything." Virginia promised she would.

That night, George couldn't sleep; he was too worried. "I might not have a chance to kiss her good night," he wrote in his diary. "Tough times, tough negative times. This one so close to the heart, so very close, indeed."

The next day, the President took a small air force jet to Greenwich; he asked his mother's namesake, Doro, to accompany him to Dorothy's Pheasant Lane home. That afternoon, while sitting at Dorothy's bedside, he held her Bible in his hands. Thumbing through it, he found old letters he'd written her from the navy and a birthday card he'd sent her when he was just a boy. He kissed her on the forehead and whispered in her ear.

"Dad needed someone to be his emotional support that day, but he picked the wrong person," Doro Bush would recall. "When I saw my grandmother in the last stages of death, both Dad and I wept unabashedly. It's still moving to think I was there when my father said good-bye to his mother, the woman who had the biggest impact on his life."

That night when he returned to the White House, Bush wrote in his diary: "I don't know that Mum knows I'm [not] President of the United States, but I do know that is not important anymore."

Later the next day, around five P.M. on November 19, Barbara got a message from George's assistant Patty Presock. His sister, Nancy, had just called. She said she felt their mother had been waiting for George's visit, because after he left, "she just let go." Hillary Clinton happened to be in the private residence at that time, reviewing decorating ideas with Chief Usher Gary Walters. Meanwhile, Barbara was at George's side as he received the credentials of ambassadors, a ceremonial duty. She leaned over and whispered in his ear, "Your mum has died."

"The next morning while I was waiting for the President, I could overhear him and Mrs. Bush talking on the phone to the president's brother, Prescott, about funeral arrangements," recalled Assistant Chief Usher Chris Emery. "When President Bush got on the elevator that evening, I told him I was sorry for his loss, and he said, 'Thank you. When it rains, it pours.' I said, 'Yes, it has poured a lot this year.' He smiled and said, 'You're right, Chris.' He then informed me they wanted a small funeral on Monday and would I please discourage people on the White House staff from attending. He knew how well intentioned they were but wanted only family members present."

The service for Dorothy Walker Bush was conducted the following Monday in the small chapel of the Christ Church in Greenwich. A letter she had written for her family back in 1981 in preparation for this day was read by her son Bucky. In part, it said:

This is a service of gratitude to God for the easiest life ever given any-one to live on this earth and all because of love. God sent into my life the most perfect human that ever lived and we had fifty-one glorious years together and he will be with me through eternity. When we first married I used to worry as I knew God's commandment "Thou shalt love the Lord thy God with all thy heart and all thy soul and all thy mind" and I knew that was the way I was loving Pres, and then it came to me that God was showing me how great "finite" love could be so that I would have a glimpse of what God's infinite love must be, and I could accept both in my heart.

Dorothy's ashes were buried with Prescott's at Putnam Cemetery in Green-wich, next to the grave site of their granddaughter Robin. Later, Dorothy's marker would simply read: HIS ADORING WIFE, DOROTHY WALKER BUSH, 1901–1992.

Dorothy's beloved sister, Nancy Walker, had suffered a stroke about ten years earlier. Dorothy had spent as much time with her as possible, first at her little cottage on Walker's Point, where Nancy began her recovery with a live-in nurse, and then eventually in a convalescent home where she'd spend her final years. The Walker girls had always been so close it was not sur-prising that Dorothy's passing marked the beginning of a steady but steep decline for the sister left behind.

Nancy had remained well-balanced and happy throughout most of her life. However, as she got older and sicker she seemed to also become sadder about the abject cruelty her father had shown her in preventing her from marrying the only man she'd ever loved. She sometimes talked about James Baker, wondering what their life would have been like had they been able to wed and have a family of their own. At one point, she kept a framed, worn photograph of him on her dresser. When she looked at the way her sister's life had turned out, all those children, all those grandchildren, it was hard to not at least wonder if her own life might have turned out differently. "I guess not everyone gets their happy ending," she would say.

Nancy Walker died in May 1997, at the age of ninety-seven.

Barbara and George H.W., holding little George, pose with Dorothy and Prescott, before boarding a flight to Kennebunkport, Maine, from Midland, Texas, on March 7, 1949. (GEORGE H. W. BUSH PRESIDENTIAL LIBRARY AND MUSEUM)

Dorothy, Doro, and George H.W. at Kennebunkport, 1962. (GEORGE H. W. BUSH PRESIDENTIAL LIBRARY AND MUSEUM)

Barbara and Doro at Kennebunkport, 1964. (GEORGE H. W. BUSH PRESIDENTIAL LIBRARY AND MUSEUM)

Bush family photo from 1966. *Left to right:* Doro, George, Jeb, Marvin, George W., Neil, and Barbara. (GEORGE H. W. BUSH PRESIDENTIAL LIBRARY AND MUSEUM)

Barbara and George—now Ambassador to the United Nations—in 1973. Barbara had just stopped dyeing her hair at this point. (GEORGE H. W. BUSH PRESIDENTIAL LIBRARY AND MUSEUM)

This is the only existing photo of Jeb Bush's wedding to Columba Garnica de Gallo, on February 23, 1974. Barbara took it with her Kodak Pocket Instamatic. (GEORGE H. W. BUSH PRESIDENTIAL LIBRARY AND MUSEUM)

George and Laura in Kennebunkport shortly after meeting in the summer of 1977. (GEORGE H. W. BUSH PRESIDENTIAL LIBRARY AND MUSEUM)

Laura and George's wedding day, November 5, 1977. *Left to right:* Barbara, George W., Laura, and George H.W. (GEORGE H. W. BUSH PRESIDENTIAL LIBRARY AND MUSEUM)

When George ran unsuccessfully for Congress in 1978, his new wife, Laura, got her first taste of politics. (GEORGE H. W. BUSH PRESIDENTIAL LIBRARY AND MUSEUM)

Family portrait, circa 1979. *Top row, left to right:* Marvin; George P. being held by his father, Jeb; George H.W.; George W.; and Laura. *Bottom row:* Columba holding her daughter, Noelle; Doro; Barbara; and Neil. (George H. W. Bush Presidential Library and Museum)

Dorothy and her son George enjoy the Kennebunkport view on August 29, 1985. (George H. W. Bush Presidential Library and Museum)

Barbara's eight years as America's Second Lady with George as VP were fraught with problems because of her troubled relationship with First Lady Nancy Reagan. Here they are in what seems like a conciliatory moment en route to Andrews Air Force Base on December 7, 1988. (Ronald Reagan Presidential Library and Museum)

Jeb and Columba pose with their children, Jeb, George, and Noelle, on August 7, 1988. (GEORGE W. BUSH PRESIDENTIAL LIBRARY AND MUSEUM)

Enjoying Kennebunkport on August 22, 1990, George and Laura with their daughters, Jenna (*left*) and Barbara. (GEORGE H. W. BUSH PRESIDENTIAL LIBRARY AND MUSEUM)

On his first day in office as President on January 21, 1989, George H.W. wanted to show off his mother, Dorothy, to the press in the Oval Office. Dorothy was eighty-eight at this time. She would die in 1992 at the age of ninety-one. (GEORGE H. W. BUSH PRESIDENTIAL LIBRARY AND MUSEUM)

George H. W. Bush's seventy-fifth birthday celebration in Houston on June 10, 1999. *Front row, left to right:* Neil, George W., George H.W., Jeb, Marvin, and Doro. *Back row:* Sharon, Laura, Barbara, Columba, Margaret, and Robert Koch. (GEORGE H. W. BUSH PRESIDENTIAL LIBRARY AND MUSEUM)

Mother-in-law and daughter-in-law First Ladies Barbara and Laura visit Bryan's House for Children with AIDS in Dallas, Texas, on October 30, 1991. (GEORGE H. W. BUSH PRESIDENTIAL LIBRARY AND MUSEUM)

Sharon Bush in April 2004 after spending the last couple of years battling Neil Bush in a messy divorce. The Bushes closed ranks around Neil, leaving Sharon to fend for herself. (RETRO-PHOTO)

Though Columba's marriage to Jeb has been complicated, they remain happy after more than forty-five years together. Here they are in Miami on June 15, 2015, after Jeb announced his candidacy for President. (UPI)

President George W. Bush and First Lady Laura Bush relax with their daughters, Barbara and Jenna, on August 24, 2004, at Prairie Chapel Ranch in Crawford, Texas. (GEORGE W. BUSH PRESIDENTIAL LIBRARY AND MUSEUM)

Laura's beloved mother, Jenna Welch, passed away on May 10, 2019, at the age of ninety-nine. Here she is with her daughter before a news conference in Austin, Texas, on December 20, 2000. (AP PHOTO/HARRY CABLUCK)

Laura and Barbara, two First Ladies in one family! While they had a complex, sometimes confounding relationship, their unabiding love for each other was never in doubt. (George H. W. Bush Presidential Library and Museum)

Barbara's marriage to George wasn't always easy, but their love story is definitely one for the ages. (George H. W. Bush Presidential Library and Museum)

George and Laura, one of America's most beloved First Couples, have been married for forty-three happy years. (The George W. Bush Foundation)

PART SIXTEEN

The Sons Also Rise

W. Runs for Governor

Barbara and George were now out of the White House and living in Houston; Laura spent two days setting up their kitchen, lining the drawers with shelf paper she'd cut by hand, all of it nice and neat and clean, just the way she liked things. Meanwhile, Barbara, sixty-eight, tried to remember how to drive a car after twelve years of being chauffeured everywhere. It wasn't going well; she was a menace on four wheels.

A major shift happened in the Bush relationship when, at long last, Jennifer Fitzgerald was no longer an issue. Once George's political career ended, so did the affair. He and Jennifer finally drifted apart. "There was never a moment when they said, 'This is it. This is the end,'" said a source who had been close to both. "They just stopped being in each other's lives. George told me, 'One day, I didn't call her back. A week later, I left a message. Then she didn't call me back. And then we just never spoke again.' He seemed fine with it," observed the source. "He also told me, 'It ran its course. She was very nice, a good person. I liked her.' I didn't get the impression it was very serious."

In all, Barbara had endured Jennifer for eighteen of her forty-eight years with George. It should also be noted here that, when contacted, Jennifer Fitzgerald denied there had ever been an affair. "It simply did not happen," she insisted.

Meanwhile, Barbara began to write her autobiography and, in doing so, took the time to really examine her life and some of her choices. She regretted wasting so much time being unhappy. It had only been when George became Vice President that she'd begun to fully understand she was responsible for her own happiness. It was the kind of wisdom that came with age, though, and she also understood that. "Try—and oh boy, how hard it is—to find the good in people and not the bad," she wrote in her book, which was published in 1994. "I remember many years ago that I wasted so much time worrying about my mother. I suffered so because she and I had a 'chemical thing.' I loved her very much, but was hurt by her. I am sure that I hurt her a lot, too. Grace Walker [Dorothy Bush's sister-in-law] said to me once, 'Think of all the lovely things about your mother, all the things you love and are proud of about her.' There were so many that I couldn't count them all. I think that I expected her to be perfect. Nobody is perfect. Certainly not me."

While she was writing her memoir, Barbara was saddened to learn that Assistant Chief White House Usher Chris Emery was fired. The reason was because he'd spoken to her in January right after the Bushes left the White House. In preparing to write her book, Barbara had some questions about her laptop, and Emery was the one who'd taught her how to use it.

Although Emery had also recently talked to Nancy Reagan, Rosalynn Carter, and Lady Bird Johnson, Hillary Clinton said he had shown "an incredible lack of discretion" in talking to Barbara Bush. She worried that he may have passed on some secrets to Barbara about the Clintons. Therefore, Emery, a father of four who made only $59,000 a year after serving three Presidents over eight years, was out of a job. According to *The New York Times*, he was only the second usher in history ever to be dismissed. Barbara was as heartsick as she was angry about it. George had also reached out to the head of his Secret Service detail when he heard that the man's mother had died and they spoke briefly. Afterward, that agent was reprimanded and transferred out of the White House. "What is *wrong* with those people?" Barbara asked of the Clintons. George suggested they just keep their distance; Barbara said, "Gladly."

Meanwhile, Barbara's sons George and Jeb had both decided to run for governor, of Texas and Florida, respectively. They were clear that if George

H.W. had won a second term in the White House, they wouldn't have gone forward with their own political aspirations. Now, though, they were free to explore their goals without having to worry about how they might affect their father's presidency. "Both believed deeply in the responsibility of public service and were also fascinated with politics and public policy," Laura would note. "And both were going into the family business. They were interested in politics because they so admired their father and politics had been his vocation. Just as some sons follow their dads into medicine or carpentry or business, they were following their father into his main profession, public service and political office."

In Jeb's run against the incumbent, Democratic governor Lawton Chiles, he was off to a rough start. When asked what he would do for African Americans, Jeb answered, "It's time to strive for a society where there's equality of opportunity, not equality of results. So I'm going to answer your question by saying, Probably nothing." Privately, George said he thought that had been a "bone-headed response." He was worried voters might "misunderestimate" his brother, employing a malapropism that would, in about six years, become one of his more famous mispronunciations. Even though competition was evident in his relationship with Jeb—and certainly his parents preferred Jeb if they had to choose which brother they'd like to see in politics—George was still happy Jeb had thrown his hat in the ring. "The Bush boys running for governor," he said. "How 'bout that?"

In his own race, George would face off against the incumbent Democrat, Texas's forty-fifth governor, the very popular and outspoken Ann Richards, an adversary of the Bush family's. She had mocked his father in the past, especially at the 1988 Democratic Convention when she said, "Poor George. He can't help it. He was born with a silver foot in his mouth." There was definitely no love lost between the Bushes and Richards.

Bush would run a good campaign against Richards, pointing out her weaknesses on policy and her inconsistent messaging, while at the same time highlighting his own themes of "personal responsibility and moral leadership." Meanwhile, she tried to belittle him, calling him "Shrub," as Nancy Reagan had done. She was right, though, when she said he had no experience—just a failed run for Congress back in 1978. He'd had little success in the oil business, had been managing general partner of a baseball team, and didn't seem like governor material. He wasn't known to read up on policy and he spoke off-the-cuff about it; sometimes he was right but often was wrong.

When Laura and George W. sat down to talk about his running for governor, he recalled, "She wanted to be sure I was running for all the right reasons, and that I wasn't running because I thought I had something to prove." Only when Laura was convinced that it wasn't about any sort of competition with his father, his grandfather, or even his brother and that what the campaign was really about was George's desire to be of service, she agreed it was the right move for him. "From the moment we decided that, yes, he should run, I knew he would win," Laura later said. "He was just different enough to make people pay attention."

Cautious after her husband's defeat, Barbara worried that George wouldn't prevail because of Richards's popularity. "George is confident that he's going to win," she wrote in her diary. "I don't think so." Of course, George knew his mother thought he'd lose; it just motivated him even more to want to win.

March 2, 1994, was Texas Independence Day, a celebration of the adoption of the Texas Declaration of Independence in 1836. George H.W. and Barbara were to attend a fund-raising event at the Dallas Loews Anatole Hotel. The former President was still incredibly busy; that year alone he would give more than a hundred speeches, campaign for forty-eight candidates, and travel to more than twenty-five states and twenty-two countries. His son had been lucky to be able to recruit him for this event.

Backstage, as father and son compared notes, Barbara walked over to Laura, who seemed a little wobbly. She had given dozens of speeches in the last year while campaigning for her husband, but it was still difficult for her. She had to steel herself to get through it. Recently, she and Barbara were in a town outside Austin and Laura needed to stress eat. "Can we get a barbecue chicken pizza at Schlotzsky's?" she asked Barbara. *"Schlotzsky's!"* Barbara exclaimed. It's a moderately priced, popular chain restaurant. "Why can't we go to a place where they don't serve food on plastic trays?" However, one look at Laura's crestfallen face and Barbara knew what she needed more than anything was a Schlotzsky's barbecue chicken pizza. "Okay. Schlotz-ky's it is," Barbara decided. "I can read that girl like a book," Barbara would say.

Now, backstage at the Loews, Barbara seemed to know exactly what Laura needed to hear. "You can do this," she told her. "You just go on out there and be who you are, Laura Bush, and I promise you those people will love you." Laura sighed heavily and then took her mother-in-law in her arms. She whispered something in her ear, probably her gratitude. Shortly thereafter, George W. and his mother were introduced to thunderous applause. A few moments later, George H.W. and his daughter-in-law walked out to an even greater response. As father and son then stood onstage gazing at each other, both felt the emotional significance of the moment or, as George W. later said, "it was a definite passing of the torch. For the first time in our family, Dad knew he wasn't going to be the center of attention. He knew it was an-other generation's time." The two shook hands, tears in their eyes.

"Mr. President," George began solemnly. "Mom."

The audience laughed.

From there, W. knew the crowd was in his hands as he jokingly spoke of having his father's eyes and his mother's mouth. He was a very different animal from his dad, animated and funny, casual and irreverent, as he talked of bringing people together and "doing something for Texas that will matter to people, that will be good for our children." Later, Laura would say, "I sat there and I watched him and all of a sudden it hit me. I thought, My God, this is what he is best at, isn't it? It struck me that night, as I'm sure it did his parents. I looked over at Bar and her eyes were wide as if she had the same feeling."

A Great Loss

While Laura Bush helped her husband campaign for governor, she also dealt with a personal crisis involving her father. She'd always had such a complex, often frustrating relationship with Harold. However, as he got older, he'd mellowed so much that she now enjoyed every moment of his visits with his grandchildren. Back when the girls were infants, Laura would cringe whenever he'd pop over unannounced. He'd knock on the door and shout out, "Are the girls up yet?" Inevitably, she'd just gotten Barbara and Jenna off to sleep, but with Harold's sudden arrival they'd be, as Laura would put it, "off to the races." She would then watch with pride as he'd cuddle the twins in his arms.

Slowly, especially over the last couple of years, it had become evident that Harold was slipping, both physically and mentally. By the end of 1994, he was extremely forgetful, not remembering the names of friends and even relatives. He no longer wanted to drive because he was too fearful of having an accident. He had trouble walking and would often collapse for no reason. On the day he forgot that George H. W. Bush had ever been President, Laura feared the onset of Alzheimer's, though no formal diagnosis was ever made. She just hoped he would be well enough to enjoy the triumph of his son-in-law's victory should George win the election. However, nothing with Harold seemed certain these days. "You know, I'll always be at your side," he told her one day over lunch. He knew their time together was coming to an end, and he didn't want her to worry about life without him.

As it happened, George handily won his election in November 1994. He was now governor of Texas, hard to believe for some considering his rabble-rousing days of old, but true just the same. Unfortunately, Jeb lost his race in Florida, and it was a real nail-biter, too; he lost by just two percentage points. It was ironic—Jeb, the son Barbara and H.W. thought was best suited for politics, was the loser and W., the one in whom they had so little belief, the victor. He was just the second Republican governor elected in Texas in over one hundred years. Still, when W. got on the phone with his father, the old man was much more despondent about Jeb's loss than he was happy about George's victory!

Unfortunately, Harold deteriorated so rapidly he wasn't able to go to the inauguration; Jenna had to attend without him. It was bittersweet for Laura then as she stood by her husband's side and watched as he took the solemn oath of office.

The next few months continued to be marked by incredible highs as Laura began to transition to her new role as First Lady of Texas and terrible lows as she watched her father struggle with hospice care at home. Then, one afternoon after collapsing, Harold was taken to the hospital in critical condition. Five days later, on April 29, 1995, he died with Laura and Jenna at his bedside.

First Lady of Texas

O h my gosh, look at this schedule," Laura Bush exclaimed to one of her
new assistants, Monica Gonzalez, as she reviewed her calendar. "How
am I going to get through it?" Laura, who was now First Lady of Texas, was
in her small but elegantly furnished three-room office on the bottom floor of
the Capitol building across the street from the governor's mansion. Monica
smiled. "Oh, you will, Mrs. Bush," she said. "You always do."

With shaky hands, Laura went into her purse and pulled out her box of
Winstons. Monica frowned; she didn't like it when Laura smoked simply
because she worried about her health. "Okay, look. I'm just going to have
one," Laura said, lighting a cigarette. She put it to her mouth and took a
deep drag. "My God. This is *so* good," she said as she exhaled a thick plume
of white smoke. "How can something that's so good be so bad for you?"
she wondered. She then spent a few minutes savoring every second of her
smoke. "Okay, that's that," she said as she put out the butt in an ashtray on
her desk. She took the box and tossed it into the trash can, saying, "I'm good
to go now, and that's it. No more cigarettes for me."

Twelve hours later, after a long and hectic day, Monica found Laura rum-
maging through the trash. "Is it still here?" she asked hopefully. She was
looking for the Winstons. "I'm so darn happy right now," she exclaimed as
she fished the box out of the trash and took a cigarette from it. "I promise,

just this one," she told Monica as she lit it. This time, though, when she finished, she put the Winstons in her purse.

The next morning, it was the same routine—the enjoyment of a single cigarette, the tossing of the box into the trash followed by the pronouncement that she was "good to go." This time, though, while Laura was gone Monica took the box and emptied its contents into the trash. Then she doused the cigarettes with a cold cup of coffee. That night when Laura rummaged through the trash looking for the box, what she found instead was a real mess. "Oh no, Monica," she cried out in dismay. "What happened here?" Monica smiled sheepishly. "I'm just looking out for you, Mrs. Bush," she said. Laura forced a smile. "Okay, well, I guess I'm glad someone is," she said with resignation. Then she looked at the mantel, and who should she see smiling back at her from a photograph framed in silver? Dorothy Bush. "You didn't know her," Laura said with a smile, "but the fact that you're looking out for me pleases her to no end."

It was this kind of humanity, this sort of "everywoman" characteristic, which Laura Bush exhibited every day of her time as Texas's First Lady. "She had a way of understanding people and what made them tick and what their vices and virtues were," said Monica Gonzalez, "because she was one of them, what with her smoking habit and her other little vices and insecurities and her love of family." Monica technically worked for the governor's mansion; Laura had another functionary, a personal assistant named Andrea Ball, known as Andi, who was the only person actually on her staff. "She was one of us," said Monica of Laura. "There was no difference other than her title and maybe her wealth, but no difference in her humanity."

Laura and George now lived in the Texas governor's mansion in Austin, an impressive Greek Revival–style structure. This was the most luxurious of environments, full of the finest pieces of furniture and art along with precious early American antiques. A grand, elegant staircase connected its first two floors. Laura would learn that there was no changing any aspect of the downstairs with its deep yellow, blue, and red motif. It was verboten to do any alterations of this floor, most of which was made available to the public and through which about 25,000 tourists traipsed annually. She would one day learn it was easier to get clearance to change the White House's décor than it was the governor's mansion.

Laura was surprised to find that in a house so large with such incredibly high ceilings and enormous scroll columns, her family's private quarters would be no bigger than a medium-size apartment, and certainly smaller than the house in which the Bushes previously lived. They had to give away most of their furniture, "but in the end," Laura would say, "it was worth it just to have this great moment in our lives. It felt unreal."

Laura kept it simple in their private quarters, which she'd had painted a pale gray. She decided to bring her own kitchen table rather than allow the cats to ruin the one already there, and there was no keeping the furry little animals off that table, either. After it would get completely scratched up, Laura would cover up the nicks with a marker made for just that purpose, which sold for a couple of bucks in a drugstore.

The family had two cats at this time: Ernie, a big orange tabby who'd been a stray but now ruled the mansion—and also did most of the damage on the table—and India, a sleek black cat. Once, India, who was Barbara's favorite, disappeared somewhere in the mansion—they *hoped* it was in the mansion, anyway—while the teenager was in Europe. "We have to find that darn cat," Laura said, "or Barbara's going to lose her ever-lovin' mind when she gets home." Monica Gonzalez assured her they would find it. "Lord willin' and the creek don't rise," Laura said, using one of her mother's old Southern expressions.

All over the mansion, in every room, Monica put up signs that read, "Lost cat. Please call . . ." with her cell phone number. Luckily, India showed up on its own just before Barbara's return. "Thank God," Laura said as she hugged the cat. "The suspense of how this whole thing was going to turn out was killing me."

"She loved fresh flowers, everywhere, especially orchids," recalled Monica Gonzalez. She had a couch in the living room that she liked to change seasonally, but instead of actually switching it out she had new slipcovers made for it, one for each season. 'Why buy a new couch when you can just do this?' she asked. She was very frugal. In her bedroom, she had a large king-size bed for her and Mr. Bush. There were two round tables, one on each side of it, with long silk covers to the floor, and both tables were stacked with books, flowers, and framed photographs of family members. She had additional closets built in their room, and also in some of the others, because storage space was limited to what one might have needed back in the mid-nineteenth century when the place was built.

"I remember that she was obsessed with 409, the cleaner. She always had a bottle handy and would take it out and start wiping surfaces. 'I would say, Mrs. Bush, we have people here to do that,' and she would say, 'I know. But this is therapy for me.' Or she'd walk into a room and run her hand on the mantel of a fireplace and find that it was dusty, and she'd say, no, this should not be. Then, she'd get out the lemon Pledge and go to town. Or you might see her vacuuming, and you would say, 'Really? Mrs. Bush? Really?' and she would say, 'Yes. Really.'

"I also remember that she liked to surround herself with positive people. For instance, she had this one friend who was a name dropper and a society climber and just so difficult to be around. She would say, 'Monica, so-and-so's coming over, and I'd really like to limit my time with her. Would you come in and tell me I'm going to be late for my next appointment so we can make it as brief a visit as possible and get her out of here?'"

Shortly after moving into the governor's mansion, Laura had a conversation with her good friend Adair Margo, who would, in about twenty years, become the First Lady of El Paso. "You know, I never really aspired to be someone," she told her. "By that, I mean, you know, *someone*. I never thought it mattered if you were the best at something. I always felt you don't have to be the best to live a good life. All I ever wanted was a nice, normal life."

"Well, look at your life now," Margo said. "This is not normal at all, is it?"

"I just keep thinking there must be a reason for all of this," Laura said, gazing around at her opulent new surroundings. "Maybe this has been my destiny all along. To be of service. Does that sound ridiculous?"

"No," Margo told her, "not at all. In fact, it sounds wonderful."

So, how could she best serve? That was the question on Laura's mind when she and George moved into the governor's mansion, and it was her primary concern for the next six years. Just as Barbara had done as America's First Lady, Laura focused on a platform dear to her heart, which was literacy. She spent the next six years developing literacy programs that would enrich the lives of not only young people but Texans of all ages who found reading a challenge. "It was her idea to convene a summit of researchers on how to improve reading instruction," said Margaret Spellings, George Bush's education aide who would become secretary of education in Washington. "They were dazzled that she was so well-informed and so interested that they were coming to Texas, of all places, to talk about cutting-edge research."

It would be tough going at first. "I remember when she was the newly selected First Lady of Texas and hadn't moved into the governor's mansion yet," recalled Susan Byerly Nowlin, who was Laura's "big sister" in their sorority at Southern Methodist University, "and there was a very large organization in Dallas called the Dallas Woman's Club, a private club started in 1922. They bring in speakers on a regular basis and you can have lunch and listen to incredible speakers. Laura called me one morning and said, 'I've been asked to speak in Dallas at the Dallas Woman's Club, and I'm a little nervous so I really want to look down the first row and see some of my friends. So may I invite you to be my guest?' Of course, I was thrilled and honored. She invited about eight of us.

"So we were all seated in the front row and they gave this lavish introduction about 'today's speaker,' and Laura was just, well, to be candid, she just wasn't comfortable from the start. While she slowly walked from her seat to the stage and then up its stairs and across it to a podium in the center, it was as if she were wading through molasses. I thought, 'Oh my gosh, she's really nervous, isn't she?' As she talked, her neck just got redder and redder, and those of us who knew her well thought, 'Relax, Laura. Don't let these snooty society women get to you,' but it just wasn't her thing. She did well, don't get me wrong, but it wasn't an award-winning moment, because when you're not comfortable the audience isn't comfortable, either. I had a feeling though that she was going to work on this thing, knowing her as I did, and find a way forward as a speaker in time."

"First, though, she needed to take care of her mother and make sure she was okay now that she was on her own," Adair Margo recalled. "Laura had a picture in her dressing room of her mother, Jenna, who was just a cute girl at the time it was taken, holding a burro by its reins and with a little friend named Catherine 'Kitty' Kistenmacher. I would look at that picture and get lost in it. Laura, Jenna, and me and my mom were such great friends. My mother, Betty Ruth, was younger than Jenna and, due to Jenna's ties to El Paso, we spent a lot of time there together. Laura would go to El Paso sixteen times as First Lady of Texas, often bringing Jenna along.

"I have this specific memory, and I have told it to Laura several times, of Laura coming to El Paso for an event with her mom. I met them at the El Paso International Airport, and I remember Laura holding her mother's hand and steadying her as they walked down this long hallway at the airport, very slowly, very deliberately. It felt so loving to me, I just had to stand there and watch how sweet Laura was to her mom, how caring she was.

"No matter her duties as the wife of the governor—and she had many, believe me, she was very busy all the time—the foremost thing on her mind other than her kids and her husband was her mother," concluded Adair Margo. "Family meant everything to her, and that never changed. 'I think people sense that we Bushes are all about family values,' she told me after she moved into the mansion, 'and I think that's one of the reasons they voted for George and Jeb, and also one of the reasons they voted for their father so many times. The public gets lots of things wrong about us,' she said, 'but not that. *That* they get just right.'"

Born for the Job

As its governor, George W. Bush would be consumed with Texas's well-being for the next six years. He would often make decisions popular in Texas but maybe not in other states, such as when he signed into law the bill allowing people to carry concealed weapons. He also spearheaded Texas's largest tax cut up until that time. He raised the salaries of teachers and funded organizations to prevent domestic violence. He spoke out about alcohol and drug abuse, usually not citing his own history. He wasn't sure going cold turkey was a method he wanted to endorse for others. He wasn't big on environmental issues, but thanks to certain regulations he passed, Texas was well on its way to becoming the biggest producer of wind-powered electricity during his time in office. He was popular with his constituents and handily won reelection in 1998.

"Laura disagreed with George on several points," said Virginia Mason, who was still friendly with the family even though Dorothy Bush was gone, "and I think it took her a minute to figure out how to proceed in that regard, too. He was pro–death penalty and would put more people to death than any governor in Texas history [at that time], 152 executions to be exact; 150 men and two women. She was anti–death penalty. He opposed gay marriage and gay adoption. She did not. They respected each other, though, and found a way to make it work, not only out in the world but at home. They would tease each other. Mrs. Bush gave as good as she got. 'Oh, Bushie, you can say what you want, but you know the truth and *it's not that*,' she'd tell him. She could really put the guy in his place."

Monica Gonzalez, who eventually ended up moving into the governor's mansion with the Bushes, recalls that one of her jobs was a task that would become obsolete because of the internet. "I would get to work at five in the morning and cut out every article about the governor from ten to twenty different newspapers," she recalled. "I would then neatly paste them onto white sheets of paper and have this compilation of clippings on his desk before he got to the office in the morning. These were, essentially, his CliffsNotes of what was being said about him and his policies that particular day."

One morning as Monica was finishing her clippings for George, Laura walked into her office. With the tip of her finger touching her mouth as if she was in thought, she said, "Listen, I have an idea, and maybe you can help me with it. The girls are fifteen now," she continued, speaking of the twins, "and in moving here to the governor's mansion I realized I have boxes and boxes of memorabilia, photos of the girls, letters, so much stuff . . . pictures of my mom and dad. I just can't get through it all. I would love it if you could put together a set of memory books for Barbara and Jenna. I'll order the books if you'll fill them. Can you do that?"

Monica said she would be happy to compile the books. A week later, Laura presented her with thirty blank scrapbooks, a set of fifteen for each daughter, one book for each year of her life. Barbara's were forest green with gold trim, to match the green Kate Spade wallpaper in her bedroom. Jenna's were red with gold trim, her favorite color. This promised to be a whole lot more work than Monica had ever imagined—*thirty scrapbooks?* "There were boxes and boxes of stuff to go through," she recalled, laughing. "I thought, My gosh, does Mrs. Bush have to save *everything*?"

"Should I go over all of this stuff with you," Monica asked, "and we can figure out what you want in the scrapbooks?"

"Oh, heavens no," Laura said. "If you do that, I'm just going to be in the same boat I'm in right now, which is sinking. Just do your best. I trust you."

"So I got right to work," Monica Gonzalez recalled. "As I did, Mrs. Welch, Laura's mom, would come and sit with me and go through the letters she and Mr. Welch had written to their daughter back when she was in college. 'How great is it that the girls will get to know their grandfather better through these letters?' she said in her very soft-spoken way. 'Are you enjoying this work?' she asked me. When I told her I was, she said, 'Well, a family's history is everything, isn't it? Appreciating who we Welches are to one another is one of the things I think we most have in common with the Bushes.'

"I had to sort through it all, put everything in chronological order and organize it by year for each girl. What a job this was; it took me six months.

"Finally, when I was finished, I presented the thirty scrapbooks to Mrs. Bush. She loved them. What happened next is what most impressed me. She called the twins into her office. 'Look what Monica made for you,' she told them as she handed over the scrapbooks one by one. 'Aren't these great? Didn't she do a good job?' My eyes filled with tears. 'Thank you for doing this for us, Monica,' the girls said. 'We can't believe you went through all this trouble for us.'

"Because my mother was a housekeeper and I grew up around a lot of wealthy people, I know that they usually didn't give credit where it was due," Monica Gonzalez said. "Most people in Mrs. Bush's position would have just given the scrapbooks to her daughters and taken full credit or, at the very least, not have been so specific as to who was responsible. But Mrs. Bush always credited everyone on her staff for whatever it was they did for her and her family. That meant a lot to us."

While raising her daughters and making sure their family history meant something to them, Laura continued to grow in her new role as the state's First Lady. Calling on her experience as a teacher and a librarian, once she decided to open her heart and mind to a purpose bigger than educating children in a library and instead speaking in front of hundreds, even thousands, in an auditorium, it was as if Laura blossomed. She sponsored forums on cognitive learning, brought in speakers who were top researchers in the field, and hosted luncheons at the mansion for teachers and professors. She started the Texas Book Festival in 1996, highlighting authors from all over the state and allowing them to mingle with readers who enjoyed their work. She traveled all over Texas, sometimes with her mother and other times with her mother-in-law, getting to know the people who had voted for George and also coming to an understanding with Democrats who didn't support him.

When Virginia Mason attended a formal ball at the governor's mansion, she was stunned by Laura's new composure. "She grew into the role in such a big way, and so quickly," she recalled. "I was standing with Barbara and we were just gobsmacked as we watched Laura mingle with the crowd. First of all, she looked gorgeous in a little lime green strapless number. But it was her self-confidence that most struck us. 'I remember when George brought her home,' Barbara told me, 'I thought to myself, well, this poor dear will never fit in with us Bushes. She'll last five minutes in this family. Well, just look at her now.'

"Barbara was proud of her. She told me she missed being in the White House, that it had given her so much purpose, and now that she saw Laura doing the same kind of thing here in Texas, it made her envious. 'I usually don't envy people,' she said, 'because I have such a good life. But a woman who finds herself in a position to serve is a woman I envy, and my daughter-in-law has a servant's heart. She and I, we're the same.' I said, 'You should tell her that, Mrs. Bush. She'd so love to hear it.' And she said, 'Oh, no. We don't do that.'

"I also found it interesting that when Laura came over to greet us, she and Barbara held each other at just a slight distance while embracing. Yet, when Laura hugged me, it was a real hug, in very close. Also, when she and Barbara spoke, there was a strained formality between them. I knew that they had their way, she and her mother-in-law, and that it wasn't exactly intimate as much as it was respectful."

It's also worth noting that, with the passing of the years, Laura still had the same friends, people like Regan Gammon, Peggy Weiss, and Ethan Marshall. "I think what kept her sane and happy was that she maintained friendships she had from way before she was a Bush," said Monica Gonzalez. "She wanted people in her life who treated her like just Laura, not like the First Lady of Texas. These friends from West Texas kept her grounded. She knew she could trust them."

Laura's Midland friend Cindy Schumann Klatt recalled, "She called one day and my father answered the phone. He said, 'Cindy, some chick named Laura is on the line.' She was calling because she wanted to have a high school reunion at the governor's mansion. She asked if I would take care of it because I'd handled all of the reunions over the years. So that's what I did, I organized a reunion at the governor's mansion, and not just from our class but from some of the other classes too where we had mutual friends.

"Laura said, 'Oh, it's going to be a gorgeous weekend. We're going to have sunshine and a lot of fun.' We had conversations about it almost every day. All of the invitees had to be cleared with the Texas Department of Public Safety detail, the guards protecting the Bushes. That was interesting, getting that done. You'd find some people had pretty embarrassing problems in their past, and you'd then have to tell them they couldn't come, but it was a strict screening for all 304 students and their spouses.

"So, we got up there to the governor's mansion on a Thursday night. The forecast was for beautiful weather, but that afternoon it started pouring down rain. George had people to put up tents and floors, but it was still a mess. All of the women had fancy dresses on and ended up wading in mud. It didn't matter, though; we still had fun. George greeted every single person, stopping and taking pictures. While he wasn't much of a dancer, Laura stayed out on the dance floor and danced with us all night long. It turned out to be a great reunion."

One of those invited to the party was Benjamin Franklin, Mike Douglas's best friend who had once tried to get Laura to face Mike's mother while parked in front of their farm. He was on the guest list, and Laura didn't ask to have him removed. "She was nice, cordial . . . I mean, she was okay," he recalled. "It wasn't some great moment, it was quick and she moved on and so did I." Another guest was Judy Dykes Hester, who had been in the car with Laura when she had the accident. "A marvelous night full of great memories of Texas," she said.

"I didn't see Laura as much as I once had," recalled Ethan Marshall, also at the reunion, "but when I did, it was always the same with us. 'Can you believe this?' she whispered in my ear just as I was leaving. I told her, yes, I actually could believe it. 'You were born for this job, Laura,' I told her. She smiled and kissed me on the cheek. 'I don't know about that,' she said. 'I'm just figuring it out as I go along.' As a bunch of people rushed over to her to meet her, she got swept away by the crowd. She turned and looked at me over her shoulder as she was being pushed along. Then she smiled and mouthed the words *Call me*."

Laura Grapples with the Past

S he figured it had to happen one day. It was inevitable, wasn't it? But still, Laura Bush was completely thrown when her thirteen-year-old twins came to her to ask her about . . . the accident. "How did you learn about this?" Laura wanted to know, trying to stay calm. They explained that one of the officers from the Texas Department of Public Safety detail had mentioned it to them in passing.

"Here's what happened," explained that officer, who'd been working the governor's detail for almost ten years. "I wasn't even supposed to be protecting the girls; it was someone else's job and I was filling in. They were upset and complaining about their curfew, typical teenage stuff. I said something like, 'Well, you know, your mom is just being cautious because of that thing that happened when she was younger.' I thought for sure they knew about it, but when I saw the looks on their faces I knew I was dead wrong. I then tried to backpedal, but those girls were so smart. They wanted to know more, but I didn't tell them more. I said, 'Don't worry about it. It's nothing.' I had already said too much, though, I'm afraid. I'm not sure how they put the rest of the story together, but apparently they did, and then they went to their mom with it."

Now cornered, Laura had no choice but to explain to Barbara and Jenna details about the tragic accident that had claimed the life of a good friend of hers so many years earlier. Laura tried not to cry as she told the girls her story, but it was difficult. Soon, all three of them were sobbing.

"Once I became a mother myself, I thought more about the Douglases," Laura would later recall. "I began to understand how devastating their grief must be. On some level, only when I had children could I begin to comprehend the enormity for them of losing Mike. Only then, when I could imagine that it was Barbara or Jenna. Looking back now, with the wisdom of another forty-five years, I know that I should have gone to see the Douglases; I should have reached out to them. At seventeen, I assumed that they would prefer I vanish, that I would only remind them of their loss. But in retrospect, I think all of us—not only me but all of Mike's friends—should have been more solicitous of them. We weren't."

"I think that what happened to her when she was a girl is the reason that, as a woman, she was so sensitive to the feelings of others," said Adair Margo. "I remember, once, a friend of young Barbara's committed suicide. It was tragic, this young boy. . . ." Adair was referencing a friend of Barbara's who had tragically hanged himself. Barbara, who had a crush on him, was devastated by his sudden death. It would be years, actually, before she'd reconcile it. "I was scheduled to stay at the governor's mansion," Adair recalled, "and Laura called me and said, 'Adair, I know you always stay here, but do you mind staying somewhere else this one time? I hate to ask but, you see, Barbara has lost a friend and I think we need some time together as a family.' I said, 'Oh my gosh, of course. This is how we should all be, setting time aside for family when it's most necessary and important.' I think that after what happened to Laura, she made the decision that never again would she shy away from being there when she *should* be there, for her friends and for her family. The first thing she did after the boy's death was go and see his parents and express her sympathy."

However, after her talk with Barbara and Jenna, Laura wanted the agent who had slipped up with them fired.

"When the governor called me and asked to see me, I knew exactly what it was about," recalled the officer.

He walked into George's office and found him sitting behind his desk wearing blue jeans and a denim shirt with his feet up on the desk, in cowboy boots. The agent thought he would be asked to sit down; he wasn't. While standing before the governor, he immediately offered to turn in his resignation. George shook his head no and said, "But you should understand that Mrs. Bush is very angry right now, and so am I." He was very protective of his wife, he said, and when she was upset, so was he. The agent began to explain himself, but after about thirty seconds, George took his feet off the desk and started working on some paperwork. Without looking up at the agent, he then said, "Go. We're done here." At that point, he started chomping on a homemade version of Chex Mix, which he always had in a canister on his desk and to which he was pretty much addicted.

"'I *said*, that will be all,' he told me as he tossed some of the Chex Mix into his mouth," recalled the officer. "When I finally left his office, I knew for sure I was finished."

While George agreed with Laura that what had happened was appalling, he wasn't sure the guard should be terminated. Laura decided to give it a couple of days and then see how she felt.

Two days later, she arranged for him to come to the governor's mansion to meet with her. The two went up to the second-floor private quarters and sat at the kitchen table. Laura fixed him a cup of tea. She then asked a series of questions about his life. Did he like his job? Why had he joined the Texas Department of Public Safety detail? What had drawn him to such a responsibility? Was he married? He was. Did he have children? He did. Today the agent refuses to go into detail about their talk, feeling that the specifics should remain private. All he will say is "We didn't talk about the accident and we didn't talk about the fact that I had tipped off the twins. She didn't bring it up. She just wanted to know me, everything there was to know about me. Then she got up and said, 'Thank you for coming,' and walked me down the stairs and out the back entrance. I didn't know where I stood with her when I left."

Laura decided not to have the officer terminated. Too many lives had been ruined because of the accident of so long ago, and she didn't want this man's to be another of them. She told one person on her staff, "He's willing to die for my kids. How can I hold this mistake against him? I don't want to be that person. I don't want this job to turn me into that person."

"I was very, very grateful to them both for not sacking me," the agent now says of George and Laura Bush.

The revelation of this closely guarded history raised another issue for Laura. Who else knew about it? She had long ago told George not to tell his parents. He finally confessed that he had told his father years ago, but he'd asked him not to tell his mother. "Please, Bushie. *Of course* he did," Laura exclaimed, according to one account.

Laura couldn't help but be troubled by the fact that Barbara had probably known about the accident all these many years but had never discussed it with her.

A perfect arc to this story would have been for Laura to go to Barbara and open up to her about the accident. This heart-to-heart might have then been the beginning of a new and much closer relationship between them. But real life isn't quite so simple.

According to people who know her best but who would only speak on deep background because of the sensitive nature of the subject, Laura decided to leave well enough alone. She knew Barbara admired her as a loyal wife who always supported her husband's political ambitions. Honor, duty, discipline, and sacrifice mattered to Barbara Bush, and certainly Laura had demonstrated each of those traits in the years she'd been married to her son. Importantly, Laura also knew Barbara thought she was a good mother to the twins. Though they disagreed from time to time, she knew that they really did look out for each other. Was all that enough to set Laura's mind at ease? In the end, it would just have to be.

First Lady of Florida

By the end of 1998, Columba Bush was forty-five. She was still very eye-catching, with short dark hair—sometimes colored a lighter shade—intelligent brown eyes, and a dazzling smile. While she had been wildly gorgeous as a teenager, now, as a Bush wife of almost twenty-five years, her look had morphed into a more dignified kind of beauty. "I have never been a social person," she said. "I love silence," she added, sounding a lot like her sister-in-law Laura. "I like to read a good book and go for a walk." She and Jeb now had three children, George Prescott, twenty-two, known as George P.; Noelle, twenty-one; and Jeb Jr., fifteen, known as Jebbie.

By this time, 1998, Columba's mother, Josefina, was seventy-six and unwell. A year earlier, she had lost a leg to diabetes. She had been living in Mexico when she became ill and was soon moved by the family to Florida. Her other daughter, Lucila, now also lived in the state, just a few miles from Columba. She was still married to John Schmitz, the man who'd been with the sisters when they first met Jeb in Mexico. Josefina's son still lived in Puerto Vallarta.

Jeb had run unsuccessfully for governor in 1994, and as far as Columba was concerned, once was enough. The campaign had done damage to her marriage; Columba was even overheard saying, "I didn't ask for this." Jeb would later admit he had neglected his family. Columba found herself alone with three teenagers as her husband traveled about the state meeting interesting people and living an exciting life. Echoing her mother-in-law's sentiment when Barbara was trying to cope with Jeb's absentee father, Columba felt she was missing out on life and that he was having all the fun. Jim Towey, who went on to work in the George W. Bush administration and become a close friend of Columba's, observed, "She knows the good and bad of being around politics. It's opened the door to extraordinary experiences for her. But she's paid quite a price as well."

When she was on the campaign trail and was forced to speak in public, Columba was terrified. *The New York Times* noted she "vastly preferred watching Mexican soap operas to attending fund-raising events." Al Cardenas, a leader in the Republican Party of Florida in the 1990s, confirmed, "She would come to some of the big political dinners and do some rallies, often speaking in Spanish, but her focus was on trying to give the kids a normal life."

It was total chaos at home before, during, and after Jeb's run in 1994. First, her son George P. got into a fracas with a girlfriend and plowed his SUV into the front yard of her family's home. He wasn't arrested; no charges were filed. Then Noelle was accused of shoplifting, arrested, and fined. It had also become clear that Noelle had a drug problem, a very serious matter for her for years to come. Meanwhile, young Jebbie would be caught in a mall parking lot with a teenage girl, both naked from the waist down. The police report cited "sexual misconduct," though no charges were filed.

Columba wasn't happy when Jeb told her he wanted to try again for governor in 1998. He wasn't a quitter, he said, and still wanted a career in public service for his state and wasn't open to discussion. While Jeb had always been the boss, lately Columba had begun to resent it. She was asserting herself more often, and he didn't like it when she put up a real fight about his running for governor.

Back in the 1970s, after Jeb met Columba and made his transformation from bad boy to accomplished adult, he became serious about his life. His brother George was a slacker for much longer. But people seemed to respect George more. George ran for governor and won. Jeb ran, too, but lost. Now, with George talking about the presidency, Jeb was talking about again running for governor. "They have always been competitive, those two,"

Columba said. "I think they drive each other, actually. Of the brothers, they
are the two who have the most in common. They push each other without
even knowing it."

Barbara felt Columba should just accept that she had married someone
who was destined to become a politician. She encouraged her to come up
with "one great speech" and deliver it in both Spanish and English. Barbara felt that because Colu was bilingual, she had the potential to reach a
wide, diverse audience. Back in 1988, Columba had appeared in a Spanish-
language commercial for George H.W. when he was running for President,
and Barbara thought she'd done an admirable job, just as she'd done giving
her nominating speech at the Republican National Convention.

When Jeb decided to run for governor in 1998, the Bush women tried to
rally around Columba, but she wasn't open to it. She felt her relatives were
trying to force her to be happy as a political wife. "In the end, she knew it
fell on her to fix her own life," said one of her friends. "Struggling to come
to terms with Jeb's political ambitions would prove to be a very lonely experience for her, though, if not for her Catholic faith."

"No one prepares you for a life in politics," Columba later said. "But
what was helpful to me was having a very strong faith that I got from my
mother. When you're strong in faith you don't lose hope. You may think,
things are really bad now, but I'm going to pray. And you pray, 'God, please
help me with this situation.' Then you get clarity and understanding. One
of my prayers is, 'If I'm here it has to be for a reason. So please help me.' My
mother gave me a good example through her faith. I'm sure she spent hours
praying. She never loses hope."

In the end, Columba decided to make it clear that her support of Jeb
would be predicated on one condition, and it was the exact same one
Dorothy, Barbara, and Laura had at one time placed on their own husbands,
Prescott, George H.W., and George W. "You cannot abandon this family,"
Columba told Jeb. She felt he had done just that in 1994, and she wasn't
going to allow him to do it again. "As your wife, I will support you publicly,"
she told him, "but only if you promise to support this family privately. This
family means everything to me."

Grateful, Jeb then agreed to send her on a trip to Paris as a show of appreciation. Why, people wondered, would Columba need his permission to go to Europe? Jeb had always been very controlling. Moreover, he had been notoriously cheap for years, as everyone in the immediate family well knew. He was constantly worried about how much money Columba spent on clothing. Perhaps because of her new rebellious posture, she was dipping into the bank account a lot more.

Jeb and Columba were now quite wealthy. His real estate partnership with a Miami developer had made him a multimillionaire, and a number of other smart investments had paid off well. Therefore, there seemed little reason for him to be so concerned about how much his wife might spend on dresses and jewelry.

Jeb won his second bid for governor of Florida in 1998. Once she was officially Florida's First Lady, Columba Bush had to move from multicultural Miami, which she loved, to the state's more traditional capital, Tallahassee, for which she had mixed feelings. "If people in Tallahassee were looking for a Southern belle in that job of First Lady," Jim Towey said, "they had the wrong woman."

Still, Columba knew what she had to do in her new role; she would follow the examples of her mother-in-law, Barbara, and sister-in-law Laura and immediately set out to determine her platform. Noelle, who was now the spitting image of her mother, was still struggling with addiction, though. Columba had been at odds with her for as long as she could remember. Noelle was always rebellious; Columba just wanted her to make better choices. It was heartbreaking for her and Jeb that she was still using, and it had caused a great deal of domestic angst. Columba decided to become an advocate to heighten awareness of drug abuse and how it impacts families. She joined the board of the Center on Addiction and Substance Abuse at Columbia University and hosted Florida's annual statewide prevention conference. She wanted to know all there was to know about substance abuse, visiting hospitals, rehabilitation centers, and even prisons. "She was always unseen in this, and hence the general view was that she wasn't a very visible First Lady," recalled James R. McDonough, who was named by Jeb as Florida's first drug czar in 1999. "We covered thousands of miles, though. We did it for eight years."

"I've seen firsthand the terrible consequences of drug abuse," Columba said at the *"Soy Unica! Soy Latina!"* rally at South Miami Middle School. "My heart is with all who suffer from addiction and the terrible consequences for their families." She also spoke in Spanish, just as Barbara had suggested. This was in October 2002, just two days after Noelle was jailed for violating the terms of her drug treatment program. She'd been found with a dime-size rock of crack cocaine in her shoe and was taken away in handcuffs to serve a ten-day jail sentence at the Center for Drug-Free Living in Orlando. This was the same treatment center she'd entered eight months earlier after being accused of posing as a doctor in order to get a prescription for Xanax. "My daughter, unfortunately, is ill, because drug addiction is an illness," an emotional Columba said to admirers at the South Miami Middle School. She looked on the verge of tears. "She's been fighting it for years," she added.

Drug addiction awareness was not Columba's only platform. Just a few months after Jeb was sworn in, she contacted the Florida Coalition Against Domestic Violence. "I would like to be helpful," she said. "Do you think it would be purposeful for me to be helpful?" Columba was inspired by her and her mother's experience with her abusive father to raise awareness of domestic violence. She would spend many hours with victims, comforting them and talking to them about their futures. In the years to come, Columba would host fund-raisers and even appear in public service commercials—in both Spanish and English.

She was fearless in the causes for which she chose to advocate. Barbara and Laura had played it safe with literacy, but Columba took bigger risks, putting herself out there to raise awareness about drug addiction and domestic abuse. She found great satisfaction in it, too, and was really not reticent to talk about her own experiences. It was as if she even found the work somehow cathartic. She always found herself racing to one event or another, posing for pictures, accompanying Jeb to functions. "Since my husband ran for office, we live under such pressure that I don't see my mother as often as I'd like," Columba said at the time. "Most people don't understand and don't believe it. They'll say, Can you come for dinner? And I'll say, I don't think so because we have a crisis here. And we have crisis after crisis after crisis after crisis. And these are things I can't say to my mother because of her health. She would only worry more and more."

Jeb wasn't always able to keep his promise to be present for his family. Through her own work, though, Columba grew to understand that being a public servant wasn't easy or predictable work, and that others would often need him as much as she did. "Yes, there were times when I wished he had been home more, and there were times I wished he had put down his Black-Berry," she would recall. "Then he would read me some of the emails he was receiving. They were emails filled with concern, frustration, sometimes fear, and once in a while anger—and I knew he was doing exactly what he was born to do: lead."

Columba's Revolt?

It was a summer evening in June 1999, and there she stood in the customs line at Atlanta's Hartsfield International Airport. Columba Bush had just returned from the five-day trip to Paris promised to her by her husband out of gratitude for having supported his gubernatorial campaign. The agent asked how much she intended to claim in overseas purchases in order that a duty could be applied to the items. Without hesitating, she said she'd purchased five hundred dollars in merchandise. But when the agent inspected her passport, a flurry of shopping receipts fell from it. He perused a few and then summoned another agent. The two then pulled Columba out of the line and escorted her to a private area. When someone added up the receipts, they came to almost twenty thousand dollars! The agents rifled through her suitcases and discovered that she'd purchased a good deal of couture clothing, some still with tags on it. They were able to match some of the receipts to the merchandise. She was fined $4,100, which was about three times the amount of duty that would have been assessed on the merchandise, had she claimed it as required by law. She wrote out a check and was on her way. No arrest was made.

The story immediately made the press. "Florida's First Lady Fails to Report Paris Goods," read the headline of the *South Florida Sun Sentinel*, just one of the hundreds of newspapers that covered it. "I deeply regret this mistake and am sorry for exercising bad judgment and can assure everyone this will never happen again," Columba said in a statement.

Why would she do such a thing?

With the passing of the years, a remarkable thing happened in Columba's marriage to Jeb. He became very much like his father in that he was given to making decisions without consulting his wife. He was slightly worse than George H.W. in that he seemed even more controlling. For instance, early in their marriage, Jeb put Columba on a strict budget. However, she wasn't a frivolous person; she certainly wasn't raised that way. Yet Jeb treated her as if she was always about to bankrupt them. This was a real twist because when they first married, Columba had so much influence over Jeb that his parents didn't even understand it.

Not surprising, Dorothy Bush had never been in favor of this kind of dynamic in a marriage. One day at Kennebunkport in the 1980s, she and Columba were on their way to the tennis club on their mopeds and afterward planned to go shopping. Just as they were pulling off on their scooters, Jeb said something to Columba like, *"Don't spend a penny more than what we agreed on."* Dorothy stopped her bike and backed up so that she could face her grandson. She then reminded him that Colu was his wife, not his child. Jeb didn't say anything to defend himself. He just uttered, "Yes, Ganny," and bowed his head.

All these many years later, Jeb was still monitoring Columba's spending and, lately, she seemed to be getting a little fed up with it. Some of her friends say what happened in that immigration line was a form of revolt. "This had been building for years," said one friend of hers. "Are you kidding? *For years.*"

It made sense that Columba was trying to make some kind of statement, not necessarily to abscond with untaxed goods. Surely if she'd really wanted to avoid paying duty, she would have had a better strategy. But she'd tucked away all her receipts in her passport, where they were bound to be found, and then she didn't even take the price tags off the clothing she'd purchased! It really seemed as if she wanted to get caught. If so, maybe she didn't fully realize the ramifications of her stunt and the headlines it would generate. But she was the governor's wife. What else could she expect?

Once the story was out, Columba was truly embarrassed. One friend, who refuses to ascribe motivation to Columba's actions, did concede: "She didn't think it all the way through. Put it that way. If she had, she never would have done it."

"All it took was one lie," wrote David Nitkin of the *South Florida Sun Sentinel,* "to transform the popular image of Florida's first lady from soft-spoken attention-shy spouse to tax dodging, big spending cheater. Ask any Floridian what he or she thinks of the governor's wife today, and the description is likely to be devastating."

Columba's cursory apology wasn't enough to satisfy most people. "They have come nowhere near to a full explanation of what happened, and that is the first thing people are owed," said Tony Welch, spokesman for Florida's opposing Democratic Party. "One of the things you get from all of this is you get evidence that he [Jeb] ain't an everyday Floridian. His wife is on a five-day shopping vacation in Paris, but he wants to tell me he is tuned in to inner-city problems, that he wants to help our public schools with vouchers [meaning taxpayer dollars for private school tuition] and I'm not buying it." Someone else noted that the $19,000 Columba spent was "more than what about 35,000 state employees earn in a year."

"There is no logical, single explanation for it," Cory Tilley, the governor's spokesman, finally admitted when pushed hard.

"They want answers. They want answers," people kept telling Columba Bush. "Well, they're not going to get them," she reportedly said, "because I have made my statement." Jeb had other ideas. Feeling pressured, he finally had an aide explain that Columba simply didn't want him to know how much she'd spent on her vacation. He then personally added, "It was a difficult weekend at our house." This statement just made things worse. It made it sound as if she was afraid of her own husband.

"The embarrassment I felt made me ashamed to face my family and friends," Columba would later say in a speech to the Central Florida Make-A-Wish Foundation, in July 1999. "It was the worst feeling I've ever had in my life."

Barbara was mystified by what had happened. She waited until the last weekend in June when the family converged at Kennebunkport before she demanded to know what in the world was going on. Jeb said he didn't want to discuss it, and Barbara let it go. She would never embarrass Columba by asking her directly, especially since Columba was so mortified that she locked herself in her bedroom the first day of her visit and wouldn't even come out for meals. "Well, I'm sorry, she can't stay in there forever," Barbara said. "She has to eat. This is ridiculous."

After a few hours, Columba's sister-in-law Sharon, Neil's wife, knocked on the door and coaxed her to take a walk. The two women have never said what they discussed, but Sharon helped Columba come to terms with the scandal. Sharon's marriage to Neil had its own challenges, and she was able to talk to Columba in a way that might have eluded her other sister-in-law Laura. Neil was the black sheep of the family, always in some sort of financial trouble. He had big dreams, most of which never seemed to work out, leaving him and Sharon constantly in debt. If anything, Sharon may have been able to tell Columba that she should thank her lucky stars. Jeb might be tight with their finances, but at least they had money. Whatever the sisters-in-law discussed, Columba felt better about things. Jeb was grateful to Sharon for helping Columba, and he let her know it.

George W.'s Presidential Marathon

At the same time Jeb Bush was elected governor of Florida, his brother George won his second term as governor of Texas. All through his campaign, people kept asking him if the presidency was next on his agenda. George wondered himself. On the morning of his second inauguration, he was with his mother at the First United Methodist Church in Austin and had a conversation with her about possibly running for higher office. "I'm really struggling with this," he told Barbara. "Well," she said. "Make up your mind, then."

That same day, the sermon at church was about God summoning Moses. "Like Moses, we have the opportunity, each and every one of us, to do the right thing, and for the right reason," said the minister. Barbara caught George's eye and mouthed, *He's talking to you.* George later recalled, "It was a liberating moment, because I kind of did make up my mind right then. Serendipitous. Or maybe it was meant to be."

It would actually be some time before he made up his mind.

"I was privy to conversations and so I know for sure he didn't want to run for president," said Monica Gonzalez, Laura's assistant. "But so many Republicans kept coming to the governor's mansion to talk to him about running, saying, 'We need you, we need you.' I remember Karl Rove—who had really convinced him to run for governor and had sort of shaped him in many ways—coming in and talking to him. Mr. Bush told him, 'It's going to have to be something I pray about.' I know his daughters didn't want him to run. Definitely Mrs. Bush was against it. 'No, this is not anything I want,' she told me. 'Life in politics in Texas is nothing compared to what I know it's like in Washington. So, no, it's not for me and I hope not for George.'"

Laura felt political campaigns could be intensely cruel, especially since she had seen her father-in-law criticized unfairly in the media by the Clinton campaign. Though she had campaigned for George, she had her heart set on private life after his second term. "Laura told me she fervently prayed about it and came to the decision that this was what her husband was supposed to do, maybe not what she wanted to do, but what he was compelled to do," said her friend Adair Margo. "She felt she was part of a calling. So, yes, she eventually did do an about-face and decided she would support him in it. I knew she would."

On Sunday morning, March 7, 1999, George W. Bush announced in a press conference at the governor's mansion that he was forming an exploratory committee with the intention of possibly running for President. Three months later, on June 12, he finally declared his candidacy in Cedar Rapids, Iowa. "I am proud to be a compassionate conservative," he said. "I am running so that our party can match a conservative mind with a compassionate heart."

Soon, the presidential campaign was in full swing; the next year would be exhausting. Before hitting the trail, George and Laura had to trade their Texas Department of Public Safety detail for Secret Service. "I was assigned to fly with the major press corps as a liaison between the Secret Service, the staff, and the media," recalled Denny Schlindwein, one of the new agents replacing the safety detail. "So when the candidate flew, the media would be in the following plane, and that's where I would spend a lot of my time, ironing out problems and making sure we all got along. Sam Donaldson, Chris Wallace, *Time* and *Newsweek* and Reuters, all of those guys. Also, I was the shift leader for the Missus [Laura]. So everywhere she went, I went."

Before hitting the road, the Secret Service agents met with George and Laura. Schlindwein recalled, "All three shifts and bosses had to meet the protectees, so we were invited to the governor's mansion in Austin. Our shift stood at the bottom of the staircase as Governor and Mrs. Bush descended. He went down the row of agents, asking our names, where we were from, saying 'Welcome aboard,' that kind of thing. She followed alongside him, very nice, smiling, shaking hands. As I met him, I said, 'You know, I protected you a couple years back when your father was President. I called you George back then. Now I guess I have to call you Governor.' He said, 'Yup. And with any luck, you'll soon be calling me Mr. President.'"

"Campaigning for office is like running a marathon, day after day," Laura would recall. "You wake in darkness and sleep when the local news anchors are just signing off. You sleep in motels and hotel chains, on a hard pillow one night and a soft one the next. Or you sleep upright on the plane itself. Your life is packed between the two sides of a suitcase. Even the press sometimes has it easier than the candidates. If a reporter catches the flu, he or she can hop off the trail for a day or two to recover. But not the candidate. If George or I got that same flu, we couldn't get off; we had to keep traveling to every event. We drove in motorcades with flashing lights and sirens, traffic shunted to one side. Days and weeks collapsed into a blur."

The public seemed fascinated by the differences between Laura and Barbara whenever the two made public appearances together. In December 1999, with the Iowa caucuses weeks away, they gave their first joint television interview on ABC's *This Week*. Their banter was easy and natural but also became a bit tense when they discussed George. "You have said he's, in temperament and personality, a lot like his mother," remarked the interviewer Cokie Roberts to Laura.

"Careful," Barbara said with a warning expression.

"That's right," Laura replied.

"Careful," Barbara again said.

"Well, they're both feisty," Laura continued, ignoring her mother-in-law. "They both like to talk. They're funny. You know, I think there are a lot of characteristics that they share."

"And you said he's incorrigible?" Cokie asked of George.

"So's Bar," Laura added.

"Exactly," Barbara agreed. "I mean, I'm not going to argue with that."

The playing field was finally whittled down to George Bush and the

Democratic candidate, Vice President Al Gore. By this time, Laura had been assigned three agents, plus her shift leader, Denny Schlindwein. "My first impression of her was how polite she was," he recalled. "We'd get out of the car and I'd open the door for her, and she'd say thank you. We'd then go to our destination. When she'd come back to the car, I'd open the door for her and she'd say thank you. After a day or so I said, 'Mrs. Bush, you need to understand something. You don't need to say thank you every time I open the door for you. That's my job, ma'am.' She smiled and said, 'Well, *you* need to understand something. Whenever you open a door for me, I will say thank you. That's just the way we operate around here.'

"While in the car, she could've just sat silently like most people we protect. But, instead, she would lean in between the seats and talk to me and the other agent. 'So, what's your wife's name?' 'How many kids do you have?' 'What are their interests?' She would remember everything you ever told her, and weeks—months even—later, she would ask about your wife by name, or inquire about one of your kids' hobbies.

"She was also very strong-minded," he said of Laura. He remembered a time the Bushes visited a church in Austin. When the visit was over, George left the premises and got into the car and waited for Laura. After about fifteen minutes, she was still talking to people in the vestibule. Impatient, George told Denny, "Look. Go in and get Mrs. Bush, will you? Get her out of there. We gotta go." Denny walked back into the church and found Laura surrounded by parishioners. He leaned in and whispered, "Mrs. Bush," but before he could finish, she whispered back, "I know, I know. George wants me to come out. Well, you go back and tell him that when I'm done talking to these people I'll be out, and tell him not a second sooner." The agent then trotted back to the parked car and peeked into the half-open window. "Governor," he began. George cut him off. "Don't tell me," he said. "Let me guess. She said that when she's done talking she'll be out, and not a second sooner." The agent laughed and said, "Correct, sir." George smiled and concluded, "Never let it be said I don't know my own wife."

It would be a hectic four months, one stop after another, one speech after another. Then, about halfway through the campaign, the *Star* tabloid published the first true exposé of Laura's 1963 car crash. The last time any newspaper had covered it was when it occurred, and she was referred to as Laura Welch in those local reports. In the intervening years, no one had ever made a connection to the well-known Laura Bush, which does seem incredible given her many years of high-profile public life.

Laura had feared this moment of revelation for many years. "When it came out, most of us wondered if it was even true," said agent Denny Schlindwein. "Mrs. Bush confirmed it for us while we were on a flight. 'Yes, it did happen,' she said, 'and it tragically changed the trajectory of the lives of so many people.'"

While the story made headlines, to everyone's surprise it didn't adversely affect the campaign because Laura was so genuine in expressing her sadness and remorse. People seemed to understand.

The week the story came out, Barbara made a few stops with Laura on the campaign trail. As earlier stated in the prologue of this book, one Secret Service agent remembered that the two were sitting side by side when Barbara turned to Laura, reached out, and touched her cheek tenderly and then held her hand. "Though no words were spoken, so much was said," recalled the agent. "Watching them, I felt the history there, the understanding, the sense of family."

Even with the present scandal regarding Laura in the background, the campaign had to continue. Barbara went on the *Today* show to make a few critical observations about the behavior of Bill Clinton in office that had led to his impeachment and also made it clear that Al Gore could never restore dignity to the office the way her son could. Jeb traveled all about Florida drumming up votes there, as did Columba. Laura went to schools to give speeches and read to students. Meanwhile, George H.W.'s participation was limited for fear that the son would be too tightly linked to the father's detractors. Instead, H.W. played a strong role in the background, making important strategic decisions.

On November 2, just five days before the election, when George had a reasonable lead in the polls, a story was leaked that George had once been arrested for a DUI in Maine. This incident had occurred almost twenty-five years earlier, before he and Laura were married.

The issue of George and his drinking and possible drug use had already been raised, earlier in August. "Not only could I pass the background check and the standards applied to today's White House," he told reporters at a press conference, "but I could have passed the background check and the standards applied on the most stringent conditions when my dad was president of the United States." Up until that time, he had repeatedly refused to answer specific questions regarding rumors of cocaine use. "I believe it is important to put a stake in the ground and say enough is enough when it comes to trying to dig up people's backgrounds in politics," the candidate told reporters at a follow-up news conference in Columbus, Ohio. "I'm going to tell people I made mistakes and that I have learned from my mistakes," he said. "And if they like it, I hope they give me a chance. And if they don't like it, they can go find somebody else to vote for."

Three months later, this new story now broke about his DUI. If he was being so open, his critics asked, how had this arrest slipped his mind? "Now, in an election where character was a key issue, the last four days were being devoted to questions about George's character," Laura recalled. "I called the girls at school before they heard the news from someone else."

Laura wasn't exactly thrilled with George's response to the story. "When I was young and irresponsible," he said, "I was young. And irresponsible," a phrase he would also use when the issue of whether or not he ever used cocaine came up. Laura felt his words made him sound worse than he'd actually been in his youth. This was the kind of response that could turn an election. As she recalled it, "the polls soon showed that George's three-to-five-point lead had collapsed into nearly a dead heat." Later, Karl Rove would say he believed the story actually cost George about a million votes. Barbara put a positive spin on it when she reflected upon it. "Frankly, I think that instead of the effect that some hoped for," she recalled, "this might have reminded people that George had the discipline to give up drinking and that he was strong."

If George lost his race, a lot of people in his circle felt he would have accepted it after the initial disappointment. "All through the campaign he never thought he had a chance against Al Gore," said his Secret Service agent Denny Schlindwein. "For him, it was just a gamble, and he was willing to throw the dice and see how it would all work out."

"I only ran because I have nothing to lose," George told Denny one day while on their daily jog. "I don't have a long-term, family-influenced political game, so that makes it easier. In other words, I don't have to worry that if I fuck this whole thing up a dynasty will come to an end."

"He said that his family wasn't like the Kennedys," recalled the agent. "'I'm not JFK, Jeb's not Bobby, and my father ain't Joe Kennedy pushing us along. My father's message to us always was, "We'll raise you to go out and excel and succeed and all we expect is that you do your best and win if you can." That's a better message than "Son, you gotta do this shit because if not you'll fuck up the dynasty."' Plus, he said, he had work experience, and 'when did Kennedy ever have a job? I've worked hard in my life.' Not that he had a problem with the Kennedys necessarily, he said, 'I just ain't one of 'em. My whole life isn't politics. My whole life is Laura and the kids.'"

Denny Schlindwein concluded, "He wanted to serve, don't get me wrong. He had great ideas and policies, but his life was bigger than that, or maybe simpler is the better word. If you really wanted to make W. happy, all you needed to do was make sure he had a pickup truck, a dog, a cigar, a can of beer, and a chainsaw, and, for sure, he'd be in seventh heaven.

"Once, we were pheasant hunting and he realized he was late for an event. We were two hours away from it. We got in the car and he said, 'Step on it, pal. I got me a big function tonight and if I'm late, Mrs. Bush will pluck me like a pheasant.' I was going way, way over the speed limit, and he was whooping and hollering like a Midland teenager, saying, 'Go. Go. Go. Faster. Faster. *Faster.*' That was the W. I knew.

"The day before the election, I said, 'Governor, I need to tell you something. I've protected six men that have run for President or Vice President.' He said, 'Oh yeah? And how'd it turn out for them?' I answered, 'They all lost, sir, every last one of 'em.' He looked at me with a surprised expression, laughed, and said, 'Dang! Why'd you have to tell me that, Denny?'"

While George didn't feel pressured to win, he had to admit it would be "nice as hell to do it." Once he'd imagined himself behind that massive desk in the Oval Office, it was very difficult, impossible actually, to let the dream go. Laura wouldn't let him, either. She kept telling him, "You are meant to be President of the United States, and you *will be* President of the United States."

The Bushes Wait for
Life-Changing Results

On the night of November 7, 2000, the Bush family congregated in the governor's mansion to watch the election results on television. Barbara and George were present, as were Jeb and Columba and a host of other family members, including some grandchildren. As Barbara knitted and listened to an audiobook on the couch in the small living room, Laura tried to stay busy in the kitchen. Jeb and George continued to work the phones. The next few hours were a whirlwind of confusing events. At around eight P.M., major television networks called Florida for Al Gore. However, within two hours, they began to retract that calculation. By two o'clock in the morning, Bush had taken the lead and networks now projected him not only the winner of Florida but also of the presidency! Everyone whooped and hollered, especially when Gore called to concede. "Is this possible?" Barbara, who seemed dazed, asked Laura. "I think it is, Bar," Laura said, seeming to disbelieve it. "I think it is." Columba was so overwhelmed she sat in a chair in a corner and began to cry. "It's okay, honey," Jeb kept telling her. "It's okay." She said, "I'm just so happy, and it's just too much, Jeb. It's too much."

The celebration didn't last long. A little more than an hour later, everything changed again when it was reported that Florida was actually too close to call. *"What does this mean?"* Columba asked desperately. George W. chuckled. "It means I ain't President," he said. "What the heck kind of fiasco election is this, anyway?" Jeb asked, especially when Gore called Bush back to retract his concession.

Everyone was exhausted. "Okay, look, I'm done," Barbara said after Gore's call. "I have to go to bed." Laura agreed. Jeb and George were reluctant to call it a night, though, and wanted to sit in front of the television to see if things again might change. Laura went to George and put her head on his shoulder. "Bushie, would you rather win? Or go to bed." He smiled at her. "I'd rather go to bed," he said, looking beat. "Hopefully, this will all be decided by morning," he added.

It would be more than a month before the election would finally be resolved. There would have to be a voter recount in Florida amidst numerous legal challenges and talk of ballot issues—"hanging chads"—and other inconsistencies in Jeb's state. (He recused himself from the process, incidentally.) It would be a long, torturous wait.

During this time, Laura and George retired to their country home, Prairie Chapel Ranch, just outside of Crawford, Texas, which they'd purchased a year earlier and which Laura was still in the process of decorating. This lovely three-bedroom house and a guesthouse sat on 1,600 acres of beautiful West Texas prairie land. It was here in this comfortable one-story limestone structure that the Bushes and some of their friends would try to relax during a time when they didn't know what the future would hold for them. "That was a little tough, to say the least," recalled Secret Service agent Denny Schlindwein, who continued on with George and Laura after the election, "when the Bushes were in limbo."

One day, George and Denny were on their regular morning jog when Denny turned to him and asked how he thought the election would ultimately be resolved. George smiled and, not breaking his stride, answered, "I gave it my best, and now we just have to let the chips fall where they may, I guess."

Denny nodded. "It's been a tough road for you," he said as the two men ran along a beaten-down path. "But I have so much respect for you. You love America. You're doing it for your country, sir."

George laughed and patted the agent on the shoulder. "Well, actually, I'm doing it for you, Denny," he said with a twinkle in his eye. "I just don't want you to go out a loser, pal."

For the next few weeks, Al Gore continued to lead in the popular vote, but George in the electoral college. In early December, the Bushes returned to Austin for the holidays at the governor's mansion. "Every Christmas, Laura invited seven of us to a Christmas luncheon to spend the day with her and see how the governor's mansion was decorated," recalled her friend Susan Byerly Nowlin. "She did such clever things every year. She always invited different artists from all over Texas to decorate a room. They'd get a lot of recognition for making that room their Christmas room that year, and show their art in there. This was Laura's sixth year as First Lady of Texas.

"The seven of us showed up at the mansion, and there were cables running down the front sidewalk, out the gate, and right past where we were standing. It turned out they were conducting a television interview for *60 Minutes* about the election, the topic being along the lines of 'You thought you had it in the bag, but now maybe you don't.' Laura's private secretary came out and said, 'Oh, here you all are. Mrs. Bush has been waiting for you. What are you doing standing out here?' I said, 'Well, we're certainly not going in there with this interview going on,' and she said, 'Oh, no, no. Mrs. Bush wants you to come inside.' She then took us to the room where the interview was being taped. My first thought was that Laura needed to concentrate and probably wouldn't want us standing there. But she was so over being nervous about these things by this time. Gone was the woman who had given that speech at the Dallas Club whose neck kept getting redder and redder as she talked. Watching her be interviewed, I was struck by her poise and realized that the last six years had taught her so much."

Finally, on December 12, the Supreme Court, by a vote of 5 to 4, halted the Florida recount. The final tally was incredibly close. In electoral votes, Bush had just five more than Gore, 271 to 266. However, in popular votes, Gore had 50,996,582 to Bush's 50,456,062, a difference of just 540,520 votes in Gore's favor. The electoral college is what matters in choosing the winner: George Walker Bush was officially the forty-third President of the United States.

PART SEVENTEEN

Triumph and Tragedy

Four Chains

T hank you for doing this," Laura Bush was telling a Secret Service agent. "I appreciate it." It was about three in the morning on a frigid winter night during the third week of December 2000, about a month until George's inauguration. Laura was now in Washington with the new title "First Lady–Designate." She wasn't living in the White House yet, but rather staying across the street at the historic Blair House when not traveling down to the governor's mansion to help with the packing of the family's belongings. "I guess I could get in trouble for this, ma'am," said the agent. "I'm not on your detail." She nodded and said she understood; she actually knew him from her father-in-law's detail. The head of her detail was now an agent named Ron Sprinkle.

According to what the agent would later recall, he and Laura were standing on the semicircular driveway in front of the north side of the White House, the most popular Pennsylvania Avenue vantage point viewed by onlookers from a distance on the other side of a six-foot-plus wrought-iron fence. Pennsylvania Avenue had been closed to all vehicular traffic ever since the Oklahoma City bombing during the Clinton administration in 1995. However, pedestrians were still permitted.

Behind Laura and the agent was a line of thick lime-colored hedges, and then, stretched out like a lush carpet, the sweeping North Lawn. The perimeter was dotted with trees, each stately and ancient. In the middle of the lawn was a circular pool with a graceful fountain, its perimeter outlined by red, white, and purple flowers. Pointing to the spray of water, Laura said that back in the 1800s there had been a statue of Thomas Jefferson in its place, during the Lincoln administration. The agent would later recall thinking it made perfect sense to him that a former librarian would know the history of the executive mansion of the President of the United States.

The night was serene and peaceful, blessedly quiet with just ambient street noise emanating from the distance. The water splashing from the fountain was the most noticeable sound. The sky was a cloudless arc of black velvet sprinkled with stars. Laura seemed struck by the silence. The air was crisp and fresh. It was cold—she could see her breath—but it must have felt good.

The two gazed up at the White House's eight stately white columns— three on each side, four in the front. They studied its classically elegant prostyle portico; the lunette fanlight over the gracious entrance; the large chandelier hanging by its long chain; and the majestic, V-shaped roof. Lifting their eyes, they would have noticed the American flag flapping in the sky high atop its gleaming metal flagpole. The entire white structure was lit by bright spotlights, causing it to have a glow so bright it must have appeared magical. The history of this home must have been on Laura's mind because, according to the agent, she seemed swept away. "I've been here a million times, coming and going from different events, Governors Association dinners hosted by the Clintons and such," she said softly, "but it feels like I've never actually *been* here. I don't even know how many rooms are in this place." She'd soon learn there are 132, give or take.

Laura observed that usually at official events she was never able to take the time to just be in the moment. The agent nodded. "I've actually never looked at this place in this way, either," he said. Rarely had he ever taken the time to just stand in front of it and really look at the White House, and he'd been on the job for more than fifteen years. Laura had wanted this time alone in front of the executive mansion because, as she explained, she'd probably never have the chance as First Lady. She remembered when her mother-in-law was living here and decided to take a casual stroll to the front of the White House in the middle of a summer's day. It caused such a fracas with the Secret Service, Laura said, it almost felt like a national emergency. The agent smiled. "Yes, well, that doesn't surprise me, ma'am," he said. Laura also mentioned that Barbara had told her protective detail to "get lost" so that she could pose for pictures with the tourists. "That doesn't surprise me, either," said the agent, shaking his head in amusement.

"Can I have a few moments alone?" Laura asked. "'Fraid not, ma'am," the agent answered. However, he offered to back up a little. She smiled and nodded her thanks. He then walked about two feet from her and stood in place, scanning the area around them.

The agent recalled watching her as she took a deep breath and then exhaled deeply, as if *finally* rescuing a second just for herself. She had always been a loner, but now she was a private woman in a public life, and grateful for any time to herself.

Perhaps her thoughts went back to a time when a little girl lay on a blanket in her backyard with her mother gazing up at the wide vista of twinkling stars and talking about the possibilities of life outside Midland. Now that child was a grown woman standing before the grand house in which she would live as the nation's First Lady. What an incredible journey it had been. She was excited about the future but also felt some trepidation. But the timeless aspect of this house, which had stood for more than two centuries, had to reassure her that she, George, Jenna, and Barbara would not only thrive but also be well protected within its walls.

Laura continued to stand next to the base of one of the two columns on the side of the portico. She gazed up at the neoclassical lantern with its six curved frosted-glass panels. "Four chains," she observed, turning back to the agent. She was referencing the heavy metal fetters designed to keep the fixture from twisting or swaying in the wind. "They keep it steady, you know," she said. He nodded. "One chain for each of us," she concluded with a smile. "One chain for each of us," she repeated, this time more to herself.

It was getting colder; she hunched into her jacket and hugged herself as the breeze grew sharper and rustled through the trees. Despite the frigid air, she didn't seem to want to leave.

"Another couple minutes?" the agent asked her.

"Yes," the First Lady–Designate decided. "That would be nice."

A First Lady Finds Herself

With her husband now President, Laura Bush would bring to the White House the same charm, imagination, and class she'd shown as Texas's First Lady, but in a way that was displayed on a global stage. She had learned from her mother-in-law's example that the only way to thrive in this role was to completely devote herself to her platform. In both Barbara's and Laura's cases, it was literacy, and Laura also advocated for the women of Afghanistan and their children.

Not since the nineteenth century had a woman been the wife of one President and the mother of another, and that was Abigail Adams. However, she had died six years before her son John Quincy Adams was elected in 1825, so she didn't live to see her daughter-in-law, Louisa Catherine Adams, be First Lady. Barbara Bush was the only woman in American history to actually see her daughter-in-law follow her in the role of First Lady.

Laura would be a very different kind of First Lady. Barbara was homespun with a simple wardrobe, stripes and polka dots and colors that some people found reassuring. Laura was more refined, with a couture wardrobe that was sleek and tailored. "I wanted to look elegant, to appear my best at events here and abroad, and not to glance back later at White House photos and silently cringe," she later recalled. "I really felt for Hillary Clinton, who spent years having the press write nasty things about her hairstyles. It unnerved me enough that I paid with our own money for someone to come to the White House and blow-dry my hair almost every morning, just so I could try to avoid a bad hair day."

"Laura is so simple in what she wears privately at their ranch and elsewhere," observed her longtime friend Susan Byerly Nowlin. "However, as she'd seen with every First Lady, when you get to the White House, you have to become focused on fashion, and you find yourself doing the designers a pretty big favor by wearing their dresses. She ended up with the most beautiful clothes I'd ever seen. She had her taste and designers adhered to it. She didn't want anything low-cut, for instance. Oscar de la Renta was so conscientious about that, and so fabulous to work with. Each designer put his or her incredible gift of flair into whatever they were doing for Laura. I know she favored de la Renta. A designer Laura also liked a lot was Lela Rose, who designed the dresses Barbara and Jenna wore at the inauguration. Laura understood fashion was a big part of being a First Lady and not something she could take lightly. 'All eyes are on you in this job,' she told me, 'and you really have to give them something to appreciate.'"

Barbara was more outspoken than Laura and always said what was on her mind. She was beloved for it, too. Laura was much more circumspect. There were times when people really didn't know what she was thinking, and she was perfectly fine with that. She didn't think it was necessary to be transparent. Her job wasn't to help shape policy as much as it was to support her husband in his platforms. Maybe as a result of not being as outspoken, her poll numbers were never quite as high as Barbara's. She didn't care.

Even if she didn't influence policy, Laura was not content to remain quietly in the background. Like most modern First Ladies, she was an active participant in her husband's presidency, as she had always been in their marriage. George agreed and would always seek his wife's counsel, rarely if ever making an important decision without allowing her to privately weigh in. This isn't to say he would always do what she suggested. However, he viewed his presidency as a part of his life from which his marriage was not excluded. "The White House is just for now," Laura would tell him. "The marriage is forever."

The dynamic between most mothers- and daughters-in-law can often be dicey, and that of Barbara and Laura was no different. They didn't always agree.

Barbara didn't like the floral arrangements that were being planned for a luncheon early in the administration. As she leafed through a thick book of designs, she suggested a different sort of arrangement and Laura dutifully took notes. Barbara then called down to the basement flower shop to give a few instructions to the chief florist, Nancy Clarke. But then when it came time for the meal, Barbara saw that the arrangements were exactly as Laura had originally intended. Barbara was a little offended, but she let it go.

There were also a few more major conflicts. When Laura first moved into the White House with her longtime assistant, Andi Ball, Barbara felt Andi was too inexperienced to handle the job. She had done well for Laura in the governor's mansion, but at the White House in the new role as Laura's chief of staff, she seemed in Barbara's estimation woefully out of her depth. Barbara told Laura she should replace her before things got out of hand. Laura said she didn't think it was necessary. Barbara refused to accept that answer and continued to push the issue. One day, in the middle of this contretemps, Barbara was walking down a hallway in the White House when she was intercepted by Laura. With a smile on her face and not breaking her stride for even a second, Laura linked arms with Barbara and led her to the small Queens' Sitting Room, where a few people were working. "May we have the room?" Laura asked. After the staff quickly gathered their things and cleared out, Laura closed the door. The two women were inside for about five minutes before the door opened again and Barbara shot out of it like a cannonball. Laura exited with calm self-assurance a few moments later. She told one of her aides, "I was clear with her about Andi. I just told her, 'Look, this is not your decision, Bar, it's mine. And I said, *no*.' She agreed to back off."

Laura's new lead social secretary, Catherine Fenton, was also key to her success. Cathy, as she was known to all, had been the deputy social secretary for Nancy Reagan and Barbara Bush. With her capable staff of eight, she planned all the Christmas parties, Medal of Freedom ceremonies, congressional balls, state dinners, and other activities at the White House, always complicated by the rigid protocol required. "You are in the middle of this nonstop whirlwind," Fenton said. "What you're reading about in the newspapers is happening all around you."

One ongoing conflict with Barbara involved Laura's children, especially when it came to Jenna, who tended to be more of a handful. Barbara continued to believe Laura was too lax and, if it had been up to her, both girls would be disciplined more often. But Laura held her ground where the twins were concerned. "Laura would, of course, always side with the girls, no matter what the conflict was," said George W. "Look, the girls, when they were teens, they could ruffle feathers, and Mother's feathers could be easily ruffled."

When Jenna, at nineteen, was cited for underage drinking in Austin shortly after her father was inaugurated, Barbara was very unhappy about it.

In February 2001, Jenna's Secret Service agents watched as she and a friend went into a bar even though the agents realized both were under the legal drinking age. As they sat in a car outside the bar, they saw the girls leave and two undercover Austin police officers cite them with what turned out to be an MIP (minor in possession of alcohol). Laura later recalled, "We [she and George] told her [Jenna] that this would be a lesson, and one that she had learned the hard way. Her friends might do something wrong and not make headlines, but she did not have that luxury."

Barely three months later and just weeks after Jenna pled no contest to the charge, she and her sister, Barbara, went to another bar in Austin and tried to order cocktails. When asked for her identification, Jenna pulled out a fake identification. The manager could've just denied service and told the twins to be on their way, but instead she decided to call the police. According to the officer's report, she said, "I want them to get into big trouble." When the police arrived, the Secret Service agents in their cars outside ran into the bar and tried to talk the officers out of giving the Bush girls citations, saying, "Don't worry, they'll never come back here. We promise." In the end, the police decided to write the girls up, leading to the classic *New York Post* front-page headline "Jenna and Tonic."

Barbara Bush had sharp words about the fracas, not for her grandchildren, but for Laura. Barbara wrote in her diary at this time, "The thing that really bothered me or bothers me is the fact that the girls (especially Jenna) are rude to their mom and dad." She later wrote both grandchildren a letter to chastise them about their public behavior and to remind them that the country was watching and that they should now begin to think about more than just themselves. When one considers how well the twins would turn out, though, it seems clear that Laura knew what she was doing. However, the occasional reminder from Ganny that the world had expectations of them probably didn't hurt, either. Jenna and Barbara took it well; they loved and respected their grandmother, but they also knew who was in charge.

To some people, it felt like Barbara was still in charge even long after she was out of the White House. One longtime staffer recalled that, during her son's administration, when some employees heard Barbara was in the building they would try to make themselves scarce. He equated the experience to being a youngster in a new school and having your very strict former teacher come to visit. "On one hand, it was nice to see her again," he said, "but on the other," he concluded with a chuckle, "not so much.

"Once, Barbara Bush and the First Lady—Laura Bush—were on their way to the Oval and I happened to be on a break and sitting on the corner of my desk and talking on the phone," said this staff member. "They stopped right in front of me. Barbara Bush made a slitting motion with her hand across her throat that told me to hang up, so I did. She then said to me, 'These desks are not for sitting on. In fact, my understanding is that this is precisely why they make chairs.' She pointed to a chair and said, 'Oh, look, there's one now. *Sit on it.*' I jumped off the desk and sat in that chair like I was a scared ten-year-old.

"As they walked by, I heard Laura laugh and tell her mother-in-law, 'My God, Bar. You're the worst.' And she smiled and said, 'I know. I'm pretty awful.'"

Laura's First State Dinner

On September 5, 2001, President George W. Bush and his First Lady, Laura Bush, hosted the first of four state dinners they would give during their first term. Their honored guests were President Vicente Fox of Mexico and his wife, Martha Sahagún de Fox. Fox was the first winning opposition candidate since the election of Francisco I. Madero back in 1910; he would serve from 2000 to 2006. He and George had been friendly going back to his days as governor of Texas.

This was an exciting occasion for Laura Bush and she would take great pride in the final result, though the careful and sometimes tedious planning caused her no small measure of anxiety. While she wasn't nervous before her own wedding, this event truly rattled her. "A state dinner is far more intricate, an elaborate display of hundreds of moving parts, from guest lists to menus, which require an advance tasting, to table seatings, arrival protocols, and choices of linens, flowers, china, and silver, even the champagnes and wines," she would recall. "And traditionally all of this falls under the purview of the White House Social Office, working with the Office of the First Lady. If the four-hour evening is flawless, it is only because of the hundreds of hours that have been invested beforehand. No detail is too small."

Whereas a state dinner hosted by the Clintons could have had a guest list of as many as seven hundred, Laura decided she wanted to keep her first one smaller and more intimate. She decided to host it in the State Dining Room, which seats about 130 people. Typical of Laura, she decided to include some of her good friends from Texas, including Adair Margo. Throughout her time in Washington, she'd always like having people around who acted as touchstones to her past, or at the very least to Texas. It made her feel comfortable and not so much a stranger in her own (white) house.

Around this same time, George appointed Adair Margo chairman of the President's Committee of the Arts and the Humanities, and she would also be appointed by Secretary of State Colin Powell to the U.S. National Commission for UNESCO. A few years later, she would receive the Presidential Citizens Medal from President Bush, who cited her "strengthening of the international relationships from Mexico to China." She recalled, "I'll never forget that Laura, who maybe felt that since I'd never had a presidential appointment before and was a little overwhelmed by it, said, 'Listen, one reason for this appointment is just so we can see you as much as possible. We just want you in our lives, so there's no pressure here. This is about friendship more than anything else.' That just released me in so many ways. I realized I didn't have to change the world, you know?

"In years to come, Laura would have these house parties at the White House; all of us from Texas that she knew and loved would attend," she recalled. "Sometimes the gatherings revolved around book fairs she would host. It was very interesting to know the ins and outs of the White House. I learned, for instance, that Chief Usher Gary Walters couldn't go to bed until all of the White House's guests had retired for the night. But we Texans would just stay up all night long, gabbing and catching up. It wasn't fair to the usher. Laura would always tell him, 'Look, Mr. Walters, this obviously isn't going to end any time soon. Go to bed and get a good night's sleep. We're just fine here.'"

Upon inviting Adair Margo and her husband, Dee, to the first state dinner, Laura also suggested they bring along Adela Gonzalez, who had been the Margos' housekeeper for thirty-five years. It speaks to the ties that bind Laura to people of so many different cultures and stations that Adela was the mother of Monica Gonzalez, the woman who'd been Laura's assistant in the governor's mansion in Texas.

Adela, who hailed from Toreo, Mexico, had given birth to Monica out of wedlock. She was hired by Adair Margo when she sought work as a housekeeper to care for her child. Mother and daughter then lived with the Margos for Monica's entire youth. They even paid for her college education. After her graduation she went to work for Laura in the governor's mansion. Monica was the subordinate who had helped Laura organize her family's photographs into scrapbooks for the twins. When Monica left Laura's staff to be married, right before the presidential campaign, Laura hosted a farewell party for her. Adair and Dee then paid for the wedding, and Dee walked Monica down the aisle.

"Bring Adela," Laura suggested when she invited the Margos to the state dinner. "She can hang out with Maria and keep her company."

Maria was her longtime housekeeper, Maria Galvan, who had immigrated to Texas from a small Mexican village with her daughter in the mid-1980s. She had worked as a maid in Austin before being hired by George and Laura in 1995, just as they were moving into the governor's mansion. After Maria taught herself English, George strongly encouraged her to get her citizenship, which she did. The Bushes both grew to love her and brought her with them to the White House as part of "the family."

Adair did as Laura suggested, and that's how she and Adela Gonzalez ended up spending the next seven nights in the White House. "The day we got into town," Adair recalled, "Laura and I were sitting on the Truman Balcony off the Yellow Room, and she said, 'Let's just wait here and watch Marine One land with the two Presidents,' meaning Bush and Fox. It was such a gorgeous view with the Washington Monument in the background, as well as the Jefferson Memorial. You could also see the Potomac River on the horizon, and airplanes landing across the river at Washington National. I said, 'Oh my, yes, but let me go get Adela. She shouldn't miss seeing this.' So I went up to her room but couldn't find her. I searched everywhere. I was so aggravated because I really didn't want her to miss this incredible opportunity. I couldn't imagine where she was, though, but I didn't want to miss it myself, so I ran back down and joined Laura on the balcony.

"Marine One lands on the White House South Lawn directly below the balcony, and we're watching as they let down the stairs, and the marines all stand at attention as President Fox walks down, followed by President Bush. The two Presidents salute the military and it's official, ceremonial, and breathtaking. And we look closer and closer until Laura says, 'Wait. Hold on a second. Is that Adela down there?' And sure enough, there's Adela Gonzalez standing at the foot of the stairs, and she has Maria Galvan with her. 'What in the world are *they* doing down there?' I asked, astonished. We just laughed and laughed. And that's how my former housekeeper, Adela, and Laura's present housekeeper, Maria, ended up having their picture taken standing between two Presidents in front of Marine One. 'Just exactly as it should be,' Laura said, delighted. 'Good for them.'"

It turned out that her first state dinner was a smashing success for Laura. She wore a full taffeta skirt of red lace over pink silk and an off-the-shoulder bodice that was designed and custom-made for her by Arnold Scaasi. A large rhinestone necklace was the perfect accent. George wore a sleek black tuxedo—with cowboy boots. The afternoon before the event, Laura put on the dress and went down to the flower shop to show it to Nancy Clarke, who headed up that department, as she had for six administrations, including Barbara's. As Nancy was admiring the gown, George happened by. "What are you up to, Bushie?" he asked his wife, using the nickname they often called each other. She said she was showing the dress off to get some opinions about it. George took her in from head to toe. "*That's* what you're wearing?" he asked. "Really?" Yes, she said. "Well, I think you should wear black," he said. "This is a pretty formal event, you know?" Laura disagreed. "It's Mexico," she said, "and I want to wear something colorful." George shook his head and smiled in a teasing fashion. "Trust me, Bushie. Go with black. I know what I'm talkin' about," he said as he left the room. Nancy Clarke recalled, "Mrs. Bush and I rolled our eyes at each other but didn't say anything. Of course, she wore the hot pink dress and looked gorgeous in it."

The table design in the State Room was created by Nancy Clarke and social secretary Cathy Fenton. The floral displays on each table, along with tapered cream-colored candles in elaborate gold holders, were white hydrangeas, roses, and lilies with limes. Laura decided to go with a gold-and-white color palette, and in that regard made use of the gold-rimmed china that had been commissioned by Hillary Clinton back in 2000.

The menus on the tables were printed in English and Spanish—the first ever bilingual menu at a state dinner—and outlined a meal consisting of Maryland crab and *chorizo pozole,* summer vegetables, pepita-crusted bison, poblano whipped potatoes, fava bean and chanterelle ragout, and a salad of gold and red tomatoes with mâche and microgreens. For dessert was served a mango and coconut ice cream dome topped with peaches and served with a red chili pepper sauce and a tequila sabayon. Executive Pastry Chef Roland Mesnier recalled that his dessert featured "sugar figures of tropical hummingbirds with red breasts and green moiré plumage."

As the 130 guests—including Clint Eastwood and Plácido Domingo, both favorites of Laura's—enjoyed their meal, Adela Gonzalez and Maria Galvan had dinner in the private kitchen. The next day, Adair told Adela, "I wish you had been there. You missed such a fantastic meal. Let me tell you what we ate." Adela laughed and said, "I know exactly what you ate because Maria snuck heaping helpings of each course into the kitchen for us. So we ate what you ate."

It had all been a little more sophisticated than what Laura ordinarily liked, but since it was her first state dinner she compromised some of her culinary tastes. Still, she had preapproved each dish during a series of tastings—customary for Presidents and First Ladies prior to such events. Over several evenings back in July, White House chef Walter Scheib sent sample courses up to the President's Dining Room, where George and Laura indulged. Then he would go to them for their feedback. Sometimes his ideas worked, sometimes they didn't. For this state dinner menu, for instance, he had intended on a blue cheese and bacon salad with a fried filled-and-rolled corn tortilla; he tried to cater the menu to what he'd heard was President Fox's taste. However, Laura felt the cheese was too pungent, and she didn't like the consistency of the tortilla. She was happy with the crab stew, though. Meanwhile, George liked the bison he sampled. Step by step, the menu was created.

In the years to come, Walter Scheib would be struck by just how different Laura was from the previous First Lady he had served, Hillary Clinton. Laura's tastes were simpler. In addition to the Tex-Mex foods she enjoyed, she would very often ask for chicken pot pie and buttermilk biscuits, or roasted beets—she would have had beets for every meal if possible. There was also a minted fresh pea soup she favored which she started wanting to have served at almost every function; Scheib eventually suggested that maybe they should cut back on the pea soup before guests got tired of it. In terms of desserts, Laura hated the idea of strawberries dipped in chocolate, feeling there was nothing creative or interesting about it. She told Roland Mesnier that as long as she and George were in office, she never wanted to see a single chocolate strawberry, "so please just think of something, anything, else." He did: pears poached in grenadine, which she enjoyed.

"Where Mrs. Clinton wanted to see the best of American food and wine and entertaining, Mrs. Bush's mantra was that she wanted to serve food that was 'generous, flavorful, and identifiable,'" recalled Walter Scheib. "She also steered clear of anything that might be perceived as highbrow. I once presented a menu for a special event that featured a twenty-five-year-old balsamic reduction. After reviewing it, she noted on the menu that was returned to me that we could use the reduction, but not the name, which she found pretentious."

In her book *An Invitation to the White House*, Hillary Clinton would refer to Walter Scheib as "a culinary teacher." Laura made it pretty clear from the start, though, that she didn't need any sort of food instruction. "Mrs. Bush had no desire to be taught; her taste was defined and set, and that was how it was going to be," he recalled. "[She] wanted everything we did to have an unpretentious, down-home feeling. Our ambitious picnic menus [under Hillary] were replaced by menus featuring braised green beans, Texas green chili, and hominy casserole and fried catfish. There was a whispered sentiment around Washington that the Texas style the Bushes brought to the White House was a step backward."

Following the state dinner meal, opera star Dawn Upshaw gave a performance in the East Room—the same room in which JFK once lay in state and Richard Nixon gave his resignation speech—followed by dancing in the Grand Foyer. Afterward, everyone adjourned to the Truman Balcony, where Laura and Adair had earlier watched the Presidents arrive and, from there, they enjoyed an incredible twenty-minute fireworks display designed by the famous Zambelli Fireworks company. The bursts of color were so noisy, 911 lines lit up all over the city from people who thought the White House was under attack, ironic considering the national tragedy about to unfold in just six more days.

For the next week, Adela Gonzalez had free rein over most of the White House, with Maria Galvan as her guide. "It was a surreal time I will never forget," she concluded. "Then, on the morning of September 10, we kissed Laura goodbye, and Adair and I left Washington thinking, wow . . . did all of that just happen?"

For her part, the new First Lady felt satisfied by her first state dinner; it had gone as planned, and having a good friend from Texas present made it all the more relaxing and fun for her. She later remarked that it was "in a lot of ways, the culmination of what I thought it would be like to be the wife of the president, to live in the White House." Little did she know that this early, happy experience in the White House would be the last of its kind for quite some time because, truly, everything was about to change.

9/11

George W. Bush's presidency would be completely shaped by the terrorist attack on New York and Washington on September 11, 2001, and then by the subsequent resulting conflicts in Afghanistan and Iraq.

On September 11, Laura Bush was scheduled to give a speech at the Capitol before the Senate Education Committee. She had been invited to do so by Senator Edward "Ted" Kennedy of Massachusetts. She'd be only the fourth First Lady to ever testify before Congress. After her speech at the Capitol, Laura and Ted were scheduled to host the members of Congress and their families for the annual congressional picnic.

Laura's in-laws had spent the night at the White House in the Queens' Bedroom. They were scheduled to leave early to fly to St. Paul, Minnesota, where both were to give speeches. Then they were set to go to Texas for the kickoff of the new Houston Texans football team. Laura barely saw them when they arrived. She was always amazed at how hectic things could be at the White House. Barbara and George had dinner elsewhere with friends and retired for the night. The next morning, Laura made it a point to have breakfast with them before they left for their trip. When a functionary told her that her day was too tight for an unscheduled breakfast, she said, "No. You make time for family. That's what we do." By the time the Bushes left that day, their son was also gone; the President was visiting the Emma E. Booker

Elementary School in Sarasota, Florida, in an appearance relating to his education platform.

Laura raced out of the White House to her car that morning with her chief of staff, Andi Ball, and Bush's domestic policy adviser, Margaret Spellings. As they walked, her Secret Service agent, Ron Sprinkle, whispered in Laura's ear upsetting news: A plane had just smashed into a tower in Manhattan. She was alarmed, thinking it was probably a small jet accident that would likely result in casualties. "What a shame," she said. "Those poor people." It was while driving to the Capitol that she and her agent heard that the North Tower had been hit first, followed by the other tower. By the time they got to the Capitol, just a two-mile drive, the whole world had changed around them.

Ted Kennedy was in his office with the television blaring in the background and the tragedy unfolding during a live broadcast when they arrived. He attempted to regale Laura with stories about his mother, his youth, and his brothers, talking about Kennedy family lore, seeming completely oblivious to what was being reported on the news. While he spoke, Laura looked over his shoulder in horror at the white plumes of smoke billowing from the towers. All she wanted to do was to tell Kennedy to stop talking for just five minutes so she could figure out exactly what was going on. "I felt my skin start to crawl," she recalled. She would later wonder if maybe Kennedy simply couldn't cope with another tragedy given his life's story and was doing everything he could to avoid acknowledging the truth of what was going on in Manhattan. Finally, when President Bush came on the screen, Laura raised her hand to silence Ted. They then watched as George made a brief statement. A few minutes later, they heard the terribly shocking news that a plane had hit the Pentagon. What was going on?

All Laura wanted was to get back to the White House as soon as possible. As she and her staff were walking as quickly as their feet could take them to their car, Ron Sprinkle got a call on his walkie-talkie. Change of plans. Laura needed to get down to the basement immediately. She and her team and the agent then raced down the hall and down a dark staircase to the bottom level. Everyone was in an absolute panic. No one knew what was happening, only that this day was turning out to be the stuff of nightmares.

By this time, Laura's Secret Service detail was joined by a SWAT team and, with guns drawn, they hurriedly pushed the panicked First Lady along to an underground entrance and then practically shoved her into a car waiting for her there along with the rest of her motorcade. Off they went—red and blue lights flashing, sirens blaring, walkie-talkies crackling—not to the White House, which had, by this time, been evacuated, but to the nearby Secret Service headquarters, which would be entered via another underground entrance. Once there, they put Laura in the basement in a small conference room with blank walls and no windows. It was there that she would have a chance to watch news broadcasts and realize the full extent of the unfolding terror. "I watched the replay as the South Tower of the World Trade Center roared with sound and then collapsed into a silent gray plume, offering my personal prayer to God to receive the victims with open arms," she recalled. "The North Tower had given way, live in front of my eyes, sending some 1,500 souls and 110 stories of gypsum and concrete buckling to the ground."

Laura immediately telephoned her daughters—Jenna at the University of Texas and Barbara at Yale—both of whom had already been taken to secure locations by the Secret Service. She called her mother to make sure she was okay. Getting in touch with George was impossible, given the pandemonium—he was on Air Force One, heading for Washington—but she kept trying. She couldn't believe despite all the technology available to the government, it took her three tries before she finally reached the President in the air on a secured line. George was shaken and wanted to make sure his wife was safe. He wanted to return to Washington immediately, but everyone agreed it wasn't safe and he'd have to make several stops along the way to wait out the time.

Once the President finally arrived many hours later at the Secret Service headquarters in Washington, he ran to Laura and pulled her into his arms, holding her close and stroking her hair. Never, he said, had he been so glad to see her, and she felt the same. The Secret Service suggested they take them back to the White House, where the Bushes could spend the night in a basement bunker, but George decided they would sleep in their own room.

Once back at the White House, Laura became worried when she couldn't find Maria Galvan. One of the agents said he thought he saw the house-keeper in the White House theater on the lower level. Laura doubted it. Why would she be watching a movie at a time like this? Eventually the Secret Service located her; she was fine and staying with someone from the White House's flower shop on Capitol Hill, a few miles away, because she hadn't been able to get back into the White House.

That night, George Bush addressed the nation to ask for prayers for all who were grieving and whose "worlds have been shattered." He urged "all Americans from every walk of life [to] unite in our resolve for justice and peace. America has stood down enemies before, and we will do so this time. None of us will ever forget this day . . ." Afterward, he and Laura retired to their bedroom, where they would be together for the night, as always.

About a month later, George told a reporter for *Newsweek* that he had been so exhausted that night, he went right to sleep. Laura didn't like the way that sounded. Later she'd have a chance to set the record straight in another interview, if not directly, then in a vague way that at least sounded more appropriate. "I was up at night, I was worried," she said of this dark time in her life. Then, pointing to her husband sitting at her side, she added, "He was too. I knew it."

"You Will Be Remembered, Laura"

By September 22, just eleven days after the national nightmare, Laura Bush had attended funerals and memorial services and had visited victims in hospitals while also making numerous television appearances. George headed a country that was preparing to go to war. Exhausted, she was now at Camp David on a Saturday, finally with a moment to collect her thoughts.

The President was with Laura, too. He'd been uncharacteristically tense, especially in the face of news outlets reporting that, just weeks earlier, he'd completely ignored credible intelligence that a terrorist attack on American soil was all but inevitable. George felt he had let the country down. He had failed America, he believed, and he was determined to never let that happen again.

When they'd landed in Marine One, George was dismayed to see that the landing zone was completely lit up. He complained to CO Mike O'Connor, telling him the lights served to make him and his family targets, "and if you don't shut them off by morning, you'll be running laps around the camp." However, the crew couldn't figure out how to extinguish the lights and ended up just frantically destroying all the connections with wire cutters.

The Bushes weren't alone at Camp David. In addition to their children, George had convened what Laura would later call "a council of war," which included Secretary of State Colin Powell, Secretary of Defense Donald

Rumsfeld, National Security Adviser Condoleezza Rice, Treasury Secretary Paul O'Neill, Attorney General John Ashcroft, FBI director Robert Mueller, as well as a number of generals, all of whom were guarded by at least a dozen Secret Service agents.

On Monday, Laura was scheduled to meet at the White House with some of those whose loved ones had perished on Flight 93. This was the plane that had been hijacked and brought down by al Qaeda terrorists in a field in Shanksville, Pennsylvania. This visit with their grieving families wouldn't be easy, Laura knew, and there'd be dozens more meetings like it in the weeks and months to come, just as emotional, just as gut-wrenching.

On Tuesday, she was scheduled to go to New York and give a speech at Madison Square Garden to three thousand Learning Leaders, volunteers who donate their time to students and schools. Then she would visit an elementary school in Manhattan whose young students had been traumatized by the attacks. After that, she was to visit Engine Company 54 and Ladder Company 4, which had lost fifteen firefighters.

"She is responding to it as all other Americans do," said her press secretary, Noelia Rodriguez. "If you can reach through the media, to help them be comforted and consoled at this time, then that is a tremendous responsibility that she wants to fulfill."

This would be Laura's life for months to come, these kinds of poignant meetings where it would be her job to soothe the heartbroken and buoy the spirits of those whose lives would never be the same. Never had a First Lady carried such a burden, but then again never had anything like September 11 ever happened on our shores. She wanted to talk to Barbara.

Laura hadn't had a chance to talk to her mother-in-law since the catastrophes happened. Barbara and George had left the White House the morning of the eleventh for St. Louis but never made it there. After the attacks, they were grounded in Milwaukee. All planes had been instructed to fly to the nearest airport and stay put until air traffic control felt it safe to clear them for travel. Barbara and George checked into a cheap motel and had dinner that night at an Outback restaurant: "they have good food and the service is fast," Barbara explained. The next morning, they flew to Kennebunkport.

Laura and Barbara spoke on the phone for only about ten minutes, and it was a memorable call. Her mother-in-law told her she had seen many of her speeches on television, and had also seen a recent appearance on Oprah Winfrey's program. "Children take their emotional cues from their parents," Laura had said on that show. "They need a very calm and relaxed atmosphere at home. Of course, we can't explain terrorism. We really can't. It's just a horrible, evil thing, but one good thing out of this is we've seen so much good. Americans are strong. They are very resilient. We see that every single day." Barbara was impressed, not just with that appearance but with all the many news clips she had seen as well. She wasn't often impressed these days. When Barbara saw Laura tell a news anchor that she believed parents should turn off their televisions and focus on family time instead, she thought it was such sound advice and exactly what people needed to hear.

The way Laura managed to keep her composure on every program while talking with such common sense about coping with tragedy really moved Barbara. She knew from her own experience that Americans held Laura to a higher standard than they did most people. She was expected to be brave, courageous, and unshakable. It wasn't easy. But that was the job, and she felt Laura had truly risen to the occasion. "Of course I feel, like everyone does, sadness and anxiety," Laura had said on another show. "I also feel, I know, everything is being done to make sure America is safe. Because I know that, I feel reassured."

"You will be remembered, Laura," Barbara told her when she had a chance to talk to her. "You *deserve* to be remembered."

By the time Laura hung up, she had tears in her eyes. She felt honored and humbled to hear those words coming from a woman whose approval had always meant so much to her. For a time afterward, Laura Bush just sat still, letting Barbara's praise continue to wash over her.

War Games

In October 2001, about a month after the terrible attacks on New York and Washington, President Bush announced the first round of bombs and missile strikes against Afghanistan. Sixteen months later, in March 2003, he would give Saddam Hussein and his sons a forty-eight-hour deadline to leave Iraq and avoid war. They didn't comply. He later told his staff he was going to kick Hussein's "sorry motherfuckin' ass all over the Mideast."

Two days later, "U.S.-led coalition forces began high-precision bombing strikes on Baghdad," Laura would recall. "Less than twelve hours later, Americans and Iraqis had their first skirmish on the ground. We were at war." This conflict continues to drag on, all these years later.

The two biggest issues of the Bush presidency are the so-called weapons of mass destruction (WMD), which Bush claimed as a primary reason to go to war, and whether Iraq had direct links to al Qaeda. Where WMD are concerned, we now know they didn't exist, despite the fact that in August 2002, Vice President Dick Cheney insisted, "Simply stated, there's no doubt that Saddam Hussein now has weapons of mass destruction."

"I knew the failure to find WMD would transform public perception of the war," George wrote in his book *Decision Points*. "The reality was that I had sent American troops into combat based in large part on intelligence that proved false. . . . No one was more shocked or angry than I was when we didn't find the weapons. I had a sickening feeling every time I thought about it. I still do."

Some believed Bush had delegated too much authority to Cheney, who had been secretary of defense under his father, or that maybe Cheney found a place to exert his own power and then exploited the opportunity. "There was this vacuum for George Bush about his foreign policy, his defense policy," noted the historian Barbara Perry. "He had no ideology in those spaces, so those with strong views obviously saw the opening there, or the vacuum, and they filled it."

Whatever his motivation, Cheney continued to insist on WMD and on links between Hussein and al Qaeda even as evidence mounted to contradict both notions. In addition to putting faith in him on the subject of WMD, Bush just believed him on the issue of the link between Hussein and al Qaeda, too, and continued to act largely based on his assertions, this despite the fact that in 2004, the 9/11 Commission concluded no "collaborative relationship" between Iraq and al Qaeda.

Many people have wondered how much influence President Bush's parents, the former President and First Lady, had on him and on his policies during this most difficult period in his presidency. The historian Jon Meacham, in his excellent book about George H.W., *Destiny and Power,* wrote that the father felt that the son relied too heavily on people like Cheney and Donald Rumsfeld, his secretary of defense. Still, even though he didn't agree with the escalation of conflict, he didn't inject himself in his son's administration.

It's interesting that the personal history between father and son had always been that of W. wanting to please H.W. Not this time, though. Now the son had risen as his own man . . . his own President. Not only was George not concerned about his father's opinion, he felt that H.W. had left unfinished business with the first Gulf War by allowing Saddam Hussein to even survive it. The time had now come to settle things with "shock and awe," and the son believed he was just the President to do it.

Though W.'s father may have backed off, his mother didn't. True to Barbara's nature, whenever she had an opinion, she let her son know it. She completely agreed with her husband that George was being swayed by people in the White House who didn't know what they were doing. Some who had worked in H.W.'s administration—men whom Barbara respected, like former National Security Adviser Brent Scowcroft—had actually tried to talk her son out of going to war, but George didn't want to hear it. "These men know what they're talking about," Barbara told him, but to no avail.

Barbara wasn't a fan of Dick Cheney's. She thought his heart surgery had somehow affected his thinking. He just wasn't the same, she argued. He was angrier and power hungry, and she didn't like it.

One day, she confronted George and let him know how she felt. "I don't approve of any of this," she told him. *"None of it."* She said she was sure that Cheney was behind most of his recent decisions. "Why are you letting this crazy man control you?" she asked. She reminded George that his father, as Vice President, had always been very respectful of President Ronald Reagan. He never would have interfered in policy in the way Cheney was.

George didn't hesitate to put his mother in her place. He told her that all the calls he was making were his own, and that if she took issue with his Vice President then she also took issue with him. He didn't want her to buy into the narrative that he was being manipulated by Cheney or by anyone else. "There's only *one* President," he told her. He was forceful and adamant.

At this point, Barbara likely didn't know what to think. These were her son's calls? Not Cheney's? That revelation only made it worse for her. It now felt to her that his presidency was going off the rails. However, she took his admonition seriously and decided that he was right. She should probably stay out of it.

As always, Laura supported her husband unequivocally. As far as she was concerned, each decision he made under the shadow of terror was the correct one. "It's not easy to govern," she would say, "and people didn't understand the pressure George was under."

"She couldn't have been more calm and resolved, almost placid, which was very reassuring to me," George said of Laura in recalling this difficult time. "I can't imagine what it would be like had Laura been hysterical, highly emotional. Never did she say, 'Get me out of here! What have you done this for? Why are we here? It's your war, see you later.'"

Laura also appreciated it when George's true personality shone through;

the fact that the President was still, at his core, the same ambitious, young man she'd met so many years ago made her smile. However, she didn't like it when he said he was going to catch Osama bin Laden "dead or alive." She mockingly asked him, "Bushie, are gonna *git* him?" Later, she would explain, "I just didn't much care for it." George would be more specific about her criticism. "She didn't want to see me become too bellicose, react with bloodlust. I'll tell you this: she's not a shrinking violet. She doesn't get mad; she gets pointed. If I do something that needs to be toned down, she'll tell me." He later joked of that "dead or alive" line, "Well, at least they understood me in Midland."

There were many times George didn't want to discuss any of what was going on, and she had to draw him out to know what he was thinking. "He would be tired or frustrated or angry, and become incommunicative, especially around all the weapons of mass destruction controversy," said one good friend of Laura's. "She had a way of just not pushing, of letting him come to her when he needed to, and he usually did. It was good that they had a firm foundation to their marriage before they got to the White House, because these were the kinds of challenging times that really tested that relationship. They got through it, though. Laura always took the position that whatever it was would one day pass and, at the end of it, they'd still be together. She tried to keep it all in perspective."

"He did not want to invade Iraq," Laura Bush would write of her husband in her memoir, "but most of the global intelligence community was telling him that, the next time, a 9-11 could happen with chemical or biological weapons. We had been brutally attacked once; he would not allow it to happen again."

Going Undercover for
the Bush Twins

Twenty-one-year-old Barbara Bush was a senior at Yale University listening to a professor drone on and on in class about something she knew wouldn't matter to her in a few weeks' time but was also curriculum she'd need to ace an upcoming exam. When the class was finally dismissed, she walked to the back of the room on her way out and made eye contact with a young, dark-haired student. He was wearing blue jeans, a Yale T-shirt, and flip-flops. When he saw her looking his way, he quickly averted his eyes. *Interesting,* she may have thought; the last time she'd tried to engage him, he did the exact same thing. She made a mental note of it.

Unbeknownst to Barbara, this man in her classroom was no student; he was actually an undercover Secret Service agent named Jonathan Wackrow, and Barbara was his chief protectee. She knew she had Secret Service protection, and she was good at spotting the agents. Usually they were men in suits with walkie-talkies standing outside in the hallway—not men who were undercover in her classroom. This was new.

Back in 1998, when it was becoming clear that many people wanted Barbara's father, George W. Bush, to run for President, one of the reasons he gave for his hesitation was that he didn't want to ruin his daughters' lives. He realized that if he was elected, Barbara and Jenna would be college students during his administration. What would their lives be like in school if they were followed everywhere by Secret Service agents in black suits talking into walkie-talkies? "We were really independent kids, and the thought of Secret Service agents following us all the time was terrifying," Jenna later told *Texas Monthly*. "But when it came right down to it, we thought he should run because he would be a great president. How unbelievably selfish would it have been for us to say, 'Please, Daddy, don't do it because we're nineteen and it might affect our life negatively.'"

After 9/11, security concerns for the twins had to be ramped up. "Barbara and Jenna were then targets of al Qaeda, and we knew it," recalled Jonathan Wackrow. "Because there was a lot of intelligence being generated at the time about it, we had to take it very seriously. The global threat environment had changed dramatically after 9/11. It made protecting someone outside the confines of the White House extremely difficult. I always thought it interesting that we put the President and First Lady in the White House on eighteen acres of fortified property, and when they were out in the world they had a regimented schedule all of us knew by heart and were able to follow. Yet their daughters lived completely unstructured lives that were impossible to predict. They wanted pizza at midnight? Fine. We had to figure it out, and most of the time, if we did our job right, they didn't even know we were figuring it out."

"My agents lived a dual life," daughter Barbara Bush recalled, "living mine along with me and also living their own lives when they returned to their wives and husbands and homes during off-duty hours. Yet they would still be debriefed on my every move. They knew if I spent the night out and wasn't coming home until the next morning, and if I made a late-night run to a diner for pizza. I would even bet they knew who my crush was. It could not have been easy for my detail. Most people living under Secret Service protection—dignitaries, presidents, officials, actual *adults*—go to offices and have predictable schedules. I was a college student, so my schedule was about as predictable as the motions of asteroids."

After 9/11, Jonathan Wackrow became part of the undercover team that, for the duration of the Bush administration, protected the Bush daughters, primarily Barbara while she was attending school at Yale but also Jenna when she was in New York City away from her studies at the University of

Texas. Like their parents, the sisters also had the Secret Service agents in businesswear, men and women they would come to know well because of their constant close proximity. Wackrow, though, was one of the undercover agents they didn't know, a person in the crowd wearing plain clothes, blending in and protecting them without their knowledge.

"My job was to integrate into the young Bush women's ecosystem," he recalled, "so, in other words, if they were in a restaurant, I was eating at the table next to them. If they were in a nightclub, I was in the nightclub, too. When Barbara attended class at Yale, I went to class at Yale. I like to joke that I attended Yale for four years, so how come I don't have a degree? I was in my early thirties at the time, so in a college environment with a grad school where students were a little older, I fit in pretty well. But it took a lot of collaboration and coordination to organize this kind of protection with law enforcement entities, in this instance the Yale University police and the New Haven police.

"The whole point was for us to be unobtrusive, to not interrupt their lives," he recalled. "We tried to hide in plain sight. It's a protective model where you're either following or leapfrogging ahead of the protectee, or you're always within eyeshot of her, but you're not obvious.

"For the Bush twins, I had to predict anything that could come up," he recalled. "As well as having my head on a swivel for that horrible shooting incident or explosion or car ramming, I had to also consider the possibility of a medical issue. What if she had a heart attack, or if she fainted or tripped and fell? How would I then immediately respond with the proper medical care? That was as important as an outright attack."

During his time guarding the Bush twins, Jonathan Wackrow says he noticed the special relationship they had with their grandfather. He recalled, "What I saw was George Bush Sr. acting as a father figure during the time his son was so keenly focused on being President. Especially in Barbara's senior year, the former President leveraged his contacts to help her get jobs, but doing it in a way that was as her grandfather and not as a former President. I would take her to various job interviews in New York and the manifest would say that he, the former President, had 'connectivity,' in other words he knew the individual she was seeing and had set up the interview. I wished my grandfather had the ability to do that when I was her age."

After the twins got older, the job of protecting them became even more complex because it took on international dimensions. For instance, Barbara volunteered for almost a year at an AIDS hospital in South Africa. Later she worked in the educational programming division of the Cooper Hewitt Museum in New York. In 2005, Jenna taught at an elementary school in a low-income Washington neighborhood. Then, the next year, inspired by Barbara, she worked as an intern with the Latin American division of UNICEF. A year later, she would write a book, *Ana's Story: A Journey of Hope*, about an HIV-positive teenage mother she had met while volunteering. Both girls were smart and dedicated, despite any scrapes they may have gotten into along the way. Neither has any regrets about those missteps, either, other than the unhappiness they may have caused their parents—and grandmother. "I loved my life," Jenna says today. "I didn't want to be in a cage. I wanted all of the same experiences as everyone else, and the fact that I was criticized for it, that they made jokes about me, well, that came with the territory. It certainly didn't stop me or my sister from living our lives. As for the agents, we liked them. I mean, we really did, the ones we knew, anyway. They had a job to do. We had *lives* to do."

"I wasn't a babysitter," Jonathan Wackrow concluded of his years guarding the Bush daughters. "I wasn't there to give life advice. I wasn't their father. When you're with protectees for as long as I was with Barbara and Jenna, certain assumptions can be made along those lines.

"Once when they were in California, they went skydiving. The First Lady called the detail leader, absolutely furious because he had allowed it. But, no, we're not going to tell the girls, 'Mommy said you can't go skydiving.' There's always a sense from the parents of 'No worries. The Secret Service will keep them out of trouble.' Not my job. They were going to get in trouble; they were young people with minds of their own. My job was to let them live their lives, allow them to make their mistakes within reason, give them the freedom to get into trouble with their folks over their bad decisions . . . and keep them alive in the process."

Rebel Wife

Life had not been easy for Sharon Bush for a number of years. It was actually difficult to remember when she'd last been happy in her marriage to Neil, it had been such a long time ago. The two married in 1980 and, by 2003, had three children: Lauren, Pierce, and Ashley, nineteen, seventeen, and fourteen, respectively. (Lauren would have a successful career as a model.) After his Silverado scandal in 1990 and the subsequent failing of Neil's oil-drilling company, JNB Explorations, his family fell onto hard times, which then became the catalyst for friction in their marriage. Neil went from job to job—a gas exploration company, a cable television news company, a firm that sold oil storage tank covers—making money here and there before each company would inevitably go out of business. He seemed never able to keep his head above water. He continued to blame his father's and now his brother's presidency for his many problems, insisting that he wouldn't be under such scrutiny and subject to such high expectations if not for his family's high profile. He had actually toyed with the idea of politics himself, but after his well-publicized business failures, those aspirations wouldn't amount to much.

Neil, forty-eight, was actually a smart, ambitious person who just seemed in need of a good break and always felt in the shadow of his wealthier male relatives. In a deposition, Sharon would compare him to his brothers

George and Jeb and, in doing so, refer to him as "the weak link." She further explained that she didn't mean she envied George or Jeb, though, "because they were engaged in the public arena to such an extent that they neglected their families." This seems to be true of Jeb, but it's difficult to find evidence to support such an allegation where George is concerned. "I was frustrated that he wasn't home . . . and he wasn't making money," Sharon further stated of Neil. "I said, 'Why can't you figure it out like Marvin has?'" Marvin Bush, who Sharon claimed was "very rich," was the youngest Bush brother and at the time ran a private-equity business in Virginia.

After many years of enduring it, the strain of Neil's marriage to Sharon had reached a breaking point by 2001. He felt like a failure and, apparently, also felt Sharon viewed him as one. Their constant battling had become a real issue in the extended Bush family.

Maybe, considering the tumult, it wasn't surprising that Neil would stray when he became involved with someone named Maria Andrews. Maria, about ten years his wife's junior, was a three-year volunteer in Barbara's literacy foundation office in Houston. She was a gorgeous, dark-haired woman who'd been born in Mexico and grew up in North Carolina. She'd been married since 1988 to a wealthy oil and gas entrepreneur named Robert Andrews, and together they'd built his very profitable business from the ground up. They lived in a sprawling $2.8 million hacienda they'd built, coincidentally, just a few miles from Neil and Sharon.

While Maria and Neil had seen each other around Barbara's office, they didn't actually become acquainted until January 2002 at a fund-raiser for Jeb at the St. Regis Hotel. Apparently, there was an immediate attraction between them. By April, they realized they were in love. In a letter to her, Neil called Maria "a loving, caring, energetic, low maintenance, sexy, passionate, intelligent, level-headed woman." It would appear that Maria did something for Neil that Sharon wasn't able to do: She gave him confidence. She told him he was a powerful man who'd had a few knocks in life but had survived despite them. He was a good father, a good person. She suggested he not try to compete with his brothers, that he find his own way. For Neil, after years of feeling so beaten down by life—and by his wife—Maria was a godsend. He didn't want to take a chance on ever losing her. He wrote to her in

February 2002: "Everyone is sympathetic to my situation. You will melt like butter into our family. The Bush thing is a blessing and a burden for in-laws but your temperament and nature are such that you will have no problem."

Realizing now more than ever that his marriage was irreparably damaged, Neil moved out of the modest four-bedroom home he shared with Sharon in a residential area of Houston and into a small apartment. Sharon was crushed. While she had not been happy with him, they did have three children and she felt that for their sake they should continue to try. She pleaded with him to change his mind and even appealed to mutual friends to get him to do so, but because he seemed happier than he'd been in some time, no one wanted to intervene. Apparently, he was trying to show restraint, though. In later depositions it would be revealed that he and Maria were not intimate until January 2003.

In May 2002, Neil asked Sharon for a divorce in an email he sent while in Dubai working with yet another company, this one called "Ignite! Learning" that specialized in interactive programs for educational purposes. He told her she was a "world class mother" and that "our kids are a reflection of this." However, the fact that she kept harping on his not making enough money coupled with her belief that "Dad's influence will be the magic answer to our financial woes cause me consternation." He wrote that they were "almost out of money" and that he had "lost my patience for being compared to my brothers, for being put down for my inability to make money, and tired of not being loved." He was sure she felt the same way. He also wrote that the answer to her numerous queries as to whether he had "another lover" was no, but that he had made "an emotional (not sexual) connection with another woman," and he was glad he had done so, too.

Agitated, especially by the revelation that he'd met someone else, Sharon went to Barbara for advice. She wasn't exactly helpful. "Well, that's for you and Neilsie to work out," she icily told her, adding, "You talk to your mother, and Neilsie will talk to me."

Later, maybe feeling that her security in the family was being jeopardized by the failing of her marriage—and probably also worried about her talk with the matriarch—Sharon wrote a congenial note to George and Barbara to assure them of her loyalty. She wrote that though this was a terrible time, "I would be remiss if I did not write you both to tell you the deep and abiding respect and gratitude that I have for you. The past 22 years have been the most incredible years as a member of the Bush family, the best years anyone could hope for. I want you to know from me personally that I will uphold the honor and respect associated with the Bush name."

Soon after, Sharon went to Kennebunkport with her three children. It was at that time that she began to more fully realize that her place in the Bush hierarchy had slipped. She was dismayed when none of the family members came to see her at her bungalow or invited her to their homes. The family had already circled wagons around Neil, leaving her on the outside. It hurt. "From the beginning, you had to choose sides," one family member said. "And you didn't choose Sharon's, not unless you wanted to end up in the same boat with her. Sad to say, but that's how it was."

In the weeks and months to come, the slights from the family would mount. It was clearer than ever to Sharon that, with her divorce, she would be going up against Bush power and Bush money and would have no support from any of them. Married for almost twenty-three years to a Bush heir and having borne three of his children, she found this turn of events completely unacceptable. Feeling desperate and alone, she then began to lash out in ways that made her seem unstable. For instance, at one point, she ran into Neil and Maria in a restaurant. She lost it. She called Maria terrible names, screaming at her that she was a "Mexican whore" and "Mexican trash." She asked her, "How do you sleep at night, breaking up a family?" It was awful, and Sharon would say she later regretted it. When Barbara heard about it, she was shocked. She couldn't believe Sharon would act that way; it seemed so out of character. She spent a lot of time trying to find a rational explanation for an irrational act, and finally decided there was no way to comprehend any of it. Rather than reach out to her, though, Barbara continued to keep her distance and just hope Neil would find a way to deal with her.

On August 26, 2002, Neil filed for divorce from Sharon, and Maria also filed to dissolve her marriage to Robert. Soon after came a lurid revelation in a deposition that Neil sometimes, while married to Sharon, had sex with strangers during business trips in Taiwan and Hong Kong; "whatever happened,

happened," he said. It seems obvious that these women were prostitutes, though Neil said he didn't pay them and they didn't ask for money. He also said he soon hoped to be paid $2 million for acting as a consultant to Grace Semiconductor Manufacturing Corp., cofounded by the son of Jiang Zemin (the general secretary of the Communist Party of China). This was even though he admitted he had no educational background whatsoever in semiconductors. In the end, he didn't get the money, but still, it sounded like he tried to make a deal based more on his brother's presidency than his own experience. These revelations made headlines. Barbara blamed Sharon, not Neil, reasoning that had it not been for her fighting Neil tooth and nail, none of these disclosures would have been made. Also, in light of these stories, she and George had become worried about how it might impact the President and First Lady.

At the first divorce mediation, Sharon was offered a paltry thousand dollars a month in alimony, plus 75 percent of all cash and liquid assets, worth approximately $500,000, plus residency in the couple's house. She would also be given 75 percent of the proceeds of the sale of the home, which was projected to sell for at least $850,000.

A thousand dollars a month? The Bushes were wealthy beyond all reason, and everyone knew it. Maybe Neil didn't have the money, but *someone* did. After being married for more than two decades to one of the members of the Bush dynasty and bearing three children for whom she'd been the primary caregiver since Neil had often been off trying to make a buck, Sharon knew she had to start getting serious about taking care of herself.

Pressure Tactic

In the spring of 2003, an associate of Sharon Bush's contacted Lou Cola-suonno, a publicist with the small boutique firm called West Hills Partners in Manhattan. He was also a former editor in chief of the *New York Post* and the *Daily News*. "I basically got a cold call saying, look, Sharon Bush is having big-time trouble with the Bush family because she's now in the midst of a gnarly divorce from Neil," he recalled. "She would like a little help with her image and maybe a public relations campaign to help in her divorce."

Colasuonno flew from New York to Houston to meet with Sharon in the office of her attorney. Sharon was still just as blond and beautiful as ever, a diminutive woman of fifty with large and luminous blue eyes and, as Colasuonno would soon learn, an oversized personality. Lou was present for about five minutes when Sharon angrily blurted out, "The Bush family is trying to screw me. And Neil's threatening to throw me out and give me nothing. And he's now with a Mexican woman. And her kid? It's Neil's!"

Colasuonno was completely thrown. He regarded her with astonishment for a second or two and said, "Mrs. Bush, I don't really know you. But the first thing I can tell you is that if you go around town making these kinds of statements, that's going to be a problem."

Sharon calmed down; she seemed to appreciate the good advice. She was overwhelmed and emotional, as Colasuonno could well see. She then

J. Randy Taraborrelli

played a tape of a conversation with Barbara she'd apparently recorded surreptitiously. Colasuonno figured Sharon thought it would make Barbara sound heartless, but he felt it just made Sharon look bad. "My husband and I have done everything we could for the children," said Barbara on the tape. "Neil's a grown-up. It's between you. You're two adults."

Colasuonno arranged for Sharon to meet with the popular biographer Kitty Kelley, who happened to be writing a book at that time on the Bush family, scheduled to be released in about a year. "I figured if Sharon had half a brain and room-temperature IQ she would have seen a lot of stuff and would have some pretty good stories about the Bushes," the publicist recalled. "So I arranged a lunch at a restaurant on the West Side of Manhattan for her, Kitty, and me." The PR flack thought that if the Bushes heard that Sharon had met with Kelley and maybe were also told that she was writing a book of her own, this information would encourage Neil into a better settlement.

"Kitty, of course, being Kitty, could make a pet rock talk," Colasuonno recalled of their meal together in April 2003. "Sharon loved her. She blabbed on and on about the family and even said that W. had snorted cocaine at Camp David while the old man was President. I almost fell off my chair when she said it. When the book was finally published [in September 2004], Sharon completely recanted that story. But I was sitting right there with her when she said it. I don't know if it's true or not, but I do know that's what she said."

The next day, Lou Colasuonno helped source a lengthy article about Sharon in *The New York Observer*—"W.'s Sister-in-Law Schleps Tell-All About First Family"—which just so happened to be the day of the second divorce mediation. "In her book, sources said, Ms. Bush hopes to show that Barbara Bush has exercised a good deal more control over the family than previously revealed," claimed the article. It also gave details of Sharon's lunch with Kitty and the hope that she would provide information for her book. After it was published, Neil suddenly offered a substantially better settlement. Now she would receive $2,500 a month in alimony, and for the next four years $1,500 a month in child support, plus 75 percent of the proceeds from the sale of the house and 50 percent of any stocks and other property.

"If there was ever a cause-and-effect situation," said Lou Colasuonno, "I would say this was it."

It wasn't much considering the family's wealth. However, Sharon realized it was probably the best she could do. Still, it seemed unfair and she wasn't happy about it.

Sharon's Appeals Fall on Deaf Ears

Barbara and George worried about how the bad publicity relating to Neil and Sharon might affect their son the President and the First Lady. Family values had always been a platform of the Bush administrations, and Sharon made sure to question those principles in every interview. How could anyone argue with her, though? The family had been touting such principles going all the way back to Dorothy Bush, and here was one of their own at odds with everyone else, and she was raising three Bush children. It was difficult to escape the notion that something could have been done for her to prevent this public airing of dirty laundry.

Sharon felt she had always had a good relationship with her famous sisters-in-law and their husbands. After all, they were family and had been for more than twenty years. There had been a history of births, weddings, divorces, and wins and losses, all of which meant the world to her. She hoped her relatives felt the same way. Therefore, she sat down and wrote to Laura and George, telling them that she still believed in "the family values that you both, Jeb and Columba, Bar and Gampy preached to the masses." Therefore, she didn't believe "that children should grow up in a divorced home." She said she'd lived "a straitlaced life and been a devoted wife and mother. Now I reach out to you to support me and my children as I am scheduled to go to trial in April. . . . Never in my wildest dreams, after

22 years of marriage, would I ever have believed that I had to fight for my dignity and financial stability."

The President was immediately clear that he and Laura shouldn't respond. However, Laura liked Sharon very much and thought maybe a private note from her would be appropriate. The concern though was how could she be sure Sharon would keep the note confidential and not somehow use it to her advantage? In the end, though, she decided George was probably right; they did not respond.

Sharon also wrote to Jeb, though not Columba. She wrote that she remembered how much he appreciated "the help I gave you with Columba when you had some very rough times in your marriage. I remember your thankfulness and appreciation towards me when I took the time to spend with Columba in Maine—getting her out of the bedroom—taking her on walks and even getting her into the swimming pool when she was embarrassed about the jewelry incident at customs." She said she loved Columba and was "happy to do that for my sister and brother in law of 22 years. I have to tell you," she added, "how disappointed I am in you and your family."

Jeb, too, decided not to respond.

Sharon's divorce from Neil was finalized on April 28, 2003. Shortly after, Sharon sent an email to George H.W. asking him to lend her $467,000 so that she could pay off the balance of the house she and Neil owned on Memorial Drive in Houston. She was living in it as per their divorce agreement. She said she believed the property, valued at a little over $800,000, would appreciate in the next few years to more than $1.5 million. At that point, she said, she'd sell it, repay the loan, and split the balance with her former father-in-law. Barbara and George both knew Sharon had a stringent divorce arrangement with Neil that she could sell the house to the highest bidder and split the proceeds with him. However, that bidder was not supposed to be her, and the proceeds were not to be split with his father. "She thinks she's being slick," Barbara said, "but this is not smart, dragging us into her problems again."

She felt that Sharon's request was just another example of her trying to maneuver things behind the scenes to her advantage. She and George had given Neil and Sharon money in the past. They'd given them about half a million dollars a number of years ago to bail them out of a tight spot. Neil couldn't pay it back, and they didn't expect him to, but they were also not inclined to give him or his ex-wife any more. As a rule, George and Barbara usually did not dole out money, no matter the problem. Regarding Sharon's missive, Barbara thought they shouldn't even respond to it. More specifically, she was afraid to respond to it. She suggested to George that they send it on to Neil and stay out of the line of fire. George disagreed, but only in the respect that he felt it would cause more hard feelings if he didn't respond. Barbara said she felt things couldn't get much worse, and maybe she was right.

Barbara felt it best that George not respond to Sharon's email. Barbara was trying to get past her anger, but it was tough for her. Her daughter-in-law was a formidable and persuasive woman, she reasoned. Why couldn't she just find a way to move on, or at the very least keep her private business to herself?

"But she's just trying to *survive,*" Columba told one relative of her sister-in-law. "I'm not sure Bar understands what that's like. I'm not sure *anyone* in the family understands what that's like." Maybe Columba was thinking about her own mother, Josefina, and what it took for her to extricate herself from her marriage, how much strength it took for her to find her way forward. How had they all allowed Sharon to slip through the cracks? None of it made sense to her, but with the battle lines drawn as they were, apparently even she didn't feel comfortable reaching out to Sharon.

In the end, George and Barbara collaborated on a letter to Sharon, which was signed by George. First off, the letter said that George would not enter into a deal with her without Neil's approval, especially if it differentiated from their divorce agreement. He felt she should sell the house, he wrote, and purchase a cheaper one with the proceeds: "Several people I know have bought 3–4 bedroom houses at a cost of less than $300,000," he noted.

Then he (and Barbara) wrote that he understood how difficult the divorce had been for her, but it was time for her to buck up and get on with her life. She needed to find a job, he wrote, and "close the unhappy chapter with Neil." This was easier said than done, he admitted, but, "Often, lacking tons of money, people have to start over to find true happiness." He was certain, he wrote, that the children would be happy in a new home she could afford, and that she would "give the kids, in the future as you have in the past, all the love you can muster." He closed by saying, "Barbara and I will always be there for them should some special need arise. Sharon, I really hope your life ahead is full of happiness—I really do."

When Sharon considered how much money the Bushes had, this note had to have been difficult for her to accept. However, she also must have known that Barbara and George firmly believed that their money was their money, not Neil's, and certainly not hers.

Sharon would later find another way to get the money for the house, from "a friend," she would say, though she was never specific. However, she wasn't yet done in her quest for justice. She was now determined to prove that Maria's two-year-old son, Alexander, had been fathered by Neil and not by Maria's former husband, Robert. If she could do so, it might give her some leverage to go back to the well for a better settlement because she would have proven that Neil had been unfaithful to her before they were officially separated. Dragging an infant into the fray and arguing that the man who says he's his father isn't just so she could get more money? This was hardball, and she had to know it.

Sharon, acting even more desperate than she'd been before her settlement, met with a friend of Maria's and gave her a handful of Q-tips and asked her to swab the child's mouth in order to collect DNA that could be tested. This friend refused to do so and told Maria and Neil about it. Sharon later said she regretted the request, but felt the legal system would let her down in regard to the test. At some point, she plucked some of Neil's hair while he was helping their daughter with her homework. She would later say that the sample wasn't for any DNA test, but rather so that she could have it tested to learn if Neil was doing cocaine. (The cocaine test came back inconclusive.)

In September 2003, Robert Andrews sued Sharon for defamation, insisting that he had fathered Alexander and she had no right to tell people otherwise. He was asking for damages in the amount of $850,000.

The stress took a toll on Barbara, who woke up one morning with chest pains. She was alarmed, as was her housekeeper, Paula. Her blood pressure was sky-high, and the doctor asked if she'd been under any unusual stress.

She said she hadn't been, but George disagreed. He felt the problems with Sharon had really affected his seventy-eight-year-old wife. He told Paula that Barbara cared for Sharon a lot more than she let on, and that she was also stunned by Sharon's request for a DNA test for little Alexander. Barbara didn't know how she would ever look the boy's mother in the eye again and thought that Sharon's actions had reflected poorly on the entire family. "We're better than that," she said.

In January 2004, a judge ruled that the DNA of Robert, Neil, and Alexander was allowed to be tested. In the end, it would turn out that the boy was Robert's, not Neil's. Though Robert's suit against Sharon was eventually dismissed, the damage done by this time was incalculable.

That same month—January—Sharon saw Barbara at a party celebrating the opening of Super Bowl week. Sharon was with her daughters, Lauren and Ashley. They ran to embrace their Ganny; she hugged them both tightly with tears in her eyes, delighted to see them. Sharon stood off to the side. When she caught Barbara's eye, a smile flitted across her face, her eyes sparkled a little, and Sharon asked very sweetly, "Remember me?" Barbara's demeanor so immediately cooled, it could have chilled the air around her. With hard eyes, she met Sharon's gaze directly. "Yes, Sharon," she said. *"I've been reading your depositions."*

Neil Bush and Maria Andrews finally wed on March 6, 2004. "We love Maria," George H. W. Bush said of his new daughter-in-law as Barbara looked on, smiling. "This is a very happy day in the Bush family."

In time, Sharon Bush would do what Bush women always somehow managed to do: She would figure out a way to survive, and, in her case, it would be thanks to product endorsements and other work. She is also the development director for Cristo Rey Brooklyn, a high school that focuses on assisting disadvantaged children. In taking back the reins of her life, she would also get past her anger, which she felt she had to do not only for herself but for her children.

On November 30, 2019, Sharon married financier Bob Murray in New York.

PART EIGHTEEN

Passages

Other Sides of Laura

In April 2004, the time had come to move Laura's mother, Jenna Welch, into an assisted living facility in Texas. She would turn eighty-five in July and had slowed down a lot in the last couple of years. She was still generally healthy though showing signs of cognitive decline. She and Laura remained incredibly close, and Jenna was well loved by everyone in the family, especially by her granddaughters, Jenna and Barbara. Laura took great pains to make sure her mother was involved in every aspect of the relocation and used the time it took to box up a lifetime of memories as an opportunity to further bond with her. She knew that these moments would be the stuff of memories in years to come, and she wanted to make the best of them.

Jenna was content in her new, small apartment. "She'd always been the kind of woman to find satisfaction in whatever circumstance she found herself," said Ethan Marshall. "I was with Laura once and some other friends were going on about their mothers and how disgruntled they always were with every little thing. Someone said, 'Oh, you know what that's like, don't you, Laura?' And she said, 'Well, actually, I don't. My mother's a tough Texan like me, and we don't complain.'"

"Jenna's being in the retirement center was actually a little bit difficult," recalled her and Laura's friend Adair Margo. "I think what made it worse is that at first they had a lot of mother-daughter gatherings there, but soon the mothers started passing away and all that was left was just Jenna. Laura would go to visit and it would be hard to see her all alone. But she would always go, always. She would try to keep her spirits up."

At this same time, Laura's daughters, Jenna and Barbara, both graduated from college. First there was a celebration dinner in Austin, attended by their grandmother, as well as Regan and her husband, Billy Gammon—yes, Laura's old friends from Midland, still a big part of her life. The next night was the celebration for Barbara in New Haven at a party hosted by George's good friend and former Yale classmate Dean Richard Brodhead.

Both daughters wanted nothing more than to campaign for their father when the big push for his second term began. This would be their first time on the trail with their parents, and they'd enjoy every second of it. They were effective, too, well-spoken and persuasive about the father they adored without reservation. They felt his policies were sound and believed he was constantly misrepresented in the press; he had made some tough decisions regarding the war, they felt, and should be praised, not criticized. On the road, they demonstrated the kind of strength and resiliency that had always been the hallmark of Bush women. There were those times when a cynic would say something critical or unkind about their parents, campaigns being brutal and this one no exception to that rule. Jenna and Barbara would sometimes be offended almost to the point of tears. However, Laura would warn them that to take any of it personally wouldn't do them or their father any good. Politics was no place for sensitivity, she told them.

She knew what she was talking about. Critics had said Laura was "plastic," that she had "no emotions," that she was "subservient to her husband." Before George even took office, *The New York Times* wrote of Laura, "Some historians predict that the first lady she may come to resemble most is Mamie Eisenhower, whose division of labor was simple: 'Ike runs the country and I turn the lamb chops.'" Yes, Mamie had actually made that statement, but she couldn't have turned a lamb chop if her life depended upon it; she had servants who cooked for her. She was actually very effective in running the White House residence, even if she had been in the Oval Office only four times in the eight years of Ike's presidency, and only when she was invited.

Why? Because she said she had no reason to go in there. "People always underestimate first ladies," she said.

Laura once lashed out at an adversarial reporter when he was making assumptions that she had no influence in the White House. "Please don't think you know me," she said testily. It was uncharacteristic of her to be so touchy; the journalist looked at her and smiled as if he thought she was joking. "I'm very serious," she told him. "Are we clear?" When he apologized and said, "I didn't mean to overstep," she said, "Fine. Then don't." She was later sorry she'd been so sharp. "Don't lower yourself," she would always tell her daughters. "You have to rise above it. If not, it'll eat away at you little by little."

Laura had influence when she thought she could make a difference. When Dick Cheney accidentally shot a friend, Harry Whittington, with a shotgun while quail hunting in Texas, Laura thought the White House was stonewalling reporters by not being forthcoming about it. It looked bad to her, and she had her chief of staff, Anita McBride, call Andy Card, George's chief of staff, and tell him that the White House needed to be much more open and answer questions. "This isn't the time to be cagey" was the message Laura passed on. It was received, and Cheney did speak to the press.

Laura would sometimes scour newspapers looking for inaccuracies about her husband that she might clear up, or other misrepresentations she thought might reflect poorly on him. For instance, *The Washington Post* once ran a picture of George standing before the presidential seal giving a speech. The way it was shot, though, only the tips of the eagle's wings were visible behind his head. It actually looked like was wearing horns. Laura had one of George's counselors, Karen Hughes, contact the newspaper's editor to suggest that they be more careful about this sort of thing in the future lest Arabs wanting to paint George as the devil be given ammunition to use for that purpose. She didn't much like it, though, if she was painted as having too much influence on George. When Hungary's *Nepszabadsag* newspaper asked her if she advised him, she said, "Obviously, I'm not his adviser. I'm his wife."

In April 2005, Laura showed the world just a little more of who she was, at least in terms of her sense of humor. When she spoke at the White House Correspondents' Dinner, her speech was a revelation to a lot of people in that it showed a side of her not seen by many other than her close friends. A few highlights:

> *George always says he's "delighted" to come to these press dinners. Baloney. He's usually in bed by now. I'm not kidding. I said to him the other day, "George, if you really want to end tyranny in the world, you're going to have to stay up later."*
>
> *I am married to the President of the United States, and here's our typical evening: nine o'clock, Mr. Excitement here is sound asleep, and I'm watching* Desperate Housewives. . . . *Ladies and gentlemen, I am a desperate housewife. I mean if those women on that show think they're desperate, they ought to be with George.*
>
> *[That] brings me to my mother-in-law. So many mothers today are just not involved in their children's lives. Not a problem with Barbara Bush. People often wonder what my mother-in-law's really like. People think she's a sweet, grandmotherly, Aunt Bea type. She's actually more like Don Corleone.*

The audience loved her. She closed on a serious note:

> *I think when you marry someone, you unconsciously are looking for something in your spouse to help fulfill something in you, and George did that for me. He brought fun and energy into my life and so many other things. George is a very good listener; he's easy to be around; and on top of it all, he's a loving father whose daughters absolutely adore him.*

Her speech was written for her by Landon Parvin, who'd been writing for Presidents and First Ladies for many years. It was the one and only speech he had ever written for Laura. "Bush 43 told me a couple of times that even Putin enjoyed it," he recalled.

"It was the President's idea to have her do this," Parvin said. "Last year, we had gotten a lot of flack for the comic moment where we made light of weapons of mass destruction, so we wanted to do something this year that would be easier to take, and that was Laura.

"I had met with her a number of times in writing the script, tailoring it to her and to what she thought people might find humorous about her marriage. I remember that in the White House residence, near the bedroom, there was an enormous jigsaw puzzle on a table that she and the President had been working on for months in their spare time, and I thought, how interesting is that, the way they still do those kinds of things together?

"She showed me that she has great instincts for comedy. On the way to the venue, I went over it with her and she was cool as a cucumber, not at all nervous. Brad Freeman, one of the Bushes' top supporters and fund-raisers, was in the car with us afterward, and he was going crazy, he loved it so much. She was pleased."

Listening to their mother and keeping their wits about them, the Bush girls would do well on the campaign trail. Good news did come the family's way when Jenna met a campaign aide from Virginia, Henry Hager, who made her very happy. Their quickly blooming relationship was a light, personal relief from what was a tough race between her father and the Democrat, John Kerry, and his running mate, John Edwards, but in the end, George Bush and Dick Cheney won a second term.

Before the inauguration, George and Laura hosted a black-tie dinner to celebrate Barbara and George's wedding anniversary. Sixty years. It seemed incredible. All their family members were present: Jeb and Columba, Marvin and Margaret, Neil and Maria, Doro and Sam, the President—in cowboy boots—and Laura, and most of their now-grown children, Barbara and George's grandchildren. They posed for a memorable family portrait in the Red Room of the White House, everyone in formal gowns and tuxedos, looking for all the world as if they were one of the happiest families in America, and in many ways, maybe they were. They had survived, anyway, and that was really saying something considering some of the more challenging moments that had come their way, both politically and personally.

By this time, George was eighty and Barbara was seventy-nine. Had their marriage been perfect? Obviously not. However, Barbara said that the things she had once worried so much about disappeared with the passing of the years, just as the people who'd once presented such big problems became those whose names she couldn't even remember. "And you look across the table," she said, "and there he is, this man who's been there for all of it and you think, how'd I get so darn lucky?" She adored George Bush more, she said, than she had ever in the past, "and that's a lot, believe me."

Another Four Years

Later that month, in January 2005, George W. Bush was inaugurated for the second time for another four years. In his stirring speech about freedom for all men, he intoned, "America will not pretend that jailed dissidents prefer their chains, or that women welcome humiliation and servitude, or that any human being aspires to live at the mercy of bullies."

It would be during George's second term that Laura would have the opportunity she'd long wanted, which was to go to Afghanistan and see firsthand the dire conditions of women and children there. "Women have been denied access to doctors when they're sick," Laura had said back in November 2001 when she delivered the president's weekly radio address, a first for a First Lady and devoted by Laura to the plight of Afghan women. "Life under the Taliban is so hard and repressive, even small displays of joy are outlawed—children aren't allowed to fly kites; their mothers face beatings for laughing out loud. Women cannot work outside the home, or even leave their homes by themselves."

Her trip to Afghanistan was an incredible, even if sometimes gut-wrenching, experience for Laura, and visiting the President, Hamid Karzai, and his wife, Zeenat, in the presidential palace was something she'd never forget. While there, she had an opportunity to speak to students, to understand their society, and also to thank the troops in Bagram. It was the utter devastation of every place she visited, though, that stuck with her. This was just one of many international trips Laura took during her husband's second term—she later went back twice more. She would also visit the Middle East, India, Pakistan, and Africa, to which her daughter Jenna accompanied her. Laura would be hard-pressed to think of a country she didn't visit during those eight years—seventy-seven in all. Not bad for a girl who once said she never wanted to leave Midland.

Also, that year, the El Paso Community College re-dedicated its library on its Northwest Campus as the Jenna Welch and Laura Bush Community Library. It's in Canutillo, where Jenna grew up. Laura decided to let her mother have all the glory of that dedication, realizing that if she went all eyes would be on her. "Jenna went and she pulled the string to let the canvas down," recalled Adair Margo, who was one of those who'd first discussed the idea with the president of the college, "and when she saw the banner she said, 'Oh my gosh. My name is first.' That was so cute. And I thought, my goodness, all of the big and important global things that happen when a woman is First Lady, how interesting is it that it's these little things that mean the most to a family. I know Laura was delighted that her mother had this honor, just delighted."

In August 2005, Hurricane Katrina hit New Orleans, a category five and one of the deadliest storms of our time. Today many people feel George W. Bush's presidency was irreparably damaged by his response to the tragedy, which, at the time, was judged woefully inadequate by many of his critics. Also, in what would turn out to be a terrible public relations miscalculation, he was photographed looking mournfully out a window on Air Force One at the devastation below. In his book *Decision Points*, he wrote, "That photo of me hovering over the damage suggested I was detached from the suffering on the ground. That was not how I felt. But once that impression was formed, I couldn't change it."

At first, the war had actually helped Bush's approval rating, as often happens with wartime Presidents. But then as it raged on, people began turning against it, especially when it was speculated by some news analysts that the Middle East policies of both Bush 41 and Bush 43 really had more to do with securing the oil in the region and maybe trading military aid for it than with any notion of peace. Rumors about the Bushes and Saudi Arabia—the largest oil exporter in the world with about 25 percent of all known oil reserves—have run rampant for decades.

As a result of Katrina, Bush 43's approval rating plummeted to 50 percent, the lowest of his presidency. Making things worse for him was Kanye West, who felt he was speaking for African Americans when he famously said on a live television fund-raiser, "George Bush doesn't care about black people," referencing those who were disproportionately the storm's victims. George was stung by the comment, as was Laura. He later called it "one of the most disgusting moments of my presidency. He called me a racist. I resent it. It's not true." By 2007, his disapproval rating would increase to 65 percent, making him the second most unpopular president in the history of modern polling, right after President Nixon, who was at 66 percent.

Laura and Barbara both felt George had done the best job he could under the circumstances, and they blamed bureaucratic red tape for most of the Katrina problems. Barbara then made things worse by her commentary in an interview.

"Almost everyone I've talked to says, 'We're going to move to Houston,'" Barbara said when she visited residents of Louisiana who'd been displaced and were now being housed in the Astrodome, in Houston. "What I'm hearing, which is sort of scary, is they all want to stay in Texas. Everyone is so overwhelmed by the hospitality. And so many of the people in the arena here, you know, were underprivileged anyway, so this is working very well for them."

They were underprivileged anyway? This is working very well for them? It was unfortunate. Barbara was widely criticized for being completely out of touch and even heartless. When Barbara expressed concern that the negative attention might somehow further damage her son's already troubled presidency, Laura called her to tell her not to worry about it. However, Barbara was still weighed down with regret, more than Laura had ever seen from her. "It's not what I meant at all," Barbara sorrowfully told her daughter-in-law. "I know, Bar," Laura said. "I know."

Laura felt terrible about it. It was as if no consideration was being given of Barbara's long and invaluable history of service. Even at her advanced age,

Barbara was expected to be eloquent and well-spoken, no matter how she may have felt—if she had a headache, if her eyes hurt, if she hadn't gotten enough sleep or if she simply wasn't at her best. It was a heavy load for her to carry.

Meanwhile, things just kept getting worse. "The ongoing war really took its toll on the family," Marlin Fitzwater, George H. W. Bush's press secretary, said at the time. "There was no end in sight. You had to wonder what 43 could have achieved if not for this war going on in the background the entire time. In January of '07, when he announced some twenty thousand more U.S. troops to Iraq, a lot of people said enough is enough. It looked like there was no way out, though, once we were in."

Nancy Pelosi, the leader of the Democratic Party in the House of Representatives, declared around this time, "Bush is an incompetent leader. In fact, he's not a leader. He's a person who has no judgment, no experience and no knowledge of the subjects that he has decided upon. Not to get personal about it, but the president's capacity to lead has never been there. In order to lead, you have to have judgment. In order to have judgment, you have to have knowledge and experience. He has none." (She would have similar comments to make about President Donald Trump in less than ten years' time.)

It didn't help when the economy sloped dramatically downward. By the time President Bush left office, his approval rating was lower than it had ever been, and much of America was eager to see the back of him.

It lightened the mood at the White House when, on Saturday, March 29, 2008, Laura Bush organized another high school reunion. This was really a full-circle moment for her in that many of her friends from Midland joined her at the White House. For instance, there was Judy Dykes Hester, who had been in the passenger seat when Laura had her car accident in 1963. Also present was Jeanie Pendleton Bohn, the close friend who brought Laura's homework home to her while she was recovering. Regan Gammon was there, Laura's best friend who stood at her bedside and tried to console her that terrible night. Jan O'Neill was there, too, the woman who matched Laura with George at a barbecue at her home; she actually helped Laura organize the reunion. So many of Laura's friends from Midland attended and, as Judy Dykes Hester put it, "After all we'd all been through over the years, to think we were in the White House with Laura, and she was First Lady, well . . . I guess you just never know how life is going to work out, I guess."

There were people at the reunion who did not agree with George's policies relating to the war. Some were downright angry about it. A few tried to engage Laura on that level, but she wouldn't have it. "Maybe you and I can talk about that some other time," she told one old former classmate who seemed to think the invitation to the White House was an invitation to debate the issue of weapons of mass destruction. "Right now, though, we're going to dance. Okay?"

"You all mean so much to me and George," Laura Bush told her friends at the end of the evening, her Texas drawl still so prominent. "Thank you all for coming so many miles just so we could spend this time together."

Another happy occasion occurred on May 10 when Jenna married Harry Hager at the Bush ranch in Texas. Her grandparents Barbara and George were present, as was Jenna Welch. George walked her down the aisle as Laura wiped away tears.

In a few more months, George and Laura would celebrate their thirty-first anniversary on November 5. Where had the time gone? What a wild ride it had been, from Texas to Washington. It was time for a change, though, and the First Couple knew it. They'd given it their all in Washington, and maybe it was enough or maybe it wasn't, but it was all they had. Now they were ready get out of Dodge and give someone else the chance to figure out the world's problems.

Goodbye

In November 2008, forty-seven-year-old Barack Hussein Obama II was elected the forty-forth President of the United States.

Before he left office, President George W. Bush invited every person who worked at the White House, from those in maintenance to the florists, secretaries, butlers, painters, and telephone operators, into the Oval Office for a group photograph. Most of them had never even been in the Oval before, and some had worked in the White House for as many as fifty years. Some were crying as they posed for that picture, they were so overwhelmed by the experience. George and Laura had long thought of these trusted employees as family and, in a way that was so very Texan, wanted them to know they were appreciated.

On his last day in office, the outgoing President and the incoming walked out of the Capitol and down its long flight of stairs, flanked on either side by military men in full uniform; Obama in a red tie, George in blue, both in long black wool coats. They stopped at the foot of the stairs to wave. They were then joined by Laura Bush and Michelle Obama, who had descended the stairs arm in arm, Michelle in a sage-colored wool-lace ensemble with green leather gloves and Laura dressed in creamy white. Then, with Michelle at Barack's left and Laura at George's right, they joined hands and walked toward Marine One, smiling and laughing with one another and looking for all the world like the closest of friends. It had been a long and vicious campaign, as is pretty much always the case. Many of the critical statements that had been made by Obama about Bush had enraged him and Laura. It just seemed like Obama had more criticism for President Bush than he ever did for his opponent, Senator John McCain. Though Laura knew George had been wounded by much of the discourse, she also knew that this was how the game was played.

When they got to the green-and-white chopper, George raised his right hand a little to suggest a firm and hearty handshake in the offing; Obama met his hand in the air and shook it mightily. As their wives looked on, the two men then embraced. It's what America is really about in these historic moments, a smooth transfer of power, which, no matter how bitter the road taken to get there is a destination that matters more than anything else. The two men said a few words to each other as Obama patted Bush on the back.

Laura then embraced Michelle and, as she pulled away, kept her hand on Michelle's shoulder while they spoke. Laura knew what Michelle's life would be like now, and as she would later say, she envied her because, truly, it had been such an honor to serve her country. The last eight years had been filled with many unforgettable experiences.

While Michelle and George kissed each other on the cheek and embraced, Laura hugged Barack. Then she walked up the few metal steps to the chopper, followed by George. The Bushes stopped at the top of the stairs and waved to all the onlookers. A few moments later the helicopter rose into the air and, now back at the foot of the Capitol, Barack and Michelle—joined by the new VP, Joe Biden, and his wife, Jill—stood and waved goodbye to the Bushes.

Inside Marine One, accompanying Laura and George, were his parents, ready to take their son and daughter-in-law home, away from Washington and back to a simpler and maybe even happier life in Houston. They had done their best, two generations of Bush men and their wives, each with a story to tell unique in and of itself but threaded by a common theme: White House ambitions, and all the political machinations it took for them to get there were fleeting. Who they were to one another in their marriages and with their families and the choices they'd made in their personal lives were what mattered. In the end, what makes the story of the Bushes so compelling is the family's adherence to those values. It was always the women, though, who made sure no one ever lost touch with what was really important.

Trump Versus Bush

September 16, 2015. Seven years had passed since George Bush had left the White House. Now his brother Jeb would make a run for the top job.

Columba Bush was standing in a backstage area of the Air Force One Pavilion of the Ronald Reagan Presidential Library in Southern California's Simi Valley, site of the second debate of Republican presidential aspirants. While surrounded by an intense huddle of her husband's campaign workers, she fanned herself with a waving hand and complained about the temperature. She wondered if it was purposely being kept warm so that the candidates would appear to be sweating, which would certainly make for dramatic television. Her husband, Jeb, had just confronted Donald Trump, the New York real estate developer and reality television show host, on a number of cultural and political issues, including immigration. It had been clear from the constant expression of consternation on Jeb's face that the entrepreneur had pretty much walked all over him. "But he doesn't have any *facts*," a frustrated Columba vented to one of her husband's staffers about Trump. "I don't know what he has, or why people like him." She was angry and didn't seem to care who knew it. "He's mean. He's ugly. He's awful," she concluded, "and the way he acts, well, Bushes have never acted that way."

During the heated debate, Trump had been asked about an earlier retweet of his comment suggesting that because Columba hailed from Mexico, Jeb had a "soft spot" for that country, one that tended to weaken his immigration policies. At that, Jeb took umbrage. "To subject my wife into the middle of a raucous political conversation was completely inappropriate and I hope you apologize to her for that, Donald," he said.

Though Trump conceded that Columba, who Jeb announced was in the audience, was "a lovely woman," he said he wouldn't apologize to her, "because I did nothing wrong."

Jeb continued, "So here's the deal. My wife is a Mexican American. She's an American by choice. She loves this country as much as anybody in this room. And she wants a secure border. But she wants to embrace the traditional American values that make us special and make us unique. We're at a crossroads right now. Are we going to take the Reagan approach, the hopeful optimistic approach, the approach that says you come to our country legally, you pursue your dreams with a vengeance, you create opportunities for all of us? Or the Donald Trump approach that says that everything is bad, everything is coming to an end."

Trump countered with, "Jeb says that they [immigrants] are coming into our country as an act of love. With all of the problems we have, the people coming in, this is not an act of love."

What Jeb had said, back in April—and maybe with Columba's father in mind—was: "The dad who loved their children, was worried that their children didn't have food on the table and they wanted to make sure their family was intact, he crossed the border because he had no other means to work to be able to provide for his family. Yes, they broke the law, but it's not a felony. It's an act of love. It's an act of commitment to your family." The fact that Trump saw it differently and wanted to make an issue of it at the debate spoke loudly to the differences in the candidates' views on immigration, and also to Trump's eagerness to keep the conservative base fired up over this long-controversial issue.

Earlier, Trump had criticized Jeb to Breitbart News for speaking in Spanish on the campaign trial. "He should really set the example by speaking English while in the United States," he said. The topic came up again in the debate, with Trump reiterating that "this is a country where we speak English."

"Unbelievable," Columba said of that comment after the debate; the Bushes had always spoken both languages in their household, and their children, for the most part, learned Spanish before they'd even learned English. "What is wrong with speaking both languages?" Columba asked. "How disappointing is he as a person?"

Donald Trump would remain a thorn in Jeb's and Columba's sides, just as he would in that of everyone else hoping to run for high office during this time. The 2015–2016 presidential cycle was nothing short of the Donald Trump Show with his bold, angry, and often insulting pronouncements. Ultimately, though, it said a lot about the political climate at the time—one in which the loudest voice was the one most paid attention to—that there was no way to ignore him. Somehow, Trump was managing to tap into the wants and needs of a disenfranchised middle America, a large swath of the population who'd expressed disillusionment about "the system" and who believed it would take someone radical, an "outsider," to fix it. Many people began to champion Trump's rabble-rousing, rebellious nature, wanting more of it and believing that America would be the better for it. So much for the "compassionate conservatism" Jeb's brother had campaigned on in 2000 or the "kinder, gentler nation" his father had aspired to back in 1988.

During Bush's 1988 campaign, Donald Trump thought he'd make a good running mate for George H.W. and mentioned as much to Bush's political strategist Lee Atwater. He then sent George a letter and offered to go on the ticket with him as his Vice President. George didn't know what to make of it. Was it a joke? He decided not to validate the suggestion with a response. Now, almost twenty years later, Trump was campaigning for the Republican nomination for President against George's son Jeb and was the front-runner.

How, the Bushes all wondered, had it come to pass that a television star and real estate mogul ended up with so much political power? Or as Laura Bush observed, "Celebrity is a particularly poor model for politics. At the White House, there is no off-season hiatus or a director to yell, 'Cut, that's a wrap.' The demands of not just the nation but of the world are fierce and unrelenting."

On December 15, 2015, in yet another debate, in Las Vegas, Jeb Bush tried to lay down some ground rules. "Donald, you're not going to be able to insult your way to the presidency," he said as Trump pulled a face that suggested, *Oh yeah, wanna bet?* Jeb continued, "That's not going to happen. Leadership is not about attacking people and disparaging people. Leadership is about creating a serious strategy to deal with the threats of our time."

According to sources familiar with the family, when George and Laura called Barbara to ask what she thought of Jeb's performance that night— both of them on the line at the same time—the matriarch was lukewarm about it and said she felt much of what Jeb had to say lacked specificity. Also, there were so many potential candidates—nine in all—she felt he looked a little lost on that stage.

Jeb had been toying with the idea of running for President for at least ten years. People in the Bush family and in its orbit had long thought he, not his brother George, should have been the first to run for high office. While Jeb always seemed more serious than George, what he didn't have was George's charisma and energy. Jeb's always had a laid-back style that now seemed completely out of place in a Republican Party that had been all but hijacked by Donald Trump. Jeb was serious and levelheaded, not hot-tempered and not bombastic, like Trump, who gave him the mocking nickname "Low Energy Jeb."

It wasn't just a Trump problem, though. Jeb also seemed to pale in comparison to some of the other candidates, like Ted Cruz, Marco Rubio, Chris Christie, and Carly Fiorina. In the end, Barbara said she just wanted Jeb out of the race. She felt that enough Bush family members had been President— two was enough for her, apparently—and some other family should have the chance to put forth one of its best. "We had our time," she said. "Enough." Mostly, though, she was revolted by the idea of her statesman son being used as a punching bag for someone like Donald Trump, a man with no political experience who, as she put it, "sounds to me like he's never even read a book."

After Barbara did a couple of television interviews and voiced her opinion that Jeb should back off, he was very upset with her. "What the hell is going on?" he asked her. Mother and son then had a couple of heated telephone conversations about it. He needed her support, he said, not her discouragement. It was embarrassing, he told her, to have the still-popular and beloved Bush matriarch speaking out against his campaign. Barbara said she would stop. After that, she did try to be more publicly supportive. However, she couldn't shake the instinct that it just wasn't Jeb's moment. She could so clearly see what was going on, not only with the Republican Party but with the country as a whole, and realized that, as much as she disliked him and wished he'd just go away, Donald Trump was here to stay. Plus, she felt Jeb would just inherit all his father's and brother's enemies. She didn't want that for her son.

Columba was also slow to come to terms with Jeb's wanting to be President. It wasn't something she would ever have wanted, especially after leaving the Florida governor's mansion for a quieter life in 2007. When asked if she and Jeb discussed policy, she said, "Never. We talk about our daughter and sons and cats and dogs and silly things." She would sacrifice her freedom and privacy and go out of her comfort zone for Jeb if being President was truly what he wanted. How could she stand in his way? She eventually agreed to it, but only if he promised to spend time every week with her, their children, and their grandchildren, the all-too-familiar demand made by Bush women over the years who were worried about the impact of politics on their families.

Laura felt sure Columba, who would be the first Latina First Lady, and only the second one born in a foreign country, could rise to the challenge of once again campaigning for her husband. "I did give her advice," she told CNN's Alisyn Camerota. It was the same advice Barbara had given Columba years earlier: "I told her she should get a really good speech and give it. She could do it in English and Spanish. I think that's a huge advantage for her and could be a huge asset for the Republican Party to reach out to Hispanics in our country. And she'll be great. She's shy but I think she'll be a really wonderful asset to Jeb. She doesn't like the spotlight particularly, but I have to say, I didn't either. I got used to it."

During the campaign, there was a bit of drama about Columba's extravagant shopping taste. *The Washington Post* revealed that she once took out loans to purchase almost $100,000 worth of jewels at a Florida jewelry store, including two pairs of diamond stud earrings set in platinum, an eighteen-karat white gold and diamond Bulgari bracelet, and an eighteen-karat white gold and diamond necklace. Columba and Jeb made no public statement about the report.

The Washington Post exposé on Columba didn't make much of a dent. It was full steam ahead for Jeb and Columba, just as had been the case many times over the years for Bushes on the campaign trail.

In February 2016, after Jeb Bush lost the Iowa caucus and it didn't look good for New Hampshire either, he decided to recruit his ninety-year-old mother. Previously, he didn't want to invoke his family's legacy. He knew his brother had left office an unpopular President. Some political pundits felt Jeb would have been better served to link himself to his father's presidency, which was now more respected than his brother's. However, not wanting to seem to exploit his family's name, he dropped "Bush" from his campaign posters altogether, using just "Jeb!" Even Donald Trump thought it was a bad idea to drop his last name from the campaign posters. What was probably an even worse idea, though, was trotting out "Mother" for television appearances.

On CBS News, being interviewed by Norah O'Donnell with Jeb at her side, Barbara opined that she thought Jeb had been too soft during the debates. "Why don't you interrupt like the other people do?" she asked him. Jeb looked as embarrassed as a ten-year-old being told to toughen up by his hard-nosed mom after losing a schoolyard brawl.

"But I've gotten better at interrupting, Mom," he protested weakly. "C'mon!"

Unfazed, Barbara continued, "He's so polite. We brought him up that way. And he does not brag like some people we know." When O'Donnell asked, "Who are you talking about?" Barbara answered, "I can't remember." She didn't even want the word "Trump" to roll off her lips. "I'm not getting into a spitting match with him," she said. "He can spit farther than I can." She also observed that Trump was "like a comedian or a showman or something."

In another interview, with CNN in February and again with Jeb at her side, Barbara was asked what she thought of Donald Trump and answered, "I don't think about him at all. I think about Jeb, the *qualified* candidate." She said she was "sick of Trump. He doesn't give any answers as to how he will solve problems. Instead, he makes faces and says insulting things. He's said terrible things about women. I don't understand why people are for him. I'm a woman. I'm not crazy about what he says about women."

The problem with putting Barbara and Jeb side by side was that Barbara came off as the stronger, more effective politician. In a final slap to Jeb, Donald Trump went on the record saying she should have been the one running for President, not her son.

Trumping Jeb

Despite his mother's best efforts, Jeb Bush came in fourth in New Hampshire whereas Donald Trump crushed it. South Carolina was no better, and by the end of February 2016, Jeb realized there was no way forward for him and he would never win the nomination. He therefore reluctantly dropped out of the race.

After Jeb's announcement, Barbara called Columba and told her she was proud of the way she had handled herself during the campaign, always at Jeb's side and never lowering herself to publicly speak out against any of his adversaries. She said she thought she'd make an excellent First Lady, when the time was right.

While Columba was disappointed for Jeb, she also had a lot on her mind at this time with her beloved mother, Josefina, suffering from Alzheimer's. Jeb had confirmed the years-long battle about six months earlier at an event in Portsmouth, New Hampshire. "My mother-in-law has dementia and she's ninety-four years old," he said. "She's a gift from God; she's the most beautiful woman I've ever met. Just totally faith-oriented, just the sweetest, nicest person." Bush had also said several times during his travels that he supported more federal funding for Alzheimer's research.

Columba had insisted that Josefina not be sent to an assisted living facility, preferring that she be able to remain in her own home in Miami, cared for by her and her sister, Lucila. It was not easy, but both daughters felt strongly that it was what their mother deserved. Josefina is still battling the disease as of this writing.

On November 8, 2016, the hope that Donald Trump might be relegated to the past was dashed when he won the presidential election against Democratic candidate Hillary Clinton. Trump had defied all the odds and all the polls, too. Barbara tried to come to terms with the win this way: "He won the Electoral College [306 to 232] but not the popular vote, which he lost by three million. So, that tells you something." She couldn't go too far with that logic, though, since her son hadn't won the popular vote either in 2000; he lost it to Al Gore by 540,000 votes, though he did win the electoral college 271 to 266, which is how he became President.

Trump's victory was disheartening for just about everyone in the Bush family, except for maybe Jeb's eldest son, George P. George P. is today forty-four, has two young sons with his wife, Amanda, and serves as Texas Land Commissioner. A veteran of the war in Afghanistan, he voted for Trump because he thought his policies were in line with the Republican platforms. He had worked hard for his father's campaign, though, as did his younger brother, Jeb Bush Jr., who is now thirty-seven and has two young children with his wife, Sandra. Meanwhile, Jeb's daughter, Noelle, now forty-three and living free of her addiction for a number of years, did not play an active role in the campaign.

On January 20, 2017, Donald John Trump was inaugurated as the forty-fourth President of the United States. His inaugural address was viewed by many as a dystopian view of America, full of dark sentiment that was maybe not so much inspiring as depressing:

[But] for too many of our citizens, a different reality exists: Mothers and children trapped in poverty in our inner cities; rusted-out factories scattered like tombstones across the landscape of our nation; an education system, flush with cash, but which leaves our young and beautiful students deprived of knowledge; and the crime and gangs and drugs

that have stolen too many lives and robbed our country of so much un-
realized potential. This American carnage stops right here and stops
right now.

Trump's supporters said he was merely pointing out the hardships faced
by many Americans. His critics were appalled; why did he have to be so
bleak on a day that was supposed to encouraging? After Trump finished,
George W. Bush leaned over to Hillary Clinton and famously said, "That
was some weird shit." Looking at history, though, Trump's speech echoed
aspects of George's own father's inauguration speech on this exact same day,
January 20, in 1989. On that morning, George H.W. had intoned:

There are the homeless, lost and roaming. There are children who have
nothing, no love, no normalcy. There are those who cannot free them-
selves of enslavement to whatever addiction—drugs, welfare, demoral-
ization that rules the slums. There is crime to be conquered, the rough
crime on the streets.

Perhaps Trump's dark speech was a harbinger of things to come in his
administration: his presidency would be rife with so much controversy
there'd barely be a moment for the country to catch its breath between scan-
dals. In December 2019, he would become just the third President in the
nation's history to be impeached. A sarcastic Laura Bush would privately
observe to one good friend of hers, "Well, *that's* a big surprise, isn't it? Can't
imagine how *that* happened."

After the White House

Today Laura and George Bush live happy and content lives on their Houston estate as well as in their Crawford country home. She remains an advocate for same-sex marriage and *Roe v. Wade*, especially now that she no longer has to be concerned about how to square her personal beliefs with Republican platforms. She strongly opposed President Donald Trump's policy of separating families at the Mexican border, and was vocal about it. "I live in a border state," she wrote in an op-ed for *The Washington Post*. "I appreciate the need to enforce and protect our international boundaries, but this zero-tolerance policy is cruel. It is immoral. And it breaks my heart."

For his part, George stays publicly apolitical these days, enjoys painting with watercolors, and has shown much of his work during television interviews. He put in his time in government, had his victories and also his defeats. While many still disagree with polices put forth while he was President, especially having to do with the country's engagement in a war that continues to rage to this day, he's been admired for the way he's comported himself since leaving office. Many have learned to embrace him. In a rare public statement on current events, in May of 2020, he called on Americans to put aside partisan differences during the onslaught of the Covid-19 pandemic. "Let us remember how small our differences are in the face of this shared threat," he said. "We rise or fall together and we are determined to rise."

In 2010, Laura wrote her autobiography, *Spoken from the Heart*, in which she finally was able to write about the death of her friend Mike Douglas back in 1963. Now the personal history she had held close for so many years was something she would find herself discussing openly in television interviews. No longer shackled by the sadness and pain of that terrible time in her life, she was finally free to be candid about it even if, by her own admission, she would never be free of the guilt it caused her.

Laura's beloved mother, Jenna Welch, died in Midland on May 10, 2019, at the age of ninety-nine. What an incredible life she'd had, always showing courage in the face of adversity and inspiring not only her daughter but her granddaughters as well, not to mention the many friends and relatives who loved her. She rarely had a cruel or judgmental word for anyone, not easy in the world in which she found herself due to her daughter's marriage.

Meanwhile, George and Laura's daughters have continued to thrive. Jenna, thirty-nine, is still married to Henry Hager, and they have three children, Margaret Laura "Mila," born on April 13, 2013; Poppy Louise, born on that same day in 2015; and Henry Harold "Hal," born on August 2, 2019. "Harold comes from my maternal grandfather, Pa," Jenna explained in a statement, "who I loved dearly and [who] was unable to keep a son long enough to name." Like her sister, Barbara, Jenna is not a Republican but rather identifies as nonpartisan. She is presently the co-anchor for the fourth hour of *Today* with Hoda Kotb, replacing Kathie Lee Gifford. She's smart, funny, and outspoken. It's not hard to imagine that if her mother had chosen a career as a talk show host, she would be a lot like Jenna.

Barbara, Jenna's twin, remains a human rights activist and is the co-founder of the successful nonprofit Global Health Corps, which focuses on universal health care. In 2017 she and Jenna wrote a bestselling memoir, *Sisters First: Stories from Our Wild and Wonderful Life*. She has been happily married to screenwriter Craig Coyne since October 7, 2018.

Neither Bush twin is a politician or has any plans in that regard. One does wonder, though, if the Bush political dynasty will continue. Besides Jeb and Columba's son George P., who still holds the position of Texas Land

Commissioner, some have felt the next great hope may be Neil and Sharon's son Pierce Bush, who in 2020 had an unsuccessful run for the Republican nomination in Texas's twenty-second congressional district. Pierce had considered running for the nearby seventh congressional district, represented by his grandfather George H. W. Bush from 1967 to 1971. He decided against it, however, going for the twenty-second district though he didn't live there and was viewed by critics as a carpetbagger. The defeat seems not to have dampened his enthusiasm for politics, though, and he's been quoted as saying he intends to "try again, since that's what we Bushes tend to do." Pierce's father, Neil Bush, is the chairman of the nonprofit Points of Light organization and still married to Maria Andrews.

Columba and Jeb are also still happily married. Some in their circle say that Jeb remains a controlling husband who continues to take issue with Columba's spending. At sixty-seven, Columba now seems just fine with it, though. "Many husbands control the household purse strings," said one of her relatives. "It isn't the big deal people think it is to have one partner take on that responsibility, and the other to learn to live with it." The Bushes seem more content than ever after more than forty-five years of marriage. "They have always adored each other, no matter their issues," said that relative. "There's a bond people may not totally understand, but it's always been there." Maybe she summed up herself and the way she has survived as a Bush wife best when Columba said, "I think in life, most things are not under our control. My life has been like that. I try to enjoy whatever comes."

Barbara Bush's only surviving daughter, Doro, is today sixty-one. She remains a philanthropist and activist and co-chairs the Barbara Bush Foundation for Family Literacy along with her brother Jeb. In 2006 she authored the bestselling book *My Father, My President: A Personal Account of the Life of George H. W. Bush*. She is still married to her second husband, Robert Koch, with whom she has two children, Robert David, twenty-seven, and Georgia "Gigi" Grace, twenty-four. She also has a son and daughter from her first marriage to Billy LeBlond, Sam, thirty-six, and Nancy Ellis, known as "Ellie," thirty-four.

When she wants to feel close to her namesake, her grandmother Dorothy,

Doro retreats to the bungalow, the single-story home on Walker's Point gifted to Dorothy by her father, Bert, on her wedding day to Prescott in 1921. Doro and her family own it today. Her siblings Jeb, Neil, and Marvin also all have homes on Walker's Point. George is the only holdout; he and Laura are happy with their ranch in Crawford.

On Their Own Terms

G od waits until you've experienced all of life's ups and downs, every one of them, before he presents you with your toughest competitor: old age," Dorothy Walker said in 1991 when she was ninety years old. "That's the biggest fight of all," she concluded, "and I will not give up the fight. So help me, I will fight it to the very last moment." In 2016, her daughter-in-law Barbara Bush was also ninety. If only she could have somehow channeled Dorothy's will to live, because by this time, Barbara had all but lost her own fighting spirit. By the end of the year, her health issues had mounted to the point where she was now on portable oxygen most of the time. Her body was wracked with pain. She was suffering terribly from arthritis in her spine, feet, and hands. Her legs also ached all the time. "I just refuse to accept this," she wrote in her diary. "I look at pictures and see a hump back." All she wanted was to just feel better for one day, to have the energy she once had and to not have to focus on a schedule of upcoming doctor's appointments. George was going through the same thing; a form of Parkinson's kept him confined to a wheelchair. He could barely speak. For a man who so loved to communicate and who always had so much to say, this condition was pure torture. "He's trapped in his own body," Barbara said at the time, "and it's the most painful thing to watch."

Somehow, it seemed unfair. Still, Barbara would never ask "Why me?"

Like the great Dorothy before her, it bored her when people complained about their health. "It's horrible to get older and have to listen to others' ailments when yours are so much more interesting," she would say with sarcasm. She also knew she and George had been blessed beyond measure with so many wonderful years together. After all, she'd already lived almost forty years longer than her mother, who had died at just fifty-four. She just always hoped that making it to the finish line wouldn't be so damn hard. She didn't want to get there before George, though. She knew he couldn't bear it, and he felt the same: He didn't want to get there before her, either.

Perhaps it was because of their present circumstances that Barbara felt the need to connect with people from their past, maybe not to say goodbye but just to be in the company of those who'd meant so much to them. One of those was Paula Rendon, who'd worked for the Bushes for more than fifty years as their housekeeper. Certainly Paula had seen it all—the good times and bad—and few people meant as much to Barbara and George. Service to the Bushes actually ran in Paula's family: her daughter, Alicia M. Huizar, had also worked for the family, and for twenty years. She was now seventy-three and residing in Houston.

"Shortly after New Year's Day 2017, Mrs. Bush's secretary called and said she wanted to see my grandmother, who was now ninety-five years old," recalled Paula Ramirez, who is Paula Rendon's granddaughter and caretaker. "Up until two years before, she had still been working for the Bushes a couple days a week. However, right before they left for Kennebunkport for the summer of 2015, Mrs. Bush told us, 'Take Paula home. Do not bring her back. She's put in her time and we love her, but she needs to retire now.' She was very direct about it because she didn't want there to be any misunderstanding. She knew how headstrong my grandmother was and that she wasn't going to retire until Barbara Bush *made* her retire. She had planned to go to Kennebunkport with them that summer, just as she had for the last fifty years—it was always May to October—so this was sad for her. But at that point, Mrs. Bush had just turned ninety and was living with such pain she couldn't imagine how my grandmother, who was three years older, could possibly work. So my grandmother reluctantly retired. It had been two years since she last saw Mr. and Mrs. Bush, so driving her to their home that day was very exciting."

When Paula Ramirez pulled up to the massive gates in front of the Bush estate, two Secret Service agents approached; the Bushes still had their protection. Paula Rendon reached into her purse and pulled a remote control out of it. She pushed a button and the gates yawned wide open; it still worked! Recognizing her, the agents waved her in.

"When we went inside, Doro, Mrs. Bush, and her nurse were there to greet us," recalled Paula Ramirez. "There were a lot of hugs and tears between Mrs. Bush and my grandmother. Then Mr. Bush came into the room in his wheelchair. His face lit up. 'Wa Wa!' he exclaimed, using his nickname for her. It was such a great moment. We sat in the TV room for a while and then Mrs. Bush had us all move into the formal dining room. When I wanted to take a photo of her and my grandmother, she said no because she had oxygen tubing in her nose and was self-conscious about it. But then her eyes welled up and she changed her mind. 'Oh my gosh, Paula, of course,' she said, and we took some pictures."

Her visitors couldn't believe that Barbara still had the needlepoint area rug on the floor that she'd worked on for many years, 1975 to 1983. "It had followed them from house to house, from country to country," said Paula Ramirez. "She also still had a pillow my grandmother had sewn for them one Christmas, poinsettias in the shape of Texas. This pillow had been in Mr. Bush's office when he was Vice President, and then it was in the Oval Office when he was President, and now here it was in their Houston home. Everyone was so old now, but they still had precious memories. Hearing them talk about the past while admiring their mementos was so touching. I think it brought them back to a better time and place. For a little sliver of time they were able to forget about their aches and pains and focus on the joy of their lives."

They all had a good laugh when Barbara told the story of a particularly inept maid who had once worked for the Bushes. She recalled how Paula Rendon would lose her patience with her and mutter, *"Stupido. Stupido."* Barbara had been afraid that the young lady would feel badly about it and one day asked if she was offended. "Oh, don't worry about me," the maid answered. "I don't speak Spanish."

When Barbara and George said goodbye to Paula at the end of their visit, they must have known it would be the last time they'd ever lay eyes on her. Barbara held her tightly. Everyone was crying as they went to the front door, Doro pushing her father in his wheelchair. Paula Rendon is ninety-eight years old and still lives with her granddaughter, Paula Ramirez, in Houston.

The rest of 2017 would be a challenging year of medical crises for both Barbara and George. In November, after yet another of the seemingly endless physical examinations that week, Barbara wearily told her biographer, Susan Page, "You're looking at what used to be Barbara Pierce Bush."

In January 2018, Barbara and George celebrated their seventy-third wedding anniversary. They had only gotten closer, especially since leaving the White House. They still saw in each other those two starry-eyed wartime teenagers who'd been so head over heels for each other that they couldn't wait to marry. He could still make her laugh, too. She'd always loved that about him. However, their quality of life had so diminished by this time, it was impossible to accept it. Barbara was so desperately unhappy, she actually started to wonder if perhaps their misery could be abbreviated if they just stopped eating. Her family members wouldn't let her entertain the idea, but by the dawn of 2018 they all realized Barbara just wanted it to be over.

Once Barbara Bush made up her mind about something, it was usually a *fait accompli,* and this time was no different. A month after taking a fall in her bedroom, she went home from the hospital and made it clear that she didn't want any more treatment, nothing that would extend her life even one more painful day. She wanted to die on her own terms. She was tired of being miserable. Feeling a little more in command of things, her attitude changed and she was more like her old self, ready to face whatever the coming days would bring. "You're responsible for your own happiness," her grandmother Lulu had said back when Barbara was just a young girl. "Take a look around," she told her and her mother, Pauline. "You've got it made! Be happy about it."

A few days later, Barbara sat down with the man who'd been at her side for more than seven decades and had a heart-to-heart talk with him. She was ready to go, she told George, and she'd been ready for some time. He told her that if that was truly how she felt, it was okay with him; he was ready to say goodbye to her. He wasn't going to worry about her either, he said, and she shouldn't worry about him. They agreed they'd both be just fine. They were grateful for the many years they'd had together.

A kiss sealed the deal.

Barbara Bush died on April 17, 2018. She was ninety-two.

George Bush would follow his beloved wife in death seven months later on November 30, 2018. He was ninety-four.

Barbara and George were laid to rest next to their daughter, Pauline Robinson Bush—"Robin"—at the Bush Presidential Library in College Station, Texas. Robin's ashes had been moved many years earlier from the original grave site Prescott Bush had once selected for her.

While it was most certainly the ending of another great Bush era, to Barbara and George's loved ones it also felt like maybe the beginning of one, too. "They believed in the afterlife," a grieving Laura Bush noted of her mother- and father-in-law, "and it gives us such comfort thinking of them in a better place and with no pain."

Laura would never get over knowing and loving Barbara Bush. She turned seventy-two the year her mother-in-law died, and had spent more than half her life—forty years, to be exact—trying to understand her. She had always known, though, that Barbara was so much more than her frustrating moments. Rock-solid and unapologetic, Barbara had always lived life on her own terms and never tried to be anything other than who she really was. She was very much like her mother, Pauline, in that respect. "I know who I am," Pauline had once proclaimed. "Everyone knows who I am and what I'm like. Nothing about me is much of a surprise."

The last time Laura saw Barbara was at her home in Houston after she was released from the hospital that last time. She sat at her bedside holding her hand, saying goodbye, but not with words, just with her presence. As Barbara lay in bed, days away from crossing over, Laura leaned in and kissed her tenderly on the forehead. "I love you, Bar," she softly told her. Barbara, her eyes closed, nodded and smiled.

Laura Bush has said that one of her favorite Bible passages is from the Book of Job. Maybe it best resonates for her when she thinks of the many years she had Barbara Bush in her life as a matriarch, a mother-in-law, a trusted companion, and a spiritual guide like no other: "You have granted me life and loving kindness," it reads, "and your care has preserved my spirit."

Epilogue

The remarkable legacies of Laura Bush, Barbara Bush, and the other women who were key figures in the Bush dynasty epitomize, in so many ways, the roles females have played over the years in American society.

Dorothy Walker Bush was a feminist long before the term was ever coined. She fought for equality in her marriage, insisting she should have a say in all decisions, especially as her husband, Prescott, ventured into politics. Her viewpoint was very different from that of her daughter-in-law, Barbara Pierce Bush, a much more conventional wife for the times. She always did what her husband asked of her, few questions asked. Happily, though, Barbara eventually discovered the power of her own voice as one of America's most revered First Ladies. Her daughter-in-law Laura Welch Bush was different still. A fascinating blend of Dorothy's feminist ethos and Barbara's traditional philosophy, hers was an equitable marriage from the very start. A First Lady during one of the darkest times in American history, Laura also demonstrated the hopeful, optimistic, and nurturing side of feminism she'd learned at the foot of her own mother, Jenna. In the end, many of Dorothy's, Barbara's, and Laura's female relatives were also great examples of strength, endurance, and independence, women to be respected and admired.

Barbara's mother, Pauline Pierce, didn't know it at the time, but a statement she made in 1940 would one day perfectly encapsulate the philosophy of her extended family. "All that really matters," Pauline said, "are the three f's: faith, family, and freedom." More than fifty years later in 1994, Barbara echoed those words. "When all the dust has settled and all the crowds are gone," she said, "the things that matter are faith, family and friends. We have been inordinately blessed, and we know that."

But perhaps Laura said it best when recalling her first night in the White House in January 2001 after George was elected forty-third President of the United States. Certainly, moving into the executive mansion was the fulfillment of George's hard-fought victory, yet something else mattered even more to Laura that night. She would recall the comfort she felt lying in bed next to him knowing that so many of her loved ones were nearby in that great house's upstairs residence. Her in-laws, Barbara and George H. W., were in the Queens' Bedroom, while her mother, Jenna, was in another room nearby. Her daughters, Jenna and Barbara, were safely down the hall. In all, twenty-three Bush relatives were fast asleep in the White House that evening, many of them on uncomfortable foldout cots. Knowing she was surrounded by so many family members felt to Laura like "the sigh of relief I would breathe back in Texas when I heard the door open late at night and I knew the girls were home and headed for bed. That inaugural night," she concluded wistfully, "I drifted off to sleep knowing that everyone we loved was safe, tucked in together under this one, remarkable roof."

The Story Behind *Grace & Steel*

Each book of mine is many years in the making, and this book is no exception. Therefore, I thought I might share with you, my reader, a bit of the history behind *Grace & Steel*.

After interviewing Barbara Bush in January 2000 for a series I was working on at the time about former First Ladies, I became inspired to write a biography of her. I found her witty and charming but also sensed a vulnerability in her that made me wonder about the true nature of her personality, and how different it might be from what was generally thought of her. At the time, I had just finished writing a book about the women who'd married into the Kennedy family, *Jackie, Ethel, Joan: Women of Camelot*. I thought perhaps a Barbara Bush biography might be the follow-up.

When I attempted to obtain Mrs. Bush's cooperation, she politely declined. She explained she was writing a memoir about her years after the White House and felt that this book combined with earlier autobiographies would serve as a sufficient body of work about her life and times. Disappointed, I decided to continue with my research anyway, especially after President George H. W. Bush told me he thought I might later be able to change his wife's mind. "Once she gets this next book out of her system," he told me with characteristic good nature, "we'll see what we see." I then spent about a year conducting interviews for that book with Bush family members and friends and associates. I was even able to get a few questions answered by President George H. W. Bush by email. I finished a first draft of that book in January 2001.

At this same time, the publisher with whom I was contracted back then asked me to write a book about the marriage of Princess Grace Kelly and Prince Rainier. This was the first time a book was ever suggested to me. Usually, they are my own ideas. Therefore, I was intrigued. I shifted my attention to that work, which was titled *Once Upon a Time*. I then went on to write several more books for that same publisher, but with Barbara Bush always in the back of my mind.

I picked up the Barbara Bush idea again in 2013, but now with the idea of expanding the book beyond her to the entire family. My publisher agreed this was a good idea and gave me the go-ahead to proceed with it. I then sought to get as many people on the record as possible and, finally, I finished a draft of that book in January 2014. However, I was still not satisfied. Something was missing. I didn't know what the manuscript lacked, I just knew I wasn't happy with it. I asked my publisher to allow me to switch topics so that I could take more time to think about how I wanted to focus the story. Believe it or not, we agreed to substitute the Bush book with a biography of the pop singer Beyoncé, which was about as different a subject as I could imagine. That book was *Becoming Beyoncé*.

Finally, in 2018, and now with a new publisher, St. Martin's Press, I was encouraged by my editor, Charlie Spicer, to return to the Bushes. This time I was determined to make it work.

In 2019, as part of my research for the newly resurrected Bush biography, I began researching the life and times of Dorothy Walker Bush, George H. W. Bush's mother. I had no idea she had been such a trailblazer. A feminist many years before the term was coined, she not only sought equality in her marriage to Senator Prescott Bush but she also encouraged her female family members to seek out the same in their own marriages. In particular, I found myself fascinated by the differences between her and her daughter-in-law, my original subject, Barbara Bush. Whereas Dorothy was ahead of her time, Barbara was *of* her time, a traditional wife and mother who believed her duty was to keep a stable home and raise her children, all the while heeding her husband's orders that she pack up and move from one city to the next as required by his work. Since this was her choice, it would have been fine for her except for the fact that she was so unhappy about it. How interesting is it, I thought, that in response to Barbara's despondency, Dorothy tried to convince her to have a stronger voice in her marriage. That's not the way generations normally work, I thought. If anything, shouldn't it have been the other way around, the younger Barbara trying to convince the older Dorothy to get with the times? Which brought me to another realization—these really weren't the "times" for feminist thinking, were they? The fact that this awakening was happening in the 1950s and 1960s, before the advent of the feminist movement in the 1970s, made it all the more compelling a story for me and, I decided, likely for you too, my reader. *Finally,* I had found my Bush family muse: Dorothy Walker Bush. It was then I realized I wanted to write about *the women* of the Bush dynasty, close to my original idea about a Barbara Bush biography but more expansive.

I became so impressed with the stories I and my research team began to uncover about the women not only of the direct Bush family but those who married into it, and their relatives—in particular their mothers. I found that there was practically nothing known about Barbara's mother, Pauline Robinson, other than the scant (and mostly unhappy) memories Barbara shared about her during her lifetime. The same held true for Laura's and Columba Bush's mothers, Jenna Welch and Josefina Gallo Esquivel. With each new interview and each new story, I became more certain that the decision I had made to focus on these inspiring women had been the right one.

When I finally finished this book in 2020, I knew I had made the right choice to keep delaying it until I was confident I was telling a story that had never before been told—and that's *Grace & Steel*, twenty years in the making.

Acknowledgments

This is by no means meant to be a comprehensive assemblage of source material. It's simply to give the reader an idea of the research used as the foundation for *Grace & Steel*.

I would like to thank the staff of the George H. W. Bush Presidential Library and Museum for their assistance with oral histories and photographs.

I would also like to thank those conscientious workers of the George W. Bush Presidential Library and Museum, again for their assistance with oral histories, photographs, and other assets. In particular, I would like to acknowledge archivist Virginia Butler.

Also, my thanks to Michael Pinkney of the Ronald Reagan Presidential Library and Museum.

I would also like to acknowledge the staff of the Webster University Library, St. Louis, Missouri.

Thank you to the Grandview Heights / Marble Cliff Historical Society.

Thank you also to the staff of the National First Ladies Library Education and Research Center in Canton, Ohio.

I also utilized the extensive White House archives, which can be found at White House.archives.gov.

Thanks also to the staff of the Birmingham Natural History Society in Birmingham, England.

Special thanks to the staff of the Yale University Library in New Haven, Connecticut, in particular the Manuscripts and Archives department.

I would like to acknowledge the Texas State Library and Archives Commission and the Texas Office of the First Lady, which is a subdivision of the Office of the Governor.

I would also like to express my gratitude to the following institutions: Academy of Motion Picture Arts and Sciences; Ancestry.com; AP Images; Associated Press Office (New York); Association for the Preservation of Historic Natchitoches; Beverly Hills Library; *Boston Herald* archives; Heritage Auctions; Lincoln Center Library of the Performing Arts, Lincoln Center, New York; Los Angeles Public Library; Paley Center New York Museum of Broadcasting; MyRoots.com; New York University Library; Newport Chamber of Commerce; Preservation Society of Newport County; Rex Features; University of California, Los Angeles.

I would like to thank Maryanne Reed for helping me locate taped interviews and transcripts from the many years of research dedicated to other iterations of this work over the years. This was not an easy task, but she did an incredible job and I am indebted to her for it.

Many Secret Service agents who protected members of the Bush family cooperated with me to make this book as accurate as possible. Some asked for anonymity, and of course it was given. Others approved the use of their names, and those names are found in the text.

My researcher, Cathy Griffin, has been working with me since 1990. We've had so much success together, and every book is a real joy and incredible experience. Cathy outdid herself with *Grace & Steel*, locating people who have never before talked about the Walkers and Bushes and convincing them to speak for the first time. Our focus with this book was to find *new* people to interview, not just re-interview people who have told their stories countless times in the past. I think we achieved that goal.

Cathy and I value our sources. My books would be nothing without them, after all. Cathy cultivates each one in the sense that she makes sure he or she knows how much we appreciate the cooperation and how we never take any of it for granted. Cathy and I agree that sources often risk a lot to cooperate with a book, and so we make it a point to never let it be regretted. Many of our sources approved their stories before publication, which Cathy and I allow because we understand how important it is to them that they be accurately portrayed.

I couldn't do what I have done over a thirty-year career as an author without Cathy Griffin at my side. I thank her.

Source Notes

Dorothy Walker Bush

I owe a debt of gratitude to Kathy M. Evans, the researcher and writer of the memoir *A Fourth City Family: The Lives and Legacies of the Walkers in St. Louis*, by the late George Herbert "Bert" Walker III, which, as of this writing, has not yet been published. A Harvard graduate, from 2003 to 2006 Bert was U.S. ambassador to Hungary in the George W. Bush administration. In 2001, he donated $1 million to Webster University. Then in 2005, because of his generous gift of $10 million to the school and university, Webster University's School of Business was renamed the George Herbert Walker School of Business & Technology.

Bert's grandfather was George Herbert Walker, also known as "Bert," the father of Dorothy Walker Bush. Therefore, the information about Dorothy and her sister, Nancy, provided by Kathy from her extensive research (and provided to me with the approval of Bert) was absolutely invaluable in helping me tell Dorothy's previously untold story. Most of the details about Dorothy found in this book have never before been published. I am grateful to Bert and Kathy for allowing me to finally flesh out the story of this fascinating woman, using as my foundation Bert's many firsthand memories of the Walker family. The kind of family history I sought to tell in *Grace & Steel* could never be told without the assistance of people like Walker and Evans. Incidentally, through her company Write for You, Kathy Evans specializes in the writing of memoirs and the researching of family genealogy to bring ancestral stories to life. If you would like to tell your story and have it memorialized for your family, she can be reached at kathymevans.com.

Sadly, Bert Walker died on January 18, 2020, at the age of eighty-eight.

For many passages in this book I drew extensively from the syndicated columns written by Dorothy Walker Bush, "Washington Life as Seen by a Senator's Wife by Mrs. Prescott Bush" and "Washington Life" by Dorothy Walker Bush. They are simply too numerous to enumerate here. Most are stored at the George H. W. Bush Presidential Library and Museum, but many can be accessed on the site Newspapers.com. Throughout the research and writing of this book, I felt fortunate to have access to such a treasure trove of material. Leave it to Mrs. Bush to leave behind, even if inadvertently, such precise accounts of her and Prescott's life together for historians such as myself.

I would also like to acknowledge the staff of the Webster University Library, St. Louis, Missouri.

I must acknowledge Robert Parrott of the Ohio Genealogical Society for his assistance.

Also, special thanks to Nancy Katzenbach, librarian at the Union County Genealogy Chapter, OGS, for all her help.

My gratitude goes out to the Texas State Historical Association for its assistance.

Thanks also to Sophie Larkin, granddaughter of Lucy "Lizzie" Larkin, for providing photographs of the Bushes' home in Connecticut in 1953, which I referred to for décor descriptions in the chapter "A Woman of Substance." She also provided the handwritten notes of Dorothy's column also found in "A Woman of Substance." With the exception of a few words, these notes are exactly as were eventually published. Ms. Larkin also provided the *Good Housekeeping* interview with Dorothy Bush—"Memorable in Many Ways," December 1953—referenced in that chapter. She also provided photographs of 12 Hortense Place, one of the homes in which Dorothy Walker Bush was raised, built by her father, Bert.

Thank you to Adair McDonald for use of her many scrapbooks relating to history of the Veiled Prophet Ball, which is described in the chapter "Dorothy's Gamble." She also provided biographical material relating to Marian Franciscus, who was crowned "Queen," and her father, James, who was Bert Walker's nemesis.

As indicated in the text, "Virginia Mason" is a pseudonym for a source who wished to remain anonymous. For purposes of continuity, she will be referred to in the same way in these notes.

Archival Material: "Editorial by David Davis Walker," *St. Louis Republic*, October 3, 1914; "Events in the Social World: Touch of Autumn in Air Attracts Many People to City Championship Golf Tourney and to Opening of Tennis Tournament—Many

New Volunteers Join Staff of Workers of St. Louis Food Administration," *St. Louis Post-Dispatch*, September 15, 1918; "Events in the Social World: The 'Dollar Dance' at Coliseum Friday Evening Is to Be a Domestic Affair of Great Magnitude for a Most Worthy Cause—Few Weddings During Past Week," *St. Louis Post-Dispatch*, May 18, 1919; "Events in the Social World: All Ears Are Alert to Whisperings as to Who Will Succeed Miss Mary Dee Jones, Queen of Court of Love and Beauty Since Last Visit of Veiled Prophet, in 1916," *St. Louis Post-Dispatch*, September 14, 1916; "Veiled Prophet Reveals Names of Some Maids Chosen for His Court: Society Whispers Also That Miss Nancy Walker Is Slated to Rule as Queen of Love and Beauty—Choice for Honor Place Reported," *St. Louis Star and Times*, October 3, 1919; "Riot of Color and Iridescence in Gowns Worn at V. P. Ball," *St. Louis Post-Dispatch*, October 8, 1919; "Misses Walker to Be Presented Today," *St. Louis Post-Dispatch*, November 25, 1919; "Society Folk in Play in Costumes of 1825," *St. Louis Post-Dispatch*, January 22, 1920; "Miss Dorothy Walker to Wed P.S. Bush," *St. Louis Post-Dispatch*, November 23, 1920; "Mrs. S.P. Bush Killed by Auto at Watch Hill," *Hartford Courant*, September 5, 1920; "Ohio Woman Killed by Automobile," *The Cincinnati Enquirer*, September 5, 1920; "Walker-Bush Wedding in Maine Tomorrow," *St. Louis Post-Dispatch*, August 5, 1921; "Dorothy Walker Bush Wedding Announcement," *St. Louis Star and Times*, August 1, 1921; "Dorothy Walker Becomes Bride of Prescott S. Bush," *New-York Tribune*, August 7, 1921; "Mrs. Dorothy Walker Weds," *New York Herald*, August 7, 1921; "St. Louis Society," "Dorothy Bush," *St. Louis Star and Times*, August 7, 1921; "Mr. and Mrs. Prescott Bush Rejoice Over Arrival of Son," *St. Louis Star and Times*, June 13, 1924; "Winners of the Inner City Squash Battle," *The Brooklyn Daily Eagle*, March 5, 1927; "George Bush's Mother's Day Tribute to His Mother," *Greenwich Time*, May 12, 1985; "Behind Every Great Man—Dorothy Walker Bush's 90th," *The New York Times*, June 30, 1991; "Dorothy Walker Bush—Molding the President," Cox News Service, July 1, 1991; "Athlete and Tough Mom Believed in Humility" by Christopher Keating, *Hartford Courant*, November 20, 1992; "Dorothy W. Bush Obituary," *Hartford Courant*, November 23, 1992; "Bush, Siblings Inherit Bulk of Mother's Estate," *Los Angeles Times*, December 5, 1992; "Bernie Yudain, Beloved Newspaper and 'Mr. Greenwich,' Dies at 91" by Lisa Chamoff, *Greenwich Time*, April 5, 2010; Samuel P. Bush Papers, Ohio Historical Society, Columbus, Ohio.

Interviews: Nancy Bush Ellis, Christopher Emery, Sophie Larkin, Myra Delcot, Louis Fraser, Sylvia Jenkins, Alberto Ferrer, Lisa Coppage, Virginia Mason.

Volumes: *Destiny and Power* by Jon Meacham; *America's Gilded Age* by Milton Rugoff.

Prescott Sheldon Bush

I, and researchers on my behalf, utilized the voluminous Prescott S. Bush Papers, stored at the University of Connecticut Library, Archives and Special Collections, at the Thomas J. Dodd Research Center. The collection contains scrapbooks (from 1952 through 1962, each disassembled with its clippings photocopied for preservation purposes), biographical sketches, newspaper clippings, information on legislative bills, correspondence, texts of interviews and speeches, press releases, and films of television appearances in 1962 as broadcast on Connecticut's WHNB.

In 1966 and 1967, Prescott Bush conducted an oral history with the Oral History Research Office of Columbia University. A copy of this oral history is available as part of the Bush Papers, and I utilized it as an important aspect of my research for this book.

I also referenced "Interviews with Prescott S. Bush by John T. Mason Jr. for the Eisenhower Project," Oral History Research Office, Columbia University, 1966, as well as "Oral History Interview with Prescott Bush, Jr.," Greenwich Library Oral History. I also accessed the Samuel P. Bush Papers from the Ohio Historical Society.

I also referenced the oral history of Timothy J. McBride, George W. Bush's private secretary, housed at the Miller Center.

Archival Material: "Appointed to National War Fund," *Hartford Daily Courant,* April 5, 1943; "Connecticut's Senator Bush Indicates Belief Only Fiscally Strong Should Be Congressmen," *The Courier-Journal,* June 23, 1955; "Ex-Senator Prescott Bush Dies," *The New York Times,* October 9, 1972; "Prescott Bush, Senator, Ike's Presidential Adviser," *Boston Evening Guide,* October 9, 1972; "How Bush's Grandfather Helped Hitler's Rise to Power" by Ben Aris and Duncan Campbell, *The Guardian*, September 25, 2004; "Paths of Power," *Time,* December 19, 2004; "Legacy: Records Show the Walker Branch of President George W. Bush's Family Included Slave Owners" by Roger Hughes, *Illinois Times,* April 5, 2007; "Genealogy in St. Louis and George Walker Bush" by Roger Hughes, Genealogy in St. Louis, November 7, 2015; "Samuel Bush Residence" (currently the Sisters' Residence at St. Raphael's), Grandview Heights / Marble Cliff Historical Society; "The Walker/Bush Family: Presidents and Players" by Jeannette Cooperman, *St. Louis Magazine,* August 20, 2015; "Sacrifice, the Bush Way: From Self to Others" by Marc-Andre Cotton, *The Journal of Psychohistory*, Summer 2016; "Prescott Sheldon Bush Genealogy," George H. W. Bush Presidential Library and Museum.

Interviews: Tim McBride, William Bush, Myra Delcot, Sal D'Orazio, Martha McCallum, Virginia Mason.

Volume: *Destiny and Power* by Jon Meacham.

There is only one true biography of Prescott Bush, and it should be acknowledged as such, and that's *Duty, Honor, Country* by Mickey Herskowitz.

Pauline Robinson and Marvin Pierce

I must acknowledge the historian Robert Parrott, president of the Union County Historical Society, for all his assistance. He provided important written material as well as photographs relating to the personal histories of Pauline Robinson and her father, Judge James E. Robinson, including ads from his campaign for a seat on the Ohio Supreme Court.

Also, special thanks to Nancy Katzenbach, librarian at the Union County Genealogy Chapter, OGS, for all her help. Among many other biographical material related to Pauline Robinson and her extended family, she provided a "Pedigree Chart for Pauline Robinson" and a "Genealogy of James Robinson," both of which were vital to my research.

I also utilized "First Families of Ohio Roster" from *The Report, Published Quarterly by the Ohio Genealogical Society*.

Archival Material: Miami University Yearbook, 1915; "Union County History of 1915," "Judge J. E. Robinson Out for Supreme Court," *The Union County Journal*, June 7, 1918; "Judge James E. Robinson: Profile," *The Union County Journal*, June 11, 1918; "Of Interest to Women: Miss Pauline Pierce and Miss Margaret Beadle Host Bridge Dinner Shower at the Jo-Ann Tea Room," *The Newark Advocate*, December 20, 1926; "Attended Bridge Party," *The Union County Journal*, July 7, 1927; "Memorial for Judge James Edgar Robinson," *Marysville Journal-Tribune*, March 22, 1932; "The Christian Citizen and Patriot," text material of workshop written by Mrs. Pauline Pierce, June 1940; "South Salon Community—Ladies Aid Society of the Congressional Christian Church Workshop," *Washington C.H. Record-Herald*, June 6, 1940; "Congressional Christian Church Minutes, Spotlight: Pauline Pierce," Summer 1940; Ladies Aid Society workshop by Pauline Pierce (miscellaneous material, 1940, 1941); "Pierce Hurt; Wife Is Killed in Auto Crash," *Dayton Daily News*, September 23, 1949; "Mrs. Lulu Robinson—Widow of Ohio Supreme Court Judge Dies," *Marysville Journal-Tribune*, January 9, 1957.

Interviews: Garret Bishop, Jessica Winter, Lisa McClintock, Linda McDonald, Donna Zimmerman, June Biedler, Posy Morgan Clark, Sarah McDonald.

Volumes: *Life Together: The Classic Exploration of Christian Community* by Dietrich Bonhoeffer; *The Family* by Kitty Kelley; *Family of Secrets* by Russ Baker; *American Dynasty* by Kevin Phillips.

Barbara Bush

In the spring of 2000, I interviewed Joan Mondale and her husband, former Vice President Walter Mondale for a story I was writing about a revised edition of her book, *Politics in Art*. I told Ms. Mondale about my idea to write about Barbara Bush, and she then told me about her experiences with Barbara when they met at 1 Observatory Circle after George H. W. Bush was elected Vice President. She then sent me an oral history she had made, which included stories about that day, as well as some correspondence between her and Barbara. I was so impressed with her. I had always thought she was marvelous and underrated and would have made an excellent First Lady. I hoped that one day I would be able to write about her and bring her to life for readers who perhaps had no idea how impressive she was, and I'm so happy that time has finally come with *Grace & Steel*.

I spoke to several of Jennifer Fitzgerald's friends, associates, and family members, all of whom asked for anonymity. While I didn't have a formal interview with Ms. Fitzgerald, I did have a telephone conversation with her in 2015 during which she insisted, as indicated in the book's text, that the affair with President H.W. Bush, "simply did not happen." I couldn't help but notice that, during that same year, she used almost the exact same phrase with Bush's biographer Jon Meacham. When he asked her about the affair for his book, *Destiny and Power,* she answered, "It simply didn't happen."

I referenced the extensive chronology of Ms. Fitzgerald's life on http://www.dkosopedia.com/.

I also referenced the transcript of President George W. Bush's news conference with Israeli Prime Minister Yitzhak Rabin, August 11, 1992, at Kennebunkport, which I secured from the Jewish Virtual Library. I also referenced the book *Call the Briefing* by Marlin Fitzwater.

Archival Material: "Miss Barbara Pierce Will Marry . . ." *The New York Times*, December 12, 1943; "Barbara Pierce Marries Lt. Bush in Rye New York," *The Journal Herald*, January 7, 1945; "Goodbye to Robin" by Amy Cunningham, *Texas Monthly*, February 1988; "Your Own True Colors," Barbara Bush recorded live at Wellesley College, June 1, 1990; "Barbara's Backlash" by Marjorie Williams, *Vanity Fair*, August 1992; "Barbara Bush's Stepmother Still Immersed in Art," *The Greenville News*, October 7, 1994; "Bush: The Making of a Candidate," *The Washington*

Post, December 5, 1999; "Barbara Bush Turns 75," *Newsweek*, August 7, 2000; "The Peripeteia, an Analysis of Reversal Speeches by Barbara Bush, Richard Nixon and Lyndon B. Johnson" by Christopher James Anderson, Graduate Theses and Dissertations, Iowa State University, 2008; "Barbara Bush Had a Good Life but a Hard One" by Mimi Swartz, *Texas Monthly,* April 17, 2018; "Barbara Bush's Children: Photos of the Family She Left Behind," Heavy.com, April 17, 2018; "How Barbara and George H. W. Bush Became Royalty in Houston" by Shelby Webb, *Houston Chronicle*, April 17, 2018; "'One Last Time': Barbara Bush Had Already Faced a Death More Painful Than Her Own" by Steve Hendrix, *The Washington Post*, April 18, 2018; "The Day Outspoken Barbara Bush Regretted Speaking Her Mind," Associated Press, April 18, 2018; "Barbara Bush Was 'First Lady of the Greatest Generation,'" Associated Press, April 21, 2018; "For George and Barbara Bush, White House Staff Became Family" by Jennifer Boswell Pickens, *The Hill,* December 5, 2018; "To Barbara Bush, Donald Trump Represented 'Greed, Selfishness'" by Peter Baker, *The New York Times,* March 27, 2019; "How Obesity and Bullying Are Connected," Verywell Family, September 14, 2019; "Franette McCulloch—A Life Well Lived, One Layer at a Time," Smith Wealth Advisers, no date.

Interviews: Barbara Bush, Paula Ramirez, Ariel De Guzman, Christopher Emery, George Hainey, Larry Ohnsman, Elsie Walker, Jonathan Bush, Garret Bishop, Linda McDonald, Donna Zimmerman, Geraldine Ferraro, Mary Ann "Andy" Stewart, June Biedler, Posy Morgan Clark, Sarah McDonald, Stephen Miller, Veronica Allday, Louis Fraser, Sylvia Jenkins, Consuela Diaz, Tomas DiBella, Dorothy Pelanda, Robert Parrott, Denny Schlindwein, Franette McCulloch, Rex Scouten, Jonathan Wackrow.

Volumes: *Pearls of Wisdom* by Barbara Bush; *Barbara Bush: A Memoir* by Barbara Bush; *Reflections: Life After the White House* by Barbara Bush; *The Coe Families of Maryland* by Carl Robert Coe; *Simply Barbara Bush* by Donnie Radcliffe; *The Matriarch* by Susan Page; *Barbara Bush* by Pamela Kilian; *Millie's Book* by Barbara Bush; *C. Fred's Story* by Barbara Bush; *The Family* by Kitty Kelley; *Trump: The Biography* by J. R. MacGregor; *White House Usher* by Christopher B. Emery.

Television: *The Late Show with David Letterman*, September 13, 1994; *Fresh Air with Terry Gross*, September 13, 1994; *Charlie Rose*, September 13, 1994; *Talking with David Frost*, September 30, 1994; *The Tonight Show with Jay Leno*, November 18, 1994; *This Week* (joint interview with Laura Bush), December 19, 1999; *Good Morning America*, March 18, 2003; *Larry King Live*, May 31, 2005; *Marketplace*, September 5, 2005; *Larry King Live*, November 22, 2010; *First Ladies: Influence and Image*, October 29, 2013; *Fox and Friends*, March 7, 2014; *This Morning*, February 4,

2016; *Anderson Cooper 360*, February 5, 2016. I also referenced the CNN documentary *The Bush Years: Family, Duty, Power*, 2019.

George H. W. Bush

I would like to thank those conscientious workers of the George H. W. Bush Presidential Library and Museum, again for their assistance with oral histories, photographs, and other assets, such as "The George Bush Collection," which includes "China File," "Personal Alphabetical Files, 1943–1983," "Business Alphabetical Files, 1954–1969," and "Political Correspondence Files, 1957–1964," as well as George Bush's "Peking Diary, Vol. 1, 2 and 3" and "CIA Files." In particular, I would like to acknowledge archivist Virginia Butler for her help with the extensive audiovisual archives, the best, I have to say, of any presidential library I utilized for research.

I also utilized the George H. W. Bush Oral History Project, housed at the University of Virginia's Miller Center. This consists of almost 425 hours of recorded interviews with cabinet members, top-level staffers, transition aides, and cabinet advisers. In particular, I utilized the oral histories of James A. Baker, White House chief of staff / secretary of state; Richard B. Cheney, secretary of defense; Craig Fuller, chief of staff to Vice President Bush; Colin Powell, chairman of the Joint Chiefs of Staff; John H. Sununu, White House chief of staff; and J. Danforth Quayle, Vice President of the United States.

I also referenced *American Experience: George W. Bush, Parts 1 and 2* on PBS, May 2020.

Archival Material: "Bush Battles the 'Wimp Factor'" by Margaret Garrard Warner, *Newsweek*, October 19, 1987; "Prescott Bush Recalls Early Years with Brother, George," *Hartford Courant*, January 15, 1988; "A Family Saga," *Down East*, August 1989; "The Bush Affair," *New York Post*, August 11, 1992; "The Woman George W. Bush Didn't Marry" by Tim Fleck, *Houston Press*, March 25, 1999; "George W., Knight of Eulogia" by Sheldon M. Stern, *The Atlantic*, May 2000; "Who Is That Little Boy in the Photograph?" *The Greenville News*, October 29, 2000; "Media Dame Rains on Bush's Parade," *Daily Mail*, October 1, 2004; "Before He Was President, George H. W. Bush Was a Pilot," Pilotonline.com, January 9, 2009; "Bush's Bald Head a Reminder of His Own Child's Leukemia Fight," *Los Angeles Times*, July 16, 2013; "Confessions of a Former White House Chef, Part One" by Hilary Pollack, Vice.com, February 5, 2015; "The Memoir George H. W. Bush Couldn't Write" by Susan Page, *USA Today*, November 9, 2015; "An American Family's Anchor to Windward" by Sophie Nelson, *Maine: The Magazine,* June 2016; "See How West Texas Oil Business Hub Midland Has Changed Through the Years" by Craig Hlavaty, *Houston Chronicle,* February 19, 2018; "How Barbara and George H. W. Bush Became Royalty in Houston" by Shelby Webb, *Houston Chronicle*, April 17, 2018; "The Tender Letters George H. W. Bush Wrote to His Darling Bar—the Wife He Adored for 73 Years" by Caroline Graham, *Daily Mail*, December 1, 2018; "Key Moments in George H. W. Bush's Life," *USA Today*, December 1, 2018; "Bush Family Tree Roots Extend to Penfield" by Marcia Greenwood, *Democrat and Chronicle*, December 5, 2018; "Public Papers of the Presidents of the United States: George Bush," George H. W. Bush Presidential Library.

From the Texas State Library and Archives Commission and the Office of the Governor, I accessed these files for this book: "Texas Governor George W. Bush, Press Office, First Lady's Speech and Press Files, 1980–2000"; "Texas Governor George W. Bush, Executive Office Records, Schedules and Calendars, 1995–2000"; "Texas Governor George W. Bush, Scheduling Office Records, Invitations, 1994–2000"; "Texas Governor George W. Bush, Scheduling Office Records, Travel Arrangement Files, 1994–1999."

Interviews: William "Bucky" Bush, Jonathan Bush, Patricia Bowman, Linda McDonald, Stephen Miller, Sylvia Jenkins, Betty Wagner, Denny Schlindwein, Richard Dupont, Paula Ramirez, Franette McCulloch, Sam Donaldson, Chris Wallace, Jonathan Wackrow.

Volumes: *All the Best, George Bush* by George H. W. Bush; *A World Transformed* by George H. W. Bush and Brent Scowcroft; *Looking Forward by* George Bush with Victor Gold; *41: A Portrait of My Father* by George W. Bush; *The China Diary of George H. W. Bush*, edited by Jeffrey A. Engel; *Destiny and Power* by Jon Meacham; *George Bush: The Life of a Lone Star Yankee* by Herbert S. Parmet; *George H. W. Bush* by Timothy Naftali; *George Herbert Walker Bush* by Tom Wicker; *The Bush Tragedy* by Jacob Weisberg; *The Bushes: Portrait of a Dynasty* by Peter Schweizer and Rochelle Schweizer; *Secrets of the Secret Service* by Gary J. Byrne; *The First Family Detail* by Ronald Kessler; *First Son* by Bill Minutaglio; *George Bush* by Webster G. Tarpley; *Ambushed* by Toby Rogers; *The Bush Family* by Craig F. Davis Jr.

Jenna Hawkins and Harold Welch

Archival Material: "Announcement of Marriage License, Harold Bruce Welch and Jenna Hawkins," *El Paso Times*, February 1, 1944; "Miss Jenna Louise Hawkins Is

Bride of Sgt. Harold B. Welch," *El Paso Times*, January 31, 1944; "Welches Announce Birth of Daughter," *El Paso Herald-Post*, November 14, 1946; "Mrs. Welch Will Give Coffee to Reveal News to Friends," *El Paso Times*, October 22, 1944; "First Lady's Mom Visits," *El Paso Times*, May 7, 2005; "A Q&A with Jenna Welch, Mother of First Lady Laura Bush" by Dan Huff, El Paso Inc., May 16, 2005; "Volunteerism Class Keeps Association Leader Busy—Catherine Kistenmacher and Jenna Bush," *El Paso Times*, January 13, 2006; "Girl Gone Mild" by Skip Hollandsworth, *Texas Monthly*, November 2007; Jenna Hawkins Welch (1919–2019), Legacy.com, May 10, 2019; "Jenna Welch, Mother of Former First Lady Laura Bush, Was from El Paso, Lived in Midland," *El Paso Times*, May 13, 2019; "Jenna Welch Passes Away at 99," *Midland Reporter-Telegram*, May 13, 2019.

Interviews: Adair Margo, Todd Southern, Donald Lane, Ethan Marshall, Harold Kelly, Harvey Kennedy, Richard Pendleton, Judy Dykes Hester, Thomas Wright, Bessie Maye, Benjamin Franklin, Jeanie Pendleton Bohn, MaryAnn Colton, James Parks, Susan Byerly Nowlin.

Volumes: *The Handbook of Texas Women* by Texas State Historical Association; *Handbook of Texas* by Texas State Historical Association; *Women Across Texas History* by Texas State Historical Association; *Spoken from the Heart* by Laura Bush.

Laura Bush

I attended the "Panel with Laura and Barbara Bush" at America's First Ladies: An Enduring Legacy conference on November 15, 2011, at the George H. W. Bush Presidential Library Center at Texas A&M University, and used my notes as well as a transcript of the proceedings for parts of this book. (I also met Laura Bush at this event.)

I also utilized the transcript of Laura's speech and Q&A at the George S. Benson Auditorium of Harding University, Arkansas, on April 16, 2018. I also referred to a transcript of Laura's interview with Larry King, May 11, 2010.

Archival Material: "Midland Boy Dies in Crash—2 Teen Girls Injured," *The Odessa American*, November 8, 1963; "Confidential Police Report with Photographs: Laura Welch Accident," November 8, 1963; "Addendum: Police Report, Laura Welch Accident," November 30, 1963; "Findings: Laura Welch Accident," Midland Police Department, December 12, 1963; "Welch-Bush," *El Paso Times*, November 13, 1977; "What Laura Wants" by Julie Bonnin, *Austin American-Statesman*, April 19, 1999; "Education Bill's Passage Is Laura Bush's First Big Move" by A. Phillip Brooks, *Austin American-Statesman*, June 22, 1999; "Laura Bush on Early Days with George

Bush," video, ABC News, November 19, 1999; "Laura Bush Ran Stop Sign and Killed Boyfriend," Associated Press, May 3, 2000; "For Laura Bush, a Direction She Never Wished to Go In" by Frank Bruni, *The New York Times*, July 31, 2000; "The Education of Laura Bush" by Paul Burka, *Texas Monthly*, April 2001; "Love Story of George and Laura Bush Holds Up in Tough Town, Tough Times" by Georgia Temple, MRT.com, February 13, 2002; "Quietly, the First Lady Builds a Literary Room of Her Own" by Elisabeth Bumiller, *The New York Times*, October 7, 2002; "With Antiwar Poetry Set, Mrs. Bush Postpones Event" by Elisabeth Bumiller, *The New York Times*, January 31, 2003; "The Poets vs. the First Lady" by J. Bottum, *Weekly Standard*, February 17, 2003; "As World Waits, Quiet on the West Wing Front" by Elisabeth Bumiller, *The New York Times*, March 17, 2003; "First-Grade Students Are Flat-Out Proud to Hear from First Lady," *Greensboro News & Record*, April 5, 2003; "Laura's Girls" by Ann Gerhart, *The Washington Post*, January 7, 2004; "Tell Laura I Love Her" by Rex Weyler, The Tyee, March 15, 2004; "Supporters in Chief" by Denise Flaim, *Orlando Sentinel*, October 20, 2004; "Laura Bush: Why Wasn't She Charged?" by suziedemocrat, Dailykos.com, October 31, 2004; "The Good Wife" by Mimi Swartz, *Texas Monthly*, November 2004; "Life at the Clorox House," *National Review*, April 4, 2006; "Behind Laura Bush's Car Crash" by A. L. Bardach, *Daily Beast*, July 14, 2007; "Laura Bush," History .com, March 22, 2010; "The Laura Bush 'Confession' Is Far from Harmless" by Gordon Duff, Salem-News.com, April 28, 2010; "Laura Bush's Classmates in Midland Recall 'Devastating,' 1963 Car Crash" by Daniel Freedman, *Houston Chronicle*, May 5, 2010; "Where I'm From" by Mimi Swartz, *Texas Monthly*, June 2010; "A Legacy of Conservation—A Conversation with Regan Gammon" Texan by Nature, no date; "Former First Lady Laura Bush's Childhood Home for Sale in Texas" by Kristine Hansen, Realtor.com, May 16, 2017; "Laura Bush's Milestones Reveal Her Leadership Style," *The Dallas Morning News*, December 30, 2018; "Southern Hospitality on the World Stage: An Interview with Laura Bush" by C. J. Lotz, *Garden and Gun*, March 6, 2019; "Jenna Bush Hager Welcomes Son with Husband Henry Hager: 'We Are Overcome with Joy'" by Charlotte Triggs and Jen Juneau, *People*, August 5, 2019; "Odessa Texas History," OdessaHistory.com, no date.

From the Texas State Library and Archives Commission and the Office of the Governor, I utilized transcripts of the following speeches by Laura Bush, from which many of her quotes in this book have been culled:

"Campaign Speech, Remarks," 1994; "The Open Forum," January 9, 1995; "Outstanding Women in Texas Government Awards," January 27, 1995; "Texas Writers' Event," March 1995; "Texas Library Association," April 6, 1995; "Presby Partners," April 6, 1995; "Safe Kids Week," Will Rogers Elementary School, Houston, May 4,

1995; "National Day of Prayer," Houston, May 4, 1995; "Round Rock ISD Co-
operative Work Study Program, Employers Appreciation Banquet," May 16, 1995;
"Amarillo College Art Force," October 10, 1995; "State Agency Libraries of Texas,"
Mansion Reception, October 11, 1995; "Media Event, Card Designs by Children of
M. D. Anderson," November 2, 1995; "Zonta International District 10 Conference,"
San Antonio Plaza Hotel, November 3, 1995; "Texas Breast Cancer Leadership
Symposium," Marriott at the Capitol, Austin, November 3, 1995; "United Methodist
Women," Dallas, November 6, 1995; "Wimberley Community Civic Club," Wimberley,
November 10, 1995; "Tenth Annual Governor's Conference on the Prevention of Child
Abuse," January 22, 1996; "Westbank Community Library Fundraiser," Austin, January
25, 1996; "Cedar Park Chamber of Commerce," January 29, 1996; "First Lady's Family
Literacy Initiative Announcement," Bowie Elementary School, Houston, February 2,
1996; "Commissioning of the West Texas Cancer Prevention Partnership," Mobile
Mammography Clinic, February 2, 1996; "Child Protective Services, Reaching for
Rainbows Luncheon," Amarillo, February 13, 1996; "Elgin Chamber of Commerce,"
February 15, 1996; "Collin County Volunteer Luncheon," Dallas, February 16, 1996;
"Texas Federation of Women's Clubs," Holiday Inn Townlake, April 25, 1996; "Cel-
ebration of Reading," Houston, April 27, 1996; "Rising Star Young Writers Confer-
ence," April 27, 1996; "City of Austin, Public Library Re-Opening," April 28, 1996;
"Texas Association for Symphony Orchestras," Houston, April 29, 1996; "Westview
Middle School Library, Accelerated Reader Program," Austin, May 9, 1996; "Texas
Medical Association Annual Convention," San Antonio, May 9, 1996; "Women's
Chamber of Commerce, Quarterly Power Luncheon," November 8, 1996; "UT M.D.
Anderson Children's Art Project," November 12, 1996; "Rainbow Room Opening,"
November 12, 1996; "Metropolitan Breakfast Club, Weekly Meeting," November 13,
1996; "Press Conference—Final, Texas Book Festival," November 15, 1996; "First
Edition Literary Gala—Final, Texas Book Festival," November 15, 1996; "Saturday
Morning Kickoff, Texas Book Festival," November 16, 1996; "Bluebonnet Girl Scout
Council Women of Distinction Banquet," May 8, 1997; "Coronelli Globe Dedica-
tion, Texas Tech University," May 9, 1997; "Angelo State Commencement," May 9,
1997; "Celebration of Reading, Houston, Texas," May 10, 1997; "Pflugerville Com-
munity Library," April 12, 1999; "Upper Valley Rainbow Room Grand Opening,"
April 13, 1999; "E. B. Reyna Elementary School, Reception for Family Literacy Pro-
gram Families," April 13, 1999; "UNT (University of North Texas) Velma E. Schmidt
Early Childhood Education Conference," April 16, 1999; "East Dallas Community
School," April 22, 1999; "Texas Library Association Annual Conference, Texas Book
Festival Awards, Dallas," April 22, 1999; "Grand Marshall, Battle of Flowers Parade,"

April 23, 1999; "Austin Museum of Art Reception," April 26, 1999; "Avance Meeting," April 26, 1999; "UT Family Literacy Center Ribbon Cutting," April 27, 1999; "Laura Bush Promenade, SMU," April 27, 1999; "ROAR State Meeting," April 29, 1999; "Celebration of Reading," April 29, 1999; "Texas Folic Acid Council," May 3, 1999.

Interviews: Richard Pendleton; Adair Margo, Adela Gonzalez, Todd Southern, Donald Lane, Regan Kimberlin Gammon, Ethan Marshall, Harold Kelly, Harvey Kennedy, Judy Dykes Hester, Benjamin Franklin, Jeanie Pendleton Bohn, Jimmy McCarroll, MaryAnn Colton, Jan O'Neill, Betty Wagner, Denny Schlindwein, Monica Gonzalez, Susan Byerly Nowlin, Cindy Schumann Klatt, Walter Scheib, Jonathan Wackrow, Richard Dupont, Landon Parvin.

Volumes: *Spoken from the Heart* by Laura Bush; *Laura Bush* by Ronald Kessler; *The Perfect Wife* by Ann Gerhart; *An Invitation to the White House* by Hillary Clinton; *Inside Camp David* by Rear Admiral Michael Giorgione; *George and Laura* by Christopher Anderson; *My First Ladies* by Nancy Clarke; *Governor's Mansions of the South* by Ann Liberman; *Destiny and Power* by Jon Meacham; *41* by George W. Bush; *Will Jeb Bush Be the Republican Candidate in 2016?* by Malcolm Stone; *First Families in Residence* by Ellen J. Uguccioni; *Inside the White House* by Noel Grove; *Laura Bush* by Beatrice Gormley; *The First Family Detail* by Ronald Kessler; *First Women* by Kate Anderson Brower; *Under This Roof* by Paul Brandus; *Upstairs at the White House* by J. B. West; *The Family* by Kitty Kelley.

George W. Bush

I would like to thank to fine people of the George W. Bush Presidential Library and Museum for all their assistance with oral histories, photographs, and other assets that I used to better understand this story. In particular, I would like to thank archivists Mary Finch and Elizabeth Staats.

I also utilized the George W. Bush Oral History Project, housed at University of Virginia Miller Center, in particular the "Karl Rove Oral Histories Part 1 and 2." (Rove was senior adviser to the President.)

Thanks to the Midland Chamber of Commerce for all its assistance.

Thanks also to the George W. Bush Childhood Home Museum (and also website) for its assistance.

Archival Material: "CIA Director's Son Charged with OUI," *Biddeford-Saco Journal*, October 2, 1976; "Born to Run" by Skip Hollandsworth, *Texas Monthly*, May 1994; "A Texas Childhood" by George Lardner Jr. and Lois Romano, *The Washington Post*, July 26, 1999; "A Place Called Midland: George W. Bush's Home Ground" by Lynn Smith, *Los Angeles Times,* September 7, 2000; "Q&A with Mark Leaverton and Don Poage, Midland's Community Bible Study," *Frontline: The Jesus Factor*, PBS.org, April 29, 2004; "George W.'s Personal Jesus" by Guy Lawson, *GQ,* January 1, 2005; "Bush Family Returns to Dedicate George W. Bush Childhood Home" by Colin Guy, *Midland Reporter-Telegram*, April 11, 2006; "How George Bush Really Found Jesus" by Craig Unger, Salon.com, November 8, 2007; "Bush: 'I'm An Emotional Wreck'" by Ronald Kessler, Newsmax.com, May 11, 2008; "Bush's Building Days Began in Midland" by Rick Brown, *Midland Reporter-Telegram*, December 1, 2018; "George H. W. Bush's White House Photographer: 'That Experience Changed My Life Forever'" by Robin Young, WBUR, December 5, 2018; Brochure: "Midland First Choice Real Estate—Homes of George W. Bush."

Of special note is the book *A History of Character: The Story of Midland, Texas* by Jimmy Patterson. Also worthwhile is the blog HistoryofCharacter.com, also written by Patterson. Also, Jimmy Patterson's interview with KCRS, September 12, 2014.

I also referred to a transcript of President Bush's interview with Larry King, July 6, 2006.

Interviews: Joe O'Neill, Richard Dupont, Charlie Younger, Denny Schlindwein, Hope Langford, Landon Parvin, James Parks, Monica Gonzalez, Susan Byerly Nowlin, Laurence Jeffrey Edmonds.

Volumes: *A Charge to Keep* by George W. Bush; *Decision Points* by George W. Bush; *Days of Fire* by Peter Baker; *Bush at War* by Bob Woodward; *The Bushes* by Peter Schweizer and Rochelle Schweizer; *W* by Elizabeth Mitchell; *America's First Families* by Carl Sferrazza Anthony; *The Last Republicans* by Mark K. Updegrove; *The Bush Family* by James Spada; *Bush* by Jean Edward Smith; *Our Governors' Mansions* by Cathy Keating; *The Texas Governor's Mansion* by Jean Houston Daniel, Price Daniel, and Dorothy Blodgett; *The Governor's Mansion of Texas* by Friends of the Governor's Mansion; *20 Years in the Secret Service* by Rufus W. Youngblood; *In the President's Secret Service* by Ronald Kessler; *Protecting the President* by Dan Bongino.

Columba and Jeb Bush

Archival Material: "Columba Bush: A Private Person in a Public Role" by Liz Balmaseda, *Chicago Tribune,* February 13, 1989; "Bush and Sons" by Tom Fiedler, *Miami Herald,* September 25, 1994; "Florida's First Lady, Columba Bush, Settles into Life in the Governor's Mansion" by Lilian Guevara-Castro, *Ocala Star-Banner,* May 5, 1999; "The Patience of Jeb" by Mark Leibovich, *The Washington Post*, February 23, 2003; "In Campaign Debut, George P. Bush Starts Small Amid High Expectations" by Lauren Phillips, *The Dallas Morning News,* July 20, 2013; "The Private Life of Jeb Bush's Mexican Wife, Columba" by Griselda Nevarez, *La Opinión*, May 20, 2014; "Jeb Bush Says His Wife Supports a Presidential Run" by Jose A. DelReal, *The Washington Post*, October 15, 2014; "The Extraordinary Story of Columba Bush" by Nick Fagge, *Daily Mail*, January 22, 2015; "Jeb Bush Shaped by Troubled Phillips Academy Years" by Michael Kranish, *The Boston Globe*, January 31, 2015; "Bush Spouse Backs Jeb, but Is Wary of Family Business" by Patrick Healy and Sheryl Gay Stolberg, *The New York Times*, February 21, 2015; "Documents Show the Expensive Tastes of Jeb Bush's Low-Key Wife" by Karen Tumulty and Alice Crites, *The Washington Post*, February 22, 2015; "Jeb Bush Struggles Under the Dynasty Thing" by Margaret Carlson, *Chicago Tribune,* February 23, 2015; "7 Things We Learned Writing a Cover Story About Jeb Bush" by Alex Altman and Zeke J. Miller, *Time,* March 5, 2015; "Jeb Bush's Forgotten Father-in-Law" by Michael Kruse, *Politico*, March 19, 2015; "Columba Bush's Painful, Unlikely Road from Mexico Toward the White House" by Karen Tumulty and Mary Jordan, *The Washington Post*, March 21, 2015; "Support Iowa's Domestic Abuse Programs" by Columba Bush, *Des Moines Register*, May 18, 2015; "Andover, Mexico and the Making of Jeb Bush" by Michael Kruse, *Politico,* May 21, 2015; "The Mysterious Columba Bush" by Hanna Rosin, *The Atlantic*, June 2015; "While Husband Campaigns, Columba Bush Meets with Domestic Violence Prevention Advocates" by Casey McDermott, *Concord Monitor*, July 9, 2015; "Columba Bush, Jeb Bush's Wife: 5 Fast Facts You Need to Know" by Tom Cleary, Heavy.com, December 4, 2018.

Volumes: *Reply All* by Jeb Bush; *Immigration Wars* by Jeb Bush and Clint Bolick; *Columba Bush: La cenicienta de la Casa Blanco (The Cinderella of the White House)* by Beatriz Parga; *Mamá* by Maria Perez-Brown; *Bushwomen* by Laura Flanders; *Jeb* by S. V. Date; *Jeb Bush Outed* by Stephen L. Goldstein; *Jeb Bush: Leader of the World Order* by Dylan Clearfield; *American Made* by Shaun Attwood and Jane Dixon-Smith; *Thank You, President Bush* edited by Rod. D. Martin and Aman Verjee; *Speaking of Freedom* by George H. W. Bush; *The Bush Crime Family* by Roger Stone and Saint John Hunt; *Jeb Bush* by the Staff of the *Tampa Bay Times*; *Conservative Hurricane* by Matthew T. Corrigan; *Who Is Jeb Bush?* by Tag Powell; *All the Best, George Bush* by George H. W. Bush; *Reflections* by Barbara Bush; *Rand Paul vs. Jeb Bush on the Issues* by Jesse Gordon; *Governors' Mansions of the South* by Ann Liberman; *Destiny and Power* by Jon Meacham; *Third Time's a Charm: The Jeb Bush Plan to Restore Our Country's Greatness* by the Republican National Committee; *41* by George W. Bush; *Will Jeb Bush Be the Republican Presidential Candidate in 2016?* by Malcolm Stone; *First Families in Residence* by Ellen J. Uguccioni.

Interviews: Columba Bush, written Q&A, March 3, 2000, Richard Dupont, Charlie Younger, Laurence Jeffrey Edmonds.

Miscellaneous

Archival Material: "The First Daughter, Doro Bush," *The Baltimore Sun*, December 9, 1990; "A Bush Wedding Is Under Wraps," Knight-Ridder News Service, June 26, 1992; "W.'s Sister-in-Law Schleps Tell-All About First Family" by Greg Sargent, *The Observer*, April 21, 2003; "The Relatively Charmed Life of Neil Bush" by Peter Carlson, *The Washington Post*, December 28, 2003; "Embarrassing Bush Divorce Papers," CBS News, January 26, 2004; "The Inconvenient Sharon Bush" by Vicky Ward, *Vanity Fair*, April 2004; "Cast Away" by Mimi Swartz, *Texas Monthly*, May 2004; "It's Gem of Fight Over 243G Ring," *Daily News*, February 13, 2008; "An Intimate Look at the Late President George H. W. Bush and His Daughter Dorothy" by Debra Wallace, *Parade*, December 3, 2018; "Dorothy 'Doro' Bush Koch, 5 Facts You Need to Know" by Stephanie Dube Dwilson, Heavy.com, December 6, 2018; "Ex Bush Daughter-in-law Speaks Out Unprompted on Candid New Barbara Biography: 'Very Ironic'" by Diane Herbst, *People*, April 3, 2019.

Interviews: Sharon Bush (March 15, 2002), Lou Colasuonno, Consuela Diaz, Stewart Powell, Christine Michael.

Volumes: *My Father, My President* by Doro Bush Koch; *Sisters First* by Jenna Bush Hager and Barbara Pierce Bush; *George & Barbara Bush* by Ellie LeBlond Sosa and Kelly Anne Chase; *Family of Secrets* by Russ Baker; *A Dictionary of American Presidents* by Michael W. Simmons; *Ana's Story* by Jenna Bush.

Personal Acknowledgments

I want to thank my editor, Charles Spicer, for all his encouragement over the years. This is our third book together, the previous two being *Jackie, Janet & Lee* and *The Kennedy Heirs*. Charles is such a great editor in so many ways, not the least of which is his commitment to the job at hand. I know I am in great hands with him, and I'm sure we'll do many more books together at St. Martin's Press.

Thanks also to Charles's assistant, Sarah Grill. My appreciation, as well, to Bethany Reis, who did a wonderful job copy editing this manuscript.

I would also like to acknowledge my domestic literary agent, Mitch Douglas, for the last twenty years of his terrific representation. Mitch is a good friend as well as my agent, and I am eternally grateful to him.

And I would like to acknowledge my foreign agent, Dorie Simmonds of the Dorie Simmonds Agency in London, who not only has represented me for more than twenty years but is a trusted friend.

Thank you to my television agent, Judy Coppage of the Coppage Company, who read the first draft of *Grace & Steel* and gave me some much-needed encouragement.

I would like to thank my attorneys, Stephen Breimer and Candice Hanson.

Special thanks also to Jo Ann McMahon and Felinda Adlawan of McMahon Accountancy Corporation.

I also want to acknowledge my television producing partner and very good friend, Keri Selig, as well as Hannah Reynolds of Intuition Productions. I would also like to thank Kimberly Currant.

I would also like to thank close friend Jillian DeVaney, who read this book in manuscript stage and offered invaluable insight. My sister, Roz Barnett, also read *Grace & Steel* in its infancy, and I appreciate her comments so much (biased though they may be).

My thanks to Jonathan Hahn, a brilliant writer, my personal publicist, and good friend. Thanks also to Lindsay Brie Mathers for her love and support.

Thanks to: Andy Steinlen, George Solomon, Richard Tyler Jordan, John Passantino, Linda DiStefano, Hazel and Rob Kragulac, Andy Skurow, Brad Scarton, Brian Newman, Scherrie Payne, Freda Payne, Susaye Greene, Barbara Ormsby, David Spiro, Billy Masters, Marlene Morris, Kac Young, Susan Kayaoglu, and Barb Mueller.

I have always been so blessed to have a family as supportive as mine. My thanks and love go out to: Roslyn and Bill Barnett and Jessica and Zachary; Rocco and Rosemaria Taraborrelli and Rocco and Vincent; and Arnold Taraborrelli. A big smile, also, for Spencer Douglas Taraborrelli.

I must also acknowledge those readers of mine who have followed my career over the years. I am indebted to each and every reader who has stuck by me. I so appreciate anyone who takes the time to pick up one of my books and read it. Thank you so much.

All my books are written with my late parents, Rocco and Rose Marie Taraborrelli, in mind at all times. I miss them.

Index